SIX DEGREES OF THE BRACELET:

Vietnam's Continuing Grip

JOHN A. SIEGFRIED

Library of Congress Control Number:		2011911364
ISBN:	Hardcover	978-1-4628-4579-8
	Softcover	978-1-4628-4578-1
	Ebook	978-1-4628-4580-4

1. Siegfried, John A.
2. Vietnam War 1961-1975. Personal narratives, American and Vietnamese
3. Soldiers-United States
4. Military History
5. Non-fiction

This book was printed in the United States of America.

Pictures by Margaret Brooks, John Siegfried, Aura Lani Hogan
Front cover by Aura Lani Photos
Back cover by Aura Lani Photos
Map by World Sites Atlas
Associated Press photo by Nick Ut
Bracelets: www.MemorialBracelets.com

Cover bracelets include as follows:

David C. Brostrom	USCG	KIA Black bracelet
Myron Donald	USAF	POW Silver bracelet
Michael John Cutri	USMC	KIA Black bracelet
Walter A. Cichon	USA	MIA Silver bracelet
John J. Donnelly	USN	KIA Black bracelet
Larry Brown	USMC	Orange Bracelet

To order additional copies of this book, contact:
Xlibris Corporation
1-888-795-4274
www.Xlibris.com
Orders@Xlibris.com
98682

OATH OF ENLISTMENT

I, (*name*), do solemnly swear (or affirm) that I will support and defend the Constitution of the United States against all enemies, foreign and domestic; that I will bear true faith and allegiance to the same; and that I will obey the orders of the president of the United States and the orders of the officers appointed over me, according to regulations and the Uniform Code of Military Justice. So help me God.

May all those who have come and gone before us, as well as those still on this earth, know that there are still many who care about the history, and the well-being, of the American servicemen and women who fought and served their country in Southeast Asia. Also remembered are the Vietnamese people, who most personally endured the horrific wrath of war on their home soil, and suffered such deep consequences. This book is dedicated to them all.

—JAS

CONTENTS

FOREWORD

Dedicated to Charles Lindewald Jr.
Master Sergeant, United States Army
Detachment B-16 Charlie Company
Fifth Special Forces Group

MSG Charles W. Lindewald, Jr.
USA 2/6/68 SVN

Ah, Cousin, could we but survive this war, to live forever deathless without age, I would not ever go again into battle, nor would I send you there for honor's sake.
— Sarpedon to Glaucus, *The Iliad*

As the singular event called the Vietnam War recedes into the dusty dimness of history, one should pause and reflect on the human story behind the numbers. War is after all the violent interaction of human beings involved in a struggle between two or more tribes of human beings to impose their will. Be it social, political, economic, religious, philosophical, or emotional, the results are always the same. A large group of people, most of whom have very little understanding of the reasons why or the consequences of, fight and struggle for one of the opposing sides in the conflict. These few bear the burden of imposing the will of others more powerful on some unlucky SOB fighting for the other side just as desperately, with just as little understanding of the real reasons for the war. All these individuals know is that they bear the burden of the battle, bear the sacrifices it demands, up to and including the ultimate sacrifice. Even if they are lucky enough to escape the culling inflicted by the Angel of Death, they must bear the scars of their service for the rest of their days. As the war fades from immediate memory, it becomes a tale of numbers, of statistics, of a select few individuals who live on as legends or heroes or villains or fools, depending on the chronicler of the story.

Vietnam is now at that juncture in the history books. Over 3 million men and women fought or served in Southeast Asia from 1 Nov 1955 to 30 April 1975, when Saigon fell—a total of 19 years, 6 months. This makes the Vietnam War the longest war in America's history to date. Over 58,000 of those who served were KIA (killed in action), MIA (missing in action), died of their wounds, are presumed dead, or were killed in accidents in country. Another 304,000 were wounded and recovered with some 75,000 being severely disabled by their injuries.

Of those dead, their average age was 23 years, and some 11,465 were under the age of 20 years old. Who knows how many Einsteins, Shakespeares, Mozarts, Jonas Salks, Madam Curies, or Billy Grahams gave up their lives in a faraway country. How many more came away with their innocence violated, their dreams shattered, their future skewed by the horrors they endured.

This book tells about some of those brave children of America, who went where they were ordered, experienced the horrors, paid the sacrifice fate dealt them, and what happened to them afterward. Pause for a moment, read their stories and . . . *remember.*

Thom Nicholson
Colonel, US Army (Ret.)

PREFACE

Dedicated to George Fallon
PFC, United States Army
Hawk Recon Platoon, 327th Infantry Battalion, 1st Brigade
101st Airborne Division

*And if it looks like we were scared to death, like a couple of kids just
trying to save each other, you should have seen it in color.*
—Jamey Johnson

On 23 December 2009, I was watching *Flags of Our Fathers*. During
the scene where James Bradley is going through his dad's World War II
mementos subsequent to his death, I was rummaging through an errant box
of my own. Uncovered was a silver bracelet; old and tarnished. Inscribed
were a name, date and other information.

After an Internet search of the inscribed name, I printed the results.
Excited, I handed them to my wife and exclaimed, "Donna, you have
to stop baking Christmas cookies and call this person now!" It seemed
appropriate that Donna call this person because her mother, Marlene, had
worn his bracelet and prayed for him and other Vietnam POWs/MIAs
in prayer groups for over twenty-four years. Since the technology didn't
exist at the time, it was difficult to learn the fate of the man's name on her
bracelet; and the bracelet somehow fell through the cracks. Marlene died
in February 2006.

When my wife called the phone number, a voice responded, "Hello." Donna asked, "Is this the home of Myron Donald?" The person replied, "Yes, ma'am." She then asked if the date 23 February 1968 had meaning to him. He said, "Yes, ma'am. That was the day I was shot down over North Vietnam." After more than an hour on the phone with retired Lt. Col. Myron Donald, or should I say USAF F-4 pilot/Weapons Operator Lt. Myron Donald, Donna decided to mail him the bracelet.

Thus, the idea of the book was born. Next up on the agenda was how to proceed. Initially, after writing Colonel Donald a letter to accompany the bracelet and then speaking to him for the first time in early 2010, my idea was to write his biography. After Colonel Donald agreed to a meeting, we met 2 February 2010, across from Davis-Monthan Air Force Base at the Pima Air and Space Museum in Tucson.

Colonel Donald's knowledge of all aircraft featured in the museum was overwhelming. He methodically explained in great detail how intended usage, troop transport, lift capability, speed, range and so on affected fuselage and wing length, thickness, and shape and so on. Finally, he explained how engine development evolved from radial to inline and "V" reciprocating engines and finally, to the biggest breakthrough, turbine engines with their huge power to weight ratios. He also discussed how combat experience and reactions to enemy equipment capabilities drove changes in aircraft design. Many of the planes flown from early on through WWII and up to today, by both friend and foe, are parked there. Air Force 1 from the Kennedy Era is also in the "bone yard" region, that area where planes are laid to rest on that hot sand and gravel of the dry Arizona desert.

Following lunch, I asked about writing his biography. Only after he probed my intentions and understood my passion for understanding a serviceman's motivations for serving his country did he agree to the idea. After all, I had never served in the Armed Forces.

Continuing discussions with the colonel led us to the realization that a compilation of interviews from Vietnam veterans, across all branches of the military, may be most appropriate in lieu of a biographical work. In addition, I needed to include support personnel including logistics, nurses, and doctors. The Vietnamese population warranted inclusion as well.

Writing this book was a journey back to the Vietnam War era. From December 2009 through July 2011, I drove through thousands of cities and towns, putting in over fifty thousand miles on US roadways, as well as flying over forty thousand miles to collect these stories. In this time period, I crossed paths with thousands of combat veterans. Of the men and women whose interviews are included, they are all mutually exclusive—each story is unique unto itself. The process that was undertaken to find these veterans, obtain permission to speak to them, and complete the interviews was overwhelming. Many veterans will only speak to those who fought and served with them. Including the men and women interviewed, they all had many regrets. However, something must have clicked when they allowed me to conduct their interview. The one common thread was the heartfelt appreciation to have a civilian expose what they experienced. But I also wanted to go deeper. With this book, I hope to make people aware of their limited overall understanding of what these Vietnam veterans experienced, as well as the aftermath of their service.

The actual questions that were asked of these folks were designed following much thought on interview construction. It was more important to know about the person, their family, and how the war impacted their lives following the service to the United States they had sworn to uphold. Only after being prompted, did they, alone, decide to embellish on actual in country experience and tell of their own personal stories.

Six degrees of separation (also referred to as the Human Web) refers to the idea that if a person is one step away from each person they know, and two steps away from each person who is known by one of the people they know, then everyone is at most six steps away, or connected, to any other person on earth.

We are all "connected." We are all joined or associated in some way, shape, or form, within those six degrees or steps. After pondering the name of the book, Colonel Donald said the following, "The more I think about the title, the more credence it has. I receive at least three or four [of my] bracelets a year from people, but the really interesting stories: I met a guy scuba diving in Mexico. He was at Khe Sanh February 1968 during [the] Tet [Offensive] when we were bombing the perimeter of the camp. He estimated we killed over three thousand NVA from the air in those passes before I was shot down weeks later. That maybe he was alive because of the USAF [and me]. The other one was in New York City when I was hailing a cab. As another man was getting out, I immediately recognized him. He was from my hometown in upstate NY. These situations happen to me all the time."

Origin of the Bracelets

The Great Depression generation and my generation, the baby boomers, are generally familiar with the POW/MIA bracelet. Originally produced in various finishes, including brass, copper, stainless steel, gold and silver, the bracelets were created to raise awareness for, and show support of, our servicemen who were prisoners of war (POW) or missing in action (MIA). Each bracelet was inscribed with a name, rank, country of loss, date of loss, and service. If you were not in the know and bumped into a bracelet "wearer," a few minutes later, you were well-schooled as to their significance.

Early on, many American servicemen returned home wearing plain brass bracelets given to them by the Montagnard hill tribesman they had fought beside in the northern regions of South Vietnam. The "Montagnard bracelet" stood for comradeship. The Americans wore it as a bond with a faraway friend who was still in danger. As the war progressed, people at home became more interested in the American POW/MIA. Carol Bates, a twenty-one-year-old sorority student, started the Voices in Vital America (VIVA) in 1970. Along with two friends and a college advisor, they began the process of making the bracelets from brass and copper donated by a fellow program member, Gloria Coppin. The intent of the VIVA was simply to drum up support for the missing serviceman and all-American prisoners of war suffering in captivity in Southeast Asia. I say Southeast Asia because not all POWs and MIAs were located in North Vietnam. There were prison camps in the South. Eventually, if still alive, the POWs were moved to the north along the Ho Chi Minh Trail.

Carol and her two friends, Kay Hunter and Gloria Coppin, marched along looking for funding. The women finally kicked off the program at the Sheraton Universal Hotel in Universal City, California. The news conference on Veterans Day, 11 November 1970, generated immediate awareness and support. Quickly, the program was receiving over twelve thousand requests a day. Proceeds were put back into the program to purchase brochures, bumper stickers—any mode of media that would publicize the POW/MIA issue. The program eventually generated sales of over 5 million bracelets, as well as support from various celebrities including Bob Hope, John Wayne, and Martha Raye. By the time Saigon fell in 1975, and the war was over, people were tired of hearing about Vietnam, and interest in the POW/MIA issue waned. VIVA closed its doors in 1976.

During the interviews, and while spending time with veterans who are still suffering in the aftermath, I came up with the idea of an orange bracelet. Approximately 60 percent of all Vietnam veterans who were *stationed* in South Vietnam are no longer alive. Some died of their wounds after the wall was built. Others committed suicide. Over time, many perished from exposure to dioxin, the most dangerous herbicide ever developed. Their rate of death well surpasses the norm. However, there are three other important groups: soldiers still alive who carry the effects of exposure to dioxin (Agent Orange), soldiers who are disabled due to the effects of PTSD (post traumatic stress disorder), and those still tending their physical wounds. All this gave me the idea of an orange bracelet. Many of the men interviewed have a combination of PTSD, exposure, and wounds that still mar them. For the four living soldiers who have allowed me to place their name on this new orange bracelet, I owe them a great debt of gratitude. A marine who died of a brain tumor in 2002 is also listed, thanks to his daughter who gave me permission. Also, I have dedicated chapters of this book to a fallen soldier (KIA—black bracelet), a prisoner of war (silver bracelet), or someone still missing in action (silver bracelet). The men with the orange bracelets also have dedications within this work.

I, too, have some regrets. When crossing paths with younger folks or professionals my age, I never fail to tell them one of my regrets is not having served this country. I've told many people that due to my fervor and respect for the military uniform, I may have been a conscript in Napoleon's or some other Army. My grandfather was in World War I, but he is the closest I have been to the armed forces via family.

Fully 15 percent of my royalties from this endeavor will be donated to various associations. The Marine Corps Law Enforcement Foundation (MCLEF) will receive support helping families of both KIA Marines and law enforcement personnel killed in the line of duty. Donations of hardbacks and e-books will be distributed to our hospitalized, wounded soldiers from Iraq, Afghanistan, and any future conflict. The Philadelphia Vietnam Veterans Memorial Society (PVVMS) and Veterans-For-Change (VFC) organization will receive assistance due to their support of living veterans and their families who require help. Finally, The United States Veterans Art Program (USVAP), the Atlanta Vietnam Veterans Business Association (AVVBA), and the North Carolina Vietnam Veterans Bridge Back Foundation will receive funding. As you embark on your journey through these soldiers' stories, also remember the millions of men and women currently serving our country. They are in harm's way, as long as the curtain is up on our world's unstable stage.

This is my first book. It may be my last, but it set me on a journey that will occupy me for the rest of my life. I hope examining these stories will change the lives of all who read them.

INTRODUCTION

Dedicated to Michael John Cutri
Lance Corporal, United States Marine Corps
Second Battalion, Third Marine Regiment, Third Marine Division

In human terms, the war was a struggle between victims: Whether a valid venture or a misguided endeavor, it was a tragedy of epic dimensions.

—Stanley Karnow

Vietnam is a small, narrow country with a coastline of about 3,444 kilometers. Its earliest people underwent the classic periods of development from Neolithic through bronze to iron. An imperial capital came into being at Thang Long circa 1000 CE (Common Era) and about 500 years later was moved to Huė. The site that was previously Thang Long is now known as Hanoi, the capital of the Socialist Republic of Vietnam.

After the establishment of Thang Long, the Viet people slowly expanded their presence toward the South, wiping out most of the ethnic Cham and Khmer, until Vietnam's boundary became roughly the shape it is today. Now, a land of a multitude of ethnic groups, of which the lowland Kinh are the largest group, Vietnam is a country incredibly rich in diverse natural resources, ranging from rubies to perhaps the largest cave complex in Asia and to a national unity that is a testament to its heritage. Archaeological research confirms the existence of a trading post near its Southwestern coast where Roman goods were in transit, coastal towns in Central Vietnam that became key trading posts with the early Malay Buddhists, the Japanese Red Seal ships that called at Hoi An, and eventually the Portuguese, Dutch, Spanish, and French.

The long association with Chinese occupiers brought to Vietnam the arts, religion, and social organization of Confucius and the Buddha. Upon the birth of Buddha in 564 BCE (before the Common Era) Buddhism became the predominant religion.

The arrival of the French turned Vietnam for a century into a colony whose people and land were to be exploited. The French ensured that their presence brought the Roman Catholic Church to the natives.

Temperatures can vary from below freezing in the northernmost part of the country to over one hundred degrees Fahrenheit in the Mekong Delta in the southern portion. The western central part of the country, called the Central Highlands, is a mountainous region with a narrow strip of useable coastal land; but in which most of the land is covered in double and triple canopies of trees and vegetation overgrowth. In the dry season, which exists from October to May, you would experience one-hundred-degree temperatures daytime followed by cool evenings. The humidity was virtually 100 percent dayside, so the chilly drop in mercury was a difficult transition through all these months.

Further north, above what would become the DMZ (demilitarized zone) at the 17th Parallel, which divided Vietnam from1954-1975, it was cooler during the day; and at times, it appeared you could see snow on the mountain ridges. The wet season in the South drew rain in such volume, that as much as twenty inches a month was not uncommon. Marshy land was mixed in with an extensive river system. Viewed from above, this river system looks similar to major interstate exchanges: circular in some spots, winding in others. Thick forests dotted some southern areas where visibility was near zero when attempting to navigate the terrain. The soil was also very different throughout the country. Red clay turned to a fine thick dust that was virtually impossible to remove from the skin in the Highlands. Once the monsoons came, the inches of clay dust became a foot of red mud.

Many foreign peoples have attempted to conquer the Vietnamese. Throughout the country's history, all the predators were never able to defeat the ethnic Kinh due to their strong nationalism. The forces of Kublai Khan learned to their sorrow in the thirteenth century that Vietnam was not a conquerable land.

When the southern third of present-day Vietnam became a French colony in 1852, it became a protectorate named Cochinchine. The central part soon followed as Annam, and the northern third soon followed as Tonkin. The French modernized the countryside by building a transportation system, and the people of Vietnam paid for this venture with their lives. When French Indochina came to an end in 1954, the southern half of the country became the Republic of Vietnam and the northern half became the Democratic Republic of Vietnam. It would take three decades of warfare for the country to be united.

The Vietnamese zeal, both in nationalism and religion, never waned through all these changes. During the turmoil with the French and their goal to catholicize the country, events spawned to reinforce the tenets of Buddhism in the South. The upheavals culminated in a self-immolation in 1963 when a Buddhist monk, sixty-six-year-old Thich Quang Duc, sat down in the middle of a busy Saigon street. After his fellow holy men poured gasoline on him, and setting him afire, one eyewitness later commented: "As he burned, he never moved a muscle, never uttered a sound, his outward composure in sharp contrast to the wailing people around him." A few months later, the country was set for major upheaval.

To this day, the vast majority of Vietnamese are practicing Buddhists.

John A. Siegfried

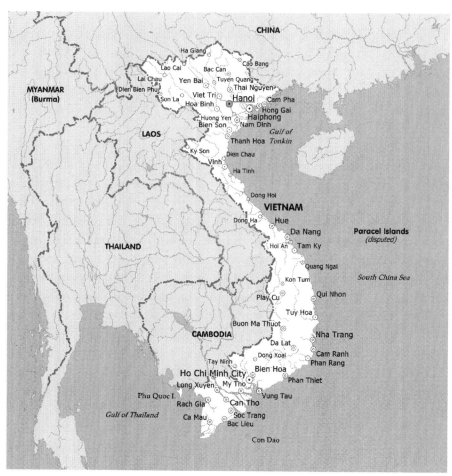

Map by World Sites Atlas (sitesatlas.com)

War remains the decisive human failure.
—John Kenneth Galbraith

The Vietnam War was the longest conflict in the history of the United States. Hopefully, this book will continue the memories of a war that affected a generation. Recently *USA Today* stated that Afghanistan exceeds this (June 2010). But it depends on when you start the Butcher's Bill, since casualties in Vietnam were in the thousands from 1955 until the Gulf of Tonkin Resolution, signed 7 August 1964, that *officially* catapulted us into the quagmire.

Even official sources can't agree on the exact start date of the Vietnam War. Vietnam Memorial Panel 01E (East Panel) states 1959. The

Department of Veteran Affairs states 1964. I took liberty splitting the difference. Although over 3,400,000 servicemen and women, who served in *all* Southeast Asia, were able to return home (including the wounded), over 47,000 were KIA along with approximately 11,000 who died from noncombat wounds. As of this writing, there are approximately 1,698 (May 2011) still listed as MIA. The greatest percentage of casualties (KIA, MIA, and WIA wounded in action) incurred by all services were from January 1967 through December 1969.

There were folks who came home as a result of an Army combat medic saving them in a hot landing zone (LZ), a Navy corpsman providing treatment for a landmine casualty, or the emergency room nurse and surgeon who amputated a limb to save a life. Others didn't incur a single combat wound. However, some vets think all soldiers who had to wade through elephant grass (sharp as a steak knife and up to eleven feet tall) should have received a Purple Heart.

There were pilots from all air services, as well as ground troops, who were imprisoned for years. Lt. Myron Donald was 155 pounds when he flew over to Vietnam from Davis-Monthan AFB in 1966. On 23 February 1968, he was standing in the middle of a rice paddy after his F-4 was shot down. Years later, after dropping to 120 pounds, experiencing treatment that only he and his fellow POW inmates could ever comprehend, including solitary confinement for six months, the Peoples Army of Vietnam (PAVN), called North Vietnamese Army (NVA) by the Americans, finally realized the political capital of a POW. Upon release, Myron was almost 185 pounds, but the collateral physical and emotional damage had been done.

No one, save for the veterans who placed their lives on the line, support personnel who experienced the debris of battle, and professionals who have counseled the thousands of men and women who returned from Vietnam, know the impact of combat on these veterans emotional, physical, and mental faculties.

Different groups of people have always viewed the war through varied lenses, and opinions on what happened have changed over time. The military brass was convinced that throwing hundreds of thousands of troops into the fray could defeat an indigent population expert in covert operations, guerilla warfare and specialists in tunneling (like the Japanese at Iwo Jima). The actual men in combat saw diminishing returns of their actions as the war progressed. Many serviceman (and officers) thought the war was mismanaged. Only recently have some US civilians come to view the GI in a different light. The exposure and effects of PTSD, dioxin, and napalm, or "jellied gasoline"—not to mention having to point a gun and shoot it at another human being—have all worn on these soldiers since their time in combat. And people are finally taking notice.

My attempt with this book is to view the war from all sides, including the Vietnamese population. The men, women and children of Vietnam were ravaged and displaced for over 35 years when you factor in post WWII conditions, the continued French occupation through 1954, post Vietnam War issues, and the South Vietnamese forced adoption to Communism.

Shakespeare wrote, "What's past is prologue." With this book, I hope to make the reader aware that our overall understanding of warfare from the eyes of the combatants is prologue to a current generation of people who will better comprehend the effects of battle on those who have sworn to protect our country. Even if a soldier did not incur a flesh wound, they may have suffered irreparable damage to their emotions, their psyche, and their soul. We civilians may never fully know or be able to comprehend this. We need also to continue to support these men and women in the aftermath of their service.

My intent with the delivery of this book was, and still remains, no different than when Ulysses S. Grant stated in his memoirs "a sincere desire to avoid doing injustice to anyone." In addition, I hope to inspire others to extend justice and gratitude to all that deserve our thanks. Conversely, my intention was never to make this book a political statement. There has been plenty published for all to form their own opinions as to why we were in Southeast Asia, and opinions on the treatment of our forces arriving on domestic soil. With all respect to Carl Von Clausewitz, his statement "War is the continuation of politics by other means" is elementary to anyone who has ever seen battle. An example of a combat situation follows Michael Kathman's story, who wrote *Triangle Tunnel Rat*:

> *I cautiously raised the upper half of my body into the tunnel until I was lying flat on my stomach. When I felt comfortable, I placed my Smith & Wesson .38-caliber snub-nose (sent to me by my father . . .) beside the flashlight and switched on the light, illuminating the tunnel. There, not more than 15 feet away, sat a Viet Cong eating a handful of rice from a pouch on his lap. We looked at each other for what seemed to be an eternity, but in fact only a few seconds. Maybe it was the surprise of actually finding someone else there, or maybe it was just the absolute innocence of the situation, but neither one of us reacted.*

After a moment, he put his pouch of rice on the floor of the tunnel beside him, turned his back to me and slowly started crawling away. I, in turn, switched off my flashlight, before slipping back into the lower tunnel and making my way back to the entrance. About 20 minutes later, we received word that another squad had killed a VC emerging from a tunnel 500 meters away. I never doubted who that VC was. To this day, I firmly believe that grunt and I could have ended the war sooner over a beer in Saigon than Henry Kissinger ever could by attending peace talks.

The interviews included are from personnel who served across all military branches and support functions. Further, Colonel Donald and the MIA family members had much of their interviews devoted to themselves, their missing loved ones, and the lives of their family members. They discussed only what they chose to speak of while imprisoned, or during the aftermath of their family member listed as missing.

All other interviews are designed to ask the same questions of each person, all of whom were in Vietnam or serving during the war. Most of the interviews were completed in person across the country—the rest over the phone. All interviewees were eventually met in person. To ensure a reasonable amount of pages for the reader, all interviews have been scaled down with contributor approval.

This book also includes interview "captions" from professionals in the field of clinical psychology, psychiatry, and behavioral analytics.

Keep in mind that data, any data, can be interpreted differently by any individual, and these interviews drove mountains of information my way. Through the course of my writing, research was done to verify as much as possible. Further, all respondents were confirmed within my reach of authenticity—it is a felony for anyone to cast themselves as a veteran (and obtain benefits as such). Finally, when extracting days, dates, and times, I could only check and recheck references. However, these references are dictated by extraction point. An example: Richard Etchberger's date of birth (DOB) was originally listed in Chapter Four as 4 October 1940. This date was sanctioned and listed on the virtualwall.org, which includes all those who are inscribed on the black granite Wall of the Vietnam Memorial in Washington DC. The designers and implementers of this site do a terrific job obtaining information for all women and men who gave their last full measure. However, the date of birth for Richard Etchberger is incorrect. Cory Etchberger, Richard's son, relayed this to me when I requested his formal approval for dedicating the Medal of Honor section to his dad.

Vietnam is the only American military engagement where the returning soldiers were summarily disgraced and eventually became disgruntled. Korea was unfortunate enough, as those vets returned to a somewhat ambivalent society more interested in the development of the TV set. For the Vietnam folks, no flag-bearing parades, no kisses and open arms from family and friends en masse—just spite, spit, and accusations that all servicemen were baby killers. They just had a job to do, and they did it. But it wasn't easy in Vietnam; it was virtually impossible to differentiate between friend and foe, villagers or VC (Viet Cong). Many who did return home led unfulfilled lives, both personally and professionally. This cost of duty cannot be measured.

CHAPTER ONE
1964-1966

The Gathering Storm

Dedicated to John Joseph Donnelly
Seaman, United States Navy
E Platoon SEAL Team 1
Task Force—116

People sleep peaceably in their beds at night only because rough men stand ready to do violence on their behalf.

—George Orwell

Many Americans were unable to point out Vietnam on a map in the 1950s. All that changed from the time Eisenhower authorized "advisors" following the evacuation of the French upon their defeat at Dien Bien Phu in 1954, to the Gulf of Tonkin Resolution in August 1964. Our military advisors in country service, beginning in the mid fifties to help train the South Vietnamese, coupled with small combat operations through 1964, set the stage for the Marine Expeditionary Force landing 8 March 1965. With the First Cavalry Airmobile insertion September 1965, culminating in the first major confrontation with the NVA (Ia Drang Valley battle 14 November 1965), these Marine and Army movements would define the opening rounds of America's longest war.

The people back home were initially supportive of our commitment to the South Vietnamese. The armed forces build up in men and material, coupled with 401 KIA by 1964, to more than eight thousand KIA by December 1966 would soon change that support structure. From 1964 through the end of 1966, we incurred over thirty-six thousand WIA as well.

Introduction to the Interviews

Navy SEALs (SEA AIR LAND) were hands down the toughest group to solicit and obtain cooperation for their time. Some interviews were "booked," then the individuals never followed up with me. Others called, but just weren't comfortable with releasing information. Like many Vietnam vets, the SEALs were wary of civilians probing for information and anyone who was not able to earn their trust. Thanks to Matt Hagerty, I was able to track down Lieutenant Gulick. John is currently president of the San Francisco Bay area SEAL Association.

To quote Colonel Thom Nicholson, SEALs are "warriors." They are a community of overachievers. SEALs are a force of choice commandos. They are expert in tactics, weaponry, and virtually all ordnance (foreign, domestic, and homemade explosives), and include some of the best endurance swimmers on the planet. Without question, they are the best maritime unit under the Special Operation Forces "net" of elite soldiers. They swim and train in cold, choppy seas, not calm pool waters. Further, their physical conditioning wreaks havoc on soldiers from all Special Forces services who are unable to complete SEAL training.

As a result of the beach-landing disaster at Tarawa in 1943, the underwater demolition teams were formed. The Navy realized quickly that ocean depth, currents, and reef evaluation were all critical to the success of any amphibious marine operation. The BUD/S (basic underwater demolition school-changed later to BUD/S for Basic Underwater Demolition/SEALS) program was established to assist in the Pacific landings from 1944 until the end of WWII. In 1962, the SEALs were commissioned for special operations. During Vietnam, their expertise was so recognized by both the VC and the NVA that there were bounties on each and every SEAL operator.

Currently there are ten SEAL Teams in the US Navy. Of all the Teams, SEAL Team 6 is the most experienced. It was SEAL Team 6 who worked with various governmental agencies and military services on the highly secretive operation to hunt down Osama bin Laden. SEAL Team 6's inclusion in the planning and execution of this dangerous OP resulted in this SEAL unit killing bin Laden 1 May 2011.

The next time you get into the shower, turn the water to tepid. Then brace yourself when it turns cool. Move the dial around to the coldest setting, and you will experience just a "tad," a nibble, about SEAL training. We all have taken wintry showers under circumstances where power is lost, or when you are down at any beach resort, the heat will force you into unusual habits. Now imagine *training, living, and working* in cold water for years. The human body can withstand far more punishment than anyone (except a SEAL, POW, or Special Forces Operator like airborne, ranger, recon and delta force) can possibly imagine. The instructors know *exactly* how long a body can tolerate fifty degree water temperature. They literally will wait until the last possible moment (before hypothermia sets in) when they order the guys out of the water. Then imagine running two miles for each meal (one up and one back). Follow this by swimming a few miles each day—sand literally in every orifice of your body. Whoops, I forgot to say one thousand or more pushups, along with the infamous flutter kicks. SEAL training is the toughest in the world. The fallout rate in a normal class can approach 90 percent. Out of a class of, say, two hundred, only twenty do not DOR (drop on request). Even in BUD/S the fallout rate is almost as high. Don't take my word on it. Read *Lone Survivor*—this story about a post 9/11 Afghanistan SEAL unit is heart-thumping, but you only have to read the first half of Marcus Luttrell's story about the training to be convinced of the above. Since reading *Lone Survivor* for the second time over three years ago and following John's interview, my morning ritual includes a cold shower in honor of the punishment the Navy SEALs live for. By the way, in the middle of winter, this shower exercise is brutal.

Needless to say, my anxiety was lifted when the lieutenant finally agreed to the interview. I was beginning to believe the SEAL "wall" could not be penetrated by a civilian. Thank you, Mr. Gulick, for not allowing that to happen.

Another interviewee found within this chapter is Hip Biker (pen name). Hip worked on the famous U-2 *Dragon Lady* (spy plane). He has become far more than an acquaintance—he is my mentor. Hip is the first person I met then interviewed for the book. Without a doubt, he is one of the most cerebral people I have ever crossed paths with. He can discuss the current price of tea in China, anything metaphysical, and all else in between. Hip can also be succinct. When I told him that he was born on a day that was highlighted by a partial eclipse of the sun, his comment was, "That figures."

During one of my business trips to Atlanta in January 2010, I was eating dinner at a restaurant in Atlanta. It was late on a Sunday evening and a man walked into the bar area and began greeting everyone. Motioning to Charlie the bartender, I asked him who this guy was. He stated to me "that's Hip." Shortly thereafter this man came over and sat down next to me. Little did I know that I was in his seat! Born in the south and raised in Atlanta, he was a gentleman and did not ask me to move. Rather, he just began conversing. Two hours later, Hip not only knew about the book, but explained to me that he was stationed in Tucson at the same airbase, at around the same time, that Colonel Myron Donald was stationed there as well! He explained his stint with the Air Force, his work on the *Dragon Lady* as a mechanic, and his tour of duty in Southeast Asia (Bien Hoa Air Force Base).

Without that trip in January, there may not be an interview here. This veteran believed in what I was attempting, which was to continue to expose civilians to the ravages of war felt by his fellow vets. Hip also successfully connected me with both Air Force and Navy personnel who fought in country. Hip Biker is his pen name because some of the U-2 technology is still classified, and he chose not to provide the readers with his real name.

Colonel Thom Nicholson is the author of *15 Months in SOG: A Warrior's Tour*. While at Borders book store in the Vietnam section, this book grabbed my attention. Colonel Nicholson's work pictorially challenges the browser to review it. Upon reading cover to cover, my next step was to locate the author for an interview. The interview followed after Thom was convinced my goals were pure. My brother Peter was recovering from prostate surgery October 2010 and asked me for some reading material. This is the first book I gave him, which was also my first book that I read *during* this project. I didn't want to go back home to reread books already perused on 'Nam; I needed a fresh dose. Thom Nicholson is an amazing man; seventy years "young" who plays more golf weekly in Denver than most. His new book, *Stagecoach Graveyard*, was released May 2010.

SOG stood for Surveys and Observation Group. Originally under CIA mandate, control went to MACV (Military Assistance Command Vietnam) in December 1963. Military jargon is literally a sea of acronyms. As evidenced so far, the military has a short form for everything and everyone. Memorizing all of them, across all services, is a feat unto itself. SOG was later changed to Studies and Observation Group—either way, the soldiers who fought under the Special Forces umbrella were some of the best of the best. Their original mission was to train and work with the indigent Vietnamese and Montagnard hill people to fight the VC and NVA.

Special Forces (SF) are the elite ground troops of any fighting unit. Although training is different than the Navy SEALs, their group consists of rangers, airborne, marine recon, and other select Army members (Delta Force was not commissioned until the late '70s). After MACV assumed control, strategically their modus operandi was unconventional warfare undercover of classified operations. Tactically, they performed reconnaissance and various other operations. They conducted cross-border operations in Laos, Cambodia, and North Vietnam to assist in disrupting the flow of material and men along the Ho Chi Minh Trail. Their losses during the war were high due to maneuvering under covert conditions; their casualties are not broken out by the Armed Services.

Nam Dong, Lang Vei, Dak To, A Shau, Plei Mei—these were just some of the places Special Forces troops fought and died during their fifteen-year service in South Vietnam. It was a stay that began in June 1957, when the original sixteen members of the 14th SF Operational Detachment deployed to Vietnam to train a cadre of indigenous Vietnamese SF teams. The first and last Special Forces American soldiers to die in Vietnam due to enemy action *in the field* were members of the First SF Group. On 21 October 1957, Captain Harry G. Cramer Jr. *(Vietnam Memorial Panel 01E Line 078)* was killed, and on 12 October 1972, Sgt. Fred C. Mick (*Vietnam Memorial Panel 01W Line 081*) was killed.

By the time the 5th SF Group left Southeast Asia, SF soldiers had earned 17 Medals of Honor, 1 Distinguished Service Medal, 90 Distinguished Service Crosses, 814 Silver Star Medals, 13,234 Bronze Star Medals, 235 Legions of Merit, 46 Distinguished Flying Crosses, 232 Soldier's Medals, 4,891 Air Medals, 6,908 Army Commendation Medals, and 2,658 Purple Hearts. It was a brilliant record, built on blood and sacrifice. Through their unstinting labors, SF troops eventually established 254 outposts throughout Vietnam, many of them defended by a single A-team and hundreds of friendly natives. By the end of 1972, the SF role in Vietnam was over.

JOHN GULICK

Lieutenant, United States Navy SEAL (Sea Air Land)
"Ready to Lead, Ready to Follow, Never Quit"
SEAL Team 1 Coronado, CA
Home of Record: Somerville, NJ
Home of Residence: San Francisco, CA
DOB: 04 July 1940
Conducted on 10 June 2010 via phone
Washington and Lee University

> *Nothing is so exhilarating as to be shot at without result.*
> —Winston Churchill

Growing Up

I grew up in Somerville, New Jersey. I was born prior to World War II and my mother's brothers served in World War II. One of them was a marine at Guadalcanal, and he didn't come back. I was imbued with the spirit of military service when I was a kid and looked up to those uncles a lot. I had a brother and a younger sister. I was the oldest, and I thought about going into the Marine Corps.

When I was a freshman in college, I started to apply to the Marine Platoon Leader Program where you go to Quantico during the summers and get commissioned as a second lieutenant of the Marine Corps. A Marine platoon leader, MROTC is what you do all year long, along with intensive programs for two months during the summers.

You do two summers, and that's equivalent to OCS (Officer Candidate School) so you get commissioned as a marine lieutenant. When I filled in an application, I revealed I had asthma, and they told me I couldn't be an officer in the military with asthma, so I'd better take the application back. Sometime later, a guy in the naval reserves told me about a program where you could go up to Newport, Rhode Island, and get commissioned that way. This time I didn't tell them I had asthma, so I got in and went through the two summer program; and at the end of the second summer in 1963, I got commissioned. I went from there to CIC school in Glynco, Georgia; and from there, I went to Air Intercept Controller School in San Diego and then to a ship in Hawaii out of Pearl Harbor. I reported there in February 1964, and a message came out; about six months later, after the Gulf of

Tonkin incident, they wanted volunteers for underwater demolition. The ship was okay, but somewhat boring. I thought I wanted a little more spice, so I thought I'd try the UDT (underwater demolition team) thing and took the test. I received orders to Basic Underwater Demolition School (BUDs) in March 1965. I completed the six-month training for underwater demolition, went to UDT 12, and got there in September 1965. I hung around there as weapons officer, so I didn't really have to do anything as it was an administrative job. I kept bugging the executive officer for an operational job and finally told him in the spring of 1966 that "if you're not going to give me an operational job where I can be a frogman with the rest of the guys, then why don't you send me to (a) SEAL team?" That was on Friday. On Monday he opened a meeting of our group and said, "The SEAL team needs an officer, they requested we send them an officer, and John Gulick has volunteered to go." I showed up at the SEAL team; in those days the acting commanding officer was a lieutenant, and I was a JG (lieutenant junior grade) at that point. The first thing I recall doing was going down to Jungle Warfare School with a SEAL team platoon that was about to deploy. The first all US SEAL team deployed in January of that year, and this platoon was a replacement. I went to Jungle Warfare School in May 1966, and from there, I also did Army Pathfinder School for about five weeks at Fort Benning, Georgia. They spent a lot of money on us.

Vietnam

I'm pretty sure we left for Vietnam toward the end of September, so I must have been in Coronado (San Diego) August 1966. In Pathfinder School, I remember one of the guys, a really good guy, who was with me in the platoon and who had gone to Jungle Warfare School with me was the first SEAL killed in Vietnam—Billy Wayne Machen (*Vietnam Memorial Panel 10E Line 19*). He was a second-class petty officer (E-5). I wondered, trying to conjure up how that could've happened. I found out when I got over to Vietnam that Billy had been killed in an ambush. A CWO (Chief Warrant Officer) named Roger Mascone picked him up and threw him over his shoulder. Machen was a big guy, and Roger hauled his ass out of there, and today they talk about no SEAL left behind. I think that really comes from the Marines, but Roger Mascone (died 2007) put that into practice without even thinking about it that day.

When I got back to Coronado, I joined up with my platoon. I was the assistant platoon leader, and they packed all my stuff that I was going to need for Vietnam. I got back from Pathfinder School on Friday and left on Sunday morning. I had to clear out, store my stuff, show up on Sunday morning, and take off for Vietnam in a Navy transport plane. I have no idea how many hours it was; we flew to San Francisco and spent the night, then to Hawaii and spent the night, flew to Guam and refueled, but I don't think we spent the night. The Navy was the same crew who had to do all the flying so we could get into Vietnam. I remember I was a little bit apprehensive like anyone would be; and when we got there, I looked around, and everything was different from my experience with the military. The planes were all camouflaged and looked like working tractor planes. I noticed the sentry boxes had a lot of sandbags around them. They had a jeep driving around that had an M-60 machine gun (.30-caliber) mounted on it, and the cartridge belt was fed into it so it was ready to go; all this indicated that it was work time. We packed up our stuff and went down to Nha Be, which was south of Saigon and on either the Long Tau or Soai Rap River. It leads down to the entrance of the Rung Sat special zone, which is between Saigon and the South China Sea. It's a big mangrove swamp, which is a tidal area. They were having a lot of attacks on shipping, which came up to Saigon from the South China Sea because that's a deep set on a deep water port. They were getting hit with recoilless rifles. The SEALs were to go in there and clean them out, which was like looking for a needle in a haystack. It was a huge area. The charts were worthless. It was just a maze of different waterways in which it was easy to get lost. The routine was to go out in patrols to cover certain areas on foot and drop off fire teams of six men and one officer to set up ambushes. I was there a week, and what we did was use a medium-sized landing craft, an LCM that had been jury-rigged and gun-decked with five .50-caliber machine guns, two .30s (caliber), and a recoilless rifle up on top of a sixty millimeter mortar pit that we created. On the top of the LCM where you normally have an open deck or cargo hold where men or vehicles can sit, we gun-decked that all over so you could walk on top. It was kind of like a mini-destroyer.

We had two platoons, and we would rotate: one would operate and one would man the boat, serving as a boat crew. SEALs now have special warfare combat crews (SWCCs). These guys operate, drive, and thoroughly know their boats. We didn't have anything like that, so SEALs were their own boat crews back in those days. They went through their own special training, but they didn't get a trident (SEAL emblem); they didn't qualify for it. I was there about a week, and I had gone out on some missions. We did some sort of Wet Ops and patrols to get our feet wet and rode the boat around. Then they were going to set us up for our first ambush. I was all set to go and was told it was on Friday. Two fire teams were going to be dropped off—one in one place and my team in another. We were driving along, on a nice, pleasant early evening. I was talking to a guy named Bill Pechecec who was actually an officer, but was manning a .30-caliber machine gun near the coxswain's (man in charge of the boat) station. We got word that we were about to come up on the place where they were going to drop off our fire team; I got my guys together and sat on the deck of this Mike (mechanized landing craft)) boat, nicknamed for LCM. I looked out; it was a beautiful scene, tranquil jungles and so green, but it was getting dark, so everything was looking gray. I looked up, and I saw this water spout about sixty feet high and thought *what the hell is that?* Well, next thing I know, machine guns opened up, because when they (our crew) thought anything was around, they'd use suppressing fire on anything that might threaten us; my job was to go to the bottom of the Mike boat and stand by with my fire team because we didn't have any positions to man. We were just supposed to wait for orders; it was awful. Everyone was firing away and I thought, *Gee, there must be something we can do.* I headed back and climbed up to the gun deck with bullets spraying and whacking off the metal, making loud noises; the sound of incoming small arms fire is still pretty damn unforgettable. I thought that I should go down with my guys because I didn't want to be around that gunfire. I climbed back down the ladder, took a step, and a second mortar comes in and hits the boat. It flattened everyone on the deck, and I got hit in the leg. I went back on deck, and all I could see are guys lying around, smoke, and intermittent fire. I remembered we stumbled into an ambush site, and I lucked out by having them drop that mortar early because my fire team was to be dropped off right where that ambush occurred. It could have happened to other people who would have been dropped off from boats at a particular spot. It's already manned and infested by the opposition, and you're very vulnerable when getting off a boat. You don't have any cover. You're just a sitting duck in the water, so some guys got chewed up pretty badly. I avoided that which was a bit of good fortune. I remember coming up on the deck, and there was a .50-caliber on the aft (towards the stern or rear) part of the boat, and I could see some tracer (special tipped bullets that illuminate and make visible the trajectory of the round to the naked eye) fire still coming from where we passed through so I got on that .50-caliber and fired, thinking, *Do I really want to shoot this .50 at these guys because they're going to shoot at me?* I fired away at them. It wasn't automatic any longer because it had been damaged from the mortar. I fired off a couple more rounds and tried to help the guys who were wounded. From there we got the badly wounded guys off on the medevac (helicopter). The rest of us took the boat back to our base in Nha Be and then I got a helicopter ride up to the Third Army field hospital near Tan Son Nhut Airfield. I spent about two weeks there.

The injury didn't hurt at all. It was like a bee sting or like having someone whip you with a towel hard. It was roughly a small piece of shrapnel in there. All they did for me was debride (clean) the wound, giving me antibiotics, and just kept me on that for a while until it appeared I didn't have any infection. They sewed me up and sent me back to the SEAL team in Nha Be on or about 20 October. We had already been in country for three weeks. There was a period of little going on because they didn't want to send us out again in one Mike boat; they wanted us to go out in a pair of boats. When we got in that situation 7 October, the mortar hit us, the engine stopped, and we were just dead in the water. The second-class engineman who was assigned to the boat went down there, and I don't know what the hell he did, but he got the engine started back up. The idea was that what if they couldn't get the engine started, and you're alone without anybody to back you, they wanted to get another boat in there. For a couple of weeks, we didn't do anything other than the usual eat, work out, and go on training runs. When the second boat came in, we started going out on missions where two boats would go together. We'd go down and board San Pans (Vietnamese boats). We did night ambushes and set those things (on fire). In fact, one time when I was at an ambush site, a fire team triggered their ambush, so there was a big "shoot 'em up," and the way they did it was if you triggered an ambush, they'd come and pick up that fire team because their positions were tipped off, and they didn't want to leave them out there vulnerable. So they picked them up, and again, the Mike boat would recon by fire. They'd open up with those .50s (caliber) and shoot to let everybody know you'd better not come anywhere near us. I didn't know how far away I was because we started to take .50-caliber machine gun fire at our position from the Mike boat—the Mike boat is shooting at us!

It was the only time I ever heard a .50-caliber going over my head, probably about 3 feet off the ground. I'm down there trying to become one with the earth, to be lower than the surface of the earth; it doesn't work that way. It's just those .50-caliber rounds sounded like a 707; they were just so loud and menacing. Within the United States, you don't hear gunfire unless you're going hunting or there's some police action. I sometimes get a little skittish when I hear a loud backfire; it can be very unsettling.

We also did some blocking operations. We were supposed to serve as a blocking force for an Army sweep through a canal with boats, and I was on one boat and some other guys were on another boat. They got into a big "shoot 'em up" on the canal though we didn't see any action, which was fine with me. That's kind of the way it went. We went on those operations, but to my knowledge, the only time my fire team was ever under direct fire was when we were ambushed the first week we were there. We walked around on patrols. We heard voices and went after the voices; they disappeared. We were never under fire again unless you count our .50-caliber shooting at us. We were in an ambush, so that's kind of like being under fire. It didn't matter who was shooting at us, it was close enough to be threatening.

We had many other insertions, but no one shot at us; we set up ambushes. These guys wanted to have some action, but nobody ever came into our ambush site. We never triggered an ambush. It was funny; I don't know how many times I was out there, fifty to seventy-five times, and you'd think out of that many times we would have gotten something. It's like going fishing and not catching anything.

I came back home February 1967. My experience in the hospital was a very difficult experience. I wasn't badly hurt at all. I was sore, but there were a lot of badly screwed-up guys in there, and everyone was young with traumatic injuries. Most of the guys in my ward were surgical cases. Some of the guys were missing legs. Some were abdominal cases or gunshot wounds. It was quite sobering to see all this and realize that I was going back to duty and I was going to be dealing with this. It's a serious business. You can be full of bravado and confidence, but once you see what the result of what some of this stuff is, it's very sobering, and it kind of wears on you psychologically—at least it did to me. I never said anything about it or talked to anyone about it. I just kind of sucked it up. So when I came back, I was really relieved to get out of there. You know what amazes me, John—I was over there with a guy named Gary Gallagher. Gary, at that point, was probably an E-4. He had been in the Navy the same length of time that I had been. He was a physically strong guy and a real good (SEAL) operator. He went on to become a master chief in the SEALs, and I think he retired in the early '90s. A master chief is the highest NCO (non commissioned officer) rank in the military—an E-9. Now, they have this thing called the command master chief. Every command has a senior enlisted man who has an administrative or honorary role and Gary was the command master chief before he got out; he made seven trips to Vietnam. If you figure that the average trip is seven months because they rotate SEALs, that's two years and four months which is equivalent to doing a couple of tours in the Army. He would've been there between 1966 and 1975. He was going to be there every other year, and it amazes me at how those guys could handle that. I thought to myself when I got back, *I've done the SEAL team and another line of work might be more to my liking.* There's nothing fun or appealing (to me) about active combat operations, yet some people liked it. I've met current SEALs who love combat operations, so it's an individual thing. Professional people who are trained and do their work in a workmanlike fashion which, I feel for sure, I did when I was in there, was the reason for getting medals for doing your job. When you're getting shot at, it's not easy to do. Nobody wants to get up and run across an open field when they're being shot at. It's your instinct to lie down and keep covered. But to get the objective covered, you sometimes have to expose yourself and take chances, which are pretty significant. It's difficult work, not easy at all.

How did Vietnam shape your life?

I applied to law school, got in, and worked my ass off. I was damn serious. I was a little over twenty-seven by then, which wasn't very old, but older than a twenty-two-year-old, a recent college graduate, and I'd been through that Vietnam thing, which was sobering. To this day, I feel I was delivered (safe) so many times; I could've been whacked.

There's one story about being out on a patrol. We found a bunker complex we were supposed to blow, and the guys bringing the explosives kicked them out maybe four hundred to five hundred yards from us in the jungle. We were out there looking for them, and this guy I mentioned before, Gary Gallagher, came up to me and said, "Listen, I just found a footprint filling with water near this stream. Somebody came up to me, and I think someone knows we're here." The question was, "What do we do? How long do we spend looking for these demolition packs?" We ultimately decided to blow the bunkers best we could with hand grenades and get out of there. Our superiors thought we shouldn't have left as soon as we did. I was tasked for the next couple of days to get those demolition packs. The senior guy in charge of the group told me he had too much paperwork, so I would have to take the guys back by myself, which I thought was not a good thing to do. The enlisted men were on the verge of mutiny, going back to a place we'd been. The doctrine was that when you're a commando outfit and go into an area where people know you've been, you'd better not go back in for a while. Let it cool off because people are going to be alert to anything you do. I've got about five guys coming up to me, angry and resentful that we have to go out into the bush. They're my constituency, and yes, they have to do what I tell them, but I need to take their concerns up the line. I have to go talk to the boss. I remember telling him we're violating doctrine, and four or five demo packs weren't worth the lives of anybody. It's not significant, strategically, to fly in and find those things when we're pretty sure somebody was in there. He said we had to go in.

He was just a senior SEAL lieutenant. He became an admiral. His name was Chuck Lemoyne. He was one of the first SEAL admirals. George Worthington was the first SEAL admiral, and I think Chuck Lemoyne was the next. He was a lieutenant, but in the meantime, I had to go back in and get those demo packs. At the same time, a little light observation aircraft called a FAC (Forward Air Controller) flew over the area where I was supposed to get those demo packs, and we started taking some ground fire. The FAC pilot called in some airstrikes, and then they started taking ground fire. The next thing you know, they figured there's a battalion (bad guys) in there, so my ten guys would've flown in, and we'd have been ground up in about two minutes, so I got lucky. When I got back from Vietnam, I felt like I'd been very lucky in everything. My friend Bill Pechecec, who I'd been bullshitting with before we got mortared on 7 October never walked again after that incident. He'd gotten some of his brains blown out. He was disabled for life, but he did have a reasonably full life. He got married and had some children. He worked as a teacher, so he did make the most of his opportunities. I could've been Bill, but instead of Bill, I had minor leg wounds. Those .50—cals that had been coming into our position could've been a little lower; one of those bullets flying around when I climbed up that ladder could've been on target, and I'd have taken one in the ear.

It's hard to get a big picture when you're down in a certain area. Something didn't seem right to me. I noticed that the Vietnamese people we'd come in contact with in rural areas were not friendly. Now this may be the Asian culture, but they didn't want anything to do with us. I noticed one day while driving the Big Mike boat with my team out on the water, some guy stands up on the shore of the river and starts firing at us with a rifle. We turned on him and started firing everything we had; the world was coming down on this guy. When we got close to the shore, the boss told me to take my fire team and see if we had hit him. We scoured the area, but nobody had hit him, couldn't find any bullet tracks or anything, but I often thought about that guy. Why would he stand up and shoot and attract attention from a big Mike boat? Maybe he wanted to draw us into an ambush, but that didn't happen—that couldn't have been the reason. I think it was just an act of defiance. He was saying, "This is my country and you don't belong here, you're western white guys and want to take us over like the French." I think that's probably what those guys were thinking; they wanted us out of there.

The military can, sometimes, define your life just as it did with a friend of mine in San Francisco who was an Army officer. It didn't define my life, but it was a major event in my life. Being a Navy SEAL was a proud time in my life. I discovered that there was a reunion on the East Coast and West Coast of the UDT-SEAL Association; I didn't really want to go. I got talked into going in 2003 and ran into three guys that were in my fire team in Vietnam. I couldn't believe it. It was just wonderful, and I keep going back ever since; I love seeing the old guys. I love that period in my life. I loved being a frogman and a SEAL. It's the best men's club, as a command master chief told me, that he knew of. It's an exclusive club that's tough to get into, and there's a certain sense of camaraderie and mutual accomplishment. What I think is really important in war is (how) to utilize people. We were simply a commando unit, but they didn't know what to do with us and what I was doing in Vietnam, was trying to figure out how SEALs could be employed. What would be the tactical use of Navy SEALs? We took our first steps there, but if you look at these books about Indochina, you see that the French and the West tend to want conventional Western-armored, air-supported military operations. They weren't going to get that from the People's Red Army. They didn't have an Air Force, and they didn't have tanks. They had some trucks, but most of their supplies came by people.

You could see that one of the things Bernard Fall thought (WW11 and Vietnam war correspondent killed during action 21 February 1967), as the French tried to fight Vietnam to maintain their presence in Indochina, was the way they were trained, the way they think, and that's what the United States does. I would think Afghanistan is a totally new and different place. There's not much cover there, but it's extremely rugged. There's cover in the sense of rocks and ravines, things like that, but, Jesus, you can't take our tanks in there. You can take the tank along the road, but what good is that going to do if the guys are a mile away up in the wilderness? You've got to go up on foot after them, and I don't know what the goal is, what are the stakes? It's a tough place to do business.

One of the things I've found out in the last four or five years, while visiting one of my uncle's who was a bombardier in the Eighth Air Force in World War II, was that my uncle at Guadalcanal had talked about taking his life. I asked, "What are you talking about?" I'd spent sixty years thinking that the guy had died from picking up diseases in Guadalcanal. My aunt said, "No, word we got was that he finally committed suicide in New Zealand after they got rotated off Guadalcanal." I went down and talked to my uncle about it, and he told me what he knew, which wasn't that much. I just paused because it's so typical how people are touched by war. This guy was a real stud. He was a marine captain and a real good guy, but it busted something in him. Guadalcanal was really nasty—a lot of Marines and Japanese died there. Looking at the HBO series, *The Pacific*, I thought to myself how sad that he made it off Guadalcanal and was probably scheduled to go back home or somewhere else, but he killed himself. What a shame, what a waste.

I think I'm okay, I don't know. I've had bouts of depression in my life; I've never been treated for it. I actually got into some VA (Veterans Administration) group-thing that was kind of interesting, but it may be genetics. I don't think it has anything to do with the war. My main thing with the war is, I'll have dreams about the boondocks and the jungle in some bad situations, and I'll feel that anxiety, but it's just one of those things. I don't think it's really affected me, but I'm not a doctor, and I've never been psychoanalyzed, but I don't think I have PTSD.

Advice to someone considering a military career

I wouldn't discourage them. I would tell them, "If you're in combat, you'd better make up your mind before you go in or you could get involved in some really nasty, unpleasant stuff." I chuckle about these reservists who are going to be deployed, and they say, "No, I didn't sign up for this. I just wanted to get paid. I wanted to drill. I wanted to go on the weekends and get the money, but I didn't want to go on active duty. I'm not going to Iraq." I think that's laughable, sort of pathetic, but people have to make up their mind. My point is, when you sign up for something, you may wind up getting more than you bargained for. Apart from that, the military is, generally speaking, a meritocracy. If you are good, work hard, and are smart, you can definitely progress and have success.

Current day

I have four sons who live in the San Francisco Bay area and one grandson. My relationships with my kids are very good. I've gotten divorced twice. I'm not currently married. I get along okay with my exes; my kids get along well with me and their moms, so it's good. My oldest is thirty-eight. The youngest graduated from the University of San Francisco as an architect major and is working at an architectural office. The oldest one is a contractor. The middle two have their own business where they make health-food juice every day and deliver it. They're not asking me for rent money, so that's good. I have practiced law continuously for over forty years in San Francisco, but I'm starting to take more time off.

HIP BIKER

Sergeant, United States Air Force
Semper Fortis: "Always Courageous"
349th Strategic Reconnaissance Squadron
Home of Record: Lawrenceville, GA
Home of Residence: Atlanta, GA
DOB: 03 January 1946
Interview conducted McKendrick's Restaurant in Atlanta, GA
    8 February 2011
Jacksonville University

> *If you gaze long into an abyss, the abyss will gaze back into you.*
> —Friedrich Nietzsche

Growing Up

I was born at Emory University Hospital and lived in Lawrenceville, Georgia. That was my first recollection of life. My parents weren't the best parents in the world. My mother was very selfish and my father was on the road all the time. They divorced when I was five, and then my mother got remarried to a drunken stepfather. I went to Robert E. Lee High School where I graduated in 1963. Then I went to Jacksonville University for the winter semester. I failed out of school in 1964. That was the kiss of death. I knew then, that if the government got notice that I was no longer in school, I was 1-A (classification), and would be drafted. I enlisted because I wanted to go into the Air Force.

I had a buddy whose brother was in the Air Force at the same time, and he said, "If you get in the Air Force, you will eat and sleep well." I said, "That sounds good to me." So I went down and enlisted in February, but I didn't have to turn in until September 24. I went to Lackland AFB in San Antonio, Texas, for basic training.

I went home on leave, then on to Biloxi, Mississippi, to Kessler Air Force Base. I was there for ten months going through radio school and learning how to repair radios. When I graduated, they asked, "Where do you want to go?" You wouldn't want to put in for California or New York. They needed to be grouped. I liked the California area, so I put in for California and Arizona. That's what I got—Tucson, Arizona. That's where I was stationed at the SAC (Strategic Air Command) Base. Mostly a SAC base, it was also a big Air Force training base, too. Off duty, I was a part-time bartender for the officer's club.

Vietnam

It was New Year's Eve 1965 about 1600 (military time—4:00 PM for us civilians) and a guy says, "The colonel wants to see you." Oh shit, what did we do? "You're going to pack your bags, you are going to 20." OL-20 was operating location 20. Barksdale, Louisiana, was Operating Location 19. He gave us orders, and we went back to our barracks, which was now under restriction. The phones in the barracks were cut off; even pay phones because when moving out, it was secret. We couldn't tell anybody: our mammas, our wives, or kids. We were gone. OL-20 was Bien Hoa AFB, Vietnam.

1 January 1966: I was deployed to Vietnam for TDY (temporary duty) for six months. I arrived at Bien Hoa, which was northeast of Saigon. If you got drafted, you were property of the Army or Marines. People don't realize that. They would take one hundred draftees and say, "Okay, you twenty are going to the Corps." Vietnam is almost like walking into a black room with no lights. You don't know what to expect. You're not trained for that. I was trained to repair radios on airplanes, not dodge mortars. I didn't do a lot of combat; I was a target. The VC would hit us with mortars and rockets mostly at night. Rarely were there any problems in the day. I would be lying in the hooch (Quonset hut), and sirens would go off. We knew something was incoming, and we just hauled ass to the bunker and literally waited it out.

If you were from a village and were going home with a VC, the VC would kill those village people. The VC ran it. There were almost ten thousand Vietnamese working on the base in the day and then they would go home at night. I am sure there was VC among the base workers at Bien Hoa.

It was tedious. It was so fucking hot and humid, we were never dry. Daytime temperatures were 108 degrees and 100 percent humidity. In the nighttime, it would get down into the 80's, but felt cool. We had a little air conditioner in our Quonset, but it didn't work half the time. We ate and slept well—that's a fact. However, because of the heat during the day, we would have to work on the reconnaissance planes in the hangars at night. The (airplane) skin was so hot you couldn't stand or touch it during the day. Some of our things (work) like the *Dragon Lady* are now declassified, but a lot of it is still classified. The drones were also designed by the CIA. The chase plane they used to train the pilots was a U-3, a Cessna 310.

We were there in support of Operation Rolling Thunder. This was a three-year campaign from 1966-1969 to bomb North Vietnam. In three years, we dropped 1,700,000,000 (that is one billion plus) pounds of bombs on North Vietnam. In my opinion, we didn't hit a fucking thing. We knocked out some bridges and some railroads, but there were four main targets: Hanoi, Haiphong Harbor, Vinh Long Province, which is the start of the Ho Chi Minh trail and Kep Air Field. You couldn't bomb a MiG (Russian Fighter Plane) while it was sitting on the ground because you might kill a Russian. You couldn't mine Haiphong Harbor because Russian ships were supplying the North Vietnamese, and we were scared to death that Russia would get involved. In my opinion, we fought Russia by proxy.

I have been tormented by that! Even the pilots ask why they kept us handcuffed during all the death and destruction. We killed two million Vietnamese civilians, plus a half a million soldiers and that doesn't count Laos and Cambodia. That is haunting! That is why I drink!

In a moment of fear, I was sitting there eating and then the siren goes off. They weren't trying to kill me; they were trying to destroy planes. If they destroyed the U-2, the unit that accomplished that feat received three years' pay—about $150 USD in the '60s.

There were no B-52's in Vietnam. They were flown out of Thailand and Guam because they were such a big target, and they would have been very easy to destroy. We did some drone work along the Chinese-Vietnamese border and saw that the Chinese were also supplying North Vietnam. We were always afraid that China might enter the war too. After the war, China stated they had no intentions of getting involved. So I wonder, when Colonel Mike (see chapter 3) and I talk, "Why didn't we hit those targets?" I think the grunts (ground troops) felt it most. I was there very early. The first combat Marines had just landed in March 1965 at Da Nang, and I thought, *We'll be out of here in a week, how can we lose?* It dragged on and on and on. I remember when the war was over, when I saw them pushing those helicopters off the sides of those carriers to make room for the Vietnamese civilians to leave the country, and they said, "Well, the Vietnam War is over, longest war we ever fought." What do you mean it's over? I puked! We're going home.

I met a guy from Texas who gave a speech in Atlanta to ARVN (Army of the Republic of Vietnam), ex-South Vietnamese soldiers. Gen. Homer Smith orchestrated that last evacuation from Saigon. He told me he was standing about fifteen meters away from the last casualties (Marines) who were killed by a mortar right before they left in April 1975. They were the last two guys (Corporal Charles McMahon *Vietnam Memorial Panel 01W Line 124* and Lance Corporal Darwin Lee Judge *Vietnam Memorial Panel 01W Line 124*) officially killed in Vietnam.

Planes were trying to take off, and people were jumping. People were in the wheel wells, hanging out of the stairs, and on the back of some of the airplanes wanting to get the hell out of there! It was then that the North Vietnamese Army came marching into Saigon. The NVA were not like our troops, but they were good.

Returned stateside 1966, then back to Davis-Monthan AFB in Tucson. I still had two years of inactive reserve. I could have been called back any time during those two years. While I was on inactive reserve, I worked for Delta Airlines on the ramp.

Being a vet stateside, I didn't talk to anybody or tell anybody about what I went through. If someone brought it up, I ignored it. I believe the movie *Platoon* (*1986*) had more to do with waking people up to the fact that the Vietnam War actually happened. There were actually wives who never knew that their husbands served in Vietnam. We wanted to put that chapter of history behind us as if it never happened. There are guys still fucked up today. I had a buddy go to the V.A. (Veterans Administration). The suicides, the PTSD, the divorce rate (I am divorced). I never had children-vasectomy. The last thing I wanted was a kid. The thought never occurred to me. Vets were the only people I could have talked to about the war and I wasn't running around much with people my own age. I ran around with younger people. All my friends and the women I dated were in their thirties. I didn't know that many vets. If I had, we would know each other for a year before we knew we were vets. It was strange, and if you did talk about it, they would think you were a baby killer.

I just meander along and try to put it out of my mind like it didn't happen. My memories have always been black and white. I have trouble sleeping at night. I have to get drunk to sleep. Knowing I took part in something that resulted in the slaughter of so many people, I kind of blame myself. I've had a guilt trip about it. I suppose if I was German, I could be a war criminal. I could have been tried at Nuremburg. What did Hitler do that we didn't? Just in a different way, same thing.

When we found SAM (surface to air missile) sites being built, we could go into the info shop and see them, but couldn't bomb it while it was being built. It had to become operational first. Why? The Russians were building it, and you might kill a Russian. That was so silly because if you don't want to die in Vietnam, keep your Russian ass out of there!

The Cold War was raging. That is why the things we did were so classified. Especially the first drones. The CIA came up. Ryan Aircraft made them; the Robins Air Force Base has a big aerospace museum there. There is a U-2 I worked on in Vietnam, and there are two Ryan drone's. They launched from the wings of a C-130.

How did Vietnam shape your life?

It made me a little more confidant. After Vietnam, nothing scares me. When I'm on my motorcycle going 120 miles per hour, I am not afraid.

I am honorable. My word is my bond. It disgusts me at times that our government allowed that slaughter. There are fifty-eight thousand names on that wall. We never had any business being in Vietnam. Kennedy wanted out, and they killed him for it.

And we lost. How in the fuck did we lose? If you saw anything in the air in America, it was friendly, and they had nothing. The MiGs made up the North. The MiG's main mission was to protect Hanoi and Haiphong. They never came south. They would have gotten their ass kicked. That was a good airplane. Colonel Mike engaged them a few times. The Vietnamese had AKs (AK-47 rifle), pajamas, and some rocket launchers on the ground. We had all of this air power and artillery and fire bases, and they ran us out. The same thing is going to happen to us in Afghanistan too, John.

Never trust the government, always question authority. A guy I knew in George Wallace's cabinet said, "It don't make a damn whether you are a Republican or a Democrat, a politician is a politician is a politician. The two parties are bullshit." The whole damn thing is corrupt. I was a little upset that when I did get out in 1968 that I didn't join the peace movement. I feel guilty that I sat back and said nothing when I should have been on a street corner with a sign, saying, "Stop this madness." Our brothers are getting slaughtered over there for nothing. I regret not marching on Washington. Vietnam was a fiasco, useless—all war has one common denominator and that is blood.

Agent Orange: I used to watch guys when they would bring in a tanker truck, just like you would see filling up at the gas station, a deadly chemical with a shelf life of years. They had nozzles and a flat bed truck with fifty-five-gallon drums and guys in nothing but fatigues pumping dioxin into these fifty-five-gallon drums. They would then be taken and put on a C-123. They would put the hoses down in them, and they would spray. All of those people are dead! When the president of Monsanto attended

Congressional hearings on Agent Orange, he swore that Agent Orange was harmless and wouldn't cause cancers. I really wanted to take a spray bottle and spray him down with his dioxin. By the man's own admission, they couldn't have gotten me for attempted murder, only simple battery, and he would be dead by now. The VA has identified fifty-nine different cancers associated with Agent Orange, some of them so rare they've never been seen before. Dioxin was a liquid used for defoliation. It worked. Since the war ended, the Vietnamese took mortar casings and made fences around the bomb craters and grew fish in the bomb craters. The dioxin has leached into the water where the fish are, babies are being born with three arms, no feet—it's horrible. In addition, five thousand South Vietnamese a year get killed stepping on mines.

I came back sitting backward facing the rear end of a C-130, that noisy motherfucker. You couldn't snooze. It took twenty-five hours to get back. We stopped in Guam then stopped in Hawaii. Then we got back; they didn't even have a bus, and the barracks were about a half a mile away. We had to carry our gear back to the barracks. They didn't give a shit. Then the hippies were protesting outside the base, but you couldn't open your mouth about that.

Advice to someone considering a military career

The branch of service might have something to do with it. What are we doing in Afghanistan? We are obviously not chasing bin Laden. Why are we fighting the Taliban? Those people are illiterate, and it's like we think we are going to turn them into a bustling cosmopolitan. I talked to guys coming home. It is like fighting in the Bible; the indigents own camels. Those in Afghanistan and Iraq have been living like this forever. It's always going to be corrupt, and all we're doing is having the whole world pissed off at us. I would advise a person to go into public service, maybe the Peace Corps. We are going to have to put down the guns and learn one day that this isn't going to get it. Someone is going to mess up one day, and we are going to destroy this world. The Middle East is a time bomb.

This Muslim thing goes back to the crusades. I don't believe in a God. I was raised a Methodist, but have been a Buddhist since Vietnam. Buddhism is the only thing that makes sense to me. Up is down and down is up. Hot is cold, cold is hot. Ugly is cute, cute is ugly. It is just perception and perspective. Long is short, short is long. Buddhism, Zen. I don't have trouble with people praying because they always pray when they want something for themselves. There's no one up there granting wishes. We create our heaven and hell right here. When others tell me that I am entitled to shit because God told me I could have it, I have a big philosophical problem with that.

It's crazy. I think Vietnam got people to talk about God and country. People over there weren't fighting for the flag or God or country. We were fighting for each other. All we had was ourselves. Now when the siren went off there was free beer at the NCO club during mortar attacks. You could go to the bunker or you could go to the NCO club and drink free beer.

You did your job and hoped that you got home. We only lost one guy, and that's not bad for the whole time. When I got out in 1968, I didn't stay in touch with anyone. I had one buddy, and he was dying. He wasn't even in Vietnam with me. He was just in the service back in Tucson. None of us kept in touch. We went our separate ways. If you did meet up with someone, you'd go, "Hey man, how's it going?" There is nothing in common to talk about. It was like seeing a childhood buddy. "I'm good, how about you? How's the family doing?" and that's it.

Doc (Carmelo Infantino) can tell you, he wasn't out there thinking about the American flag and God and country. There isn't any glory on the battlefield. There's only blood and pain and misery. You're only fighting for the buddy next to you.

We used to steal steaks and lobster from the officers club. We had no butter to eat with the lobster, and we didn't want to get caught; but then again, what were they going to do? Send us to Vietnam?

Current Day

I live in Atlanta, Georgia, in the Dunwoody area with my three dogs: Chief, Beau, and Gidget. Chief is a pit bull bird dog. Beau is an Akita mix. Gidget is a bearded collie mix.

THOM NICHOLSON

Colonel, United States Army (Ret.)
De Oppresso Liber: "To Free the Oppressed"
MACV-SOG Fifth Special Forces Group
Home of Record: Springfield, MO
Home of Residence: Denver, CO
DOB: 10 March 1940
Conducted via phone on 9 July 2010.
Missouri School of Mines, Nuclear Engineering

> *Nothing save a battle lost is more terrible than a battle won.*
> —Duke of Wellington

Growing Up

I went to eight grade schools and four high schools; my dad was involved in construction work, and we had to go where his work took us. We spent most of the time in Western and Northern Arkansas and Southern Missouri, although we took time to go to Oklahoma for a year and over to New Mexico for a year, then back to Missouri where I graduated from high school. Then I went to the Missouri School of Mines in Rolla, Missouri, to study nuclear engineering. At the end of my fourth year, I was short graduating, and so, in a fit of pique, I guess, I left school and decided to join the Navy.

I was going to join the Navy because I had seven uncles in the Navy in World War II, but when I went down to talk to them, and they found out I studied nuclear engineering, they said I'd go to submarine school. I said, "I don't want to go on a submarine." The recruiter answered, "Sorry, but that's where you're going, and that's that." I had my dander up by then and said, "Sorry, that's not where I'm going." So I walked across the street and joined the Army. I ended up in the Army because they don't have any subs and because I thought I'd like being in the paratroopers. As I finished up basic training, a guy came around to our basic training unit at Fort Ord (California) recruiting for Special Forces. He was wearing a green beret and dress green uniform, polished jump boots, medals up to his chin, "That's the most studley man I ever saw in my life. I've got to be one of those," and that's how I joined the Special Forces.

This was 1964, and it was still very early on in the war, but the point was that I was supposed to spend a year in Fort Knox, Kentucky, and then go to SF (Special Forces) training. Because of my college background, I was selected to attend OCS; from there, I would go to Special Forces. I ended up spending the year after my graduation (from OCS in Fort Carson, Colorado) as a second lieutenant, because you have to be a first lieutenant to go to Special Forces. As they were starting to ramp up Vietnam, they sent me to SF Officer's Course six months early. After graduation, which was the end of 1965, I was sent to Vietnam as an A-Team executive officer. After my return, I finished up my last semester of college, went to Ranger and Jungle School, and then returned to Vietnam for a second tour.

Vietnam

The funny part about it was when I returned for my second tour, I was supposed to go to the Fourth Infantry Division; but after I arrived, they needed Special Forces volunteers, so I rejoined the Fifth SF Group again. I was assigned to Study and Observation Group (SOG) in Da Nang, which was called Command and Control North (CCN). The Fifth Group also had a CC Central and a CC South, but I was in CCN stationed near Da Nang in the northern part of South Vietnam. When I signed in, I was briefed: "Oh, you can't talk about this. If you talk about this, we'll put you in jail and throw away the key." The next day, I could read all about our operations in *Time* magazine, explaining exactly what we were doing while we were there. The secret got out pretty quick about our mission, which was to sneak across the Laotian border to monitor infiltration of NVA troops into South Vietnam. We also put out sensors and stuff like that trying to get some idea of what was coming out of the North into the South. Our job wasn't really to interdict and stop it, but just to try to count it more than anything else.

We would actually recruit and train replacements for our people as we used them up (casualties), because we used them up pretty quick doing the job we did. I was involved with that at the staff level, and then I had a quick strike reaction company for a while. My troops were Radè Montagnard mercenaries recruited from tribes run out of their homeland in northern Laos. I did a lot of training with them, primarily, rifle marksmanship, which they didn't know much about, but took to it rather quickly. They really had great outdoor skills; they could track and move through the jungle real well, but they'd never used anything particularly modern before we got there. Their primary weapon had been a crossbow. We had to train them how to use a rifle, but they took to it right away because they saw how good it was for them.

There were also a few Army of South Vietnam (ARVN) soldiers assigned to my unit, but they didn't go out very often, and they didn't have much to do with the training. They just stayed in the rear and did what they did, paperwork or something. They weren't welcomed to go with us into the bush because they weren't dependable.

The ARVN Marines got the best men the US Marines could give. The ARVN Marines were tough like the Republic of Korea (ROK) boys; they did their job. They were trained predominantly by our Marine Corps people. I'm sure they were much better than the majority of the ARVN units. Some other ARVN units were pretty good depending on the motivation of the troops; the senior commanders set the tone. If the commanders were aggressive and took care of their troops and weren't crooked like some were, then the troops responded and they were pretty good.

I think most of us came out of Special Forces training feeling like we were really on top of our game. We really felt like we'd received some good training. We were a tough bunch of dudes, and we could handle combat; I was looking forward to it. I was going to go over there and kick some ass and the VC would be sorry they were ever born. Then you show up and you see the dirt, misery, tedium, and all the things that go into a war. Besides the little bit of combat you see, you find out it wasn't as much fun as you thought it was going to be. It was quite a shock! My unit was tasked with combat operations all the time. We did not get into nation building or any of the other "hot buttons" to win the hearts and minds of the South Vietnamese people. Once I saw American soldiers dying, any "fun" went away.

In my opinion, the SEALs are the best-trained and toughest soldiers the United States produces. They have a special mission so unique that they can really focus on it. They're highly trained and motivated shock troops. They go in fast, kick ass, come out, and go home. Special Forces (in Vietnam) were meant to go back behind the lines, stay there, and develop the people that are there into some sort of cohesive unit that can be used as a force multiplier against those people we're opposed to. So the training was different in that respect. In terms of physical training and the ability to shoot, live in the jungle, kill bad guys and all that stuff, Special Forces are very well trained and incredibly motivated. I think the SEALs are just the best there are. There's no doubt about it, for pure out-and-out warrior, SEALs are your men.

The SEALs as a unit are probably ten out of a possible ten. Delta Force SF troops are also probably 10/10, but because there are so few of them available, they impart very little power over the long haul. Special Forces are probably 8/10 as I would rate them as warriors. Delta guys are kind of the Army (version) of SEALs. I sometimes think that there's redundancy in what the services put together; I mean the SEALs could probably do what Delta does and Delta could probably do what SEALs do, but the Navy and the Army want their finger in the pie. You know how that goes. Marines want their share of the action too for that matter, so they train a unit called force recon; they're just as tough as anybody else.

How did Vietnam shape your life?

That's a good question. When I came back I was very disappointed with the way we were treated. On my bus trip from Travis Air Force Base, near San Francisco, to the San Francisco Airport, as we came out of the base, people demonstrating threw rocks and eggs at the bus. I can still remember how that hurt—how I wanted to die. I remember how enraged I was and how I wanted to get to Carson and stomp some of those hippies into the mud. However, I decided that when I got home I would not let Vietnam defeat me, even though I felt it defeated our country in some ways. I just didn't dwell on it. I just went forward, and tried not to look back. If I had problems about it, I didn't let them stay with me or drag me down. I worked within myself to get past it and then just kept on going, never looking back. I was in country from 1965 through 1966, then from 1968 to 1970. I regret it all the time; I felt Vietnam was a black mark on American history. I thought we gave up on the people to whom we made promises. I truly believe we could have won the war. If they had let us do what we wanted, I believe we could have won. I wasn't as good a soldier as I should have been. I got people hurt that maybe I could have saved if I had just been better. I wish I'd just worked harder to be a better officer because once they're gone you can't bring them back. It gets you if you let it, that's for sure. I lost a lot of friends over there and still miss them. I feel guilt that I lived, and they didn't. Funny, isn't it?

The war was a chaos that never got managed. There was no clear objective that I could ever see as to what we were doing except killing people. A perfect example of that was Hamburger Hill where we lost (KIA) 250 paratroopers from the 101st Airborne Division. The powers that be ordered them to take that stupid hill, and a couple of months later, I was in that same area. We left and the enemy just came back in like we'd never been there. Now what kind of fighting is that? That's madness.

You can pretty much be certain that all we fought *after* the Tet Offensive (January 1968 through April 1968) were NVA. (*Author-Tet is the Vietnamese New Year that is celebrated at different dates from year to year. In 1968 the holiday fell on 31 January).* We never again saw Viet Cong soldiers; we killed just about every one of them. Do the newspapers report that? Hell, no! The North Vietnamese Army was the only organized unit that we had to work against because the VC were gone. They would start to fill their ranks with new recruits, but as a fighting unit after Tet of 1968, the VC were nothing.

I was ordered to go back for my second tour. I could have gotten out of it because my brother was already there, and the Army had a regulation that brothers didn't have to serve in country at the same time. However, I felt like I had been trained for that. I knew what I was doing, and as a returnee, I was actually probably a better choice than somebody going for the first time. I didn't try to fight it; I went ahead and took my assignment. I met up with my brother while there, and we both made it home in one piece.

My unit was filled with some of the bravest young Americans that ever walked this earth; I used to stare in awe and think, *How could they do it?* It was a privilege to be in that unit and serve with those guys. It was the Command & Control North (CCN) of the Military Assistance Command Special Operations Group (MACSOG) operation. It was a MACSOG unit filled with Special Forces soldiers, and two-thirds of them were five-man recon teams. About two to three Americans and two to three Montagnard's went out and snuck through the bush looking for the bad guys. Then there were a couple of companies of reaction troops of which I was commander for a while. We went out and reacted to anything recon teams found. When you went across the border, psychologically it was harder. When they went across the border like we did and the planes flew back, you felt so alone. You had to fight the loneliness as well as the fact that there were bad guys out there hunting (you) from where you land trying to catch you, and of course, they weren't going to take you prisoner—that wasn't their objective and we weren't about to be taken prisoner.

We lost a lot of guys. The Americans were better than the Vietnamese about bringing someone home if we had a guy down. We put a lot of effort into trying to get him out even if he was dead, but occasionally, we'd leave one there for whatever reason so there were several dozen Special Forces guys among those MIAs. My very best friend was killed over there; his name was Charlie Lindewald (*Vietnam Memorial Panel 38E Line 005*). I'd known him for several years. He was killed on 7 February 1968 in Quang Tri Province. His body was found a few years year ago (2004). I went to his funeral at Arlington. It was a good closure for me. I always felt guilty

I wasn't there protecting his back like I had done in earlier assignments. I think they buried him as a master sergeant. For thirty years, he laid in an unmarked grave, but now he's home sleeping with the brave men of Arlington. I really miss him a lot; I miss them all. You try to put it behind you, not to see their faces anymore and keep on going.

Advice to someone considering a military career

I would tell them it's the most wonderful job you can have if you like it. You have to recognize that it's a big organization; it has its bureaucracy and it has its bad parts as well as its good. If you get involved in it, stay with it. If it suits your personality and meets your goals, it's the most rewarding career imaginable. I loved it.

Current day

I live here in Denver with my second wife, next to our daughter, who has some grandkids for me to play with. My first wife said I was different after Vietnam and left me. I've got four boys scattered all over the country from Annapolis, Maryland to Portland, Oregon so my family's stretched out like most nuclear families are now.

I only have one kid that went into the service; I thought more would go. One other would have gone, but he had a bad back, and they wouldn't let him in. The others said they had had enough moving around with me. My ex-wife, I'm sure, was against them going because she was bitter about how the service uprooted our family all the time.

Closing Comments

And in the end it is not the years of your life that count. It is the life in your years.

—Abraham Lincoln

Up until March 2011, John Gulick and I were faceless to each other. Our schedules never meshed on both my West Coast trips in 2010. The 21 March was the first time I saw John (on his Internet site). I e-mailed him immediately and stated that he looked good for a seventy-year-old SEAL! During the interview, my mind continued to drift toward the training documentaries I had viewed of the SEALs training in Coronado, California. How can they do what they do? The focus and inner (and outer) strength must mimic both Houdini and Hercules combined. It is now, and always will be, important for me to stay in touch with men like John Gulick. It is a good feeling calling him, and all these vets, on their birthdays. They forget I ever asked, but that was my intent, both for the reader and me. On the 235th birthday of our country in 2011, I will call John and wish him happy birthday.

Colonel Thom Nicholson was kind enough to conduct the interview with me. More so was his acceptance in writing the foreword of this book. For him to tell me "it would be my honor" bowled me over and really hit home; that maybe I was really accomplishing something here for those who served. One of Thom's comments was, "I lost a lot of friends over there and I still miss them." As his survivor's guilt kicked in during our talk, I continued to blame myself for not wearing a uniform. Joe Crescenz (see chapter 4) said to me recently, "If they would ever change the ceiling on induction in the military, we both would enlist."

And then there is Hip. We must have spent dozens of hours on the phone from 17 January until our interview on 8 February 2010, and hundreds of hours since. He is like my brother. I believe that I would be a better person if we had crossed paths earlier in my life. Hip opened my soul to the pain and suffering both he and his fellow veterans experienced. Not sure my soul can be sewn back up.

CHAPTER TWO
1967-1969

Maelstrom

**Dedicated to James "Daddy Wags" Wagner
Sergeant, United States Marine Corps
Third Motor Truck Battalion, Ninth Marine Regiment,
Third Marine Division**

*The rush of battle is often a potent and lethal addiction, for war is
a drug.*

—Chris Hodges

Operation Francis Marion. Con Thien. Dak To. Operation Buffalo. Battle of Huẻ. Khe Sanh. Operation Rolling Thunder. Junction City. Hamburger Hill. Operation Buffalo. These are just some of the battles and operations that occurred during the terrible years from 1967 to 1969. While these engagements were raging, anti-war sentiments at home began to increase from a pianissimo to a forte. The media then played the tune full blast that ultimately divided the country. My personal belief is that 1968 was the worst year in our country's history. Why?

January	Siege of Khe Sahn.
February	First Tet Offensive (beginning 31 January) rages through April
March	My Lai Massacre
April	Martin Luther King Jr. shot.
May	Second Tet Offensive—Over 2,400 American KIAs this month alone.
June	Walter Cronkite—"The war is lost." Robert Kennedy shot
July	Anti-war demonstrations continue unabated.
August	Bloody Chicago Convention
September	Media sensationalism continues to fuel the "end the war" mentality.
October	Civil rights tension culminating in the Black Power Salute at the Olympics
November	Massive Draft Card Burning.
December	Killed in action exceeds 36,000 for the war.

Over 70 percent of all casualties during the war were from 1 January 1967 to 31 December 1969. Since June 2010, I have occasionally worn Special Forces Captain James J. Amendola's KIA bracelet. His home of residence was Closter, New Jersey. Captain Amendola (*Vietnam Memorial Panel 20W Line 068*) was killed on 29 July 1969 at Tra Cu in Hau Nghia Province.

Introduction to the Interviews

There are no garden-variety stories throughout this work. Every person had a great account to tell. Why? It is *their story*. The Army interviews here include a captain, a family member whose brother was KIA, and Jim Schlegel, who was assigned to a logistics support unit in Saigon and told me I may not want to depict his story because it may be too "vanilla." Of all the services I had the honor to represent in this book, the unit that had the most esprit de corps was, by far, the Marines. By pure chance, all the initial Marine Corps interviews were of men who served during, or were in support of, the siege of Khe Sanh from 22 January 1968 through mid April 1968. Dennis Frank was the initial contact and first marine interview in March 2010. While I was canvassing, searching, for "grunts," a number of people led me to combat corps vets who served in Vietnam. Dennis's name crossed my e-mail, and after calling him, we met for breakfast in Willow Grove, Pennsylvania. Due to circumstances not within my control, Dennis was never able to confirm our interview via e-mail or hard copy. This was a prerequisite from all interviewees for obvious publishing reasons. However, because of his service, fervor, and his son's current service to our country (Captain Frank USMC HMX Helicopter Squadron that flies the president—*Marine 1*), I deemed it necessary to include this information. Dennis always receives a phone call on 4 May on his birthday.

I met Paul Ferraro and his wife at Pennsylvania Hospital one hot summer day in June 2010. One of my transcribers suggested we meet. In May 2010, we spoke on the phone while I was in San Francisco. After originally scheduling our talk immediately following his wife's hospital visit, we decided it was best to conduct the interview via phone as they had a long drive back to upstate Pennsylvania. Later on, Paul approved use of all his materials and poems that he has written (his interview has been removed at his request). Afterward, I strolled into Cookies Tavern in South Philly. While taking a call from my friend Pat Knapp who kept abreast of all my interviews weekly, I mentioned Khe Sanh in the conversation. At that point a gentleman walked over and tapped me on the shoulder, saying, "Did you just say Khe Sanh?" Answering yes and apologizing at the same time for my loud voice, he asked why. After many beers and a few shots, Forward Observer (FO) John Lang (also at Khe Sanh—Third Battalion Ninth Marines) understood the circumstances. Sergeant Lang has since provided me with a ton of information regarding the Corps, various books, and a work by his good friend and FO "trainer" Dave Martin.

Lance Corporal David "Smilie" Martin agreed to the interview never speaking to John Lang. Dave assured me later that he didn't check me out first. Because our initial meeting was a lunch in Morrisville, Pennsylvania, and after talking for three hours, Dave decided that he would do the interview. I obviously felt good about that. Dave's book *Crazy Asian War* is one of the best nonfiction works I have read on the war. He is a great American and a former career employee of Veteran Affairs who battled each and every day for his compatriot's benefits for thirty years.

Marines will sacrifice their very existence for a unit member on the battlefield. When in need, regardless of the circumstances, be they personal or combat, they are there for each other. It is a life lesson for all. Subsequent to Dennis, Paul, John, and Dave, I have met hundreds of Marines at airports, bars, reunions, planes, and trains. They are amazingly "always faithful" to one another, embracing the Marine Corps "Semper Fidelis" motto, and I have become faithful to all of them by pure osmosis.

The process to find guardsmen was very challenging. After months of trying to network, then research, then call various training facilities of the

Coast Guard, I finally found vets from Vietnam. The problem was, as with all other services, not everyone wanted to share their experiences—just too many bad memories. Plus, I was an unknown civilian to them. Finally, I found Gary Sherman, a gentleman who lives in Norristown, Pennsylvania. He directed me to Paul Scotti who, aside from being a career Guardsman, is an historian for the service. Meeting Paul in October 2010 subsequent to our interview was very rewarding. Paul is a polished professional—both an academic as well as Veteran of Foreign Service.

There have been many conversations amongst folks while I was writing this book. One repeated question is "I didn't even know the Coast Guard was involved in Southeast Asia!" In many ways, this was no different than during WWII when you watch all those D-Day landings. Guess what—some of the drivers of those Higgins Boats (Landing Craft) were US Coast Guardsmen! You just can't "land" a boat, be it a troop carrier or a huge LCT (Landing Craft-Tank) because of the currents, sea floor depth, speed, wind, and other factors. It took skill that in some ways even some Navy personnel did not possess.

The USCG 82 foot "cutters" were used in the "brown water" war, attempting to interdict VC and NVA infiltration and logistics. In 1968, the first oceangoing cutters augmented the Navy and Coast Guard surveillance forces already in Vietnam. Coast Guardsmen were also detailed to improve port security, especially in Saigon, to assist with problems involving the Merchant Marines, and to teach workmen the basics of safe handling of ammunition and other dangerous cargoes. An in country navigation system was created and the LORAN (Long Range Navigation) network was set up for Southeast Asia. The "Vietnamization" program under Nixon and General Abrams (who took over for Westmoreland) began in February 1969 and was concluded by December 1971. In all, fifty-six Coast Guard cutters served in Vietnam.

There were over eight thousand US Coast Guardsmen in the Vietnam War. Virtually all volunteered their service. They were far more involved than we civilians will ever know. If you want to get a feel of how difficult the USCG training regimen is for their elite swimmers, watch *The Guardian*. Kevin Costner and Ashton Kutcher both give terrific performances on one of the toughest school training (water) grounds in all the Armed Services. The movie will open your eyes to what we don't know about the United States Coast Guard.

Bobbie Loftus is the tax collector for Warminster Township, Pennsylvania. When first walking into her office to pay your "dues," you are met with a plethora of "I am proud to be an American." Flags abound, plaques are plentiful, and you immediately know you are in the office of a true patriot. While I was writing a book on Gettysburg in 1999, I assured her that when I would venture into another war, she would be one of my first interviews. On 5 March 2010, I honored that pledge.

Bobbie's brother was a young man who was aligned with twenty-six other Cardinal Dougherty High School graduates who were killed during their service in Vietnam. Because some underclassman enlisted into the service before graduating, the number of KIA is actually thirty. All their names are on the Memorials in both Washington and Philadelphia. The other two schools in Philly, which bore terrible loss, were Cardinal Judge High School (twenty-seven) and Thomas Edison High School. Edison "wears" the distinct robe where fifty-four schoolmates were KIA in Vietnam, the largest loss of life of any school in the country.

On a beautiful day in August 2010, I had the honor of meeting George "No Slack" Fallon in Valley Forge, Pennsylvania. While attending Medal of Honor recipient David Dolby's memorial funeral, George spoke of his service, and after my (typical) probing of his tour in Vietnam, George became interested in this work. Shortly afterward, at his home in Waterford, New Jersey, we had lunch hosted by his wife Teresa. After a few hours, he agreed to participate as an interviewee.

It was through the invitation of Commander Kevin Potter USNR (Ret.) that I attended Specialist Fourth-Class Dolby's service. A friend of my brother, Kevin and I played cards at Peter's house in March 2010. Otherwise, both Kevin and George may never have crossed paths with me.

Jim Schlegel and I were introduced as a result of Bob Hogan's (see chapter 3) insistence. They live in the same town. One of my favorite "local" drives is to go north toward Allentown, then west to the Kutztown area through the beautiful Mennonite farmlands. Regardless of the time of year, the view is consistently scenic. Retired, Jim spends time with his wife, kids, and grandchildren. He is a good man, and he graciously accepted my request to listen to what it was like being in the Transportation Command for the Army.

In order for a soldier to become part of the Special Operations Force, which includes Airborne, Special Forces, Rangers, Marine Recon, Delta Force, and Navy SEALs, you must complete the rigorous Airborne "jump" school. George Fallon met those criteria. He is a fascinating man. As his friend and unit member Bob (RO) Martin stated in his book *Spirit of the Warrior*, "George was one of those rare individuals that could find humor in the worst situations." Proud of his country, earning the Silver Star and a Purple Heart for his actions that saved his friend's life. It was after my discussions with PFC (private first class) Fallon that I came up with the idea of the orange bracelet. Subsequent to his interview in August 2010, George invited me to the annual New Jersey Chapter 101st Airborne Reunion hosted at the United States Military Academy on 3 December 2010. This reunion is in honor of General Anthony McAuliffe, hero of WWII Bastogne/Battle of the Bulge fame. General McAuliffe responded "nuts" to the German offer of surrender after the 101st was completely surrounded in December 1944. The rest is history. Unfortunately, I was unable to attend. It will be December 2011 when I can finally meet some of the Airborne, First Cavalry and Special Forces vets from WWII, Korea, and Vietnam at this West Point function.

Mr. Fallon is one of the many Vietnam veterans who suffer from PTSD, as well as exposure to Agent Orange. With the exception of Army Combat Medic Steve Knuboff, George seems to have these burdens more than any other soldier I have interviewed or met in my journey. His friend Allen Lloyd is alive today, a CPA in Florida, due to George's lifesaving actions in Tam Ky Province, South Vietnam. I finally met Allen in April, then again at the annual Vietnam veterans gathering in Melbourne, Florida in May 2011. When going to the panhandle state, there is a hot shower and room available to me complements of Allen.

A nagging question from many civilians, and quite a few paratroopers, is 'why would someone jump out of a perfectly good airplane?"

HOMER R. STEEDLY JR.

Captain (Inactive), United States Army
Semper Vigilans: *"Vigilant Always"*
Bravo Co. First Battalion Eighth Infantry Regiment Fourth Infantry Division
Home of Record: born near Bamberg, Germany
Home of Residence: Hendersonville, NC
DOB: 07 June 1946
Interview conducted at Homer's residence 28 March 2010
University of South Carolina
Website: www.swampfox.info

> *Freedom is one generation away from extinction.*
> —Ronald Reagan

Growing Up

My mother and father met in postwar Germany. Daddy was a courier, but received a serious head injury in a motorcycle accident, could no longer ride the bike, so he became a cook. While a cook, he met my mom who was a German. They got married, and I came out a year later, 7 June 1946. Daddy went back to the States about two months after I was born. He expected to send for mom immediately, but when he got home, he found out that his sisters, in order to survive since his father was an alcoholic and didn't really take care of the family, sold the farm. He came back home expecting to have a farm and a source of income; instead, he came back to find he was penniless. It took him a year to be able to afford to send for mom and me. Mom came through Ellis Island and arrived in Bamberg (yes—same town name as in Germany!), South Carolina. We were basically truck farmers providing vegetables and fruits for the Farmer's Market.

I have one brother and two sisters. There was me, my older sister Nancy, my younger brother Tony, and then my younger sister Linda. I had a pretty good childhood. We worked hard; we were poor. In the early years, when we first got back before my older sister was born, there were times when we were barely getting by. I remember times when I had supper, and I was the only one that ate; they said they were going to eat later, but I knew I was the only one that got to eat that night. I remember making flapjacks out of flour and water and the syrup was some sugar water browned in the skillet. I didn't know any better back then, but looking back, I realize what was going on. By the time Daddy got Mom over, he still didn't have any place to stay. He was only working part-time, odd jobs here and there. Mom couldn't speak English, so she couldn't get a job; and until I was about six or seven years old, times were pretty rough. They weren't bad. We didn't realize how rough it truly was in Bamberg.

I went to Bamberg High School then Clemson University intending to major in chemistry. I had been a chemistry wiz in high school. My science fair project was a rocket that went to about thirty thousand feet. It almost shot down an airliner. NASA gave me an award for it. I was expecting to do well at Clemson. Then when I arrived, I soon realized what I had been taught in that small, rural Southern farm community town was about twenty or thirty years out of date. The students at Clemson already knew about quarks, charmed particles, pi-mesons, and the like while I still saw the atom in the Bohr planetary ring model. I was completely out of my league. I tried desperately for a year to compete, but with my weak math and my weak science background, I just couldn't do it, so I dropped out and joined the Army. My intentions were to go into the Army, get a little time to get myself a high school education on my own, learn the things I had not learned, and then use the GI Bill when I got out of the service to go back to college. I guess I knew about Vietnam, but it didn't have any reality for me. I was told I was going to Alabama for training in the Chemical Corps. Then it disappeared as soon as I was enlisted.

I went to Fort Gordon (Georgia) for basic training then I was shipped out to Ft. Lewis for AIT (advanced infantry training). We were getting trained to go to Vietnam. They had a Vietnamese village set up and everything—I didn't quite understand that. Here we are in the snow training for combat in a tropical jungle. I caught double pneumonia and was in a coma for four days and had frostbite because we were camping out for two weeks in the snow getting ready to go to the Vietnam *jungles*. It didn't make any sense, but anyway that's where they trained us. While I was there after AIT, recovering from pneumonia, I worked around the base doing odd jobs. One of the officers who knew me suggested I try to take the placement test for OCS (Officers Candidate School). I was a private first class E3, enlisted man. I took the test and managed to get into Officers Candidate School and went down to Fort Benning for fifty-two weeks. I was in the same class with Lieutenant Calley (My Lai Massacre) whom everybody knows. Calley was a Platoon Sergeant in my unit. He was one of the old school "brown boot Army" style enlisted men, who took orders as the final word, not subject to interpretation.

I got out of there when I was commissioned and was sent to Fort Jackson, South Carolina, which, coincidentally, was where my wife to be, forty years later, was dancing at the USO while I was stationed there. I lived off base less than a block from where she lived. I started off training rifle marksmanship, the qualification range. About four months into that, the Army decided guys in Vietnam were having difficulty reading maps and, of course, map reading was very important. They asked me to set up the land navigation map reading course. I was the one who wrote the Army Subject Schedule. After the thirty-day leave, I was off to Vietnam August 1968.

Vietnam

I flew to Japan, then Cam Ranh Bay on the southern coast of Vietnam. From there, I took an aircraft up to Pleiku province. From Pleiku, I took a helicopter to Dak To which is on the Cambodian, Laos border area. In fact, when I got there, almost half the company were replacements because so many guys got wounded and killed during an attack. Each company was usually assigned a weapons platoon, but we had none. It was usually broken down and the personnel were put into the other three platoons so you usually only had three platoons in the field. Of the three platoons, you were running only about 70 percent strength. A squad was supposed to be seven to nine men. For us, five or six was usual per squad. Because of the shortage, we did a lot of 3-4-5 man patrols.

Our job up there was to patrol the Ho Chi Minh Trail, that network of trails that came from North Vietnam down south through the jungles through both Cambodia and Laos. We were supposed to find where they were making trails, interdict them, and stop them from using the trails. We spent most of our time out in the jungle hopping from ridgeline to ridgeline, flying from ridgeline to ridgeline to see if there was activity there. If there was, we set up ambushes and stopped them from using that trail. Then, after they had a couple of days inactivity on that trail, we moved to wherever they'd move. We sent out long-range reconnaissance patrols (LRRP), and we sent out short-range patrols also. We were a moving unit. If we were moving as a platoon-size unit, we would set up a perimeter and then send out two, three, or four men for patrols from that perimeter in various directions to cover that area. If we were moving as a company-size unit, we would set up a perimeter and generally stay there for a week or two.

In company-size units, we worked off a FSB (fire support base). In platoon-size units, you couldn't call it a firebase because we never stayed more than a day or two; we didn't want to get spotted. My responsibilities were first platoon leader, Bravo Company as a second lieutenant. Within three months of being made the platoon leader, I was promoted to first lieutenant and made the Company XO (executive officer). I was the CO's (company officer's) right-hand man. I ran the trains area and base camp and did all the legal paperwork, all the courts-martial, article 15, stuff like that. It was a staff position except I kept running back and forth between the field and the rear supply trains area. I did the payroll as well.

If I was caught up in the rear, then I would come back to the field and I would lead when the company would split into two sections. I would take two platoons and go one direction. The CO would take two platoons and go the other direction. I attended the battalion staff meetings when I was in base camp, which included the S (staff) positions-S1 was personnel, S2 Intelligence positions, S3 operations, and S4 logistics. These were the battalion counterparts to the G (general) brigade positions. Because I had that experience later on toward the end of my second tour, I worked in the battalion's tactical operations center as the S3 air-coordinating aircraft for supply, transport, and gunship support to the battalion. The S positions usually encompassed the best folks in the field prior to promotion. What was happening in Vietnam was, an officer came to the field, spent six months, and then he would be given the last six months of his tour back at base camp at some desk job or staff position at one of the battalion headquarters or in the trains area running the trains or something like that. I was rewarded with the XO position three months sooner than most people. Usually, you didn't get that until your second six months.

One of the reasons I extended my second tour was—this probably doesn't make sense to a civilian—simply because I had already begun to see what my NCOs (noncommissioned officers), my two and three tour NCOs already knew. There was a pattern you could see. A new officer would come to the field and not knowing what he was doing, he would get people killed. He would learn his lessons the hard way and people would die or get wounded in the process. The NCOs knew this was going to happen. They would try to tell him, but he wouldn't listen. Finally, he would figure out what was necessary. He would get real good for three or four months; then he would figure out he was going to the rear and get real cautious. If you get real cautious, you get people killed. Then he'd leave and another jackass would come out and make the same mistakes. It was more individualistic. We had good pointers (West Point graduates). We had good Citadel graduates. We had strong what we call ring knockers. We had good ones and we had bad ones. They had their academy rings on and would knock them on the table top calling attention to them. You would notice their damn ring. We also had some good ROTC men. The difficulty with infantry combat is that there are infantry combat leaders, and there are perfectly good officers who have no business in the field leading troops in combat. It's a different skill set leading combat than being a good staff officer back in the rear. Some people can do it and some can't. Training doesn't have a whole lot to do with it. Training is useful, but it's much more than training.

I had classic examples. I had a lieutenant that was from the Citadel, and I tried my best to explain to this young man that he needed to listen to his NCOs. He was trying to do the tactics as he was taught, classic military tactics, which you couldn't use in Vietnam in the Central Highlands, because the NVA read our classical doctrine; and if you followed it, they knew exactly what you were going to do. They could predict you, and predictability gets you killed! I kept trying, and the NCOs within his platoon tried. I kept telling him, "You keep this up, and one of your NCOs is going to shoot you because you're getting people hurt for no good reason. You're not listening to what I'm trying to tell you and you're not listening to what they're trying to tell you." It turned out that he did wind up getting shot in the back. Somebody "accidentally" test-fired a machine gun while he was taking a crap outside of the perimeter. I know it was deliberate. There's no doubt about it. I can't prove it. He didn't get killed. He was lucky, and I understand. It was self-defense. He was getting people killed. When you're getting people killed because you're making bad decisions and you're being told why your decisions are bad and you still continue acting on them, then you're the enemy at that point.

Everybody in Vietnam has a big snake experience. I mean everybody has one because there were these big anacondas everywhere. This was an Asian python that we came across. This snake, honest to God, John, looked like a log. When I first saw him, we were going up a ridgeline to search the top of the ridge. As we're going up the ridge, the column stopped. So I'm ticked. It is 100-105 degrees, really hot. We've all got these pounding headaches. The point man stopped. We're not in a good mood, and it is hard climbing. You've got to pull yourself from root to root to get up the side of this slippery red clay hill. I get up to where he is (the point man), and he's up there and he's whispering to me. He said, "It is right up there." I looked up ahead and saw a log across the trail. I said, "You stopped for a log?" He said, "No, it's a snake!" Of course, I'm right on the edge of heat exhaustion anyway. As I got closer to it, I looked at it, and there's a pattern to it. I couldn't quite make it out. I got a little bit closer to it, and I realized, "Oh my god! That is a snake!" It's a snake maybe eight feet *in diameter*, and we got up to him, and he's disappearing off the trail into one side of the jungle . . . nine feet on the other side (they can be six meters or more in length), and I couldn't see which end was the tail or the head. I couldn't tell which end was getting smaller at all. I looked at him, and he was moving. If you look real close, he's moving very slowly. Of course, the men didn't want to cross this damn snake. They're afraid they'd slip and hit it, and it'd get them, but we had to get up the ridgeline because we had to get down the ridgeline before dark to get our supplies. We hadn't had food for a day, so already we're desperate for food and water, and there's no water in the area. We had to get up to the ridgeline. There was no two ways about it. I managed to cajole and stand there and help people, grabbing their packs and pulling them up from the uphill side. I get everybody up all right except the last guy in the line. He is scared of snakes. He is not going anywhere near that damn snake. I mean, you can imagine! I said, "Listen. You have to go across the snake. At least you know where he is. If you go around him on one side or the other, we don't know, he may have a mate. At least here we've got a trail."

The snake didn't know we were there. He was that big; he was far enough in the other direction that he didn't really care. Still this guy won't budge. So I told him, "I'm sorry, but we have to go." I took off, and I went around a trail just out of sight and sat down and I waited about twelve minutes. All of a sudden, I heard, "Goddamn it . . . blah blah blah." I came around the bend, and he said, "Lieutenant, I ought to shoot your ass!" I said, "Shut up! Let's get out of here before that snake comes to get you!" He looked over his shoulder real quick, and off we went. Anyway, that's my big snake story. Everybody in Vietnam ran into an anaconda or a big python like that.

My first tour there's another story. I still get choked up when I tell this story even today. This was my first loss from my own command. We were moving up a ridgeline to see if there was any traffic. We were moving along, and all of a sudden, there was a burst of gunfire up front. I heard some M-16s go off, and all hell broke loose. Of course, we all hit the dirt and then started trying to return fire, and then it got quiet. Then Doc (combat medic Ed Gehringer) and I started moving up front to where the point man was. When we got there, there was one guy that was shot in the stomach and another guy that's shot in the—I don't remember if it was the leg or the lung, but two serious injuries. The squad that was with me had moved on up and was clearing the trail. They came back and reported later that they didn't see anyone, but that they could see bloodworms. They could see places where coagulated blood had come out of a wound and dropped on the trail. We know we got somebody seriously injured, but they (VC or NVA) had taken off with him. I get to Doc and Ed has already given this one guy two shots of morphine. The guy is screaming. He's just bleating like a lamb with his foot in a trap. Every lung full of air—he's just bleeding out. He's grabbing his guts because what had happened is that he was the slack man, the guy directly behind the point man in line. He had turned to try and warn the people behind him, and they shot him in the back, and that blew his stomach out. He's sitting there picking his guts up and trying to put them back in. I came up, and I looked at Doc and Ed looked at me. I know he's not going to make it. We're thirty minutes away from the LZ (landing zone). There was just no way. He's going to bleed out. I told Doc, "Go take care of the other guy, and I'll take care of him. Just give him more morphine for the pain." Doc said, "I can't give him more, it'll kill him!"

He had the morphine in his hand. I said, "Give it to me and I'll wait. If it looks like he needs another shot, I'll give it to him." Doc took off. Of course as soon as Doc took off, I went and gave him the other shot of morphine. He was going to die anyway. His intestines were lying all over the ground even though he had managed to get some stuffed back in. He's in a panic because he knew he's dying.

I gave him a steel pot and I told him, "Hold this over your intestines so the germs won't get in" and that seemed to calm him down. Then he lay back, and he started getting cold from blood loss. Doc came back up and told me what the other guy's status was. I think it was a sucking chest wound. We needed to get him to the LZ to get him out of there. By that time, the guy that I was working on was getting weak, getting pale. He's getting chalky looking. He's not far from, you know. He tried to say something, and I couldn't hear him, so I leaned down real close. I always got choked up. I'm sorry, John. I leaned down close, and he whispered in my ear, "Sir, was I a good soldier?" I said, "Yeah. You're a hero, son!" He said, "Please tell my parents I did good." I said, "Don't worry. You can tell them yourself. We're going to get you to the landing zone. You'll be okay." He looked up at me, and he smiled, and he exhaled, and that was his last breath.

I would say about 80 percent of the people that got killed were the new guys because they had not learned how to take care of themselves, and it happened usually within the first or second firefight. They did not understand the significance of cover, but it has to get through on that level where it becomes instinctual. So you called them nicknames like South Philly or Chucky—anything other than their real name. You didn't want to know about them. If they managed to be around long enough, you eventually picked up little details about them, but you didn't deliberately try to find out.

I spent the last three or four weeks in a battalion Tactical Operations Center (TOC). It was probably the best period of my entire life. I was a captain at this point. I have never performed at that level, before or since. My mental acuity at that time was incredible. You would come on for a regular four-hour shift. You would come on two hours early, sit there, and you were in this bunker. There were five or six radios going simultaneously, and all of them giving you vital information. There were firefights going on, sometimes two or three units at a time. You're trying to coordinate artillery, medevac, and logistics—all at the same time. You would sit there for two hours to get used to who was talking, get used to the call signs. When it was your time to come in, you would tap the guy on duty, and he would usually jump, look at you, realize what was going on, and give you the handset so that you could take over. Four hours later, someone's touching you, and then it would take you a couple of hours to calm down. You had two hours of sleep. Then you did it again. Twenty-four hours a day, seven days a week, but you did it. You felt good about it because you were saving lives. You were the guy in the sky that you had heard on the radio when you were in the field. I did that and then, all of a sudden, I left like that (the country). One evening, probably about nine o'clock, I went back to the base camp, to the trains area, got a little bit of sleep, got on a CH-47 (Chinook) helicopter, flew back down to Cam Ranh Bay, and waited about two hours there at the replacement center.

I took a commercial airplane from there and flew back. We flew to Narita, Japan, and then we were to go straight to Fort Lewis; but as we're going across the ocean, I was sitting there, and I couldn't sleep because I was wired. I looked out the window, and there's this big stream, about a two-inch stream of fluid coming out of the wing. I was thinking, "They're dumping urine or something like that." After fifteen minutes, I looked back out there, and it's still dumping fluid. I was thinking, "That can't be right." I got one of the Air Force specialists who were walking up and down the aisles, a stewardess. I pointed over there, and I said, "Are we supposed to be doing that?" She looked over where I was pointing, and she got white. She went back and got one of the military guys that were in the front. He came back, and he looked out, and he went running back up front. I thought, *Oh shit! This is not good!* When the specialists get scared, this is not good! We had fractured a fuel line and had a fuel leak over the ocean. If the instruments showed it, the pilots hadn't noticed. We ended up having to divert to Alaska. We landed, and it was sixty degrees below zero. The airplane engines couldn't be shut off because they wouldn't start again. The fuel would freeze. It's not designed for those kinds of temperatures. We landed. The Air Force personnel at the base told us we were maybe as far as seventy to eighty feet from the little hangar area. He came up to the tailgate of the aircraft, and we're in tropical fatigues. He's telling us, "Now listen. This is what's going to happen. If you fall down, do not try to get up because your skin will be stuck to the ground. When you leave the airplane, it's going to feel like your skin is on fire. Breathe shallowly through your nose. Do not open your mouth. Your lungs will freeze." He said, "Just in case you don't think I'm serious . . . ," and he spit out the airplane. The spit froze and went, "Tinkle tinkle tinkle." He took the aluminum rod that was lying on the ground out there, and he hit it against the wall, and it broke like glass. He said, "Do I have your attention now?" I said, "Yes!"

We went into the little hangar in there, and they had to work on the aircraft while it was still running and leaking fuel. They couldn't shut it off. No one got frostbite, but you could feel it burning. The second you stepped out, it felt like acid on your skin. It burned that bad. We got some coffee and waited. They finally said, "The plane's fueled up. We're ready to go again. So go back out and remember don't stumble!" Of course, we're paying real good attention this time. The surface is slippery. It's ice. These people lived there. That's their job. A bunch of crazy people!

We get into Seattle two, maybe three hours late. The people that should have been waiting to take us to Fort Lewis had given up and gone back to the base. I got back to the States, and there's nobody there to meet me. I have no money. All I have is this military pay script that we got in Vietnam, which is useless. I'm in a short-sleeved tee, and it's snowing outside. I don't know what to do. I'm walking around the airport, and there's nobody there. It's one or two o'clock in the morning. I'm trying to figure out what the hell to do. I don't even have money to make a phone call. As I'm walking through the airport, this really cute little girl, long hair, typical hippie flower child with a bouquet of flowers said," You're just back from Vietnam, aren't you?" I said, "Yes, I am." She just spit in my face and started beating on me, punching me. I mean punching hard too. I was holding her off, and I was stunned. I didn't know what to do! About that time, two security guards, out of nowhere, came and grabbed her and dragged her off. One of them came back and apologized to me and asked me what I was doing. I told him that I had been trying to find out where I was supposed to go. I just came back from Vietnam and there's no one here to meet me. He said, "Those guys left at midnight. You guys were due at eleven o'clock last night." I said, "Well, I need to get to the military base."

He set me up in the little flight lounge and bought me some drinks and was having his security people check to find out what could be done. This guy at the bar was a taxicab driver. Turns out he was a Vietnam vet and volunteers to take me out to the base; it was after midnight, and he had no fares, anyway. I found the security guard and told him this guy's going to take me to the base. He drove me out to the base, free of charge, and that's how I got back to the States. Twenty-four hours after coming out of the bush and combat situations, I'm getting beat up by a hippie and abandoned in an airport! That was my reintroduction to the world! I would love to meet that young lady. I know she regretted having done that. She had the best intentions, but went about it the wrong way.

So I now have thirty days off, and I'm staying with my parents. You have to understand, in combat, everything is intense. So every word out of your mouth is an expletive. I mean everything. It was fuck this, son of a bitch that, and damn this. It's everything. You can't talk stateside the way you talk over there. One of the reasons Vietnam vets don't like to talk about the war is that when they go back into talking about the war, they go back into that vernacular. It is very, very in your face. One night the family was sitting at dinner. This must have been the second week I was back. I spent the first week mostly sleeping eighteen hours a day and didn't want to talk to anybody, which is a classic thing for vets when they come back. I just didn't want to talk, especially bullshit, party talk. You don't have time for that.

We're sitting there, and the preacher had stopped by after church. We had a circuit preacher, so he would preach at three different churches on the same Sunday. He would have dinner with one of the families from one of the churches. He was having dinner at our house that day. Mom and Dad, brothers and sisters, the preacher and I were sitting there. We're all eating, and they were talking and talking real loud, and my hearing wasn't too good since I was still having after effects from the artillery rounds exploding. I asked somebody to pass me potatoes or something. I forget what it was. I think it was mashed potatoes. I asked twice, then a third time. Finally, I got pissed off and said, "Someone pass the fucking potatoes!" You could hear a pin drop, and my mom's quick breathing. My dad just looked over and said, "Somebody pass the boy the fucking potatoes." I just thought, *Oh shit! What have I done? Right in front of the preacher.* Daddy having been in combat himself understood exactly what was going on. My mom was not too pleased since she had never heard me use that word.

After I left Fort Campbell, I was sent to Fort Benning, Georgia, for the Infantry Officer Advanced Course, a career course that is designed to groom you for making major, colonel or lieutenant colonel. It's a prerequisite to go into the Army Command and General Staff College. I went to the advanced course and did pretty well, but got in trouble. By this time, I was totally self-confident and had a low tolerance for bullshit. When I got there, all the officers were required by the post commander to join the Officer's Club. Well, even back then, I had nothing in common with those people in the Officer's Club. Most of them were ten to twenty years older. They were drinking gin and playing golf and bridge. I was skydiving and doing pot. We just didn't have anything to talk about. I didn't want to join. They just deducted it from my pay every month. I went to the finance officer and I said, "You can't do this. That's illegal." I said, "If you do that again, I'll have to go to the JAG (Judge Advocate General) office. You can't force me to belong, and you damn sure can't deduct the fees." Well, I got counseled by my battalion commander and by my training brigade commander. I was sent to the Division Headquarters Commander's Office. Finally, the post commander called me to his office. I was standing at attention here. "Son, you're creating a problem here." I said, "No, sir, but there is a problem here." He said, "You have to do this." I said, "No, I don't. If you want to put me on court-martial, let's go because you know damn well I'm right!" CO paused. "I'll talk to you in a minute." Never spoke to me again! Never saw him again! The dues didn't come out of my paycheck anymore either! Within a year, they had quit deducting it from everybody's paycheck; it was voluntary. With a lot of pressure, of course, but it was voluntary.

By the time I finished the advanced course, the war had wound down. This was 1972. We were reaching the point where the military realized they had promoted so many young officers that they had many more officers than they were going to need in peacetime. They were trying what we called RIF: reduction in force. They came around and basically told most of us, "You're out." That's it. They had too many. Of course, the draft was terminated. The force shrank with that. A lot of them were just told, "That's it." Anyone that wanted to get out was allowed to get out immediately. Anyone that wanted to stay in had to fight for it.

I got out after nine years active duty, finishing the last three on active duty, going to college with full tuition and allowances. There was a major in

Vietnam whose life I had saved twice who owed me. When the Department of the Army sent their team down to interview all the officers and decided who got to spend the next twenty years in the Army and who would be civilians, he was in charge of the group. As I was processing through the paperwork, he saw me. "How are you doing? Glad to see you! What are you doing here?" Very cordially, I said, "Well, they said I've got a choice of going twenty years in the Army or getting out, and I don't know what I want to do for twenty years, so I'm getting out." He said, "Oh man, don't do that. Have you finished college yet?" I said, "No, I'm going to do that on the GI Bill." He says, "No no no no." I had taken maybe two and a half years of college courses when I was back in the States, so he looked on and said, "Come here, let me talk to you." He took all my transcripts, looked them over, and told me to burn two-thirds of them. He said, "Pretend like they don't exist. Bring these others in tomorrow. When you get into the line, tell them that you want to see Major What's-his-name." I don't remember the name now. I did as he suggested, and he got me full pay and allowances. I remained on active duty for three years to go to Columbus College in Georgia and get my undergraduate degree. Got out with my twenty thousand RIF (reduction in force) pay. I still had my rank in the Reserves and then I still had the GI Bill to get my master's degree. I made out like a bandit!

Saving his life twice is a story all of its own. We were all in a firebase, and the first time, I saved his life simply by defending the perimeter and doing my job. I did some stupid stuff and turned the tide. He got a Silver Star for it, but I didn't get a medal for it. He was hiding. We won't go there. About a month later, we were on another firebase and someone spotted a tiger, and when I'm talking of tiger, I'm talking of an animal. It stood almost chest high. I'm talking of a big old tiger. It was at least six hundred pounds. It was a full grown Bengal. He's crouched outside by the wire, and the major said, "There's a tiger in the wire. I'm going to shoot him." He grabbed his little .38 special. Well, that isn't going to work!

So I saw him, and I said, "Sir! You can't shoot a tiger!" I knew because I had a tiger drag one of my men off one night by the head! The tiger bit him by the head and punctured a hole through his skull while he dragged him off. The kid was sharp enough to hold his rifle and fire his M-16, and the tiger let him go. Of course, he never came back to the field again; he was really paranoid about the field after that. I knew what a tiger was and how big it was and what it could do. So I give the radio to someone else because things were quiet. I said, "Keep an ear on the radio. Come get me if you need me." I grabbed my machine gunner from my old unit on the perimeter. I said, "Bring your gun quick! There's a tiger out here, and I don't think this major knows what he's into." The major went out there, stood about as far from here to that TV. Perhaps it was about thirty feet away from the tiger. The major picked that .38 special up, fired at the tiger, and hit him in the shoulder. Now, that pissed the tiger off!

The tiger took two steps, leaped into the air, a solid fifteen-foot jump, and of course, my machine gunner just filled him full of bullets in the air. The tiger landed on top of the major, crushed him to the ground, and I came running up. I wasn't sure whether the tiger was dead yet or not. He was, but I didn't know that then. I came running up with my .45 pistol just about ready to finish him before I realized he's dead. I looked at the major, and he was either Hispanic or Puerto Rican. He was kind of dark skinned, but he was white as a sheet. What I didn't realize was that he was suffocating from the weight of the tiger. I grabbed the tiger's paw, and I couldn't even begin to roll him over. I yelled for everybody to help. We finally rolled the tiger over. The major was gasping for air. He'd been buried underneath. I mean his arm was sticking out and his head was sticking out, but all I could see was his face.

He didn't really say anything. He was in shock. He went back to the TOC. I went back to finish my shift. When I was done, he met me in the bunker with a martini and thanked me. He wanted to know who the machine gunner was and, from what I understand, bought him a case of whiskey. Then I forgot about it. Like I said, probably about a week later, I was back in the States. I forgot all about it until I saw him. So that worked out pretty good. When I got to the university, I was finishing my master's degree in sociology. I got a part-time job running a big old chain of printers on the mainframe computer, which had less memory than my whole watch has. By the time I left, when I retired, we had three-quarters of a million-dollar budget, seventeen full-time staff members, and about a dozen students. We had a Mac network and a Windows network interlaced together. We had seventeen classrooms. Nice operation.

I retired in 2003. We moved up here in 2004. Moved to western North Carolina, which is almost the spitting image of Central Vietnam, except for the fact that there's a triple canopy jungle, and it doesn't get as cold in Vietnam; and when it gets hot, it's much hotter in Vietnam in the summer than it is here. We have a similar kind of mountain range and, across the road, similar wildflowers; they were on the side of the road in Vietnam.

If it gets to 90 or 95 degrees, it's a heat wave here. People panic. Not at all like Vietnam. It's maybe 80-85 percent humidity. It gets humid at night because the temperature drops at night like it does in any mountainous area, and the humidity compresses. There were two seasons. There was a dry season and a wet season. During the rainy season, it was 90-100 percent humidity all the time. It rained probably half to two-thirds of the day. So you basically stayed wet. In the daytime, it could be anywhere from 90 to 115 degrees and 100 percent humidity. At night, it would drop down to 50 or 60 degrees, which would freeze you to death. You basically did not let it (your weapon) sit out in the sun for very long. But under the triple canopy, we didn't see sun very often.

It was incredible fatigue. Terrible boredom about 95 percent of the time, punctuated by 5 percent of the most intense-adrenaline, heart-pumping, life-or-death action imaginable. The only thing I can describe to a civilian is if you would look at *Saving Private Ryan*; the beach-landing scene. That's what combat's about. Everything's quiet, and then, all of a sudden, all hell breaks loose. People are dying left and right, and it's absolutely insane. Who lives and who dies is totally irrational: it's Russian roulette. If it's over, and you're still breathing, you survived. There's no rationale or logic to it whatsoever. Most of it is routine, boring, bullshit stuff. It's carrying an eighty pound rucksack up and down ridgelines in the hundred-degree heat, hour after hour, day after day, sleeping in the mud, just really hard, boring stuff. Then every once in a while, all hell breaks loose again, and you have to remind yourself to keep your guard up because you tend to get tired, you tend to get bored, you tend to get relaxed because you realize you haven't seen anybody in a while, and you begin to think you're not going to see anyone. Then, suddenly, there they are! Most of our contacts were what we called meeting engagements. Moving through the jungle, looking to fix and find the enemy. When we found them, all hell broke loose quickly!

The main thing was that the NVA and VC, especially in the jungle, knew where they were; they were familiar with the area. Most of them had been up and down that trail hundreds of times. They knew intimately, that at this point on the trail, there's this gully you can get into to escape. They had the tunnels and fixed positions they could get into all over the place. They knew where they were and how to get sanctuary. We had to just get around. The trouble was the jungle was so thick you couldn't just jump off the trail and run through it. In most of the places, it was so thick you had to cut your way through the elephant grass and jungle with a machete. You could not run through it. If you didn't know a path to get around through it, you couldn't get through.

In the place where there wasn't a triple canopy or the third canopy was missing, you would get jungle grass in some of the clearings, on the ridge tops, some of the ridgelines, hilltops, and in some of the valleys. It was generally six to eight feet tall and sharp as a razor blade. When you went through it, you'd all come out with your hands all cutup. Real infection problems after you went through an area with that tall grass and all because with the humidity and the heat, you'd get fungal infections. When you came through that, even though it was so hot, you had to roll your sleeves down. Usually, you walked with your hands underneath your armpits or in your pockets, and your rifle stuck under your arm.

We didn't have gloves. We should have, but who's going to have gloves for the once every three or four weeks we would have to run in jungle grass. Weight is a problem when you're carrying. We were doing anywhere from three to five days in the field living out of our backpacks. We already had seventy or eighty pounds in there, weapons included, plus the water we had to carry. You had to carry about two to four quarts of water a day just to get by. You preferably wanted more. You wanted to refill that at some point. So weight was critical. You only carried what you absolutely needed. Food was important because you had to have your strength, and water was important because you would dehydrate. And, of course, ammunition. You had to have ammunition.

Explain what you have dealt with since the war

I'm red/green color blind . . . a fact of life, not related to combat. As to visualizing things in my mind, I haven't been able to since Vietnam. My dreams are very real, but they come back to me in memory as if listening to a radio broadcast . . . absolutely no visual content at all. It has been like that since a 105 mm artillery round landed on my fighting trench and damaged my hearing. I suspect I suffered some form of traumatic brain injury (TBI) from the concussion. I do remember losing track of time for some period after the explosion and bleeding from the ears. The ringing in the ears has never gone away.

Recently, I underwent a program called brain state training. These links will help explain the process:

- http://www.brainstatetech.com/
- http://www.patsullivan.com/blog/2009/05/brain-trauma-my-brainstate-experience-update-7.html
- http://www.oprah.com/community/thread/113145

It also shut down the emotional side of my brain, in order to handle the trauma of combat. I could not afford to respond emotionally to the horrors I saw, lest I get killed in the process. Upon returning to society, I never readjusted to letting myself feel emotions. In fact, I was so afraid of losing total control over my anger at what I had been sent halfway around the world to do that I deliberately suppressed all emotions. For more than forty years, I had neither smiled, nor laughed, nor loved. I functioned in society, but the joy of life died in Vietnam.

Early into the BST sessions, I had the first visual image in my mind since Vietnam. It was quite startling. I had totally forgotten that such things are possible. No wonder many learning tasks were so difficult for me. Essentially I had to make word pictures in order to remember diagrams and control layouts. Wow! I am amazed at how well I actually compensated.

The next thing I noticed was actually laughing out loud at comedy skits on TV! Shocking! My whole outlook on life is changing since BST, and the joy of each new day has begun to return. I really hope this technology can be made available to all veterans. It is effortless, noninvasive, and subtly effective. The training is tailored in real-time to each person's own particular brain wave patterns. Through musical tones heard via earphones, the brain resets itself back to normal left/right hemispherical balance. There's no telling how many problems of daily life it will improve. The memories will never go away, but they no longer have to overwhelm me the way they used to do—thanks to Dr. Lee Gerdes and BST.

Advice to someone considering a military career

Best thing that ever happened to me. I was a very shy young farm boy and very unsure of myself. It made me into a self-confident leader of men. I can't believe that 145 people would die because I would ask them to do something. I can't believe I had that kind of command. It's the best training you'll ever get as far as growing up and getting a handle on your life, but you have to balance that with the fact that there is a chance, a very good chance, that you will see combat. If you see combat, you may die. A lot of people do. You may get wounded. You may get mutilated for life. If not, even if you don't see combat, you're going to see enough horrors of war. When you go to combat, when you go to war, the person that comes back will not be the same person that went. As your friend Hip said, "War changes your DNA." Your personality will change forever. You can't help it. You have to be prepared to deal with that. You've got to be prepared to know that when you come back, your loved ones aren't going to see the same person that left them. That's going to change them as well as the way it's changed you. You have to be able to handle that. You've got to know that the military is like any huge organization. You go in and you plan to make a twenty—to thirty-year career out of the military. You can do eighteen years and do everything right and screw up once when it's politically the wrong time, and it can ruin your career. It's not guaranteed. On the other hand, if I had to do it all over again, I wouldn't go to war because I don't think killing is right, period! End of conversation! I was a Southern Baptist. There's this little commandment that says, "Thou shalt not kill." I don't remember them putting in anything about war (as an exclusion). I really don't understand how we get around that. In WWII where we were seriously concerned about the Nazis taking over the world, that's one thing, but this was a political war, and I have problems with that even today. If you've been in that military environment, it is the greatest group of people in the world. I trust the people I served with in a way that I can't even trust my own brother. It is a bond that is so firm, so close, that it's hard to explain. When you turn your back, and you know that the guy behind you will die before he lets something happen to you, and you know that you're going to do the same thing for him, that's a bond that you can't put into words. It's a bond that when I go to a reunion, five minutes after we're together, it's like we're back sitting on top of a bunker shooting the bull again. It's that kind of bond; we'd do anything for each other. The military's a great thing. I think it's a tragedy at the same time. It is the best thing to ever happen to me. It's also the worst thing to ever happen to me. I can't recommend anybody going to the Army. I really can't. On the other hand, it's probably the most intense educational experience you'll ever have if you survive it. That's a big "if." What's the quote, "The middle word in life is *if.*"

Current day

I retired in 2004 and moved to the mountains of western North Carolina, an area remarkably similar to the Central Highlands of Vietnam, where I fought. There are even many of the same species of wildflowers along the roadsides. I spend most of my time hiking the mountains with my dog and younger friends and taking nature photographs. The rest of my time is spent tending to my aging mom and keeping up my website *www. swampfox.info* in which I am trying to tell the story of the Fourth Infantry

Division in Vietnam and all our wonderful supporting units. The site has helped so many veterans and their families connect again and begin to understand why soldiers were so changed when they returned. Your book, John, is a wonderful addition to this story. I really want the majority of the US population who were fortunate enough not to experience combat, to at least know what incredible sacrifice was made by these brave men on their behalf.

DAVID "SMILIE" MARTIN

Forward Observer (FO), United States Marine Corps
Semper Fidelis: *"Always faithful"*
Third Battalion, Ninth Marine Regiment, Third Marine Division
Home of Record: Trenton, NJ
Home of Residence: Morrisville, PA
DOB: 17 July 1946
Conducted in Morrisville, PA 17 June 2010
Dave's book *Crazy Asian War* is a must read.

> *Some people live an entire lifetime and wonder if they have ever made a difference in the world, but the Marines don't have that problem.*
>
> —Ronald Reagan

Growing Up

I was middle class. I had six brothers, so it was a large family. We are Irish German. We were taught a lot of values. I call them American values. We're taught if you want something in your life, you get off your butt and work for it. You have to be honest with everybody. You work hard, you don't do any crimes. There is no excuse for any stealing, lying, cheating, or anything like that. We were taught that you get along with everybody, but if somebody attacks you, you knock them out. At six, I came home one day with a bloody nose, and Mom gave me a straight arm in the chest. At the door, she said, "Did you win?" and I said, "No." She went, "You don't come back until you win." She slammed the door in my face. I had to find this little sucker; I knocked on doors. I finally found him, and whatever his name was, we'll call him Billy. I said, "Does little Billy live here?" The mother was happy as hell that I was there, and she went, "I'll get him," because she figured he'd clean my clock again. Little Billy didn't know that all he had to do was beat my ass one more time today, but I had to beat his ass to get home. Yes, she taught me how to be tough and how to win. You don't start anything, but if you start something or anyone else does, you finish it by winning, not by losing. He was a jerk. I kicked his butt.

As a child, I played every sport under the sun and wanted to play from morning to night. School was a pain in my butt, and I was never a great student. Unless something interested me, I would rather be outside playing. In high school, I was on a few cross-country teams—wasn't a great star. I got letters and all that stuff, and that was my enjoyment in high school. I can remember 1963, maybe 1964, in history class; they started to talk about Vietnam. I recall seeing the image of the Buddhist monks immolating themselves, pouring gasoline on their bodies and lighting themselves up. I thought that was some radical stuff, and that was pretty much it with Vietnam. Then I went to junior college. I was working three jobs just to pay for the freaking school because my parents didn't have any money, but I was still going to school. I was failing out of school, getting tired of the job, and getting tired of the hassle with the girlfriend. The Vietnam War was there! A friend of mine from the same junior college bugged me, "Let's join the Marine Corps."

One day I read this newspaper article that said, "Marines massacred on Hill 400"—whatever that was. I folded up the newspaper, barged into my friend's class, and said, "Let's go." We went down to the recruiter. He said, "When do you want to go?" and I looked at my watch, actually, and said, "Well, I have to go home and tell my parents. I could be back here in two hours." This is February 1966, and the recruiter laughed and said, "It doesn't work that fast. In two weeks, you can be in." My friend and I took the physicals; we were working out every day anyway so that was easy. We went to Parris Island, South Carolina, and then we were in the Marine Corps. It was an accelerated eight-week boot camp program back then as they needed Marines real fast for the Vietnam War. They worked us day and night, Sundays included. That must be tough on the DIs (drill instructors) because you take a normal sixteen-week program and put it into eight. They were picking and choosing what a marine really needs to know. They really keyed in on the discipline, listening, and marksmanship.

I was in the Boy Scouts and Eagle Scouts; there is a marksmanship merit badge. Every summer I went to camp, and we had .22s, so I knew a little bit about shooting. That wasn't a problem. The marching wasn't a problem. The military-type discipline was a problem because I was always a wise ass. I was the class clown; I was *the* class clown! I did everything I could to disrupt the class with jokes. It was tough to tone that down, but the Marine Corps had found a way to tone me down. Back then, it was hands on. If you didn't listen up, they literally would knock you down. It saves all that counseling, time-out, and crap. You don't want to listen to me? *Boom*, you're on the ground.

I wanted to go to Vietnam, be in the Marine Corps and be in the infantry. I wanted those three things. After boot camp, I boarded a bus in

Parris Island, South Carolina, and went to Camp Geiger, North Carolina, which is probably six to seven hours up the road. There I went to infantry training for about five weeks. In infantry training, we had an accelerated program. Infantry is infantry. We fired every weapon, walked our asses off, literally; they tried to simulate combat as much as they could. We had some sleep deprivation, we worked out a lot, and we were outside most of the time. We fired every weapon you could think of, and after that, we went home for about twenty or thirty days. We're not even in the Marine Corps five months, yet we are in California at Camp Pendleton. This was the advanced infantry training, or jungle training. They had simulated Vietnamese villages. They had pop-up targets, which were Vietnamese, and they walked us to death there. You can really walk in California. They got some hills and all this crap. Cleared there about three to four weeks and then flew directly to Alaska, down to Japan, Okinawa, and then to Vietnam. It's a couple of days, and we're in Vietnam. When we landed, it was close to 2100. The pilot did a combat landing, which was these real tight turns over the airport. The NVA and the VC are always trying to knock planes out of the sky. They could kill 180 Marines before you get into combat.

Vietnam

They had tight combat turns, which kind of neutralized the rockets because you are circling the airport in a secure area; it was pretty much a high adventure. We were nineteen or twenty-year-olds, teenagers, and now you're saying we could actually get shot out of the sky before we get to Vietnam. They opened the door, and you might have heard this from a lot of Vietnam vets. The heat was like opening an oven; it slapped you in the face. We had dumped all our sea bags on the deck (Marines always call the ground "the deck"), and we had to find them. We got processed, and in a couple of hours, we were up on this hill overlooking the base, and we can hear these Phantom jets leaving. We can hear the outgoing artillery, and we could see some incoming rockets. Going to sleep that night, it finally dawned on me that I was actually in a war! I was going, "Holy shit! I'm actually thirteen thousand miles away from home!" By this time, it's 2300/2400 at night and still hot and humid. We're sleeping on ammo boxes, not cots. The Marine Corps is a very Spartan organization. There were no blankets or sheets; it was just ammo boxes and mosquitoes. No one warned us about the conditions, this all unfolded in front of us! The next morning, we get assigned our units. That's when they started talking about the Ninth

Marines, 1/9 (First Marine Battalion/Ninth Marine Regiment) or 3/9. You start wondering, "What the hell's this about?" All of a sudden they call your name and say you are going to 3/9, one of the units that's using up most of the replacements. I asked, "What's this about replacements for 3/9?" First sergeants in the Marine Corps, back in the day, were always gigantic and always nasty. They said, "Listen you, asshole, it's because of casualties." That's pretty much the way they told you about that stuff.

One story I came to tell was 4 July around 1030 when we'd been fighting for three days. To make Operation Buffalo realistic, we only fought for six hundred yards, and we spent eight days doing that—that was about eighty yards a day. We got pushed back three times. You're talking about the USMC being pushed back tactically three times by North Vietnamese. In the Marine Corps, it always means it's smarter to move back a few hundred yards, hit them with arty (artillery), hit them with air (support), and then try and move again.

For three days, we were fighting pretty much on our bellies. When I first joined the Marine Corps, they tell you a whole lot of shit, but they also say we never leave our dead or our dying on the battlefield. You think, that's nice, that's cool. If I was dead, I wouldn't want to be left over there either. A year later, I found out what they meant by that shit. We finally get up to the bodies of 1/9, which were sister outfits. Six weeks earlier, I had been the .81 mm mortar FO (forward observer) for your second platoon of Bravo Company 1/9. I knew these guys. I knew this guy Saunders, a lance corporal that we called Sarge from Chicago. He kept showing me the picture of his wife and a year-old baby. Every time we stopped for five or ten minutes, he would say, "Did I ever show you a picture of my wife and baby?" and I would say, "Yeah, you did." And he would say, "Well, let me show it to you," and he would show it to me again. Here, six weeks later, we're out there fighting, and there was a lull in the battle. We're in a staggered column formation, had our fifteen-meter intervals covered. We're moving up toward the North Vietnamese, toward the bodies. We heard the word that we'd reached the bodies. All of a sudden, the skipper or captain said, "FO up." I told my radio operator that's not good because if there's no action and you don't want recon you don't need an FO. I trotted up to him as we are going through brush country. It wasn't "jungley," but there were hedgerows and some dried-out rice paddies.

We were within two miles of the DMZ (demilitarized zone) that separated the North from the South. I trotted up there, and he said, "You're with the bravo 1/9?" and I said, "Yes, sir, but I was with the second platoon of the 1/9. I wasn't with the whole company." He said, "We think this is Bravo Company, can you identify these bodies?" I'm looking at these Marines! Every fifteen meters, there's a dead marine in staggered formation! These guys were gunned down! It was almost a perfectly executed ambush! That was pretty much the way it was.

This was about a mile and a half from Con Thien and was fought from March 1967 to February 1968. There were more Marines killed and wounded in that battle than any other battle in the Vietnam War, and this includes the Siege at Khe San that ran seventy-seven days. Most don't even know this took place. There were a lot of units involved there as we were fighting almost daily. We finally reached the bodies. The only way you could tell a Vietnamese from a marine was by the uniform. We all had green clothes, but their clothes were a little bit different. They didn't have black outfits (like the VC). They didn't have helmets, we did. But the sizes of these bodies—they were bloated—they looked like eight-foot monsters lying on the ground. You couldn't tell a black marine from a white marine because white people turn black and blue in the tropics after three days anyway. All were bloated up, and the skin was almost ready to pop. If you have ever been to a pig roast, the skin is ready to pop . . . I went up there, and I said, "Yes, sir." He said, "You look at these people?"

"I don't know sir." He asked some guy to turn them over, so they turned this guy over, and there was a little picture; a photo sticking out of his breast pocket of his flak jacket where Sarge had always kept his picture. I asked if I could see the picture. Either he or one of his Marines reached down and pulled it out. It was the picture of the little one-year-old baby and his young wife. I'm telling you right now, I don't know where I went (mentally)—perhaps it was Mars, Jupiter, Saturn, or Pluto because I had made a connection with this guy, and he had made a connection with me. I made a connection with my mortality! I was looking at this guy, and everyone in the second platoon was freaking dead—about thirty Marines! They were all freaking dead! All I can remember is a guy tapped me on my flak jacket and said, "You know the captain is calling for you." And you're gone. I didn't hear him. All I heard was go back to your position, so I went back. I was all right after that, but that time I was gone. This was Darrell Saunders from Chicago (*Vietnam Memorial Panel 23E Line 023*). I knew him, and I can't swear to God that that was him, but why would anybody else have had that picture.

After that, we didn't disengage from that battle until 9 July 1967. We got hit with at least an NVA battalion (400-500 infantry) in our area that tried to go through us and they never made it. First, they came at us with all the artillery, rockets, and mortars. They outgunned us. They had probably 100-120 artillery pieces against ours; everything from their 82 mm mortar to their heavy "arty" pieces that ranged from 122 mm to 152 mm. The shells were gigantic. If they landed here, they would blow this whole thing up (*the restaurant where Dave and I did the interview*).

They had outgunned us, and they outmanned us by far, no doubt about it. They were highly trained soldiers, the NVA, but we were better and tougher than they were. I don't know if it's because of Western democracy, but whatever it is, I saw hand-to-hand combat within thirty to forty feet of me. I kept on looking at my rifle—somebody with an obsessive-compulsive disorder making sure it was ready, and I had the safety off. I was trying to figure out if this thing was working right, and I was watching these suckers, and there was no way to shoot guys tumbling around fighting each other. However, every time, the marine won, every single time! Either that night or the next day, when you ran into these guys who were in hand-to-hand combat, their eyes bulged. They were so pumped up. They were excited, happy to be alive. This was the experience of a lifetime, and they would tell you in an intimate detail, and you would listen every time they told you. They had these newspaper articles in all the papers like the *New York Times*, which I saved. That's how I wrote my book from these archives. They said on Buffalo (Operation Buffalo), it was fighting hand to hand, at times, when the VC broke through. When a marine ran out of ammo and the North Vietnamese ran out, whatever the hell happened, they got into it. The North Vietnamese were fighting for their lives too. They were desperate, but there wasn't one time in my tour(s) where a marine lost a fight hand to hand. I was there sixteen months and twenty-three days to be exact.

When I came back, we went to El Toro Marine base in California. It took close to four days to be processed. I got off that plane and literally began kissing the concrete runway of that air base. I was that freaking happy to be back in this country. I was that appreciative to have lived through that shit, because I knew that was a once-in-a-lifetime thing. I was as happy and thankful to be alive as any person that has ever been alive in their life. From there, they boarded us on busses with screens on it; I guess you can almost say cages. They took us from El Toro to LAX (Los Angeles) airport, and there are all these hippies.

For seventeen months, I had been in a disciplined organization. Everything was green, everything was organized, and everything was disciplined. We all thought and talked and dressed the same, and all of a sudden, people are doing what they want. It was a culture shock to me. I just sucked it up. We went to the airport and got on the plane. The plane, I'm thinking, was a military chartered plane, so everybody on board was a returning Vietnam vet. I went back to New York, landed at La Guardia, and had to take a taxi to Penn Station. This taxi driver (a right-winger) and a businessman (a left-winger) were arguing about the war. I got in, and they asked, "Just get back from Vietnam?" and I said yes, and they continued to argue. For the twenty-minute ride they were arguing. The businessman was sitting in the front with the cabdriver, and not one time did either ask me my opinion. Hell, I had my uniform on. At the end, they were actually into it, what do you mean this and do you mean that, arguing! Finally, the businessman and the cabdriver turned around and shook my hand. They knew I was there; they knew who I was. The businessman paid the fare, and the taxi driver said, "I would have given it to you for nothing." It was mixed messages, but it made me feel better. It was more interesting than anything else. Then I took the train back to Trenton. My old man met me at 2100. I only had the uniform that I was supposed to come back in, which is tropical. I extended it for a few months, so here it was 20 November 1967, and it was colder than shit. I was there waiting for the old man to show up and I was freezing.

I probably would have gone back, but that half-hour bus ride from El Toro Marine base to LAX just told me everything I needed to know about this country—nobody gave a crap! This is a big joke on me and my fellow Marines . . . nobody else knew!

How did Vietnam shape your life?

Obviously, we only live this way. We're only going forward, so I have no idea how I would be without Vietnam, but I do have guesses. I think I would be financially better off. I don't know if I'd be better off with me, as I had to go. I had to go through that war. I don't regret going.

For some of us, in the infantry, it was a horror show that you, John, couldn't imagine. It tests everything you ever were taught or brought up to believe. It tested your nerves to the max. It tested every fiber of your being. About how much guts and courage, and how much you are willing to sacrifice yourself for causes that you could hardly even explain. Mostly, the thing that really kept you going was that whatever the Marine Corps does or maybe it's all military, when they put you thirteen thousand miles away from home and all your friends are Marines that wear green uniforms and they're the only people between you and dying—you get super attached to each other. It's that mutual trust that keeps you going, that carries you through. I don't know if that's patriotism or Americanism. I think it's just a will to survive, but somehow, they found the right group of guys to go to that war and fight that war for them, great guys! We didn't abandon each other, we didn't desert each other. I have seen acts of bravery that were unbelievable, and that's the part that I don't think I'd ever be able to explain. I wish to hell I had that kind of balls. But there were some times that if I didn't call in artillery to fire, it would have been a lot worse.

I told a few of my fellow grunts (who wanted to be an FO) that they have to be the ones to find out. When you're an FO, every waking second, you spend looking at maps and thinking about grid coordinates—you're thinking about where you're at and what you have to do the next second, because when the shit hits the fan, the human mind wants to save itself! You want to get down, get as low as possible, forget about everything, but you can't do that as an FO. Being an FO is contrary to human nature. Everybody's life could depend on what you do.

The FO had 750 Bausch & Lomb binoculars that were freaking big strapped across your chest. That's the big sign. In my left hand, I had the map, I had my thumb on where we were; and every time we moved, I'd slide the map down. I had my thumb on it, so it wasn't a guess. When we got hit, I just looked at my thumb and read the six-digit grid coordinates and called it in. I had the compass hanging off my neck so that's another big sign, and I would be shooting (pointing) in all directions all the freaking time. In the right hand, I had my rifle because that's your backup weapon. You must have your rifle there. I never had a radio operator in front of me, but the guy behind me had a radio. Back then, the radios weren't cell phones. They were big clunky, heavy things with antennas. The maps were accurate if they were taken by an aerial reconnaissance, and the Air Force flew over there and took all these pictures. They tell you the distance between point A and point B, x number of meters, but they don't tell you that seven hundred thousand meters is up or down draws, up draws, triple canopy. They don't tell you the altitude, so as anybody that's climbed hills knows, you can walk straight for half a mile; but if you have to go down the hill and up the hill, that's where the maps integrity ends, and the aerial reconnaissance will, particularly in the Western DMZ area with the double and triple canopies.

Advice to someone considering a military career

I would tell them that if you feel compelled, obligated, or you want to join the military, that's fine. There are five branches of the military including the Coast Guard, and if you got some smarts, and you want to go into the engineering or the computer stuff, that's fine. If you want to go into the infantry, it has to come from within, and you have to be more mentally tough than you are physically tough. You should be physically tough because they are going to test you. You can't freaking believe how they test you. Go and sign up. If you don't want to go, don't join; it's a volunteer military. Go and deal with your life however you must. I'm 100 percent for a volunteer military. We had a few draftees in the Marine Corps, and it never lasted long. "Listen to you dumb ass," I would tell them, "I been here twelve freaking months. I'm going to listen to your freaking bullshit crying. You have to be kidding me. You better step up and do what you have to do because we have no sympathy." As my DI (drill instructor) said, "Sympathy is between shit and syphilis in the dictionary." The ones who cried the blues mostly were the FNGs (the fucking new guys). After a while, you couldn't tell the difference between the draftee and the marine that volunteered. They got squared away.

When everyone said that to them, they would walk away, thinking, *Yeah really, these miserable suckers.* I mean, look at them, our black jungle boots were white from being scraped by the brush. Our clothes had holes in them; our packs, flak jackets and helmets already had bloodstains and holes when they gave them to us. Somebody was wounded or killed that had worn them before us. What's there to bitch and moan about? We're all miserable. We're all in this shit together!

I would encourage them, and welcome those if that was what they wanted to do, knowing that they might be killed or wounded or be screwed up and all that stuff. You know something? Somebody has to do that in this country. We're the ones that go down like 2003, twice a year, to see these Marines, and we ask what it's like in Iraq or Afghanistan. They say, "I've been there two or three times." One guy we met was there five times, three in Iraq and two in Afghanistan, and I'm telling you he wasn't sniveling or crying. All he would ever say was that he wished they would slow down on these deployments, so he could have a little more time in the States. It's not like the media: Those like him believe in this shit. They believe in it because it's part of that camaraderie, or they believe in it and that's why they signed up. Earlier on, 2003, 2004, and into 2005, I would ask them,

"Why did you sign up?" and they would say, "Because of 11 September." That would almost bring a tear to my eye. The Marine Corps is trying to downsize because they are over their quota; they have too many Marines.

Current Day

I'm retired. For thirty years, I had been a benefits counselor for the State of New Jersey, but it was for the VA. Most claims go to the VA. I listened to and counseled vets, and I always told people, I didn't get the 99 percent of the vets that were doing all right. I got the 1 percent that were the drug addicts, alcoholics, the criminals, the ex-criminals, the guys with major problems, the guys with PTSD problems, the guys with the physical problems, and the homeless vets. I dealt with a lot of homeless vets; the men who really needed it. I listened to and counseled them for thirty years. I got to know a lot about them.

PAUL C. SCOTTI

Chief Warrant Officer 4 (Ret.), United States Coast Guard
Semper Paratus: *"Always Ready"*
USCGC *Point Dume* (WPB 82325), Division Twelve Da Nang
Home of Record: Brooklyn, NY
Home of Residence: Palm Bay, FL
DOB: 13 February 1943
Interview conducted via telephone. Met Paul 03 October 2010 in
    Palm Bay, FL
Paul's book: *Coast Guard Action in Vietnam*

> *He is the best sailor who can steer within fewest points of the wind,*
> *and exact a motive power out of the greatest obstacles.*
> —Sir Walter Scott

Growing Up

I was born and raised in Brooklyn, New York. I was the first son; a brother came later to give Mom and Dad a family of four. I finished high school at seventeen and joined the United States Air Force in September 1960. I attended a ten week Basic Medical Course at Lackland Air Force Base in San Antonio, Texas. From there, I went to Gunter Air Force Base in Montgomery, Alabama to attend a sixteen-week school to become an x-ray technician. My first duty assignment was Osan Air Base, South Korea, for thirteen months. I requested my next assignment to be in Spain or Germany, but was sent to Dover Air Force Base, Delaware. I finished my four-year hitch there. All my life I wanted to be in the military, while my parents preferred I go to college. Eight months before my enlistment was up, the Air Force wanted me to make a decision: reenlist, get out, or sign an extension. I wasn't sure what I wanted, so I got out. I wanted to be a veterinarian, so I went to Kansas State University, one of a few schools offering this degree. I didn't plan very well for college; I didn't have any money. Here I was out in Kansas where I didn't know anyone and living in the basement of a woman's home. I didn't have any encouragement. It was a transition shock to be sitting in a chemistry lecture class after four years of freedom in the Air Force. I left school after a couple of months and went home to Brooklyn. I worked at odd jobs, such as portrait canvassing, knocking on doors, and trying to get people to sign up for family photographs. I worked two weeks at Macy's during inventory counting ladies lingerie, but I was an x-ray technician and soon landed a job as one at the Hospital for Joint Diseases in the Bronx. After a half year of that, I became restless and quit and decided to see New Orleans. I didn't know anyone there and lived in the YMCA. This was a dismal time. You wake up in the morning and have no place to go. No one cared if you were alive.

After a month or so of this dead-end living, I decided it was time to go back into the military. Earlier, I had tried to get back into the Air Force, but they had a policy of discouraging you from getting out by making it harder for you to get back in. I tried the Army. The Army said that they would take me, give me back my stripes, and send me wherever I wanted to go. I said, "Thailand." They said, "Yes." There was one catch; I had to go through Army boot camp. I'd been to Air Force boot camp and didn't want to do that again. I decided to go to sea. I always wondered what made sailor's crazy when they went on liberty. Then I decided not to go into the Navy, because the Navy, like the Air Force, was too big, and you were more like a number than a person, so I chose the Coast Guard figuring; because of its small size, you were more like family. I went to the Coast Guard recruiter in New Orleans. He didn't offer me anything—and sent me off to boot camp! However, I had been given a choice of going to Cape May Training Center in New Jersey or Alameda Training Center in Alameda, California. Being from the East Coast and liking to travel, I chose Alameda. I found out much later that had I gone to Cape May, I would have just had to attend classes to learn nautical terminology, Coast Guard history, and the like. Alameda had a different policy. They didn't care about your prior service, you went through just like a recruit off the street doing pushups, high-porting your rifle, and all that. The purpose was to turn aimless civilians into disciplined servicemen. I wasn't alone in our company; there was another former Air Force guy and a former marine. The three of us had seaman stripes and a red hash mark for four years of active duty; for every speck of dust or scuff marks, we did extra pushups. I had two goals in mind when I joined the Coast Guard. One was to become a gunner's mate and the other to go to Vietnam. When I got out of boot camp, I was told that I couldn't be held at Alameda for the next gunner's mate opening in Groton, Connecticut. I reported to the Coast Guard base, Seattle, Washington, to tell this to the executive officer and have him set me up. He was really behind prior service people and obtained a gunner's mate school quota. I arrived at gunner's mate school in November and graduated in March of 1966. I was sent back to the Thirteenth Coast Guard District, in the Pacific Northwest, and was assigned to the 255-foot cutter *Wachusett* in Seattle. Here I joined the gun gang taking care of the 5-inch/38 deck gun, torpedoes, and small arms.

We talk about our vessels in terms of feet for size. For example, the *Wachusett* was a 255 foot long *Lake* class cutter, but in conversation, she was referred to as a "255." These and other oceangoing cutters were termed gunboats until 1967. The Coast Guard redesignated them "high endurance cutter," a term meaning that they could stay at sea a long time without replenishment of fuel and food. After six months, headquarters sent out a solicitation looking for gunner's mates to volunteer for Vietnam. I put my letter in right away. A few weeks later, I was working inside the gun mount when the yeoman came up and said, "Hey, you're orders are in." I tell him that's great: I had just put in my letter for Vietnam. He tells me I'm not going to Vietnam. I'm going to the *Modoc* in Coos Bay." What the heck is the *Modoc* and where is Coos Bay?" I learn that the *Modoc* is a 143-foot oceangoing tug that we got from the Navy and designated it a medium endurance cutter and that Coos Bay is in southern Oregon. The odd thing about these orders was that I had been on the *Wachusett* only seven months and as a junior man on the gun gang, this was at least a two-year tour of duty. Anyway, I pack up my sea bag and take a bus to Astoria, Oregon, to pick up the vessel where it was having yard maintenance done. I was greeted by guys, on the Quarterdeck, who tells me that once on board I'll never get off. I tell them, "No problem, I have a letter in for Vietnam duty." Then they asked if I was married. I wasn't. To this they said, "You will be before you leave here."

The *Modoc* with its round bottom was the worse riding cutter I have ever been on. We took a beating on winter patrols. If you weren't on watch you were in the rack. Barf buckets were tied to every stanchion. I was aboard for two months when my Vietnam orders came in. Being a single guy, I spent a lot of liberty in bars. On one of these outings, I met a woman who was a schoolteacher. She felt that she was too old for me; she was thirty and I was twenty-four. She said, "There's somebody who I'd like you to take out." I didn't want to; I was getting ready for war. No more girls, no more bars, I'm getting into shape. She kept after me until I promised to call this girl. I'm thinking that I'll take her out to dinner and that will be the end of that. She lived in Bandon, a town twenty-six miles to the south. I didn't have a car, but she agreed to pick me up. I looked around for the best place in town; that was the Sky Room overlooking the bay. I made reservations for Friday at 1900. Friday comes and I had bought a pair of civilian pants, a white shirt, and borrowed a jacket and tie. Her car pulls up in front of the cutter. I open the door and introduce myself. She asks, "Where to?" I tell her, "The Sky Room, I have reservations for dinner." Later, she told me that right then she knew she was going to marry me. The lady who greeted us at the restaurant had a little smile on her face as she led us to our table—an empty restaurant—no one makes reservations in Coos Bay. We enjoyed dinner. We danced to live music. Thirty-two days later, we ran off to Reno and got married.

I was on the *Modoc* only four months. I actually proposed on the evening I got off the cutter and went on leave. I left my wife in Oregon and went home to Brooklyn to see my parents. My promotion examination for gunner's mate second class had been sent to the Coast Guard base on Governor's Island in New York Harbor, so I had to be there anyway to take it. After two weeks in New York, I flew to San Francisco. My wife came down to spend a weekend with me before I reported to Alameda to start five weeks of pre-Vietnam deployment training. That was forty-three years ago and we're still married.

The first week was spent at the Squadron One processing center at Alameda. We got inoculations, took care of personal affairs like designating next of kin, and went through damage control drills, nuclear, biological, and chemical warfare training at a Navy facility. The second week we went to Coronado Naval Station (San Diego) for class room instruction on counterinsurgency and such. The third week we spent with the Marines at Camp Pendleton getting physically fit. We ran all the time, uphill and downhill. We fired all kinds of small arms and tossed hand grenades. The fourth week was most memorable: this was survival, evasion, resistance, and escape (SERE) training. The first class was on how to survive. We spent that evening on the beach surviving; then we were sent into the mountains to live off the land. They didn't feed us because what we caught we ate.

There were 15 guardsmen in a group of about 150, and the rest were Navy; some were pilots and some were going to become naval advisors with the South Vietnamese Navy. We were given a section of nylon parachute. This was our shelter, our bed, and whatever else. By the end of the week, we were pretty ragged looking. Now, we were primed for evasion and interrogation. On the last morning, they set us loose at one end of a large area and, at the same time, set the enemy loose at the other end. We had three hours to evade capture and try to reach Freedom Village, a sanctuary where you received an hour's respite and fresh fruit. When the three hours were up, whistles were blown and you had to come in if you were still evading. Three men had made it to Freedom Village; two of them were Coast Guard. Of the rest of the guardsmen, five were captured and the rest, including me, were still evading.

Those of us still evading gave ourselves up at the sound of the whistles and climbed into trucks. Our Communist captors were playing their role very seriously. When we arrived at the concentration camp, the people already captured are kneeling on the dirt wearing only shorts and T-shirts and being sprayed with water hoses. To get into the camp, we had to crawl through barbed wire. We threw our clothes into the pile and joined the torment. It was pretty much like that the rest of the day. They'd pull us out one by one and interrogate us. If you tried to band together, they would find the leader and take him away to break our morale. Come evening, they did the real interrogation on everybody. They put bags over our heads so we couldn't see where they were taking us. We placed a hand on the person in front of us in line and followed. They took us inside a big open building and put each of us in a small black box. Inside the box, we took off our sacks. Holes had been punched in the box to allow air. The whole time we could hear screaming and yelling; we didn't know if it was real. We heard Americans saying that the United States was using germ and gas warfare. There came a point when they pulled us out of the box with our sacks back on our heads and moved us into a narrow box on our hands and knees leaning forward; we couldn't move. After a time, they pulled us out of that box and lead us to the interrogation room; it's a small room with bright spotlights. We couldn't see the interrogator. He had our identification cards. He insulted us, our families, our service and anything else in trying to break us down. He had us doing push-ups to further exhaust our will to resist. We were asked questions, but we were taught only to give our name, rank, serial number and religion. To anything else we are to say, "Sir, my country will not allow me to answer that question." *Smack!* That answer caused them to start using us for handballs. I refused to say anything else. Finally, my interrogator tells me that I am going back into the narrow box and then coming back for more questioning. I was in that narrow box much longer this time and lost circulation to my feet. When they pulled me out, I toppled backward because I had no feeling in my feet; I was not looking forward to more interrogation. Instead they put me back in my box and didn't bother me anymore. I passed their test. If I had shown any sign of weakness, they would have kept working on me. If anyone broke down, they would not be going to Vietnam; if you couldn't handle this simulated imprisonment, you wouldn't make it in real captivity.

The exercise finally ended, and lights came on. The boxes were opened. Our captors were now our friendly instructors, but we didn't feel friendly toward them. They fed us oatmeal and an apple, which was about all our weeklong, deprived stomachs, could handle; I lost seven pounds. For the last week, we returned to Alameda to get familiar with the eight-two foot patrol boat, radio communication procedures and the like. Liz came down from Oregon for a couple of days that last week. We spent fourteen days together in the first fourteen months of our marriage. I left for Vietnam by commercial airliner and landed in Saigon 1 May 1967.

Vietnam

From Coast Guard headquarters in Saigon, they assign you to one of the three Coast Guard Squadron One divisions. Division Twelve (North) is Da Nang. In the center is Division Thirteen (Cat Lo). In the south is Division Eleven (An Thoi). The twenty-six Coast Guard eighty-foot-long cutters were split up among these divisions. These cutters were part of Operation *Market Time* to prevent the NVA and VC from moving men and supplies into South Vietnam by water. This would take place close to shore where the Navy couldn't get to it with their deep draft vessels, so they asked the Coast Guard to supply our cutters for the job. Eventually, the Navy bought an off-the-shelf fifty-foot craft they designated Patrol Craft Fast (PCF) that was nicknamed *Swift Boat,* to join *Market Time*. I was sent to Da Nang and went aboard the *Point Arden* and sleep on the mess deck overnight. In the morning, we got under way. These cutters are manned with two officers, a lieutenant junior grade (LTJG), ensign, and nine enlisted men. A South Vietnamese Navy liaison is usually aboard during patrol. I was dropped off on the *Point Dume*, my boat. I was replacing the gunner's mate on board, and the commanding officer figured it would be a good idea to bring me aboard while under way to get me acquainted with vessel and crew and to get some overlap with the outgoing gunner's mate.

After a few days at sea, we went back to Da Nang. I was now the lone gunner's mate on board. I made fifty-eight combat patrols, which lasted anywhere from two to six days with the objective of interdicting enemy movements and capturing contraband. Daily we boarded and inspected fishing junks, sail junks, and cargo junks. The enemy was most active at night. We gave gunfire support to our forces ashore with our mortar and machine guns. One example of interdiction happened when we were on an outer patrol area near the DMZ. There was nothing on the sea all around us except a sail junk with five people. When we boarded, our South Vietnamese Navy liaison inspected the papers of each person and said they were okay. Our commanding officer was suspicious anyway, so we took the boat in tow. We put one of our armed men on board and towed the boat all night. Every now and then one of us would call out, "How are you doing, Santos?" He'd yell back, "I'm fine." We turned the boat over to the South Vietnamese Navy and, sometime later, learned that the five crewmen were a North Vietnamese naval officer and four enlisted men trying to infiltrate South Vietnam.

One activity we carried out was harassment and interdiction (H&I). I remember one night we were assigned H&I coordinate's for a suspected enemy position. We set up two mortar crew sections. Usually, when we did H&I, nothing visible happened. We'd have to wait for a report from a marine unit going in there the next day to count bodies and check for damage. I was on the second gun watch this night lobbing mortar rounds at random intervals. After sending in three mortar shells, there were secondary explosions, flames, and smoke everywhere shooting up into the night. I have no idea what we hit, but it made us feel good.

I arrived in country three weeks later. There was a special operation taking place just above the DMZ. It was called Operation *Beau Charger*. The Navy was landing Marines to clear out the NVA. Our division was asked to provide an eighty-two-footer to work with a *Swift Boat* to act as screen protection to keep any NVA patrol boats from getting at our ships. Since our skipper was a well-respected combat-proven officer, the *Point Dume* was chosen. The first three days after the Marines went ashore were uneventful. The high-emotional charge of pending combat had subsided. From the North Vietnamese mainland to Hon Gio, or Tiger Island, is fourteen miles. That distance was split in half. One was called *Dagwood* and the other *Blondie*. The *Swift Boat* and *Point Dume* took turns covering each area. The night of 22 May 1967 things changed. We went to battle stations four times. The first came at 2130 when we went after a junk. We took the three black pajama-clad men prisoner and secured them on the stern; they had a front row seat for the rest of the action. We destroyed their junk. A half hour later, we're back at battle stations. The *Swift Boat* was coming under enemy fire from a North Vietnamese patrol boat near Tiger Island. At the same time, we closed the mainland to check out several enemy contacts and ended up in a running gun battle with a North Vietnamese patrol boat. I was on the aft starboard machine gun using the enemy's wake as a target reference. My loader was yelling at me, but I couldn't understand what he was saying through my talker helmet and all the exterior noise. I stopped shooting for him to drop in a fresh can of .50-caliber ammunition into the loading tray. He shouted, "Why are you firing down into the water?" I told him, "I'm not—I'm shooting at the wake." At that point, there was a lull in the shooting as the skipper maneuvered the boat, and we heard the rat-a-tat of the enemy's guns and saw little geysers of water walking their way toward the hull right below my gun. The enemy forced us to zigzag over the sea, each of us trying to get an advantage over the other. By now we were pretty close to Cap Lay where the North Vietnamese had their artillery positioned. They opened up on us with heavy guns; it was time to get out of there, and we did with haste.

I had the mid-watch, midnight to 0400. During that time, we went to general quarters again to check out contacts spotted by a destroyer. We didn't find anything. I came off watch and was not in my rack long when the battle stations gong went off again. This time there was a flotilla of junks heading to resupply Tiger Island. A thousand yards off our port side, the *Swift Boat* is in among three junks to board them. We could see his spotlights come on. Suddenly, there was an explosion and a lot of flame. Somebody yelled, "They got the *Swift*!" We moved in to assist and found ourselves among the junks, but the skipper didn't give permission to fire. He was concerned that close secondary explosions would harm his crew. There was a junk slowly moving past my muzzle. It was only fifteen yards away. I didn't know it, but my pressure on the trigger was tightening, and I let go a burst into the junk. The captain yelled, "Cease fire." About then, from another junk, came a grenade that bounced off the bow and exploded littering the forward gun crew with shrapnel. The skipper said, "Okay, let's go get 'em." We made our way among the junks firing all the time. We could see people jumping into the water. The *Swift Boat* started firing at us with its twin .50-caliber machine guns. Those guns sat right over the pilothouse where the radio was located. Our skipper called the *Swift Boat* to let them know at whom they were firing. Finally, the third time he yelled, the firing stopped. We had pretty much decimated the enemy and their supplies of rice and ammunition. The enemy's artillery had us in range again, and it was time to get out of there. Just at this point, our engines quit. We were dead in the water. I looked aft and saw this big red tracer floating toward us. It winked out, and I knew that shell was going to land smack on our fantail. I was waiting because there was nothing else to do. Just then, the engines roared. Hallelujah! We got out of there fast.

The whole coast was divided into patrol areas. On patrol, you operated alone: just one boat. If you were fired upon, you did what you could to counter it or called in help from air or sea. I was there before, during, and after the Tet Offensive. While most of my patrols were north of Da Nang, we began going as far south as Qui Nhon. Qui Nhon was good duty for the Navy; a lot of sailors liked it there. I guess it was fairly safe. That is until Tet. We pulled in there off patrol to resupply and enjoy a little liberty. We made some friends. The next time we pulled in, the base had been overrun by the enemy. Some of the people we had met were no longer alive. We went ashore armed. I remember our cook asking me to come along as an armed escort when he went ashore to dump garbage.

The Tet Offensive really tore up the NVA and VC. They couldn't mount any kind of attack after that. They were so desperate for war supplies and medical materials that North Vietnam resorted to sending down five armed trawlers at once carrying tons of supplies to its forces. Operation *Market Time* had taken away the sea as a supply route, leaving the Ho Chi Minh Trail as the sole replenishment avenue. Before the Coast Guard and Navy came on the scene, North Vietnamese trawlers ranging in size from 95 to 150 feet easily sneaked into South Vietnam, offloaded, and returned north for another load of cargo. The *Point Dume* was coming into Da Nang after a six-day patrol and found the *Point Welcome* getting ready to get under way to intercept one of these trawlers. The cutter wasn't scheduled to get under way, and her crew had been on liberty. They could not locate the gunner's mate and the electronics technician, so our electronics technician and I jumped aboard and headed back out to sea. Being in on a trawler kill was the goal of every Coast Guardsmen. I was thinking that this is a false alarm. Well, it wasn't. I got my trawler that night. The *Androscoggin*, similar to the *Wachusett* that I was on in Seattle, engaged the trawler inside the 12-mile limit. When the trawler reached waters too shallow for the big cutter, we went on the attack along with *Point Grey* and two *Swift Boats*. The trawler tried to reach the river mouth during this running gun battle, but we ran it up on the shore. We saw one crew member leave the trawler and stagger into the tree line. We were sitting about 200 yards away and the commodore was getting ready to ask for boarding volunteers when there was a small explosion on the trawler. These trawlers are rigged to self-destruct to avoid capture and we figured the attempt failed. A few moments later it blew. For a long time it rained shrapnel. I hit the deck so fast that the boatswain's mate across from me on one of the aft machine guns thought for sure I was hit. One of the enginemen, trying to squeeze under the small boat, just missed being hit by a twisted Chinese Communist bayonet. Everybody on the bow was knocked down and hit with shrapnel. The windows in the wheelhouse were broken. Aboard the *Androscoggin*, they saw us disappear from radar and thought we had been destroyed. After the heavy metal rain stopped, the boatswain's mate asked, "Where's the trawler?" I told him that we would see it when the deckhouse swung around. Well, there was no trawler, only a brown spot in the sand. We pulled what debris we could find from the sea. It wasn't much: a beehive fender, part of a hatch cover, a blue life jacket, and other odds and ends. We stayed on scene for another day while troops onshore searched the area; then we were ordered back to Da Nang. It was night, and the seas were getting heavy. During my helm watch, it was like riding in a dark elevator. We'd ride up a wave, go over it, and then we'd be falling not knowing when we were going to hit bottom. With each crash we just hoped the masking tape held the cracked windows together. To make matters worse, it was hard to hold a bearing because the compass had had a problem and was filled with vegetable oil. The regular light weight oil wasn't available. We made it back to Da Nang and got repaired. I still have some of the shrapnel that rained on us.

How did Vietnam shape your life?

I went to Vietnam with the belief that what we were doing, keeping a people free from tyranny, was worth fighting for. All the guardsmen that I served with were dedicated to getting the job done. We were given a mission, and we did it, and we were proud of what we accomplished. We didn't like the anti-war demonstrations when we returned home. The war did not have any negative effects on me. I was the same personality after the war that I was before Vietnam. I made the Coast Guard a career and retired with thirty years (four Air Force, twenty-six Coast Guard) active-duty service with the rank of W-4, chief warrant officer.

The men I saw who were engaged in the war gave it their all. They believed in what they were doing and sincerely carried out the mission. The biggest disappointment to all Vietnam War veterans was the way it ended. The politicians ran the war and then, like the cowards they are, bailed out on the South Vietnamese people. I was annoyed by the demonstrations because the demonstrators did not have a clue what they were talking about. We were fighting for the freedom of the South Vietnamese. We were fighting to contain global Communism and they just couldn't get a handle on that.

Advice to someone considering a military career

My thinking is that everyone who comes out of high school, not going to college, should go into the military. Most of us need an earnest transition period to take us from the soft living of home life into the rigors of the adult world where you don't know what's going to take place from day to day and where you must make critical life decisions. Military service instills self-reliance, confidence, and decision-making into one's character. You need a wife who is 100 percent behind you that is supportive and encouraging. I had a happy military career, in large part, to a steadfast wife. When I had seven years in the Coast Guard as a gunner's mate, she informed me that the Coast Guard was looking for people to switch their fields to journalist and urged me to do it. The change included being a spokesman to the news media and involved me in the many missions of the Coast Guard. I moved up the ranks to chief warrant officer, and my concluding assignment was Coast Guard liaison officer to the movie and television industry in Los Angeles. That was a good way to end a military career.

Current day

My wife and I have a son and a daughter. Both are married, each with two children, the standard one boy and one girl. Our son is an astronomer in Tucson, Arizona, and the discoverer of nine comets, each named after him. Our daughter is a computer troubleshooter at the Naval Academy in Annapolis, Maryland. I keep active in the Coast Guard Combat Veterans Association of which I am a co-founder.

EDWARD BRUCE SPEAR

Specialist 4, United States Army
Semper Vigilans: *"Vigilant Always"*
Delta Company Second Battalion Twenty-Seventh Infantry Regiment
    Twenty-Fifth Infantry Division
Home of Record: Philadelphia, PA
DOB: 29 January 1949
KIA: 05 October 1968
Binh Duong Province, South Vietnam
Body Recovered
Conducted at Edward's sister's home in Warminster, PA 5 March 2010
Cardinal Dougherty High School
Vietnam Memorial Panel 41W Line 016

> *Mothers should negotiate between nations. The mothers of the*
> *fighting countries would agree: stop this killing now. Stop it now.*
> —Yoshikuni Taki

Growing Up

We were all born in Boston. My dad was transferred to Philadelphia when I was six years old. With five kids, my mom was a stay-at-home mom, and my dad worked at the downtown social security office. I have three brothers and one sister. I'm the middle child, and my brother Eddie was a year behind me. Growing up in the city is a lot different than growing up in the suburbs here. We had a playground and a school right across the street from us. We used to go over there and play stick and kickball. We actually walked from home to St. Ambrose School because back then; they didn't have many buses. After grade school, we attended Cardinal Dougherty (Catholic) High School.

When Eddie graduated in 1966, he really didn't know what he wanted to do. First, he worked in a factory. Then he decided to go into the military, and he entered the service in 1967. He had been a very quiet boy. In fact, we use to call him Binky. However, we had military in the family, and I think Eddie wanted to serve his country. Our dad was in the Army in WWII. We had an uncle who was a colonel in the Army, another uncle who was in the Navy, and a cousin in the Marines. When Eddie joined, enlisted folks were not sure to which service they would be assigned, so right after boot camp, he was shipped to Vietnam. At that time things were very bad over there. My older brother, Bart, at the time, was in the Marines, but not in Vietnam.

October 1968—the news from Vietnam

Edward was stationed in what was called the Iron Triangle. This area was northwest of Saigon. Ed was killed on 5 October 1968 (Saturday) and we were not notified until the following Wednesday. Back then they just couldn't get the bodies out quickly.

The Army people came to my mom's house Wednesday morning to notify the family. I was at work. It was just my brother and my mother who were home. I believe it was someone from ROTC at LaSalle College. Then, in turn, my mother or my brother called my father. My brother called me at work; I worked for the social security office downtown. We were in a meeting, and I was annoyed that my brother was interrupting the meeting. I said, "What are you calling me at work for?" Then he said, "You have to come home, you have to come home!" I said, "I can't come home. What is the matter?" He then said, "The military is here." So I said, "Why is the military there?" Well, you just weren't in that mode and then he said, "Eddie's dead!"

I hadn't understood why my brother wanted me home. You just don't think of something like that. My youngest brother was in middle school. I don't know if Bart was just out of the military or just on leave. Thank God he was there for my mother. It was a hard time for my mother because in July her younger sister had a little five-year-old boy that drowned. Then in August, her youngest brother, who was a colonel in the military and was stationed in Texas, had a daughter with leukemia, and they rushed her up to Walter Reed, and she died. I recollect my mother coming home from that funeral saying, "One of your brothers is going to die." I remember that! Well, they say it always comes in three's. The two of them, then on 5 October, my brother was killed. It was like bedlam. We were all in shock! No one knew what to do or say. We were trying to contact my mom's brother who was in the military because, at that time, the Army told us they didn't know how long it would take for the body to come home. It could take weeks, and we couldn't wait weeks. His influence ensured that the body came home quickly. When Eddie came home, I'm not sure what Air Force base they flew him into. My uncle, the colonel who had just buried his daughter, coordinated everything.

What was sad was when the body came back from overseas, it was enclosed in glass. Well, it was a box; but from the waist up, he was enclosed in glass. We couldn't touch him or get close to him (because of all the diseases). He was embalmed and dressed in his uniform over there. When he came home, something as silly as the hair style caught your eye. The undertaker wouldn't know how he wore his hair. He put the hair back so we would know it was him. "We could look at him, but [we] could not touch him." We waited for the body. The military was wonderful. They stayed; they had the honor guard there. The hard part was the hecklers, the war protesters. Well, they were kept outside.

Everyone got into the service. There were a lot of tears, and I just couldn't believe . . . Ed was so young. My parents had an undertaker that they knew well from their church. So he did the service. I don't have much of a recollection of that next week; it is very hazy. The Foley Funeral Home on Cottman Avenue in Philly took care of Eddie. They had my parents go to the cemetery at Holy Sepulcher in Wyncote to pick the gravesite. Eddie is buried in Holy Sepulcher.

There had been talk of Eddie being buried at Arlington, but my parents decided that they didn't want him buried there because my dad didn't have a car. He had a driver's license, but he didn't have a car. My parents wanted him buried closer to home, so they could go to the grave. A few months later, they actually had a ceremony at LaSalle. That's where my parents were awarded all the medals. There were hecklers out there too.

At this point, Eddie is at peace. He is buried with my mother on one side and my father on the other side. He's right across from where there are no tombstones. My father picked it because there was a tree there, and he wanted him shaded. It sounds silly, but that's the way he picked it. He wanted a tree.

After the Funeral

I remember Bart saying he was going over there to avenge his brother's death. The military wouldn't let him because the family had already lost one member. My parents were never the same. They never really got over my brother's death. The first couple of years they weren't happy. Luckily, grandchildren came. My sister was pregnant when Eddie was killed, and her son is named Edward. Her husband, at the time, was named Edward. My brother, his first son, is named Edward. No one ever took Eddie's middle name. My mother and father are deceased now. Mom passed away in 1982;

it's been awhile. She was sixty-one. My father lived with me and, until the day he died in 2002, wore the gold star that we were given from the military. Eddie had been nominated for the Medal of Honor, which is the highest award that can be bestowed upon a soldier in the Armed Service. This was later rescinded, and he was subsequently put in for the Silver Star.

My youngest brother went into the military. He was in the Marines for a while. After graduating from Dougherty, he went to Villanova, and was in the MROTC (Marine Corps Reserve Officers' Training Corps). From there he went into the Marines. He stayed in the military for a while. Now he lives in 29 Palms in California. He is a detective for the San Bernardino police force.

I understand that Dougherty has, in fact, a picture. They have something on their front lawn for all the kids, all the boys that were killed in Vietnam. I want to know what they're going to do with it when they close the school. There were a couple of soldiers from St. Ambrose that I remember; I believe my brother was the first.

How did Vietnam affect your life subsequent to his death?

I can't to this day watch a movie on a war. I have never seen any of the movies on Vietnam or any of the movies on war. I just can't and won't watch them.

My father had instilled in us a great love for country. We are Catholic. The flag is very important to us. Our freedom is extremely important to us. I have a flag on my back window. I have a Thomas Kinkade portrait of the American flag. I have a flag outside. It was always instilled in us that freedom is not free, and my brother paid dearly for that freedom for us.

Eddie was a kid, just nineteen years old: the average age of a soldier in Vietnam. He had no idea what he wanted to do with life, what he wanted to be, or how he was going to grow up.

John, you have seen my office. It is all red, white, and blue. Freedom is the right to vote. It's all very important. In the office, when people start complaining, I simply ask them, "Did you vote?" Well, if you didn't vote, stop complaining.

Advice to someone considering a military career

Go for it! You should serve your country or, in some way, do something for your country. It might be the military; it might be politics. You should always vote, and you should do whatever you can to keep people free. A lot of people take our freedom for granted. It should never be taken for granted. In the office, you'll see a sign that says freedom is not free. It's not: people have to sacrifice their lives so we can be free.

I considered myself a child at that time. I was only twenty and married, but still like a child. Back then, people got married at that young age. That's what we did—men defended our country if our country was in war. They defended it to make people free. That's just what they did. We were all children.

Current Day

I'm an elected official, a tax collector, for Warminster Township. This is my eleventh year. Our previous tax collector died in office, and the township was looking for a replacement. It involved someone who is efficient with money, and coming from a Catholic background, I guess that carried some weight. I am fortunate to have been reelected for four terms.

Final thoughts for the interview on Eddie

Eddie was a nice young boy. That's just what he was: a boy. He wasn't a man. He never got to be a man. Do we know what he would have been like when he grew up? No. He was a good person and gentle person. He never fought with any of the members of the family or anyone outside the family. He did what he thought was good for the country. They say God takes the best at a young age, and God took him.

GEORGE FALLON

PFC, United States Army
Semper Vigilans: *"Vigilant Always"*
Charlie Co. 2nd Battalion 1st Brigade 327th Hawk Recon 101st
   Airborne Division
Home of Record: Jersey City, NJ
Home of Residence: Waterford, NJ
DOB: 04 June 1947
Interview conducted at his home in Waterford, NJ August 2010

> *If not now, then when? If not me, then who?"*
> —Hillel the Elder

Growing Up

I grew up in Jersey City, New Jersey. My parents raised us Irish Catholic. I had seven brothers and sisters. I was the fifth child and attended parochial school. We grew up in a blue-collar neighborhood and were taught to love our country. We were a rough-and-tumble family. When I was in high school, the war in Vietnam was going on. I used to read the *New York Mirror*. On the back page, they had pictures of what was happening in Southeast Asia. So I was looking forward to going to war. After a stint (one year) in the seminary, I enlisted. I didn't tell my mother, father, or my girlfriend. I volunteered for Airborne. In June 1966, I was on my way to Fort Dix, New Jersey, for basic training.

Growing up in the fifties, watching actors like Aldo Ray and John Wayne, we were mesmerized by these heroes and wanted to be just like them. When I was a kid, I played combat every day with my friend, practicing war and dreaming about someone hiding me in their duffel bag and bringing me to combat with him. I didn't realize the end game because it wasn't a game. After high school, I initially went to become a marine, but the recruiting office was closed. However, right next door, I saw a poster with a parachute and a guy hanging from it. So I went in. I went over to the Army recruiter who said, "If you go Airborne, you make $55 extra a month." So I said, "Sign me up."

My parents were upset that I didn't tell them, but they had no problems with me serving the country. My father was not in WWII due to the many mouths to feed. The Sisters of Charity did a lot for me. The drill instructor didn't upset me in boot camp because I had a nun that was harder on me than he was. I was kind of built for this, being a blue-collar all-American boy.

Vietnam

Six months after I had gone through jump school, basic training, and advanced Airborne training, I was in Vietnam (January 1967). In country, I was assigned to the 101st Airborne, 1st Brigade Charlie Company, 2nd Battalion 327th. I served from January 1967 to March 1967, at which time I changed from a line company to reconnaissance platoon: a six-man team. I was in recon from March 1967 until January 1968. That's where the story begins. What brought me to recon was walking point and resupply with another company. They called to hold up; Hawk Recon platoon was going to hook up with us. As I stood on the trail, stepping out to my immediate left was a recon guy. All camouflaged up in tigers (striped uniform). I said, "Damn, he could have killed me, I didn't see him." I said to myself, *Self—that's where I want to be. I want to be clandestine.* I went into recon, and it was a fantastic bunch of guys. All the men: NCOs, officers, grunts. The camaraderie was a given. We had to have our shit together in order to stay alive. Because of my NCOs, I am alive today.

Mike McKensey came into our unit, and we became good friends. As time progressed, we could see him changing. Once we were coming down this creek bed and one of the guys had malaria so we had to put him in a creek bed to cool him down. A helicopter took him out. We were coming down out of the valley into this open area of rice paddies. We pull over to the side, and apparently, some ARVN had been there. You could tell because it looks like a shithole; they left empty ration cans all over the place. I was leaning against a tree. All of a sudden, I see these NVA coming down the trail right behind us. I couldn't get to my weapon fast enough, so I whistled, and everybody turned around. We got into a firefight. We nicked the eight of them, one of which was a woman.

Mike went home for R&R and came back with Special Forces. He had been shot in the head, but it just clipped him. It took out a piece of his skull. They got him in the helicopter on a medevac, and the helicopter got shot down. He was shot up through the bottom of the helicopter. They finally got him out, but when we came back, I didn't see him. We heard that he was dead. Years later, I received a call at home. "Who is calling?" The voice came back, "Mike McKensey." I was shocked. They had placed him in a body bag assuming he was KIA. Only after he was back at the field hospital did someone notice movement in his bag! He was living in upstate New York and had graduated from Eastern Michigan University with an art degree. He was very talented. Mike came down to see me and had this long beard, but he said he felt guilty because after he came back, he joined Vietnam veterans against the war. He was bitter, I guess. He was shot eight times during the war.

Mike had made bronze masks, or paintings, of himself. One was a full face of him. The next one you see part of his jaw break away. His eyes were closed. In the third one, the whole side of his jaw was open, and you see the heat coming out. The last one you see the whole side of his face open, and one eye is open. His twist is, "When I went to war I had my eyes closed. When I opened them up, it was too late." He brought that to me, and he also painted a book about planes for me. Mike died of a heart attack in 2010.

Another time, we were on TOC (Tactical Operational Command) pulling security. We jumped in the helicopters and went down. As we're coming in, there was another helicopter shot down, so we were immediately in a gunfight. One kid got shot in the helicopter, never got out. Alpha Company came in for support with over a ton of choppers, almost 250 men. Then I see Captain Lauden. He's hanging on—he was literally right on top of the helicopter after he was hit (he survived). Now we're going to blow the helicopter. We can't get it out, and we're taking the guys with us. We're going to send in a recon team. This captain says, "My first squad first platoon is better than your recon. We'll send them down." They walked about 150 yards and got shot up. BOOM! So recon went down and we made five night link-ups to different units. I think there were seven or eight guys alive. It seemed they did everything right. Then on the way down, we got into another firefight. Tracers were flying all over the place. We knocked out a machine gun in a rice paddy as we came up right behind them. The day before, right about dusk, this other unit had seen NVA running up over this knoll. They sat up in the woods. The next day, a point man, an NCO and a radio and telephone operator (RTO) set out across this paddy. A creek bed was running through it. They walked across and they checked everything out. The platoon leader who later died there, Lieutenant Moore, said, "Leave the squad back here to watch our rucksacks." Apparently, the NVA were dug in on all sides and just chopped the shit out of them. Our guys got shot up. The Fourth Squad came out to break it up and they got all shot up. So when we got there it was over. The guys were all in the creek bed. One black kid who died was pointing as rigor mortis had set in. He was pointing toward the machine gun.

Next morning we head out. Alpha Company goes one way, we go the other. We're walking in some other area of operation (AO) and I was walking point all night. They said, "Fallon, you walk drag." That's the last guy. They called him "Tail End Charlie" in the Marines. "And Hoffman—you walk point." Hoffman went up to point, walks about fifty meters, and gets about eight shots right in the chest from a machine gun. He fell down and the sergeant ran out, grabbed him, and pulled him back. So now, they're firing up the trail we're on. Sergeant said, "Fallon, up front." I didn't answer him. He said, "Fallon, up front." I still didn't answer him. He said, "Fallon, up front!" I heard him, but knew there was a break in the elephant grass. I thought if I go out, I know I'll be dead, so I was hedging time. He said, "Fallon, up front!" I said, "Who, me?" He said, "No, you dumb motherfucker . . . get the fuck up here!"

Hoffman was dead (Fredrick Jean Hoffman *Vietnam Memorial Panel 27E Line 053*). His blood was on the trail, weapon lying next to it. They didn't know how big or small a unit we were. They were firing up the trail, four or five VC. Many times these dinks worked in small groups. We had on fatigues and nobody wore rank. So it didn't matter if you were the General—you were just one of the guys.

On our tactics in the field, picture a checkerboard. When we went to ground, there would be a platoon or squad in every one of those boxes. In other words, there was a space here, but there was a block behind it. If I walked through, there would be another one coming up to fill the vacuum. If we were sweeping an area: Let's say our battalion included four companies, but what happened was those companies would break down into platoons and spread out. They might put the first platoon on the right at a distance of five hundred meters, then they'd place second platoon. We were spread out so if anybody got in trouble, there were reinforcements.

We came up in force so you had to hit something. The enemy could not walk around you. When they put us in, they didn't come back for us for eight days so we didn't get resupplied. Everything was on our backs. Our patrols were called Long Range Reconnaissance Patrols (LRRPS) and the meals we ate had the same name. These were freeze-dried, ready to eat rations that were very light to carry versus the other rations used in WWII and Korea (C and K rations were canned). The line companies carried that canned shit. We carried these only when the freeze-dried rations were unavailable. The VC knew where we were inserted because some outfits occasionally were resupplied daily. At night, they'd bring in chow for the first cavalry. The next day the helicopter comes and takes a beating. We were hungry. After we were resupplied, we'd move on. These LRRP rations give you an enormous amount of protein and energy. There were four thousand or five thousand calories in each meal.

John, you asked about the mentality of some of the guys. Well, some were blue-bloods among us. Then there were blue-collar guys like me that came from all over. The Southerners—they were very proud of their ability with guns. "I can shoot a fly off a piss pot from five hundred yards." But many times a city boy was a better shot. We city boys were definitely better survivors as we sensed danger quickly. It's an instinct from growing up on the street, knowing somebody was going to jump out and kick your ass. It is engrained because somebody from a different street wanted to get you. That being said, there was an innocence of some sort in the southern boys—don't want to take anything away from them. They were good. But city guys had a killer mentality, and Airborne tended to be more aggressive than a line company. Again, individuals change as they go along. In the sense that you volunteer for Airborne, you know you're going to Vietnam. But then you're in Airborne and you click yourself up a little and you go to recon where you feel secure with the company. Now, you're putting yourself with six people. That takes balls. Some guys thought they could do it, but once they were out there and the helicopter drops them in and takes off. And you don't see anybody for eight days; it got scary for some of the guys.

In any war, the infantry had to be supported. For every man in Vietnam there had to be nine people to support that individual. So if you had a million in Vietnam, one hundred thousand were infantry. Statistically, Vietnam vets saw more combat in one year than a WWII veteran because they had more time in R&R (rest and relaxation).

Another story: We were up in Chu Lai twice as a unit. First time, they said that the North Vietnamese backs were broken and they were discouraged. That was 1967. Both sides fired mortars at each other. In that operation we killed seven hundred NVA. Then they pulled us out in August. In October, they sent us back to Chu Lai. They flew us into this hill that they had picked for the CP (Command Post). Previously it had been a Special Forces camp. We were coming in with the battalion and our helicopter was losing oil. They pulled out of formation and we landed in Chu Lai. Fortunately, our battalion went in on the hill. The Special Forces had laid mine field's whose location were not communicated to our unit. Any troopers that jumped off the helicopters stepped on Bouncing Betty's (antipersonnel mines) blowing their legs out. Our

Claymore mines were above-ground with seven hundred ball bearings in them, where the Bouncing Betty's were "dug into" the ground. A "Betty" was a mortar round (82 mm). They came up through the ground and blew about hip level.

So the NVA came up. They sent out a recon team off to the side of the hill and a recon off to the other side. We were listening and that shit's popping. Now the NVA got hit in the hill; we were sitting there. We had a five man team down from six. This guy Allen Lloyd was our sniper. He killed two NVA in the valley. Another NVA jumped back into the bush and Allen clipped him too. We sat there and all of a sudden we heard movement coming up. This guy Tex (first time in country)—we told him just let the NVA walk by. We were in these bushes and there was a clearing. The NVA had to break to come around the bush. Tex stood up and popped an NVA and they thought they had hit the perimeter. All of the horns went off and they ran right over us, up the hill and those guys shot them up there. Meantime our artillery was called in. Now they had these huge arty rounds (155 mm) that came in like a freight train. Allen got hit with shrapnel and it went down his throat. Another round came in and blew his leg off as well as part of his arm. He said, "Fallon, I'm hit." When I was right on top of him, I saw his eye; it was like white gel hanging out the side of his face. I took off my boot laces and tied his leg off. I was trying to get water for him. I crawled around and while still talking on the radio, I told them where the artillery was. I had an XM148, which was an M-79 grenade launcher that attached to an M-16; it was under my knees. An NVA was pulling a body back (another NVA soldier) and I had Allen. My heart was in my mouth. He went by and pulled the body right behind me. He must have thought I was another dink (NVA). It was very dark. We had flares all over the place. Next day, eleven hours later, they came and got us out.

Allen Lloyd lives in Florida. They amputated his leg from the knee down. Unfortunately, his eye is gone as a result of the incident. He has a glass eye. His arm is still messed up by the shrapnel of that 155 mm round: That round was scary. We were there—trees and shit all around us. After that artillery fire, there was nothing but tree stumps.

The day I got into the field was 13 January 1967. The day I went back home was the day I left—365 days later to the minute. When I got out, I was like a dog in heat. I came out and I had the guilt's. I said, "I'm coming out and leaving these guys behind." But I wanted to go home: I was caught in this quagmire. We had this big black first sergeant. I can't remember his name, but he had hands like ham hocks. I was leaving and I said, "Top" (Top is the name enlisted men call their first sergeant). I wanted to extend a hand. He slapped me and knocked me on the floor. He said, "Boy, go home. The war's lost" and I went home. He was a tough disciplined solider. WWII, Korea, Vietnam. Not sure if he is still alive, but he saved a lot of lives.

We left Cam Ranh Bay and flew to Oregon. We then jumped a direct flight to Jersey City. It was like an assembly line. You come off the plane and take your clothes off. You're still in your tiger jungle uniform. They measure you for a suit. Steak and egg breakfast following a shower. Within twenty-four hours from the time I left Vietnam, I was home. My parents didn't know I had flown in. I wanted to surprise them or give them a heart attack. I walked down the street and I saw Terrible Tom. He worked in a Jewish delicatessen and was run over by a bus when he was a child. I was coming down the street. So I said, "Terrible Tom, how you doing?" and Tommy, with the mentality of a ten-year-old, said, "Georgie, where have you been? I have not seen you in two weeks." That was my welcome home.

My father jumped off the couch when I came in. He started crying and shaking like a dog shitting razors. I'd never seen him like that; definitely caught him off balance. When I came home, I was different. My parents knew it. My mother was afraid to wake me up. Then I went to see Teresa my girlfriend. Her brother opened the door. He always used to tease her, saying, "Georgie's here." So she was all excited. From there I went to Germany with 509th Airborne. Finally, in June 1969, I was honorably discharged.

How did the Vietnam shape your life?

Teresa, George's wife, answers the question. He didn't talk about the Army. Everything that happened, he used to write in letters to me. He made me get rid of all the letters. When we first got married, we moved in and I opened up the suitcase. I said, "Look George." I had every letter; three years of them. I said, "You have history here. Every feeling, every thought he had, everything was in those letters. He made me fill a bathtub full of Clorox and throw them in. *George continues.* I didn't want anybody to see that side of me; that vulnerability.

Do you have any regrets destroying the letters?

Yes, now I do a little bit, in retrospect, but I think that was for our eyes only. In my mind, I didn't want to share that with anybody. Even if after I was dead and they had them stashed away. (*Author*): *That shows how much you love and respect Teresa.*

It's something that I didn't want to share with anybody. Being a father, I had this mentality of overprotecting myself. I couldn't accept a mistake or having done something stupid. I had seen guys do stupid things and they died; stepping on a land mine or not paying attention. To give you an example, my son Keith; he's thirty-four. When he was about eleven years old, he had just finished football practice. His friend was on another team and we had to wait to drive him home. Before the game, I saw some big kids on his friend's team and said, "Don't get in trouble," meaning be careful on the field. After the game, I was standing there, and his friend came over and said, "Mr. Fallon, Keith hurt his leg." I told him to crawl over here. I thought he'd sprained it or something. He said, "Mr. Fallon, I don't think he can." I went over and he was just laying there. He was crying and I said, "Stop crying" and he stopped. A medic nurse said, "What are you telling him?" and I said, "Shut up." If he listened to me, he wouldn't be the way he was." I was cold as ice. I should have been comforting, but I was saying you didn't listen to me you asshole. Don't come crying to me. I was tough on them all. They didn't know how to act.

When you're in a combat situation, your sense of smell, taste, hearing, everything is like a razor's edge. You have the power to give life and the power to take life. You never reach that again. I think you're an animal; the purest animal. Why? Animals survive on the sense of smell, taste, and the ability to kill or not kill. Following that, I tried to achieve that high again. I was a policeman in Camden. I went from a beat cop to a patrol cop to the tactical unit. Worked from 1900 to 0300 when all the gun calls came in. After that, I became a bomb technician.

Advice to someone considering a military career

In peacetime, I would tell them it would be a great experience in the sense that they'd meet people from every walk of life.

Current Day

I held a variety of positions following college. I worked as an insurance investigator, then the police force for sixteen years. After that, I became a sheriff officer who tracked down fugitives. Then I was offered a county government seat as Director of Central Services with direct oversight of ten divisions. I retired in 2005 as Superintendent of Roads for Camden County, New Jersey.

I have five children; Christine, Keith, Kelly, Kevin, and Christopher. Three are married, total of six grandchildren. Initially my wife wasn't prepared to have kids. Something had occurred in her womb. Fortunately, every five or six years, we had one. We have four grandchildren by my son, Keith. My daughter Christine has been unable to have children. She and her husband just adopted two little sisters. They're all part of our family now so it's very good there. All my children have done well.

JAMES SCHLEGEL

Specialist 5, United States Army
Semper Vigilans: "Vigilant Always"
Fourth Transportation Command
Home of Record: Kutztown, PA
Home of Residence: Kutztown, PA
DOB: 18 March 1950
Conducted in Jim's home 28 February 2010
Website: www.allanfurtado.com/index.html

> *Courage is not the absence of fear; but rather the judgement that something else is more important than fear.*
>
> —Ambrose Redmoon

Growing Up

I was born at St. Joseph's Hospital in Reading, Pennsylvania, 18 March 1950. I currently live in the same house in which I was born and raised. My father was a construction superintendent and traveled around the country operating different construction sites. In the summertime, we'd go along and see different parts of the country. By the time I got to high school, I still didn't know what I wanted to do. My brother before me had spent three years in the Army. He was stationed in Germany and all I remember is hearing about all the fun times he had there. The Vietnam War was going on and my brother said to me, "Look, if you don't want to go to school right now, why don't you go into the service? Sign up to be a Transportation Movement and Controls Specialist, because every time I see those guys, it looks like the best job in the Army." So, I took my brother's advice and I joined.

The Army did guarantee that I could go to school to be a Transportation Movement and Controls Specialist (TMCS). I went to Fort Jackson, South Carolina for basic and then on to Fort Eustis (we used to call it Fort Useless) in Virginia for training. Out of the one hundred guys who trained with me, ninety-seven went to 'Nam right off the bat and three of us went to Germany. I thought, "Wow, someone is looking out for me." I had come home on leave and then two weeks later reported to Fort Dix, New Jersey and then headed over to Germany. There, I was assigned to a company called the 591st Transportation Company. I had no clue what they did.

I arrived on a Monday morning and the first sergeant asked about our MOS (military occupational specialty). Our group informed him that we were Transportation Movement and Controls Specialists. He responded, "I'm sorry, but I don't have your MOS here. I'm going to transfer you to a unit where they do have your MOS, but I'm looking for truck drivers. If any of you guys are interested, I'll send you to truck driving school and a warehouse procedure school and you can stay assigned here." This particular unit was in aircraft maintenance where helicopters and small fixed-wing aircraft were repaired. As a result, I ended up being a truck driver and a warehouse worker for them. I learned about aircraft parts and all US Army aircraft Helicopter equipment. Back in those days, the helicopter outfits were mostly assigned to the transportation corps. It was the transportation corps's basic responsibility to maintain them. I believe today, helicopter outfits are now part of the Ordnance Corps. A nephew of mine who later was a Black Hawk (helicopter) pilot and an avionics specialist during the First Gulf War told me this.

After about thirteen months in Germany, the first sergeant called me and the two other guys who came to Germany with me into the orderly room. For some reason, I can remember three huge stacks of water when he said, "Well guys, I'm sending you on a trip." I said, "Yeah, where we going Tom?" He said," You're going home on leave for forty days and then you're going to Vietnam." All of our jaws dropped! I went home on leave for the forty days where I spent a lot of time with my girlfriend. The three of us then reported to Fort Lewis, Washington for two weeks of Advanced Infantry Training (AIT). Everyone who went to Vietnam had to go through extra training. You had to learn about booby traps, how to operate an M-79 grenade launcher, an M-16, and M-60 machine gun, the whole nine yards. They also took us out on convoys, attacked us, and taught us how to handle any dangerous, potentially fatal, situations. At the end of the training period, they put us on airplanes and flew us up to Alaska, then Japan, then Cam Ranh Bay in South Vietnam. Time flew during the forty-day leave and the new training period. This was nothing like Germany. I hadn't signed up for this.

Vietnam

As we landed in Cam Ranh Bay, you could see out into the thick jungle—tracers and stuff like that. "Aww shit," I thought. Then there was complete silence. The plane landed; I was one of the first guys to get off.

This huge Sergeant was standing at the bottom of the steps. He grabbed me and two other guys and told us to just stand there for a minute. Everyone else headed off. The three of us had to unload the baggage. Baggage boys, I thought-this really sucks! We could hear munitions going off in the distance. We were scared shitless! Three days later, we were temporarily put on some other movements and transportation. Eventually, I got put on a C-130. It flew a group of us to Bien Hoa Air Force Base, about eighteen miles from Saigon. From there, I went to the ninetieth transportation battalion and on to the Fourth Trans Command where I had been reassigned. However, in order to get to the Fourth Trans Command, I had to go back to Bien Hoa to catch a truck, a deuce and a half (2.5 ton truck), and go to Saigon. To this day I still don't understand why we couldn't have gone directly from Bien Hoa to Saigon.

As we pulled into the compound of the Fourth Trans Command headquarters and got off the trucks, we were told our duties. It was pretty late in the day by then so they hurried us onto three quarter ton trucks and sent us down to a place called Camp Davis. This camp is along the Saigon River, and behind it were warehouses and the other perimeter was the river. This was where I lived. The first night there was an alert. The new guys weren't assigned any weapons yet so the other soldiers grabbed us. Instead of taking us to the bunkers, they took us to the middle of the base camp where there was a bunch of flat bed trailers parked and we had to hide underneath these trailers until the alert was over—no means of defense. It lasted for about an hour. In the distance, we heard some small arm fire, but there really wasn't much—only enough to scare the shit out of us. Again!

The next day, each of us was assigned our jobs. As TMCS's, we were really transportation clerks. I had to keep all kinds of records and was on the phone all of the time. In a headquarters situation, I was on the phone with all of the different units below us. It was my responsibility to find out where they were and what they were doing. It was also my job, by using a large map in a dark room that was all lit up (like when you watch these movies of WWII where you see them pushing ships around in the ocean) to push barges around. I had to keep track of an entire river system of South Vietnam; keep track of where all the barges were. They were all US Army barges and were being pushed around by US Army tug boats carrying everything from medical supplies to ammunition and food. There were refrigeration barges. I have pictures of them. I'm going to say they weren't that big. The barges we had were about thirty feet across to about one hundred feet long.

At this particular port facility in Cat Lai, ammo ships that came in from the United States docked in the middle of the river. They weren't allowed anywhere near Saigon. They would hail three ships at a time and this was the formation they used for transporting. It was like a ferry. If one blew, they would take the other one with them. It was like dropping a small nuclear bomb. It would level everything within a twelve-mile radius. When they arrived, they would unload everything out in the river on the barges. Then they brought the supplies over to the docks, transferred it, loaded up the trucks, and hauled it to the warehouses up at Long Binh. Most of the ammunition was taken to the ammunition dump in Bien Hoa. Our unit handled everything from 5.56 MM M-16 ammunition to .30-caliber (7.62 mm) machine gun ammunition, bombs, mines, and napalm.

It just so happens I am a type 2 diabetic and I do receive a stipend from the government because of being exposed to Agent Orange (dioxin). We didn't just spray it in the jungles. It was sprayed around the base camps, the perimeters. I have pictures of the perimeter at Long Binh. There is no vegetation at all along that perimeter because it was sprayed with dioxin. I sat in a bunker one night, on guard duty, along the same perimeter, actually down the other side when a guy came along through the deuce and a half with a tank and on the back it was loaded with Agent Orange. They didn't just spray with airplanes. They sprayed with tanks, hand pumps and anything that would spread it around. Anyway, that shit leaked into the water and we drank, cooked, and bathed in it. Like I said, I was on guard duty one night and they came through spraying the shit. I got soaking wet. No one thought of any danger associated to the chemical back then.

On one occasion, we grabbed our M-16s and went for a ride. We weren't out in the boonies killing people. The TC guys just supported the guys doing that. That was our job. We had it made compared to them, and I'll be the first guy to say, I had it made, but sometimes we were in just as much danger day in and day out of getting shot, blown up by mines, or whatever—mortars, rockets as those in hand-to-hand combat. Now, I'm going to tell you a couple of stories.

Late one afternoon, there was a Major. He was in command. I don't really remember his name. He was serving on a court-martial with headquarters at Tan Son Nhut. The court-martial was over. I was driving him back up to Long Binh. He said confidently, "I checked all the intelligence, we can go up Highway 1, there's no action tonight. So, we don't have to wait for the convoy." There was always a convoy out of Long Binh. There were all kinds of security. I mean out of Newport that went up to Long Binh to the warehouse. We got about halfway up and I start hearing AK-47 shots at my rear! I put the hammer down on that Jeep! There's a bridge to go over right before you get to Long Binh on Highway 1. US Military police were waiting for guys coming through, driving like hell. The MP actually gave me a speeding ticket. "What is the matter with you guys?" I said, "We were shot at five miles down the road, you know?" The M-14 was a much heavier weapon than the AK-47 and definitely made a louder sound. You could hear this cracking sound. The Major did get me out of the ticket, but that was one night I shit in my pants, so to speak.

Another time, the VC probably weren't expecting us. Nobody shot at us. We got to Tan Son Nhut civilian air terminal, walking around with loaded M-16s. Finally, we see the major coming through the US Military customs. The son of a bitch was trying to sneak greenback dollars in the country in a money belt which he was probably going to try to sell to the Viet Cong, which is the main reason you weren't allowed to have greenback dollars. However, it still put us in jeopardy. Many of the officers often played poker for the real thing. I'm thinking, you son of a bitch. We've come down here in the middle of the night and you're trying to sneak greenback dollars into the country. There are six of us risking our lives to get you back to Long Binh. Well, we got him back to Long Binh. There was no trouble. We were lucky. Thank God nothing happened that night.

I wasn't coming home to my girlfriend because she had sent me a "Dear John" letter while I was in Vietnam. I was a little bummed out because of that but . . . the plane left Bien Hoa Air Force base on Christmas Eve around 2200. Once we got out over the South China Sea, one engine took a shit. It was a C-141 USAF Starlifter. The flight was diverted to Guam. We were able to make it because we still had three other engines. We landed and it took them four hours to swap out the engines. However, it was such a relief just to step off the plane in Guam. It was such a relief that the pressure wasn't there. I didn't have to be worried about dying because I was scared shitless from the day I stepped on the ground until the minute the plane got out over the South China Sea. Even though the plane loses a freaking engine, you have no clue what a relief it was. Anyway, I got back on the plane and flew to Travis Air Force Base in California. We got on buses and went to Oakland Army Terminal. Remember, it was still Christmas Eve for the whole twenty-some hours later. Christmas Eve for me was two days because of the time zones.

The C-141 Starlifter was the main work horse for the Air Force before the C-5 Ace. They were huge planes and very fast. When we landed, an officer said that because it was Christmas Eve and they wanted to be with their families that they wanted us to take leave and then report to another Army base to be released. Even though our papers stated that this was our release date. Some of us had been around the Army long enough and in commands long enough to know bullshit. Our orders said end time and service that day. So you are letting us out of the Army *today*. They had to go find a freaking doctor to give us a physical on Christmas Eve. We got out of the Army and had our steak dinner. I arrived at the San Francisco airport 2345 Christmas Eve. I walked up to the TWA desk and I asked, "Do you have any flights to Philly?" The lady said, "Yes, I have one." I took the seat and jumped on the plane.

Sure enough there was one seat on the left-hand side of the plane, and it was in the middle between both an Army and Air Force private. Now, I'm a Spec 5 still wearing my patches. I said to them, "I think I'd like to have the window seat." It was midnight and those two saw the patches and BOOM, out of their seats they went! I sat down and said, "Thanks guys." I fell asleep as soon as the plane was in the air because I hadn't slept from the time we left 'Nam. The plane lands in St. Louis and almost the entire passenger crew deplaned. The three of us, going to Philly, stayed on the plane. Now I had almost the whole plane to myself. The stewardess said, "Are you hungry?" I said, "Yes. I'm real hungry." She brought me this big tray of sandwiches. I ate almost the whole tray. It tasted so good. The plane landed in Philadelphia where they treated me well. At the other places, I had no problem either. At the Oakland Army Terminal, when we all got out of the service, there were guys that took their uniforms off, crumpled them up, and threw them in a corner and put on civvies. They didn't want to wear their uniform. Guess I had the problem. I'm Pennsylvania Dutch. This is the clothing the Army gave me to wear, so I'm wearing my clothing home. I got off the plane in Philly. I had called my parents from St. Louis, telling them what time to be at Philly to pick me up. I'm walking down the tarmac and the first person I saw that I recognized was my older brother. He was walking toward me, "Hey Jimmy!" and then I see my mom and my dad.

How did Vietnam shape your life?

It was my logistical military training that took me to the job I have today. I went to Allentown Business School at night and got an associate degree in general business there. I also studied traffic management through

International Correspondence Schools. I've always had, even before I went in the Army, a fascination about moving shit—transportation, so to speak. That's why I got into it. I often think about my days in the military. I often think—gee, maybe I should have made a career out of it, but then this and that wouldn't have happened. Never would have met my wife. She was a college student at Kutztown State College. She's from Slatington.

I've studied the Vietnam War, and it should never have happened. If you do your research and go back far enough, you'll find that at the end of WWII, the French wanted to recolonize Vietnam when the Japanese were kicked out. In order to do that, they had to have the support of the United States government. A Vietnamese, by the name of Ho Chi Minh, who was not Communist at the time and who actually helped American flyers and supporters during World War II, begged Truman to keep the French out. Of course, France was the ally, and France got our support. First off, the war was a big waste of human life, big waste of innocence, and a big waste of money. It should have never happened, but it did.

As far as I know, everybody that I knew who grew up in this town that went to Vietnam came back. Since then, some Vietnam veterans have passed away, one of them most recently. I can think of two, but one that I grew up with was Stevie Wagner. He was a marine over there, and he was a door gunner. Imagine that, door gunners had life expectancies of ninety minutes, but he was a mean son of a bitch. He was the kind of guy you wanted for your buddy as you were growing up. When he was done with his marine tour, the Army was looking for door gunners, and he was on Army choppers for a while. He was still in the Marines. He stayed in the Marines, but he offered his services to the Army. He died of diabetes, probably from Agent Orange. Luckily, I never lost a particular friend that was in battle.

My parents were quite spread apart in age. My dad was fourteen years older than my mother. He didn't get married until he was thirty-seven and turned forty-four when I was born. He passed away before my mother did in 1984. He was a very well-respected man in Kutztown. He was involved in the community and the church. We both worked for the same company, but he was in management. He used to run all their construction sites. He built this whole house by himself in 1949. When my mother passed away in 1994, and my family was living down on Main Street, I asked my brother (the one that advised me to go to the Army in the first place) and who had been living here with my parents because of his divorce, if he wanted to buy the house. He said no—that he couldn't afford it. He knew he'd have to buy out my half. I knew I'd have to buy out his half, but I gave him first dibs on it. I ended up buying him out. In 1994, I moved my family back home here.

Advice to someone considering a military career

Same thing I told my son. Go in the Air Force or the Navy because the technical training is terrific. Then find something on the outside that's going to pay well. If you decide not to further your education, you can still get something technical. That's what America's going to need down the road, more technical people.

Current Day

I have two sons. My oldest son, Dan, is an Air Force veteran. He went into the service right out of high school because he wanted to do like Pop and see the world. I said, "If you're going to do that, go into the Air Force, don't go into the Army." When he got out, he went to tech school, and now he's an engineer at Lutron. My other son, Andy, graduated from Kutztown in December 2001. He still works for the same company that he worked for all the way through high school, the Kutztown Bottling Works. When he graduated from college, they made him their traveling salesman. Just two or three years ago, the company changed hands. Not being familiar with the business, the new owners made him manager of the place.

Dan will be thirty-five in June, and Andy is going to be thirty-two in July. I'm very proud of them. The oldest one, Dan, has a daughter. She's going to be six months old; I am now a grand pop! When I used to pray in Vietnam, I'd say, "I want to see my grandchildren." My prayers were answered. I have strong faith in Jesus.

Closing Comments

Yea, though I walk through the valley of the shadow of death, I will fear no evil, for thou art with me.
                                        —Psalm 23:4

I will begin with Captain Steedly. In the four times that we have met, I have this feeling I have known Homer for a long time. He is another veteran who served in Vietnam that I will always admire. If his wife, Tibby, gets her way, they may be joining the Siegfrieds for Thanksgiving dinner at our home in 2011.

Mr. James Schlegel. Specialist 5 US Army. The book would not be complete without Jim. During our interview, he had to stop the tape several times. The memories flashed back to him as he spoke about his friends and what he experienced. Jim and I are close in a lot of ways. Both of us carry Pisces as our Sign, separated by only a few days on the Julian calendar and in years. Both of us are very outgoing, not afraid to speak our mind. He is a man who takes pride in his service, country, and family. I am proud to now know him. On a weekly basis, Jim sends me at least one e-mail.

Sergeant Paul Ferraro and I had a wonderful discussion over the phone subsequent to our initial meet. An author in his own right, he also provided much insight while he was talking about his Vietnam experience. His quote in *chapter 8* (Tran Minh interview—"I will never forget the look in their eyes") tells everything about how serviceman were torn between helping the Vietnamese, all the while being cautious due to never knowing who was friend or foe.

Chief Warrant Officer Paul Scotti and I seem to exchange e-mails and phone calls monthly. Paul helped me track down Coast Guard families to obtain approval for usage of the bracelets in the book. Of the seven KIA guardsmen in Vietnam, we have one honored on the copyright page as well as the spine of the book. Thanks again to Paul and his wife for allowing me to take a copy back to Philadelphia of the wonderful poem that ends the book. My goal to meet everyone in person ensured I saw that quilted piece (poem) on their family room wall.

On the business/homeowner side, Bobbi Loftus is the tax collector that everyone needs to have! On the personal side, our interview in March 2010 was poignant. Her brother Edward, as she stated, was just a boy. When a father and wife lost a son or daughter, they became "Gold Star" parents. I really have not delved into this—this topic probably a book unto itself. But she spoke very candidly about how her dad wore that "star" until his final days cut short by the tragedy of his son preceding his own death.

PFC George Fallon is a bona fide Gemini. It is wonderful when you speak to him either in person or over the phone, but don't wait for a call back. You will grow gray hair quickly. But seriously, he and I have also become very close. It was difficult taping his interview because he would bounce around a lot, which is not uncommon for vets with post traumatic stress disorder. George would delve into so many experiences from 'Nam. I just did my best to listen and let the tape recorder do its job.

To give you insight about George's persona, consider this incident. PFC Fallon originally entered the priesthood after high school. While at the abbey for one year, he got into trouble. The abbey priest promptly interviewed him after the incident, saying, "George—many are called, but few are chosen. You, sir, are not chosen." The priesthood missed out on a good man. The 101st Airborne was the ultimate beneficiary. Mr. Fallon and I will always stay in touch, because he will hunt me down if I don't attend the annual West Point Gala in honor of the 101st Airborne Division this year.

Corporal Dave "Smilie" Martin. We completed Dave's interview in a restaurant. Prior to that day, we had met and talked for over three hours. So I really went in with an understanding what this former forward observer was made of and his experience in Vietnam. Dave is a short man by anyone's standard, but a linebacker has nothing on this veteran. My thoughts were, "Wow. I would not want to be in the crosshairs of this marine on the battlefield." He was passionate about his service, his compatriots in the various units with whom he served, his dedication to the flag, and his thirty years working in Veterans Administration. He literally spent his adult life, prior to retirement, serving this country. I am not only privileged to have met him, but that we stay in touch regularly. Thank you, John Lang, for providing me the means to get to know your former "teacher" on the battlegrounds of I Corps where you and Dave served together in South Vietnam.

I Corps was the primary area where the Marines operated. II Corps was the "home" for Captain Steedly's Army units. When discussing actual combat, some of these veterans talk about the shrapnel they incurred which happens to rise to the epidermis. They will awaken, scratch an area of their body, and presto—a minute spec of metal that the dermis and subcutaneous layers of skin held hostage for years appears. In Pleiku Province, Central Highlands, II Corps area, a similar situation with the soil existed. As Homer explains in his *Chapter 7* interview, the red soil (dust in the dry season—mud in the wet season) was virtually impossible to get out of your orifices and skin. One combat Army medic actually told me that even while you were showering (maybe once a month) and you thought you were clean, while just rubbing your outer skin, the clay or dust would continue to appear. I will have to keep this in mind when taking that cold shower honoring the SEALs.

CHAPTER THREE
1970-1975

Exodus

Dedicated to Rowland J. Adamoli
Corporal, United States Marine Corps
Alpha Company, First AmTrac Battalion, Third Marine Division

We didn't lose—we were ordered out.
—from the Vietnam Memorial in
Philadelphia, Pennsylvania

In January 1970, our total forces deployed in Southeast Asia were decreasing steadily. Nixon had already begun the drawdown to satisfy the media and the Americans against the war, while introducing the Vietnamization program to transition the base of power from the United States to the South.

The number of KIA and noncombat deaths in 1970 was virtually the same as in 1966. Although 6,065 died that year, the numbers were reduced dramatically (over 30 percent) from 1969 following the massive troop reductions. Heavy action raged from January 1970 through the end of 1971 with over 51,000 total casualties. This, coupled with the intense bombing of North Vietnam in 1972, eventually led to the Paris peace talks negotiation and resolution to release the POWs in February 1973.

Although the papers stated that the war was over in January 1973, 168 more servicemen would perish that year.

The United States continued to incur casualties from the POW release through April 1975. The pictures of men pushing a helicopter off the deck of an aircraft carrier (to make room for Vietnamese civilians) will forever live in the minds of many of us from that generation.

Introduction to the Interviews

This chapter has the best mix of interviewees. One enlisted man, a lieutenant commander USN, one lieutenant colonel USAF, and a flag officer (rear admiral). All these men served in different functions and were honorably discharged, or retired, as a career officer. All three officers were consistently in harm's way. Bob Hogan was in the business of saving lives for all of the air services by ensuring parachutes were packed properly, so any pilot from any service could "walk home" if they had to eject or punch out. There are many old adages about the challenges within the Marine Corps and the Navy. A sailor provides a ride to where the corps needs to go. Yet Navy and marine pilots have to land on a moving vessel, an aircraft carrier, versus the USAF and the Army on the ground. According to aviators I've spoken to, it's a much more difficult maneuver for the former. So with all their potential differences, they have many qualities in common based on abilities and responsibilities.

In addition, instances abound where a Navy corpsman (enlisted medical service provider or HM) has been told by his commanding officer (CO) that due to all their lifesaving treatment, they belong to the USMC, not the USN. Corpsmen are assigned to a Marine Corps operating combat unit.

Bob Hogan has been my friend for over fifty years. Our yards adjoined in Glenside, Pennsylvania. My family moved from Willow Grove, Pennsylvania, to our new home in early 1958. The Hogan's moved into our neighborhood the same year. Grade school, high school, and everything in between—we were best buds. Although Bob was stationed on Guam, he saw the debris of battle from Vietnam. His father, a Navy commander during WWII, flew the Douglas SBD Dauntless in the Pacific. Mr. Hogan, who recently passed, was one of the finest Southern gentlemen I ever met. The interview process with Commander Caldwell and Admiral Roesner followed a much different path. While I was at a Veteran Assistance seminar in Pennsylvania I met a man standing at one of the booths. Although seventy-two years old, he was built like college cornerback and presented like most career military officers. After a discussion and his being inquisitive about the book, he agreed to an interview.

Michael Roesner was waiting to board a plane from Philly to Chicago on 4 August 2010. While we were being "herded" through the gate, I noticed a Navy pin on his lapel. We began chatting, both of us discussing current travel schedules. As a consultant for IBM, he flies to Chicago regularly. Then he noticed the multiple books I was carrying and asked what they were about.

The following truly shows how many of our veterans are grounded. Upon asking about his Navy pin and inquiring about being involved in Southeast Asia, he said "I was an enlisted seaman." Now this man looked like a CEO from a Fortune 500 company. So I begged the next question, "Were you a career man?" to which he responded "Yes." At this point I was really engrossed. "May I ask what rank you were at retirement?" to which he replied "Admiral." The line was fading fast to board so I closed with "So you are a Mustang?" to which he replied "Yes, how do you know about Mustangs?" Well, an enlisted man who is recommended for OCS (Officer Candidate School) and retires as an officer is deemed a Mustang. At this point, our fellow US Air "herdsmen" were being seated. He graciously gave me his business card and asked me to call him. Many of the interviews manifested themselves in this way. Caution (but interest) at first due to speaking to a civilian, then (in some cases) "back-grounding" by fellow servicemen to ensure I was above-board.

Colonel Mike McAllister flew F-4s in Vietnam—the same plane in which Colonel Donald was shot down. He has become a good friend. Colonel Mike is in great shape; sixty-six years old who has the physique of a man half his age. He runs each and every day, is a good husband, and a loving grandfather of eleven grand—and great-grandchildren. After interviewing the colonel in February 2010, I planned my next trip to Atlanta to shake his hand. So we finally met 29 March 2010 at McKendrick's restaurant. During lunch, we talked for hours. A month does not go by, since our meeting, where we don't communicate.

Due to the stringent requirements, pilots in all services make up approximately the top 2 percent of all servicemen and women. Their brains (and bravado) as well as their skill level, dwarf many of us. Maybe that is one reason Colonel Donald, Admiral Roesner, Colonel McAllister, and Commander Caldwell entered my life—to continue to learn from these men how it feels to fly.

MICHAEL S. ROESNER

Rear Admiral (Ret.), United States Navy
Non Sibi Sed Patriae: *"Not self but country"*
3rd Coastal Zone Advisor Group, Cat Lo, RVN
Home of Record: Flint, MI
Home of Residence: St Petersburg, FL
DOB: 24 October 1948
Interview conducted via phone 27 August 2010
Met at Philadelphia International Airport 4 August 2010

> *Those who expect to reap the blessings of freedom must, like men, undergo the fatigue of supporting it.*
>
> —Thomas Payne

Growing Up

I had an extremely blessed childhood. Born and raised in Flint, Michigan, I was the oldest of five children. My father was a WWII Navy veteran. He came back and built the typical post-WWII dream. We always had a comfortable home. Dad worked in General Motors factories and made a decent living, enough to put all the children through Catholic schools. I went off to the seminary in Detroit and returned and graduated from Holy Redeemer High School in Flint, Michigan, in 1966. As soon as I was old enough, I worked in the General Motors factories part-time while attending junior college and full-time during the summers. In the 1968-69 timeframe, when I finished junior college, it was time to go off and go to a school where I had to board. I needed the money, so I took a semester off to work full-time in the factories; then I was drafted into the Army. My father, of course, preferred I'd join the Navy on a four-year enlistment because he felt I certainly would have had more options, but if I allowed myself to be drafted into the Army, I'd definitely wind up in Vietnam like so many kids; the conscript being pretty much in the jungle, so I enlisted in the Navy in 1969.

I was twenty when I enlisted in May 1969. I naturally went through boot camp and the Navy's Vietnam involvement was playing very heavily in '68, '69, '70, in the riverine operations. I didn't know what I was going to do in the Navy. I progressed to second-class petty officer pretty fast, did a brief tour on the East Coast in Attack Squadron 44, came out to the West

Coast, and was in Fighter Squadron 126. Quite frankly, I was getting bored; it looked like I would be onshore duty most of the time for my enlistment, so I volunteered to go to Vietnam. At that time, Admiral Zumwalt was actively seeking youngsters that could pass the requirements for language training and the advisor curriculum to go over and serve as advisors to the Vietnamese. By that time we were withdrawing from active combat roles in early 1971. The advisor program sounded exciting to me, so I did it. I was young and single and looking for some excitement. It must have been around summertime of 1971, I did receive orders to leave the Naval Air Station in Miramar with Fighter Squadron 126 and proceed to Mare Island, California, which is where the Naval In-Shore Operations Training Center was. They trained all the Navy personnel headed for Vietnam on patrol procedures, qualified you in riverboats; and because we were going to be advisors, they'd also established Vietnamese language training as well as a curriculum called "Human Response," which was kind of an immersion into Vietnamese culture. I think they were all very good programs: I learned, in a fairly short amount of time, enough Vietnamese to conduct day-to-day business and to understand what the Vietnamese were saying. I was much more proficient at understanding what they said than speaking it. I also learned about customs and cultures, their different religions, what was rude, what things they appreciated. All this was extremely helpful to me later on because I went through basic marine patrol craft training and familiarization on PBRs (patrol boat rivers), and various other types of craft we would encounter. I went through a thorough weapons training curriculum and familiarization with virtually all small arms we might encounter in Vietnam, both weapons that the VC and NVA were using as well as American weapons when I went to Hawthorne, Nevada. It was kind of an immersion into weapons, base defense, and to get qualified on all the weapons there. They had a base defense facility set up where you and your team had to establish field of perimeters, then you'd encounter practice insurgencies where some of the instructors would attack. It was kind of exciting.

WWII, PT boats were in the ninety-foot range, swift boats were all fifty to sixty feet. PBRs were thirty-two feet; we had six people living on a thirty-two-foot boat for weeks. The SERE training was conducted in two phases. The first phase was down at Coronado Island, which was the survival piece of it. Then we were taken up to the Palm Desert in Warner Springs, and that's where you experienced the evasion and capture. They put you in a desert and you were trying to evade capture from instructors who were dressing up and imitating Communists. Then they put you in a prisoner of war camp, and after going through all of it, your mind tells you you're truly a prisoner of war. Without hurting you, they make you really believe you're a prisoner of war. They put you in those situations where you feel something like (although nothing close to) what our real prisoners of war felt: isolated, threatened, how to manage the information you have, and if necessary how to keep yourself alive—all that kind of very valuable training. The curriculum at the Naval Inshore Operations Training Center included all those phases of it. I can't quite remember them all, but I considered it to be very thorough training. After some time off, I reported to Travis Air Force Base, got on a plane, and went to South Vietnam.

Vietnam

It was the very end of 1971 when I arrived in Vietnam, and of course, we were rapidly trying to wind down. So by the time I got in country, there were no US forces actually operating riverboats. They had all been turned over to the Vietnamese. I immediately went from Saigon; after I was issued my field kit, down to Cat Lo, which was near Vung Tau and was assigned to the Third Coastal Zone Advisor Group. Cat Lo had been a very active US Naval presence at the height of Operations Market Time and Game Warden, which were insurgency, interdiction-type operations that US forces were conducting. We turned over all facilities except for two barracks. One of the barracks was used as a galley and eating/medical facility, and the rest of us lived in the remaining quarters. I think, at the time, there were about twelve Americans. At the height of the American involvement, the base probably had somewhere between six hundred and one thousand Americans. Vietnamese sailors had lots of different kinds of boats. We had Swift Boats, PBRs, and various types of amphibious craft that had been armored with weapons and howitzers on them. We had some boats that had been converted over to flamethrowers; they carried tons of napalm and would patrol up and down the riverbanks and burn off foliage. There were some French leftover, steel-hulled boats during the French occupation. They were very low in the water, very short freeboard, but they carried 20 mm machine guns on them. They had awesome firepower, but very little maneuverability and were propeller driven as opposed to the jet-pumped PPRs, so they had limited maneuvering room. That was the main operating base; that's where my support came out of as an advisor. What I would typically do is get an assignment to go join a flotilla or some operation that the Vietnamese were going to conduct. It was usually one American in a group of six boats, all of which had been American boats before, but were now commanded by South Vietnamese Naval Forces.

I never operated with US Naval Forces proper. As soon as I got there, I was instantly turned over to the Vietnamese Navy. I don't mean physically, but all my services were turned directly toward support of the Vietnamese Navy. I patrolled with them and that literally meant I lived with the Vietnamese. In the morning, I would report down to a designated point somewhere on the base. We would take off a couple days later and we went off to various places. Sometimes I didn't know where we were. Most of it, in and around a special zone, I can call to mind places we pulled into during the evening. Most of the time, there were nondescript Vietnamese river villages that if we were to spend the night on the river, we'd pull in there. Of course, the Vietnamese all knew each other. They were pretty much all related and they treated me as part of the clan.

I think the military relationship was irrelevant. It was very social, and I had a great affinity for Vietnamese people because if they didn't decide to take care of me, I probably wouldn't be alive. I ate what they ate, lived where they lived; six of us slept on a boat with no sanitary facilities. It was never designed to do that. If we ever encountered cause to fire the weapons, there were two .50-caliber machine guns up front. Most of the mechanical advantage triggering handles, that we had originally installed, had all broken and were inoperable. If we had to fire them, I had to go forward to charge them. The Vietnamese didn't have enough heft to do that and then go back and start operating weapons in the back of the boat. Typically, .50-caliber weapons will seize up and jam sometimes, so you had to take them to the rear and charge them. Most of the time what I was doing was helping them maintain weapons. The boats were in great shape when they were turned over to them, but I'll say, I don't mean to be unkind . . . maintenance of mechanical things, including weapons was not high on their list of priorities. Therefore, their ability to fight deteriorated including the speed (of the boat) they could reach. For food, we'd typically get that from the fishermen. Vietnamese in that area got by on fishing. I don't want to say they were pirates, but whatever these boats were would come from their fishing areas. If they crossed the boats we were on, they'd always manage to get a basket of shrimp and other seafood. The seafood was totally delicious. It was handed to us, but I never saw any money being exchanged. The only thing I could figure was it was part of the territory in Vietnam, and so we lived off seafood. Consequently, I lost a lot of weight;

a combination between the heat and dysentery because you pretty much had it full-time when you were there. Sometimes if we didn't have fresh seafood, we pretty much ate dried fish and rice because it was available. We cooked it on a stove using diesel fuel. When you had to go to the bathroom, there was a rope tied to the aft of a .50-caliber machine gun mount. You kind of put your feet above the transom, held on to the rope, and hoped they didn't have to speed the boat up too fast to take care of business. That was pretty much what life was like when I was out there on patrol with the Vietnamese. I'd return back to Cat Lo where I had a nice room. You could choose any room you wanted, as there were only twelve of us there to get a shower and eat chow. We had a US Navy cook. The Army paid us in local currency and MPC (Military Payment Certificate) because I lived off the economy. So they paid me in Vietnamese money. We had a bar there and that was always nice. Most of the time, I was with the Vietnamese out on the boats boarding whatever village they had rafted up for the evening. I spent a lot of time at weddings, funerals, and family events.

How did Vietnam shape your life?

That's an easy question, but a complicated answer because I don't know what I would have been like had I not gone to Vietnam. When I came back in the summer of 1972, I was a very different person. First, I was not bitter, and I was not resentful. Part of it, I think, was because I was in the Navy. I had chosen to do this. There were some very tough times in Vietnam. Tough physically and environmentally—heat like you cannot imagine all the time, day after day. What I realized when I came back was how much of the world is different from the United States and how lucky we are to have what we have. I came back and could have immediately returned to my old job at Chevrolet, so I did. I could've taken a month off, but I didn't because I wanted some money, and I wanted to get out of the Navy because I had had enough of Vietnam. I remembered coming home from work one day and telling my dad, "I think I need to go back in the Navy because I don't think I belong out here." I felt lucky to be out of Vietnam and back in the United States because you had dreamed about it, but I felt absolutely out of place. Except for the veterans that were in the factory working with me, there wasn't anybody who could relate to the experiences you get in combat or living in a combat zone. It's so intense that normal, everyday life seems incomprehensible. I told you, John, that my dad was a very patient kind of guy; he'd been through WWII himself, so we had that in common.

Dad was in the Navy. He was in the Armed Guard if you were familiar with that. He served with a Navy gun crew on a militarized civilian ship in a convoy division.

A friend said, "You heard of the GI Bill? You get two years of college before you go back in the Navy, get your degree; and if you still want to go back in the Navy, well, God bless you. It'll be paid for and maybe you can go back in as an officer." So I said, "Well, okay, I'll give it a try." I always loved Northern Michigan, so I talked to some folks about joining Northern Michigan University. I loved it, and I applied. I went up there, sailed through the last two years of college, met my wife, got married, finished my senior year of college, and decided to go back into the Navy. This was 1975 before Saigon fell.

To describe the war, the first words that come to mind are illogical and bizarre. It's a shock to leave a place like Michigan in the winter time and be in Saigon during the hot season. It was so hot over there, you had a tough time functioning. I felt very alone which is one of the things that concerns me about the removal of combat forces in a place like Iraq where you're subject to attack all the time. It is more dangerous than ever and that was the environment that I was in. Had it not been that I understood enough of the Vietnamese language to understand what we were getting into on a day-to-day basis, I don't think I would have survived. It was incredibly dangerous, but I didn't feel any impending danger, mostly because . . . I don't know how to explain it. It was probably a combination of youth and just the feeling that you're invulnerable sometimes. Although there were several times I was wondering if we were going to make it through the day. I think the services themselves, including the Navy at the time, did not nearly do as good of a job as they do today in minding and taking care of human resources. There were weeks that the Navy had no idea where I was. There was no communication on the boats except for HF or VHF radio. If I had been captured, and there was no one from the Vietnamese side to come back and report on it, nobody would have known. To this day, they wouldn't have known. This wouldn't happen today. I felt very alone. I felt completely divorced from the US Navy because I was assigned to the Vietnamese Navy on patrol when I went back to Cat Lo. I didn't do much there except eat up, think up, clean up, and do it again.

I had a commanding officer. I don't know his name and that ought to tell you something. He was a lieutenant. I saw him maybe once or twice; he told me what was expected of me, and I went off and did it. I was a good sailor and would file a written report at the end of the patrol. I think as long as I showed up for patrols and filed my reports that was enough for him. Periodically, I would get instructions. This is an actual case . . . he would get all the patrol advisors, about a dozen of us, that were actually out on the rivers, "I want every one of you guys to take a case of concussion grenades with you and use them up while you're out there," meaning the concussion grenades are supposed to be effective against sappers (VC trained in explosives) swimming, so our technique was to throw a lot of hand grenades in the water. Frankly, that was an idiotic approach, but I went out; and I made sure by the time I came back, I pulled the pin on a bunch of hand grenades. It's a great way to go fishing by the way.

Not to cast aspersions, but I stayed as far away from the US Army as I could. There were still some operational learning units out there. Most of those guys were so high on marijuana and heroin—it was incredibly prevalent so I pretty much stayed away from those guys. I figured I was much more likely to stay healthy with the Vietnamese. I had no problem with alcohol when I was up there on the river unless we were tied up on the village and I had a lot of people around me. I kept myself capable of taking care of myself mostly because I had no one else to depend on. I was armed to the teeth. I did have one incident that cured me from some initial bad habits. Our job was to stop river traffic and search for contraband, weapons being ferried back and forth to the VC, but most of these boats had families on them. When I first got on patrol, I had a pistol. It was a .38 revolver and I kept it around the back of my pants; usually I didn't wear a shirt. After a while, I didn't wear pants anymore. We lived on the river in shower shoes and skivvy shorts because it was so damn hot. I was onboard a Sampan that had a family with kids on it. I was lifting up the floorboards looking underneath there for contraband. When I'm down in the boat, the Vietnamese had twin .50-caliber machine guns trained on the boat. A little kid in the family pulled my pistol out of its holster and I didn't even feel it. Next thing I hear is this yelling, a high pitched excited Vietnamese exchange going on, screaming, and I look up and the guys are about ready to open fire. They would have ripped that boat apart because that little kid was waiving my gun around, innocent. Fortunately, I got the gun back and everybody was crying. I never carried that thing again. I could just see they would have opened up and that whole boat would have been in splinters, me too, and all those people killed. That was what life was like: It was bizarre, it was surreal, but, at the same time, it was the way of life. Once you became accustomed to it, it's what you expect.

The hardest part, honestly, was coming back in 1972. What I remember was indulgence—the clothes, the drug culture, everything going on in the United States at that time seemed so out of place to me. Then I went up to Northern Michigan University, and one thing I think was really good is that they recognized they had a lot of returning veterans, and they set up dorms for those over twenty-one. That's when I went to Spooner Hall at Northern Michigan University. The place was absolutely full of recently returned Vietnam veterans. Although we were experienced, we had a hard time, and we paid a pretty heavy price. Still, we had a great time because we had money, and we were all on the GI bill. I pulled through with flying colors. In fact, last year, I was their distinguished Alumnus for 2009.

I was commissioned in 1975 in Pensacola right after the fall of Saigon and started flying out of Redding Field. I was going through the second phase of flight training. The Navy had a lot of aviators, and as typically happens after a war, they scaled back. The only way to get a regular commission was out of the academy or an ROTC program. The USNR is the Navy reserves.

I was full-time active duty, but I was commissioned USNR as we all were back then. You had to serve four years before you could apply for augmentation into the regular Navy. In flight training, I flew T-34 Mentors first and then I was out at Whiting Field flying T-28s, which was essentially a WWII fighter. It was a big piston radial engine trainer aircraft. It became apparent that this was not going to become a long-term future because they were literally putting people up. My flight instructor whose obligated service was up was not picked for augmentation, so he had to go home. I liked flying, but I didn't have to do it to be fulfilled in life. Because I had a business degree, I applied to the supply corps to see if they would take me. They were accepting guys converting from the "line community" over to the supply corps. They took me and augmented me immediately and made me a regular officer, which meant I didn't have to worry about being told to go home after four years because I had given up flying. I did have to compete for promotions, of course; and if you weren't promoted in the officer ranks, you'd have to go home. But it gave me a whole new lease on life in the Navy, and the rest is history.

I was a captain and the deputy commander of the Navy Inventory Control Point for Aviation. Then I became deputy commander for Ships & Submarines and Nuclear Reactors in Mechanicsburg, Pennsylvania. After a few more-challenging responsibilities, I was selected for admiral. I had served as a supply officer on the USS *Carl Vinson*, a Nimitz Class carrier. I was the supply officer of the USS *Harry E. Yarnell*, which was a Leahy Class Cruiser. Then I was staff commander of US Naval Forces Pacific. Then I served aboard a multitude of ships on a temporary or short-term business. After thirty-nine years and seven months, I retired in November 2008.

Advice to someone considering a military career

This question is posed to me all the time. I believe you experienced it there in Philadelphia, and it happened to be a flight attendant. She and her son are still corresponding with me. He will be reporting in September and wants to be a SEAL naturally. That's why parents who don't have military experience in the family are always apprehensive. But this is the thing I usually tell parents when they say, "Oh yes, my son/daughter wants to join the military." They must have done something right as a parent, because so few of the American youngsters who are eligible chronologically, meaning by age, are allowed to join the military because of either physical, educational, or moral issues. The fact that their kids are eligible to be in the military means they're in at least the top 30 percent of all the kids in the United States. The other thing I tell them is the biggest change that I've seen in the military over forty years are the quality of the people in leadership. You have to volunteer to be in the military today; you have to work really hard to stay in the military because you have to compete for promotions and if you don't advance, you won't be allowed to stay. The technical requirements are so different than they were when I first came in.

I have no problem at all with the notion of National Service for the American youth. I think it would be an important step in the right direction toward establishing some sort of accountability for all of the benefits that you get by birth, as opposed to some sense of ownership or equity that does not include services in the armed forces. The armed forces are called on to do things because we're so well organized and capable like fighting forest fires, you name it. The US military is the best since the Persian Gulf War.

Current day

I have been married since May 1974, and my wife and I have two sons. We have a son who is a civil servant working for the Navy in Philadelphia. The other is a naval officer stationed aboard USS *Lake Erie* in Pearl Harbor who was promoted to lieutenant commander. They both went to Northern Michigan University as I did. I am very proud of them both.

MIKE MCALLISTER

Lt. Colonel (Ret.), United States Air Force
Semper Fortis: "Always Courageous"
421st Tactical Fighter Squadron
Home of Record: Lawrenceville, IL
Home of Residence: Atlanta, GA
DOB: 22 January 1944
Interview conducted February 2010 via phone
Met Mike 29 March 2010 Atlanta, GA
ROTC University of Oklahoma

> *John: thanks so much for including my friend, Tom Burton (first lieutenant USMC, Vietnam Memorial Panel 31W Line 099) in my dialogue today. We were brothers in spirit, if not in blood, and his death still gives me pause.*
>
> —Colonel Mike McAllister

Growing Up

I was born in Lawrenceville, Illinois. My dad was a B-24 instructor pilot at George Field, Illinois, which was near Lawrenceville. He went over to the China-Burma-India (CBI) Theater immediately after I was born. My mother and I went back to the Bronx where my grandmother and aunt lived. For the first four years or so, I was in the Bronx. Then we moved around the country on assignments with the Air Force. He eventually became an Air Force medevac pilot and remained in the Air Force for twenty-six years. Wasn't much fun growing up under his command, but then I was hard on my kids. It's quite a trick to balance being a warrior on one hand and a good dad on the other. I'm doing better as a grandfather. I had wanted to be an Air Force pilot from the earliest time that I can remember. I saw the life that my father had, so it was comfortable to me. I liked the camaraderie and the adventure—that was my goal and I never swerved from it. I had good grades in high school and went to Oklahoma University where I got my degree in chemistry, but rarely used it except for making bran muffins by scratch. I got my degree and my commission as a second lieutenant going into pilot training at Vance Air Force base in Enid, Oklahoma.

Undergraduate Pilot Training (UPT) was a one-year flying training course. In those days, you got your pick of aircraft based on your ranking in the class. I was tenth out of fifty-five, so I received an assignment to the F-4 in March 1968. This was just before Johnson called a halt to the bombing of North Vietnam. This was also right after the Tet Offensive. My dad had been in WWII and the Korean War. I wanted my shot at it, so I went for the fighters. My instructor was an F-4 pilot who had also flown the Phantom in combat. He encouraged me, and I was lucky enough to get the plane I wanted.

Vietnam

I was a distinguished ROTC graduate at the University of Oklahoma. My service covered a period of about twenty-seven years, but I completed twenty-four years of active duty. I was at Da Nang, a US base in northern South Vietnam where the predominance of my missions were working with the Army (close ground support) or working on the Ho Chi Minh trail. I had maybe ten or twelve missions into North Vietnam, but in 1971, no one was going into Hanoi. I escorted gunships at night and bombed along the Ho Chi Minh Trail in the daytime. Probably half the missions I flew were in support of the ground troops. This included close air support, troops in contact, and tactical emergencies.

The F-4 was a great airplane for its time. I have over three thousand flight hours in the F-4. I never had to walk home (punch out), and it did a great job of turning JP-4 (jet propellant) into noise. If I didn't have any bombs left, I could make a lot of noise and scare people, which I did on occasion. At Da Nang, I flew lots of close air support using a 20 mm Gatling gun, our unfinned napalm and snake eye, which is a five-hundred-pound retarded bomb. These are all weapons that allow a pilot to get close to the ground before firing/releasing ordnance so that there is less chance of hitting the good guys. When I was down in the "weeds," I'd be looking for targets on the ground based on the FAC smoke and/or verbal directions—referencing some landmark in the immediate vicinity of the target. I flew 292 combat missions.

On my last mission, my second tour, the (temporary duty) tour to Takhli RTAFB (Royal Thai Air Force Base), Thailand, I was hit by an automatic weapon round through my empty wing tank. That's the only time my airplane was hit by anything other than some salt spray. The internal fuel tanks were self-sealing, but this is a fuel tank that hangs down under the wing. If those tanks had been full of JP-4, there would have been "a big fire!" I was also bombing in Cambodia on that mission. I believe that President Nixon took some heat for ordering those missions. I was bombing around a Buddhist Pagoda somewhere near the Tonle Sap, a big lake in Cambodia. The Rules of Engagement (ROE) directed us not to hit any religious buildings. The bad guys would hide in the Pagodas and shoot at us from there. That's probably where I got hit—trying to get as close to the Pagoda as I could without hitting the building. Then somebody got off a good shot at me.

I recall my only encounter with a MiG. I chased one into North Vietnam one night. I had the Russian fighter on radar, but I didn't get clearance to fire, so I turned around. It was a classic rope-a-dope ploy by the pilot, who was trying to lure me into a chase. Another flight continued after the plane disappeared off the radar. F-4s committed to an intercept; then the sky was lit up with antiaircraft artillery (AAA) fire. The other flight barely escaped the trap and landed right after me at Da Nang. They had burned so much fuel escaping the AAA barrage that their engines flamed out as they were clearing the runway. This was most definitely a case of discretion being a better part of valor. That's about the closest I got to a MiG. I was pretty much an "air to mudder." We were primarily air to ground (support) squadrons. We would go out there and drop things off the airplane, let them hit the mud, and hopefully, some bad guys too. As far as our guys, far too many were killed or missing in action (MIA).

The most traumatic loss that I experienced was my best friend from high school and college. His mother treated me like I was another son. He was a marine helicopter pilot. He flew Sea Stallions, the CH-46. While he was in Vietnam, he crashed in the South China Sea while doing a test flight on a CH-46. That was my first experience with death from the war of someone close to me. To this day, when I hear TAPS, I just melt. I go right on back to that time, because we were best buddies. I couldn't deal with that, and it's still painful. His name was Tom Burton. He was commissioned through the Marine Corps platoon leader's course (PLC) at Quantico. CH-47 is a Chinook that the Army uses. The CH-46 is older and has a piston engine. It looks similar to the Chinook, but they call it the Sea Stallion. The Marines used it as a troop carrier. Boeing made both planes.

Another story, at Homestead Air Force Base in 1968, there was a squadron formed from different bases just for the purpose of deploying to Southeast Asia. Our squadron headed to Phu Cat Air Base in Vietnam. All of us were trained together, and we were going to deploy in the summer of

1969. As it happened, an EC-121 was shot down over the Yellow Sea a few days before we were to deploy. Our squadron was diverted to Kunsan AFB, Korea, for six months where I met Dick Somers (Major Richard Keith Somers, KIA 25 February 1971, *Vietnam Memorial Panel 04W Line 006*). After we returned to Homestead AFB for training, we went to 'Nam almost immediately. We ate breakfast together on this fateful day. I was going out on my first "dollar ride," getting an orientation tour over the Ho Chi Minh trail. He was going out on a regular combat mission. On the weapons panel of the F-4D, the bombing indicator lights would sometimes indicate that there was still a bomb left under the wings when there wasn't.

He saw the light and made one more pass. Before he was able to complete it, a .51-caliber round came through the canopy and took his head off. The back-seater (weapons systems operator) WSO, who recovered the airplane, was a good stick (pilot). As soon as he saw the blood all over the cockpit, he knew it was either pull out or hit the ground, so he recovered the airplane and flew back out over the coast where he punched (ejected) out himself and my buddy. An Army helicopter crew picked them both up. That was traumatic for me, being my first taste of combat. Eleven months later, I was on a plane to Sydney, Australia for R&R. The guy sitting next to me, an Army pilot, was the man who picked up my buddy. He gave me a lot of detail about the incident that I hadn't heard before. It is amazing at how small the world is. Another "connection" as your book title indicates.

I completed a year at Da Nang and came back to the states in February 1972 where I was assigned to an F-4 unit at Holloman Air Force Base in Alamogordo, New Mexico. In March 1972, the North Vietnamese started the Easter Offensive. I was back in Southeast Asia in May 1972 with the Holloman wing, but this time at Takhli Royal Thai Air Force Base. In response to the NVA's Easter Offensive, the United States deployed many combat units back to the Hanoi area, and things started to heat up. Then our losses started mounting up. A big mission for the Fourth Tactical Fighter Wing (TFW) was to lay down a chaff corridor for the fighter bombers, to confuse the North Vietnamese radar operators; that was a "hang your ass out" mission. They had many losses. My old wing at Da Nang also suffered tremendous attrition. I thought I had given those wingmen some good survival strategies, but several young pilots that I had trained at Da Nang were no longer with us. I later found out some of the reasons why. We had a squadron commander, who was on his third combat tour and wanted his MIGs, in the latter portion of my tour. He had flown the F-105 and the A-1E on his previous tours and came back as a squadron commander in the F-4. Some of these deaths were attributed to him because with his fangs out, he had forgotten that he was putting his wingmen in undue jeopardy. A few years later, I was training F-4 pilots at Homestead AFB, and he came through as the base beautification inspector, a dead-end job to nowhere. I think karma took a hand.

Having grown up with the Air Force and having listened to all of the stories, my eyes were wide open. I don't feel that my government pulled the wool over my eyes. I know other guys felt betrayed when they got over there because it wasn't what they were expecting. I knew it was going to be a war and people get hurt. The shock was when I got to Da Nang and went to a little snack bar they called the No Hab Kitchen. *No hab* was pigeon English for "we don't have." I tried to order something off the menu, and it was, "No hab this, no hab that;" and finally, all I could get was pizza or fried chicken. That was the biggest trauma for me since I am half-Italian, and I like my good wine and food, but I didn't get any of that over there.

I came back from my first tour through SEATAC (Seattle Tacoma Airport) and LAX. I don't remember any personal confrontations with anybody. I just walked through the airport, got on a plane and went on my way. I walked back into the world where guys had long hair. I actually enjoyed flying in 'Nam because I could fly at night with all the external lights on my aircraft off. There is something eerie about flying over a country in the middle of the night, and there is not a single light on the ground and only interrupted, occasionally, by bombs that were exploding and tracers coming up. It was like the boogey man was down there waiting for you. When I came back to the States, lights were everywhere, and I just enjoyed flying. Back in the States, I was never confronted with any kind of disparaging remarks, no "baby killer" or anything like that. No one put up signs in front of my house. I would turn on the news and see the protesters though. I still have family members who thought I was in the Army. Many civilians don't really think about the military one way or another, we're all lumped into one big bag—Army, Air Force, Marines, Navy, Coast Guard, military.

How did Vietnam shape your life?

I decided to resign my commission after the war because of what my service was turning into. We were putting up sheet rock and painting buildings. Looking back, I wish I had spent more time doing that because I could have had a trade after I got too old to fly. I had done my thing in Vietnam.

The peacetime Air Force was looking for officers, but I never really looked at myself as an officer. When I went back in, I had a much broader perspective on the whole thing. It also helped that Reagan had just been elected president, and money started pumping back into the military.

It's easy to second-guess—being a Monday morning quarterback. With all the guys I knew that got killed over there or are still MIA, I just wonder what we achieved. My wife works for a company that has Italian-designed furniture, and furnishings that are built in Vietnam.

Advice to someone considering a military career

To borrow from Dickens, "It was the best of times, it was the worst of times." They should particularly know about the worst times. I have talked to some who changed their plans and went another route. Some pressed on with military service. During my ten years of flying in the airlines, my young first officers asked me about the war, and I would just tell them how scared I was at times and what it was like to be away from home for months and years. Some kids don't realize what their getting into. They look at the movie *Top Gun* and think that's the way it is. I would rather have a guy go in with his eyes open than one who goes, "Holy cow, I didn't expect that!"

Current day

I live right outside Spaghetti Junction, which is on the northeast side of Atlanta. My wife and I each have two children from previous marriages. Together we have eight grandchildren and three great-grandchildren. None of them ever considered going into the military. I think I cured them of that. They are all in other fields. I flew for Atlantic Southeast Airlines (ASA), the original Delta, for ten years. When I hit age sixty, I had to retire under the FAA's age sixty rule. I have done some recruiting for ASA since my retirement in January 2004. I have met some young pilots who came out of the military or wanted to join the military. Some of them could never understand my views on the war. If I told them it was a mistake, they didn't want to hear it. They wanted to hear that you saluted smartly, did your duty, and carried on. Today, I enjoy spending time with my vet buddies, Hip and Doc. It took us many years to find each other, but it's always a good time when we're together. I know there are demons lurking in the back of my soul. I try to let those sleeping dogs lie. I went through it, had my eyes open, and I'm still standing.

ROBERT BEVAN HOGAN

Sergeant, United States Navy
Non Sibi Sed Patriae: *"Not self but country"*
NAS Quam Squadron
Home of Record: Jacksonville, FL
Home of Residence: Kutztown, PA
DOB: 13 June 1953
Interview conducted 20 February 2010 in Kutztown, PA
Kutztown University

> *A man who is good enough to shed his blood for the country is good
> enough to be given a square deal afterwards.*
>   —Theodore Roosevelt

Growing Up

I was born next to the Jacksonville, Florida, Naval station in 1953. My father, being a WWII naval pilot, moved around a lot. After I was born, Dad was stationed in Guantanamo Bay, Cuba. Castro was a rebel and had not yet taken over the country. We stayed there until 1958. In March, the whole family got on a Navy freighter and sailed from Cuba, past the Statue of Liberty, into New York Harbor. We were all dressed in flip-flops and summer clothes. My mother went to a Good Will and bought coats for us and took us straight to Saint Patrick's cathedral. There is a picture with all of us with our bare legs, flip-flops, and old overcoats standing on the steps of Saint Patrick's Cathedral.

We came to Glenside, Pennsylvania, and met our good friends the Siegfried's. Our backyards touched each other. It was my first contact with John. We lived there for three years. Dad then got stationed in Pittsburgh, Pennsylvania, as a Navy recruiter. He couldn't fly anymore because he couldn't pass the flight physical. He was losing his hearing from the years of flying in front of the engines. In 1963, we moved to Savannah, Georgia, and he was the CO of the recruiting center.

Dad retired from the Navy after twenty-eight years at the rank of commander in Savannah. That summer (1966) our family camped across country. We went the southern route, came home the northern route, and wound up back in Glenside late summer.

John and I were back at St. Luke's grade school together. We graduated from there and went to Bishop McDevitt High School. When I finished, I had no aspirations, against my parents' wishes, to go to college. I just wanted to see what the world was like, so I got a job at the shore in Avalon, New Jersey. At the time, the country was embroiled in the Vietnamese conflict, and Nixon had devised the birthday lottery system. I registered for the draft and was classified 1-A. On 13 June 1971, I got picked number three out of the hat. If I didn't enlist, I would have been drafted, and I wasn't really gung ho—"Let's go kill some gooks." I wasn't that type at first, but I wasn't about to run to Canada either. The war was winding down. Nixon was trying to get us out. We were on the tail end. In 1972, Nixon was saturation bombing the North, and it was more of an air war at that time. They were pulling troops out as you remember, but I still had the chance of going into combat. I figured I would serve my country. I'll do it in the Navy and be safer.

The GI Bill was attractive to me. I didn't want my parents to have to struggle to pay for my education. They had three daughters they were sending to school. I said, "I'll go in, and if I want to go to school, the military will pay for it." In November 1971, I came home and had Thanksgiving dinner with the family.

I was an airman recruit, which was my first rank coming out of a boot camp. I was an E3, a PR-2 (parachute rigger second class). While I was in there, they got away from serial numbers and went to Social Security numbers.

On 1 December 1971, I went to the Naval Air Station in Willow Grove and enlisted in the Navy. A week later, I was issued my uniform and went to boot camp. The Navy was transitioning their boot camps from the Great Lakes to Orlando and San Diego. Boot camp assignment (location) was dependent on where you lived. Great Lakes were torn apart and Orlando wasn't built yet, so I was one of the few Navy school classes to graduate in Memphis.

I finished accelerated boot camp in midspring 1972. I finished P school (prep school) in Tennessee; in the summer, I was sent to Lakehurst, New Jersey. This was the old blimp base where the Hindenburg crashed. We learned how to sew and how to pack parachutes in the old blimp hangars. We needed to learn how to work with oxygen equipment—anything that had to do with a pilot's survival in the air if he had to bail out. We had to learn how to issue life rafts, life preservers, and small arms; we were issued .45-caliber handguns. The Navy eventually turned that over to the Airman Ordnance (AO). They created a special rate just to take care of all the guns and weapons in one place. I was in rigger school until late 1972.

Guam

I caught a flight directly to NAS (Navy squadron) Guam. The Navy considered Guam as sea duty because you were on an island. I was attached to the base. They were called Ships Company. I wasn't attached to any squadron. Guam had two main Navy squadrons, the VQ1 and the VQ3 on the island. VQ stood for reconnaissance. We were responsible to maintain all the equipment. I had a Navy chief who I answered to who was responsible for our paraloft. He was a freaking alcoholic. He was fed up with being in the service. His job really was to oversee us and inspect every piece of equipment that went out of that loft. He got tired of my calling him all of the time to inspect the chutes, so he turned me into a quality control guy. I was the youngest PC inspector in the Navy at the time—not even rated yet. When you get your "crow" in the Navy, that's your bird, everyone on the squadron punches you in the arm. Nail it, pack it on there, tackles your crow. I was still an E3, an airman apprentice and was a full blown Navy PC inspector. I had to get certified.

My training was very interesting. They figured if you're going to pack a chute for others, you're going to pack your own chute and jump it. We want you to be responsible and know what it is like to be responsible. It was the only school in the world where your first jump was a free fall. They call it the dope rope, static line. Static lines are when you hook the ropes to the ceiling, jump out, and the line pulls your chute for you. Lakehurst was the only place in the world where the students jumped and pulled their own ripcord by themselves with no buddy with them in the air. We jumped out of a C-121 with all the seats ripped out. We sat ready against the bulk heads. Our instructor said, "Okay, let's go." We all lined up, the green light; we all went out—one thousand, two thousand, and pull thousand. At the time, no other service did that anywhere in the world for the first jump. The Navy never lost anybody until the year I was there. A marine wrote a suicide note, went out, and never pulled the rip cord. The Navy was in charge of the operation, but the Air Force used to have the job of doing most of the packing for a lot of the planes in Guam and anywhere else. They gave it up. The Navy decided to have a military operational force where I went to jump school. I was with Navy SEALs, underwater demolition teams (UDT), along with the Coast Guard and Marines.

The SEALs used to bust their ass all the time. The UDTs are a step below the SEALs. They are guys that couldn't make it to through the entire SEAL training regimen, but they were so well trained they became UDTs. The

UDTs didn't go through Hell Week (last week of SEAL training), but they were very skilled in demolition and under-water operations. For the first time in my life, I am not just with Navy guys. I am learning with Marines. Not one of these people had seen combat, they were all young kids—my age. We became really good friends. It was a very good experience.

I left school, got shipped out to Guam, and attached to a squadron. I was the PC instructor in this paraloft and the VQ squadron's job. The mission in Guam was to fly A-7s, which was a two-engine jet aircraft. It would fly over Vietnam and take infrared and pictures and movies of the terrain and then it would land in Thailand, refuel, and fly back home. A-7s had a seven man crew; navigators, photographers, and two pilots. It reminds you a lot of an F-4 when you see it, very similar in shape like the drop wings. It had the same engines, the same power plant that the B-52s had—a powerful plane. I should know more of it, but I didn't. I was just worried about how much dope we could smuggle on it.

They were top secret planes, and they could not be searched, which is the key to what we might get into later. It was an open funnel for dope access from Thailand, fly it over Vietnam, and land on an airbase. Those guys would fill the film cans up with pure heroin, come back, then fly back to Guam; and we would take those film canisters off the planes and throw into our cars and bring them up. It was incredibly strong, and the Navy and all branches of service had a horrible problem with drug addiction because of that. I didn't realize it until I got involved with it that I was doing a lot of it. Eventually I came down with hepatitis so bad I almost died. I was in intensive care for two weeks.

I was in Guam, and all my guys were out on the flight—they were all air crewmen. I was a ground guy. We had P-3s in our squadron too. If a plane got shot down or crashed, we would go out in the P-3s to look for them, and they needed all hands to look out the window for wreckage. All the guys were away, and I was at home. I lived off base, and I was getting really sick. I was feeling really run down. I started getting jaundice, but I didn't think anything of it. One night, I was lying in bed, and I broke out in this horrible sweat, and I just shit myself, and it was black everywhere. I got up to take a piss. It was dark—it was horrible. I was so weak. I plopped back onto a big water bed. I will never forget it. It was covered with bile. That was the hepatitis. It was my organs failing. Luckily, one of the crewmen came home and said, "Oh my god." Terry Voorhees, I'll never forget him. Torrance, California. Terry came in, cleaned me up, and got me to sick bay, which is a twelve-mile ride. Doctor stripped every bit of clothing off me looking for tracks. He thought I was shooting up heroin, but I wasn't. I was smoking and snorting it. Intravenous was quicker, but it is also very deadly because of hepatitis C, which you can get from the (dirty) needles. The only way you can get hepatitis C is from intravenous use or alcoholism.

I was put into the hospital. I spent two weeks in what they called the "junky ward." I was in there with Marines and Air Force guys from 'Nam. There was about ten of us, and I never saw the true effects of heroin when I was in there. Because we were so infectious, they put us in a ward by ourselves. Their buddies were smuggling stuff into them. My liver was the size of a football, swollen up out of my side. I was flat on my back and couldn't move for a week. I was in critical condition. I was kind of in a coma trance kind of thing, I remember all this commotion and seeing a light next to me. The guy next to me was cooking up a spoon, cooking the stuff up because heroin will liquefy when you get it to a certain temperature, especially the pure stuff. Anyway, thank God, I made it through that. I got myself healthy. What saved my life was probably my being youth as I was only twenty years old.

I was in ICU a week and a half. My total stay in the hospital was almost three weeks. My parents didn't know until I came home. They were the only ones that knew. I wasn't proud of it. They knew I was screwed up. I was a knucklehead for doing that. One thing good about the Navy is the recognition they had a serious problem. They didn't send a bunch of guys home addicted on heroin. The Navy started what they called operation Golden Flow. I was put into what they called the 3×5 program. I had to piss into a bottle three times a week. I recall Chief Dean sat me down, saying, "Hogan, do it. It's the only way to prove to me you're clean and you're good to go back to work."

This process cleaned my record right up. I went back to work packing chutes and doing everything I had to do. However, after going back to work and not being tested anymore, I smoked pot, a lot of it laced with heroin, what we called Thai sticker. It came from Thailand, so we called it Buddha. Thai stick is the female bud of a marijuana plant wrapped around the stick with twine and dipped in liquid heroin and then packed in bricks so it looked like a sandwich. There were twenty sticks to a brick. The Thais made it because it was like an incense stick. They would light it, and because it was dipped in heroin, it would burn very slow with a thick smoke. To them, it put the Buddhists into a state of mind for prayer. Of course, the Americans came over and abused it. I have never heard of it here. I brought twenty bricks home with me. Because I was parachute rigger, I was kind of untouchable. No one would mess with a rigger because they packed their parachutes. We had free run of the base, and they never searched our shit. When I went home, I had a big wooden crate and put all my personal stuff in it. Some guy came up to it and looked in: "Everything looks good." They nailed it shut. I had so much dope in that crate.

When the parachutes were brought back in, we would rip them apart and put them all back together to the Navy's specification. There is a history card in every parachute. Every parachute had to be repacked every six months, the history card signed off, and then I would give it my PC stamp. We had history cards on aircraft, and any maintenance that had to be done on the planes. All the life preservers, life rafts, and all the parachutes were our jurisdiction. We would go into the cockpit and remove all the oxygen regulators and put them into a big atmospheric tank so you could test the regulator to make sure it worked properly. Liquid oxygen was used in the jets because they would go way above twenty thousand feet. We took liquid oxygen, pump it (it was like a filling station) into these tanks that were then put into the aircraft and then converted into oxygen for the pilots up in the atmosphere—very dangerous stuff to work with. Remember Apollo One (Wally Schirra), and then one of the subsequent launches where the astronauts burned up on the launch pad-that was all liquid oxygen. Just one little spark, and everything burns.

In the military, you get thirty days vacation every year, which is pretty good. I think you had to use it or lose it at the time. A lot of guys never took leave, and they would save up the money for whenever they got out of the service. These were the smart guys, not knuckleheads like me who blew it all on drugs. We go on R&R; we would go to Anderson Air Force Base, and I got a MAC flight. The big thing was to go to Thailand. That is where the women and the drugs were. The Air Force had a base in Thailand, which was right on the Thai/Cambodia border, and it was a highly guarded base where I saw canine dogs. The coolest thing in the world was I saw my first Black Bird there. The Black Bird was the U-2 of the time. Everybody was arguing at the time, remember McNamara was saying, "We're not going into Laos" or "We're not doing this." Well, the Black Bird was flying missions over there taking high-resolution photos; that was its mission, no markings. It was black with nothing but antennas on it. The plane flew-in, they fueled it, re-rigged it, and ripped the chutes out. It was a long, roundabout story, but we flew over hostile airspace. We took off from Anderson, and we went in to Kadena, Okinawa. Kadena is a major marine base; we are still there. The Okinawans hate us. We landed in Kadena, refueled, and flew over Laos and Vietnam to U-Tapao Air Base. That is about the closest I ever got to the Cambodian border.

When you first get to Guam, they don't know where to locate you, so they put you in a transient barracks with no windows or doors. It has jalousies to keep the rain out. There is a bunk and a lock. I'm in a transient barracks that are all lined up parallel to each other, and they are connected by little breezeways. They have a roof over them because it rains twice a day in the tropics. It is my first night in Guam, and I am sleeping on my back; and all of a sudden, I feel this horrible smash to my head. I see a flash of white light. It is like my head explodes. I wake up. I think I am dying. I think a bomb went off! There were three Marines in my room, and they are pummeling me. One had a board and the other one had his fists, and they are beating the crap out of me. The other one was going through my locker, ripping through my stuff, pulling shit out. "What the fuck?" I jumped up; I thought I was dying so I went into my kill mode! I got one by the throat and was beating him in the head! It's a horrible brawl. They had come in through the fire escape, but they left out the back.

There was an officer in the group of barracks (whose) job was to watch over the barracks. The officer of the day (OD) came back, saw me, and went, "Oh my god." My nose was broken, my lip was split, and I had a large split over my right eye. I was a mess! Bloody pulp! I didn't know what happened. I didn't know these guys were Marines, I figured that out later. They took me to the hospital; they reset my nose, put a splint in it, sew me up, and got me all put back together. They deny me back to the transient barracks, I got to bed. "We'll talk about it tomorrow," he said.

He came back the next day to do a report. The barracks next to me had a second floor and a bottom floor. I had known that barracks was full of Marines. So the next night, I was all bandaged up, and I went to the enlisted man's club. I got really drunk. I came back, and I stood outside the marine barracks, and I called the whole fucking barracks out. "You motherfuckers!" I said. "You can come now, I am awake now!" I heard this (*sound effects*-loud noises-men running in the barracks). They had to rush the doors. The guys who were guarding the barracks, the sergeant of arms, had to lock it up, so these guys couldn't get out. I was right outside the window. "Come on, he's a fucking cunt." I staggered back to my bed and passed out.

The next day, I got up, did my duty during the day; then I went to the enlisted club again. It was a sea of tan (Marines). I think you could have heard a pin drop when I walked in. They're all at the tables; the bar was full of them, and some were raw recruits. Then there were some guys, their hair a little longer, looked crustier, and were smoking cigarettes. So this gunny sergeant, I will never forget this big guy, went, "He's cool." I went walking over, and he went, "Hey, man, sit down. Look, you are one crazy motherfucker. Do you realize we had to bolt those doors to keep these motherfuckers from coming out and killing you, dude? I will never ever forget you."

He had already done two years. He said, "This is what's happening here, man." The bottom floors were the guys going, and the top floor were us poor bastards that survived coming back. They had these guys jacked up to kill. He said, "Let's go out and beat up some sailors tonight." They had this problem; they had to keep those guys caged in. They were like animals! They just couldn't wait to get on a transport fast enough. He said, "These guys are all smoking pot now and shit." They showed these guys movies every night. John Wayne, you know, "Kill! Kill! Kill!"

It was by design, and this blew my mind. He said, "We are the poor bastards upstairs, our corporal will kill us if we go down and tell them what's real." We were all out smoking joints together, and they're telling me this. "These guys are all at the bar, and they are going to listen to their veterans. If I call these dogs on you, man, they'll kill you right here." Rest of the night went great, we got drunk—trashed—and that was it. We became very good friends. Guam was a big detox area for those guys. I would hang out with them. These guys were traumatized. I did my two years in Guam.

Northwest Orient had the contract to fly guys back to the mainland. They landed in Saigon City wherever, loaded the poor bastards up, took off, landed in Guam to pick up any other guys who had already detoxed or who was getting released. I was being sent back home the last day in July 1974, a week before Nixon resigned. I got on that airplane, and it was full of pot smoke. These guys were all combat vets. They were climbing over the seats, grabbing the chicks in the ass, the attendants—they loved it. There was no law on that aircraft, never forget it, long as I live. The pilots weren't going back there to tell them to shut up. They said, "Let's just get them in there." So we flew to Travis Air Force Base, which was a major point of debarkation. They had little gray school buses pick us up and take us to San Francisco.

First, nobody is going to relate to what I did; I didn't talk about it. When I came back to Travis Air Force Base, I got off the plane, and it was fifty-five degrees. I had flip-flops, swim trunks, and an island shirt and carried my sea bag. You could come back however you wanted to, civvies, guys on that plane were like half-shirt open, and they didn't give a shit. I had no coat, nothing. I had been in the tropics now for two years. So I was shivering in the phone booth. I called my Uncle Bill. He came, picked me up, and had a Pendleton wool jacket he put around me, and we went drinking to warm up. At the time, Elmo Zumwalt (chief of naval operations) allowed beers in the machines in the barracks. Soda machines had beer in them. Zumwalt allowed that when I was there; then changed it all when I left.

How Vietnam shaped your life

I felt like I was in my forties when I came back because I had seen so much. I didn't feel like I was twenty-one or twenty-two, and I didn't see anyone killed. I can't imagine the guys who really saw a lot of stuff. I walked the streets of Bangkok, tripping on acid, hooker on each arm, and I was twenty years old. I was on a motorcycle up on the hills in northern Thailand hanging out with Buddhist monks.

It was very bad. Of course I went crazy over there. I came back and had to go to Thailand for two weeks. I came home, and the big joke was—go to take a piss and you start screaming because you're blocked. All the pus and that shit that build up with gonorrhea or syphilis—they call it the drips. Puss is actually dripping out of the end of . . . was bad, but he's good now. I saw that, and I went, "Oh fuck!" Sure as shit got to the infirmary. They take your dick, and they smear it on a little slide like we had in chemistry class. The guy looking at it went, "How much were you fucking over there?" I said, "Five times a day." He went, "Jesus Christ, you're a lucky man."

When I was in Guam, you might as well have been a priest. There were no chicks around. That's why we would go to Bangkok all the time. The Doc went, "Hogan, you are lucky. You got what they call NSU [remember the song called "NSU," nonspecific urethra]. We don't know what the fuck this is."

"Basically," he says, "your dick is tired-out, worn-out. Just give it a break, man. Take this tetracycline and call me in two weeks."

It wasn't a fucking war. I mean, WWII, it was, "Take that beach, let's take that island." A lot of guys were high in those companies. This was late in the war. A lot of them had the shit beat out of them because they're on the (combat area) perimeter and they're smoking pot. Now, it was pretty much on the level.

Sappers would come, and I would hear a lot of Marines I hung out with say, "They would come in at night, we would hang out during the day, and it was just boring." Then Charlie would infiltrate at night, after the Tet Offensive, in 1968. They're all over the South. Just kill anything that moved—it didn't matter anymore. I knew guys who were on the gunboats. This one first-class seaman who was in my paraloft did six months on a gunboat. He said, "We shot fucking monkeys, kids, anything that moved. It didn't matter. We just opened up on it. Didn't know who was ARVN or VC."

Those guys would scare kids. It was just guerilla warfare, and we couldn't win. Years later, when I moved up here to Kutztown, I worked with a lot of Vietnam vets with Carolina Freight carriers.

One of these guys, Denny, died. I know it was Agent Orange. He was a tunnel rat. He told me that. All he had was a flash light and a .45; they would hold him by his feet because he was so small and put his head down in these tunnels. You have probably heard of these guys; they just start shooting. The VC were master tunnel diggers. Look at the ordnance we dropped on Hanoi, and they were still running around in tunnels and shit like that. It is just pathetic to answer that again—just a sad waste of life.

Advice to someone considering a military career

I really feel this from the bottom of my heart. I don't want kids to go in and have to do military. If they want combat, then give them the option to do it. I think if we are in a war, which we are now. I think it should be mandatory for every kid coming out of high school. I really believe that. I didn't force my kids to do it, but I gave them that option if they wanted to, and none of them took it. I really think it shapes you; you really need to have everything stripped of you. I was in boot camp, no stalls in the bathroom, everybody shit in the showers and shine together like cattle. It really makes you realize that everybody is the same. It is just the discipline that I got from there that really made me a survivor later on in my life. I just really feel that everybody should have to do some form of service for our country, even if they are just screwing in light bulbs in the barracks for two years.

Girls and guys, I am all for equality. I think women belong in there. If you are gay, who gives a shit? "Don't ask, don't tell" is a big issue now. I don't care who you are, what you are, what your orientation is. I think it is good for everybody to do some form of service even if it is like a Peace Corps kind of a thing for at least two years for our country.

Current Day

I wasted a lot of time. I came home, and like I said, I felt older. I felt like I became a young father. I was twenty-two. I married a twenty-year-old woman. We had two kids right away, and it was like, I am ready, but nobody else is. I felt like I was able to handle family. I had just matured. I don't know what you call it, but I was glad I was alive, and I wanted to have a family and kids.

I moved up here to Kutztown in 1977, thirty-three years ago, and had Erin. She'll be thirty-three, Bobby is thirty-one. That marriage ended around 1983. Got remarried to my current wife, Cindy; I had to get an annulment from the church since I am a Catholic. Cindy and I were together, and she became pregnant with my youngest daughter, Aura, who is now twenty-four. The church still wouldn't allow me in. Aura was born that June, and in August of 1986, Cindy and I got on my Harley and went to the Justice of the Peace and got married. The oil line broke on the way there, and Cindy had a white shirt on with white jeans, and oil sprayed up and down her back. I had oil dripping off my boots. I pulled the Harley up front, and we were late because I always am.

In 1988, I finally got an annulment. It took a lot of string pulling. It is very difficult to get through the Catholic Church. I was able to get married in the church, and that happened on 13 February 1988. We moved into my current house in that same year. I raised my children, and everybody is up and gone—three grandsons. Erin has two boys, and Bobby has one.

JAMES T. CALDWELL

Lt. Commander, United States Navy
Non Sibi Sed Patriae: *"Not self but country"*
Helicopter Assault (Light) 3 Squadron "Seawolves"
Home of Record: Charlotte, NC
Home of Residence: Doylestown, PA
DOB: 07 June 1937
Interview conducted in Doylestown, PA 19 March 2010
Lees-McRae Junior College
Website: www.seawolves.org

> *Man is only great when he acts from passion.*
> —Benjamin Disraeli

Growing Up

I was born in Charlotte, North Carolina. My father was a carpenter. We lived out in the country about six miles north of Charlotte on a big farm, although my father did not farm. We had over one hundred acres. It was a nice, growing-up environment. From an early life, I always wanted to be a pilot. My planning was always to get into a four-year school, get into the ROTC program, get my commission through the college system, and become a pilot in one of the services. My college days started at a Presbyterian School in the mountains of North Carolina. Lees McRae Junior College was a two-year program. I believe they had two hundred students when I was there in 1956-1957. It was a very expensive place. Father had a deal with me, my brother, and my two sisters—in that he would pay for the first two years of college, and then we were on our own for the last two. In early 1957, I was a sophomore in college. I had already been accepted to North Carolina State in the engineering department, and I get my draft notice. After talking to the draft board, I had no choice. I had to serve.

It was a mandatory draft country-wide. They gave me and my other friends that had draft notices a little time to join the service of our choice. My first choice was Air Force. I passed everything except the physical eye test. I always thought the Air Force had the most airplanes and the biggest choice. Being in the Navy was my second choice. I flunked the color-blind test. In less than a week, I was back in the same city with the United States Navy, and I passed everything. I got accepted into the Navy Pilot Program as a cadet. In this program, you had to have at least two years of college, and they promised to educate you while you were in the military, which they did. Thanksgiving Day 1957, I was off to Pensacola Florida to begin my pilot training. I wanted to be a jet pilot. I got as far as advanced training in Texas flying the Navy first swept wing aircraft—The F-9F Cougar, a wonderful aircraft—loved that aircraft. The Cougar was grounded with several fatalities back-to-back. They ground the aircraft to determine what happened to prevent it from happening to someone else. It took longer than it should have to come back up again. It was at least three or four months before we heard anything. They were talking about sending us students out into fields that I particularly didn't want—like blimps and seaplanes. I wanted to fly jets. My second choice was helicopters. A group of us got together and had an audience with the admiral. We asked him if we could transfer back to Pensacola, Florida, to get our wings in helicopters. He didn't even blink, saying, "When would you like to leave?" In a way, we were solving his problem. He had several hundred students that he had to take care of; five were out of there the next day. That's where I got my wings in September 1959, and my very first squadron was in Quonset Point, Rhode Island, flying in submarine warfare arena. That was my specialty while I was in the Navy.

In 1961, the end of my four years was coming up, and I decided to get out. I had a job offer with New York Airways, which was a helicopter service between the various airports and Manhattan waterfront. The United States Navy Bureau of Personnel called me up and said, "Don't do that. We would like for you to stay in the Navy. We've invested so much money training you. We'll give you your first choice of duty, wherever you want to go." I said, "Okay, I would like to go to Pensacola to be a flight instructor in helicopters." They said, "Done!" For the next three years, I flew three different kinds of helicopters and enjoyed this very much.

The Bell was the primary; the first helicopter everybody flew. The little helicopter that you saw on television in the early 1960s in *MASH*, for example, was a Bell. I also flew the Sikorsky H04S. While I was there, we received the H34 also built by Sikorsky. I helped write the training syllabus for that model while I was flying in Quonset, Rhode Island. My three years was up, and I went back to Norfolk, my second seagoing squadron. By the way, training command is shore duty. No seagoing. We went out to take students to check them out on how to land on an aircraft carrier. At that time, it was the USS *Lexington*, which was tied up in Pensacola.

We didn't see much sea duty because our new ship, the USS *Intrepid*, which is now a museum in New York City harbor, was taken away from the antisubmarine warfare arena and sent to Vietnam as an attack aircraft carrier. We didn't have a ship, but we did go out on Gemini recoveries. I was the backup, pickup pilot for astronauts Michael Collins and John Young. That was a fascinating week and a half seeing them come in on their descent from space. John Young actually turned out to be the astronaut with the most flights, and the most time in space, of any astronaut to this date in the United States Navy. Michael Collins later on became the executive director of the space museum in Washington DC.

I went to an organization called TACRON. This would not have been a choice of mine; *Tacron* stands for Tactical Air Control Squadron. On a moment's notice, we had to control live aircraft, live bombing runs in event of an amphibious assault somewhere in the world. We're talking John Wayne, early-WWII movies by this time. I was amazed they still had this as a mission, but I was there for almost three years in the Mediterranean and four months in the Caribbean. I was away from my family a lot. That was not a good cruise. I was being told by Washington that because I was coming off four years of sea duty, I'd get my first choice wherever I want to go. So I chose Monterey, California, for my postgraduate school. At this point, I didn't even have a degree so I could get my degree and perhaps stay on for a master's. Getting ready to go, we're starting to pack, and I got a telephone call, saying, "We just changed your order." With less than two weeks to leave town, they changed my order to the Alternate National Military Command Center in Fort Richie, Maryland. It was the underground command post where the president, his staff, joint chiefs, and his cabinet go in the event Washington comes under a major nuclear attack. It had life support for thirty days. In those days, they had three command posts. They had seagoing, airborne, and shore. I was in the shore base. The Air Force plane was airborne 24/7, which was the airborne command post.

It was a fascinating job. It included all of the Armed Services. I got to know a lot of real good friends with other military branches, their experiences, high-level stuff. When we had meetings, we briefed so many "stars" (generals and admirals across all services) it hurt your eyes to look into the audience. Most of it was practice! You had to be ready! I had a funny experience here. We were about three miles from Camp David. This one Sunday, I took the children into church, and my three-year-old son had kept grabbing on the neck of the guy in front of me who turned out to be the secretary of Defense, Melvin Laird. After the service, I said, "Mr. Laird, I am so sorry." He said, "Don't worry about it, what's your son's name?" He was so nice. It was in 1968-1970. A lot of dignitaries would be spending the weekend there, and I'd see a lot of them at church.

Vietnam

I got orders from there to my helicopter squadron, HAL-3, which was headquartered in Ben Thuy, South Vietnam. I got a call from the Navy department personnel, saying, "Commander, we'd like to talk to you about your orders," and I said, "What orders?" The person on the phone said, "Your orders to Vietnam." They had sent me my orders but never received them. I came to find out I was due to leave in less than a month for my workup training to go to Vietnam.

My wife couldn't believe it. I went to escape and evasion school. I went to weapons training school. I went to Fort Rucker, Alabama, to learn how to fly the Huey, which is the gunship we flew in Vietnam. All of that took place in about three months and—*boom*—I was in Vietnam. This consisted of river patrol boats, PBRs, barges, all different types of Navy vehicles, all different types for brown water, Navy-going vehicles. You didn't see anything bigger than a very large barrack ship.

Our main purpose was to conduct close air support when our riverboats came under attack by the VC. A river patrol squadron would consist of a dozen boats with four or five guys on each boat. The Mekong Delta went straight up to Cambodia. If you look at a map of that part of Vietnam, there is nothing but waterways, rivers, and canals everywhere because of the rice. I was on a river called the Vam Co Tay that split into two rivers: one went to the right of Parrot's Beak and one went to the left. We were situated right on one of them. My detachment was responsible for those two rivers, and the Parrot's Beak River coming out of Cambodia because a lot of infiltration came down that way.

I was in my uniform when I landed in San Francisco. There were no bands playing, no crowds waving. There was no reaction at all. It was just like we were a commercial flight landing in San Francisco. I got off the plane, and nobody was there. I walked down into the terminal. This was 1971. When I came home, I always wanted a war trophy, and I got one. I had a special bag made up to carry a weapon, and as soon as I got on board in Saigon, I handed it to the flight attendant, and I said, "This is a war trophy. Can you store it for me?" She said, "No problem." As I got off the airplane, I was carrying this gun. As I was walking through the terminal, people were moving out of my way. It was a Chinese-made SKS, the primitive version of the Russian AK-47.

How did Vietnam shape your life?

When I came back, I had roughly eight more years of service. I spent five of that right here in Pennsylvania at the Naval Development Center in Ivyland. I was having so much fun here. I decided to extend and extend. I got married the second time. It was a nice place to have shore duty. So I retired out of this area and went down to Philadelphia. The Naval Air Technical Services Facility—which primarily had the responsibility of all handbooks, drawings, etc., for all military airplanes and missile systems—was my new base. I had a hundred-million-dollar budget in 1969 for buying handbooks for Navy and marine corps aircraft and my department. I had one hundred people working for me. It was fun, but I didn't fly. I was riding a desk. My coming home was uneventful. Nobody stood on me, yelled, or screamed.

I'm glad I went. Would I do it again? Absolutely! Did we have a reason for being there? Absolutely! The reason for being there, in my mind, was that we were trying to prevent the Communists overtaking all of Vietnam. It was the same thing as in Korea, North Korea vs. South Korea. We did a hell of a job. We weren't allowed to do the job we could've done to end the war. If you're fired on, your helicopter and your crew have to get permission from a higher authority to return fire. That's no way to run a war. That happened to me a lot.

One of our missions was escorting tankers up the Mekong River all the way to Phnom Penh, Cambodia. We invariably took fire going all the way up. We could not return fire unless we got permission from the airborne command post out of Saigon. There was one command post controlling the whole operation except for our little river patrol. We didn't go through anybody for that. We did our own thing.

Advice to someone considering a military career

I would tell them absolutely, but so far, I've struck out on that completely. I may have had an influence on my kids getting into the Naval Academy, but nobody ever wanted to go into the military. I don't have a problem with that, but I would recommend it. The military system is a great place to serve your country. To work, regardless of whether you're a pilot or you work on submarines. Regardless of your mission, it's a great place to be. I spent twenty-one years in it and loved every minute of it. I've seen the world. I've met friends that I still communicate with via Christmas cards, Facebook, and the whole nine yards. It was good. Would I do it again? Yes. I would do it again. My father was too young for WWI and too old for WWII. He was in construction. He was building aviation facilities in great places like Norfolk, Virginia, during the early parts of WWII. My dad would have loved to have been in the service. He was so excited when I asked him to go to Pensacola to pin on my wings when I got commissioned.

Current Day

Right now, I'm seventy-two years old. I'm still working, and I have no intentions of retiring. I'm working because I enjoy work. I have a total of five children. My first wife died of cancer a number of years ago. Two of my three kids from that marriage live within an hour of me here in Pennsylvania. One lives in Easton, and one resides in Buckingham. My second family, I have two boys. One is an electrical engineer for Lockheed Martin, graduated from Penn State. He works out in King of Prussia. My second son is a CPA working out in Philadelphia in forensic accounting. Right now, he's in New York City for six months. I have ten grandkids. Eleventh one is on the way and supposed to be here in November. It's a big family, a great family.

Closing Comments

Some people sure have short memories. And those who are too young to know need to be taught.

—www.sermonspice.com

I have known Bob Hogan since 1958. The reason people called Bob "Bish" in his younger days was due to his being baptized by a bishop in the Catholic Church. My daughter was two when she met him, and since she didn't understand his name, Donna, my wife, would say, "It's Bish—like a dish!" It seems only yesterday that our families met fifty-three years ago. Bob's interview may be both disturbing and dubious to some people, but he is as honest as the day is long, and every Gemini that I know is a straight shooter. Of all the souls I have ever encountered-to quote Spock from *Star Trek,* who also know Bob personally or professionally, not one of them has ever spoken negatively about Robert Bevan Hogan. I believe it comes from Southern breeding. He was sincere enough to tell me things that none of his friends *ever* knew, including me. The war is over, but Bob will wear its scars for the rest of his years. His free spirit nearly cost him his life. However, I am convinced that same independence has kept him alive since 1974. By the way, I have never called him Bob directly. Rebel, Savannah Silver Head (he looks like Terry Bradshaw), Odd Bob Hogan, yes! But only Bish when we are not kidding around.

Commander James Caldwell and I have had lunch thrice in the past year. He has blessed me with many books that have assisted me throughout this effort. I believe that if Colonel Mike and Commander Jim stood side by side, you would take them for brothers. Six years is the only variable that separates the two. Both men are full of life, and I am happy to have become their friend.

Admiral Michael Roesner is the only flag/general officer within this book who was interviewed. I achieved my goal of obtaining that military rank/level complements of that plane ride to Chicago last year. Many military and civilian men reached out to their cadre of contacts to find me a general officer, all to no avail. Some things you just have to do yourself! To think a man enlists in the Navy, performs one of the more dangerous jobs in the war, and ends up retiring a two-star "upper rank" Admiral is amazing to me. Remember George Lucas's (along with writers Leigh Brackett and Lawrence Kasdan) script line for Yoda in the second *Star Wars,* "Try not. Do, or do not. There is no try." Michael S. Roesner fulfilled that life attribute that we can all learn from.

After all my discussions, in person and over the phone, with Colonel Mike McAllister, I want to fly an airplane! Don't care if it is a Piper Cub, a vintage WWII Dauntless or a Gulfstream. Mike told me he would get me "up close and personal" with some of the newer aircraft on my next trip to Atlanta, and he better keep his word. My first book signing will hopefully be in a UH-IH Bell Helicopter from 1965 on the Marine Corps Birthday, the evening of 10 November 2011 in Philadelphia, home of the United States Marine Corps. It will go well into the morning of Veterans Day, and this Huey is a rotary wing aircraft that I would also love to fly as well. Colonel Mike and I reach out regularly. Currently, he is hiring pilots for Delta Airlines. There is no one better than a fighter pilot to measure the gut of a man who wants to fly commercial planes.

The "dating" of chapters 1 through 3 was challenging. After speaking to many veterans, they all agreed that the years listed in each chapter were accurate relative to the title of that chapter. Even though the war was declared over on 23 January 1973 by the government and the papers, the fighting persisted, while the wounded and killed continued. On their first day of combat, almost 1,000 Americans were killed. Even on the *very last day* of their tours, 1,448 men died.

Finally, I'd like to issue a warm, happy one-hundredth anniversary to the United States Navy in 2011. Let's toast Messrs. Gulick, Caldwell, Roesner, and Hogan for their service to our country.

CHAPTER FOUR
Medal of Honor Recipients

Valor and Bravery in Battle

Dedicated to Richard Etchberger
Chief Master Sergeant, United States Air Force
1043rd Radio Squadron

There are two tangible symbols of selfless sacrifice. There are tangible symbols representing the ultimate offer of one's life for others. One of those symbols is the Cross of Christ and the other is . . . the Congressional Medal of Honor.

—Paul Harvey

The Medal of Honor is awarded by the president in the name of Congress to a person who, while a member of the military, distinguishes himself or herself conspicuously by gallantry and intrepidity at the risk of his life or her life above and beyond the call of duty while engaged in an action against an enemy of the United States, while engaged in military operations involving conflict with an opposing foreign force, or while serving with friendly foreign forces engaged in an armed conflict against an opposing armed force in which the United States is not a belligerent party. Incontestable proof of the performance of the service will be exacted, and each recommendation for the award of this decoration will be considered on the standard of extraordinary merit.

Early in the Civil War, a medal for individual valor was proposed to general in chief of the Army, Winfield Scott, but Scott felt medals smacked of European affectation and dismissed the idea. The first formal system for rewarding acts of individual gallantry by the nation's fighting men was established by General George Washington on 7 August 1782. Designed to recognize "any singularly meritorious action," the award consisted of a purple cloth heart. Records show that only three persons received the award: Sergeant Elijah Churchill, Sergeant William Brown, and Sergeant Daniel Bissel Jr. Public Resolution 82, containing a provision for a Navy medal of valor, was signed into law by President Abraham Lincoln on 21 December 1861. The medal was "to be bestowed upon such petty officers, seamen, landsmen, and Marines as shall most distinguish themselves by their gallantry and other seamanlike qualities during the present war."

Shortly after this, a resolution similar in wording was introduced on behalf of the Army. Signed into law on 12 July 1862, the measure provided for awarding a medal of honor "to such noncommissioned officers and privates as shall most distinguish themselves by their gallantry in action, and other soldier like qualities, during the present insurrection." Although it was created for the Civil War, Congress made the Medal of Honor a permanent decoration in 1863.

As of 29 May 2011, 3,444 men and one woman have received the Medal of Honor—of which 85 are living, 55 serving in Vietnam. During the Vietnam War, there were 247 Medal of Honor recipients—154 posthumously.

The highest awards that can be issued by service preceding the Medal of Honor are as follows:

Army: Distinguished Service Cross (includes Special Forces, Rangers and Airborne and Delta Force).
Navy: Navy Cross (includes SEALs)
Marine Corps: Navy Cross
Air Force: Air Force Cross
Coast Guard: Coast Guard Cross (as of 2010—formerly Navy Cross)

The current Medal of Honor is a five-pointed bronze star, tipped with trefoils containing a crown of laurel and oak. In the center is Minerva, personifying the United States, standing with left hand resting on fasces and right hand holding a shield blazoned with the shield from the coat of arms of the United States. She repulses discord, represented by snakes. The medal is suspended from the flukes of an anchor. There is also an authorized ribbon and rosette to be worn in lieu of the medal. The Medal of Honor ribbon is blue with five stars, two at the top and three at the bottom. The six-sided blue silk rosette bears thirteen stars and is worn on *civilian* attire. Medal of Honor recipients may also wear the medal itself around the neck of civilian attire for special occasions. There are three types as of this writing: the Army Medal of Honor, the Navy Medal of Honor (covering the Navy, Marines and Coast Guard), and the Air Force Medal of Honor.

Roger Donlon, Colonel, US Army (Ret.) was the first American to receive the Medal of Honor during Vietnam. Captain Donlon was awarded the medal by President Lyndon Johnson on 20 November 1964 for his actions on 6 July 1964 in the Nam Dong Valley of South Vietnam.

> *And it is not the big strong guys that are the heroes. And I still don't understand that term (a hero) except somebody who does something—it is ordinary people doing extraordinary things under extraordinary circumstances . . .*
>
> —Company Combat Medic, Steven Knuboff

Introduction to the Interviews

I had the honor of meeting all the living recipients of this award from Vietnam listed in the Acknowledgments section. Michael Crescenz and Richard Etchberger are recognized here through the efforts of Richard's son (Cory Etchberger) and Michael's brother (Joe Crescenz). Colonel Walter Marm tried to steer me toward Vietnam Medal of Honor recipient Sergeant David Dolby, literally weeks before he died. Sergeant Dolby's PTSD and physical condition prevented him from completing an interview. The strain of five tours in Southeast Asia was too great.

Michael Crescenz attended one of three Philly schools (Cardinal Dougherty) that lost at least twenty-seven graduates during the war. Cardinal Dougherty just closed its doors in June 2010 due to falling admissions. Thomas Edison High School had the highest KIA rate in the nation. Father Judge lost twenty-seven boys as well. After being reinterred to Arlington National Cemetery a few years back, Michael's name surfaced through my friends Barbara Cunningham and Mike Tierney. After more scouring, I located Joe and asked him to speak for his brother.

Joe Crescenz was the most outgoing of all the participants in this book. I can't count how many times he said thanks for honoring his older brother.

What a surprise to learn that my daughter Heather teaches at the same school where Valerie Crescenz (Joe's wife) has instructed for years!

I uncovered Walter "Joe" Marm in Edward Murphy's book, listed in the bibliography. Colonel Marm seemed interested, and we agreed to speak at a future time. Many weeks went by when my wife, Donna, and I were invited to the New Jersey MCLEF gala in Atlantic City. Joe came up and said hello. I realized who he was—that we had already spoken on the phone! Three weeks later, at his home in Fremont, North Carolina, we completed the interview in his den.

Michael Crescenz and Colonel Marm are the only stories enclosed in this section, but I am grateful to have met all the other men who served their country. These men, who wear the pale-blue ribbon adorned with the Medal of Honor, are American icons from the battlefield. They wear the medal not for themselves, but in honor of those who did not make it home, as well as for all those who currently serve the United States in uniform.

MICHAEL CRESCENZ

Corporal, United States Army
Semper Vigilans: *"Vigilant Always"*
Alpha Company Fourth Battalion Thirty-First Infantry Regiment
    196 Infantry Brigade Americal Division
Home of Record: Philadelphia, PA
DOB: 14 January 1949
KIA: 20 November 1968
Posthumous Medal of Honor Recipient
Vietnam Memorial Panel 38W Line 016
Interned: Arlington National Cemetery Section 59, Grave 3226

Crescenz was the only Philadelphian to be awarded the Medal of Honor for his actions in Vietnam. The decoration was posthumously bestowed on the 1966 Cardinal Dougherty High School graduate for his actions on 20 November 1968. The nineteen-year-old corporal was serving as a rifleman with Company A of the 4th Battalion, 31st Infantry, 196th Infantry Brigade, Americal Division, in the Hiep Duc Valley, near Chu Lai, Quang Tin Province. Crescenz had worked as a shipper for a parts distributor before enlisting in the Army in February 1968. He was shipped to Vietnam in September 1968. He was survived by his parents and five brothers.

Official Medal of Honor citation reads,

> Corporal Crescenz distinguished himself by conspicuous gallantry and intrepidity in action while serving as a rifleman of Company A. In the morning his unit engaged a large, well-entrenched force of the North Vietnamese Army whose initial burst of fire pinned down the lead squad and killed the 2 point men, halting the advance of Company A. Immediately, Corporal Crescenz left the relative safety of his own position, seized a nearby machine gun and, with complete disregard for his safety, charged 100 meters up a slope toward the enemy's bunkers which he effectively silenced, killing the 2 occupants of each. Undaunted by the withering machine gun fire around him, Corporal Crescenz courageously moved forward toward a third bunker which he also succeeded in silencing, killing 2 more of the enemy and momentarily clearing the route of advance for his

comrades. Suddenly, intense machine gun fire erupted from an unseen, camouflaged bunker. Realizing the danger to his fellow soldiers, Corporal Crescenz disregarded the barrage of hostile fire directed at him and daringly advanced toward the position. Assaulting with his machine gun, Corporal Crescenz was within 5 meters of the bunker when he was mortally wounded by the fire from the enemy machine gun. As a direct result of his heroic actions, his company was able to maneuver freely with minimal danger and to complete its mission, defeating the enemy. Corporal Crescenz's bravery and extraordinary heroism at the cost of his life are in the highest traditions of the military service and reflect great credit on himself, his unit, and the US Army.

The presence of any Medal of Honor winner [sic] is sufficient to bring generals to their feet saluting.
                                    —Richard Condon and George Axelrod

Growing Up

We grew up in West Oak Lane in Philadelphia. Our proud parents raised six sons of Italian/Irish heritage. My father was a WWII Army veteran of the European Campaigns, and none of his sons ever knew what he did in the Army. After returning home, he married our mother, a girl out of West Philly. Pop went back into the beer business with my Italian grandfather, Charles Sr. I know they were proud of all their boys.

Michael was very competitive with Charlie. They had that connection that the first two siblings would always have in a family growing up in the 1950s and 1960s. Mike was one hardheaded SOB. We all had our tempers, but that boy, when you saw him lose it, he'd go bazonkers. I was a witness to some of the fist fights. All my brothers were very athletic, but Charlie and Mike were very gifted. Charlie was so fleet of foot and so fast that he would get Mike so pissed off, bop him a couple times like a kangaroo, and then do a beeline. Mike would chase his ass down through the house, and Mom would be screaming, saying, "Wait until your father comes home, he's going to give it to both of you!" It was good growing up, but Dad was really tough on them.

Growing up, no one ever thought they'd have to worry about another war, especially a war like Vietnam. Korea was bad enough, and my father never really spoke much of the Korean War. Most of those men who saw action in WWII didn't either; they knew it was hell for those guys, but I don't think our fathers or mothers were prepared to see what was to come when Vietnam broke out. It was tough for my dad and mom to see their sons going into the service. Charlie tried one year at community college in Philadelphia. He said that wasn't for him, so he grabbed his buddy Dick Downy with whom he played baseball in the sandlots in Philly, and they went on the buddy system in the Marine Corps. We were one of three families in the neighborhood that lost a brother, a son, and a grandchild. Now they're on that wall in Philly and DC to be remembered for their sacrifice to our nation.

Vietnam

Before you knew it, Charlie got his orders to go to Vietnam and was in country around March 1967. I do remember this: When Charlie came home from 'Nam in early 1968, he came off the tarmac with one other marine, and how ironic that this marine grew up in our same neighborhood. They were the only two guys who came off this plane that were in a military uniform. Nobody was there to greet them; no one really cared except for our family. Mom and Dad made sure that my two younger brothers and I got up early to get ready to go down to Philadelphia International to greet Charlie. We didn't know what time he was coming in, but we waited, and then there he was. I know my parents were very excited. Of course, we took the other marine home; he lived on Limekiln Pike in West Oak Lane, directly across Saint Athanasius Parish, the Roman Catholic Parish in which we grew up. We dropped that marine off before we went to Mass, since it was on a Sunday morning. I was astounded that this marine told my parents that his mother and father didn't even know he was coming home.

When Charlie came home, our brother Mike, who graduated Cardinal Dougherty in 1966, entered the Army in February 1968. I think he got out of boot camp at Fort Bragg May 1968. Charlie came home in early 1968; Mike was sent over in September. If you joined the service, you had a choice. If you were drafted, you didn't know where you'd go. I worked with a guy in the school district, and he saw that happen because he was a draftee into the Army. I've heard of other guys being shanghaied into the Marine Corps down at the recruiter's office, but Charlie and Michael both volunteered.

Before Michael was shipped off, Mom and Dad had a big family gathering with friends, neighbors, and guys Mike and Charlie grew up with. I'll never forget this: we found out that Michael proposed to his high school sweetheart, and she accepted. At first, I think Michael wanted to get married before he went overseas. When we had the party, Mom had begged him not to, and my mom finally approached her father-in-law, who finally put some sense in him. My Italian grandfather convinced Michael that if that girl really loved him, she'd wait. Michael said, "Okay, Pop-pop, I guess I'll have to wait."

Michael's Sweetheart

A lot of people asked if I have a contact with his girlfriend. I don't. When we were finally going to have Michael reinterred down at Arlington, there were veterans of the war that didn't even know us, and that's one of the few things they asked, "What happened to his sweetheart?" Maybe there were similar circumstances for a lot of those men when they came home, or they received Dear John letters, possibly a failed marriage or when they came home, their high school sweetheart didn't want to be with them anymore. Who knows? We lost contact with Christine. We called her Chrissy for short. She actually stayed around and visited our family, stayed with my mother and father for a couple days or a week at a time down in Sea Isle City (New Jersey) even after Mike was dead.

She loved our Michael so much, and she didn't know how to break away. My mother finally pleaded with that young lady. "Chrissy," she said, "please get on with your life. You have to start all over again, you're too young. Don't let my son bury you, you're too young." She eventually did, and the last we ever heard of her was in the mid seventies. I may have still been in high school when she finally told my mom and dad good-bye. The last time they heard from her, I think she settled in Connecticut, and she was getting married. She was a sweetheart, an only child, and her mom and dad loved our brother too. Mike was like the son they never had. It literally broke their hearts. So the war just didn't affect the immediate family, it affected a lot of other people who knew Mike.

Motivation for entering the service

I think it was to follow in Charlie's footsteps, that he felt, "Hey, if Charlie can do it, I can do it." Michael did boot camp at Fort Bragg (North Carolina), and then he did some advanced infantry training (AIT) at Fort Ord, California. Then they shipped him back to Fort Benning, Georgia, for additional training. After all that, I guess he got his orders, came home for a little R&R, and that's when they shipped him out. He might have been out on the West Coast. One of his buddies on the plane was Bob Gleason. He survived his tour in 'Nam. Bob just retired a few years ago. I've met Bob a few times, most recently back in July 2009 at a reunion for the 196th Light Infantry Brigade, Americal Division. They were in the Central Highlands and saw a lot of action. They fought with the Marines during those battles.

When Bob Gleason saw the death of Michael in the Stars and Stripes, he said part of his heart was ripped out. He couldn't believe it because they wanted to stay together, but they were separated when they arrived in country. The officer's job there was to divide these guys out into the different companies if they thought the guys were too chummy.

Pete's Turn

My brother, Pete, went into the Marine Corps in 1970. Pete joined the Marine Corps on the buddy system with Charlie Gillis, and that never works out. Pete was more of an observer, and he was very close to Michael. I know he respected Charlie growing up, and I know he cared for Charlie, but he really looked up to Michael. Pete was a tough kid, but he wasn't as tough as Michael or Charlie. Pete liked to party and have a good time—he always told a good joke. He was the funny guy, and I think, out of respect to Charlie and Mike, he felt he had to join also. If the first two did it, then he'd have to do it, and if that was his motivation, then God bless him. I kind of wanted to go, but being the fourth, and having the first three in during the war, my mom had a conniption when she saw me wanting to serve. She must have seen me as her so-called scholar. She told our father that the government was not taking another one of her boys, and that I was going to college!

Mom didn't want another one of her sons involved in Vietnam, but they wanted the bodies, so Pete joined the reserves as a marine and was never sent out of the country as far as I know. The day Michael was brought home and we buried him, it was the early part of December 1968, but Pete, I think took it so hard that, to this day, Pete still has a very hard time dealing with it. Pete has had a rough life.

Arlington

This was a real turning point for our family. I think Pete has gotten to a point in his life that he knows it was a good thing that we reinterred Michael at

Arlington, but at first, he was very opposed. When I told him that we were going to get Michael exhumed out of Holy Sepulcher, Pete didn't want it done. I explained, "Pete, you have to understand, Mike belongs with his brothers in arms." He just didn't want Michael disinterred. Charlie, my two younger brothers, and I had no problem. My younger brother Steve, who served over four years in the Coast Guard postwar, thought it was a wonderful idea.

When I first brought up the subject to my brothers, I think they thought it would never happen. If it hadn't been for all the support we got from the Medal of Honor Society and many VFWs in Pennsylvania and New Jersey, other veteran's groups like the Gathering of Eagles, various veterans biker clubs such as the Patriot Guard, Rolling Thunder, Second Brigade, the Vietnam Marine Corps Brigade, the Philly Motorcycle Cops, and American Legion Posts like the one in Toms River, New Jersey, it might not have. These groups raised monies to help get Mike down to Arlington. The archdiocese of Philly gave me a very hard time about exhuming the body at first, but we finally got it done with the help of Bishop Joe McFadden, who actually grew up in Philly and played basketball with an old friend of my older brothers. My friend, Denny Luminella, and his business partner, Jim Terry, gave us a break on their funeral home costs to inter Mike down at Arlington. I didn't want Mike to be alone at Holy Sepulcher forever. No one else in the family was going to be buried there with him. At Arlington, he will have his resting place looked after. People started coming out of the woodwork to help, and I began to realize that this meant a whole lot to the 'Nam vets, who never got a "welcome home." This was the funeral they couldn't attend when they were overseas, the respect they didn't get when they came home. I see a difference in my brothers. It's like we could finally make peace with what happened.

Mother

She always supported us as best she could as she was a saint. It was hard for Mom when she lost Michael. I look back and wonder if Michael was the apple of her eye, but I know Mom always loved every one of us equally. I know she loved Charlie because she always missed having him around. She would ask, "Joseph, have you heard from your brother Charles? I know he's working down near Atlantic City." Every once in a while I would get on the phone, call up Charlie, and say, "Hey, Charlie, do you think you can visit Mom and Dad in Sea Isle? You're only a half an hour away." "Hey Joe,

I'm busy. I'll get over there when I can." Charlie just couldn't visit Mom and Dad as much as he would have liked. Looking back, Peter was very affected. He served in the corps and got discharged. I know Pete had a lot of problems. He made a lot of mistakes in his life, but Pete has straightened out and is doing well.

1968 was a hell of a year. I think you said the worst year in our history. The year 1969 was really no better. That's why I believe when you meet more of these men and women that served over there during that time, they're the ones that just . . . I don't know how to put it—you respect their space, you respect their quietness. If they want to talk, they're going to talk. It was just a hell of a time because my buddies and I were growing up around this. Some of my buddies' older brothers came back, and the poor guys looked like living skeletons. They were gaunt in the face. I just couldn't believe how much weight these guys lost. Some of their teeth were half-rotted out.

There were no hero's welcomes for these guys. Most of them were lucky to even have their families give them a coming home party. It was just a very strange time in our American history for our service people. When they came home during that time, I just couldn't believe the stuff I witnessed as a thirteen-year-old kid. I was shocked to see some of the crap that some of these men were getting from the general public.

I saw two soldiers in their dress greens up at the old Gimbels in Cheltenham. I was walking with my mom, and I was around twelve at the time. I couldn't believe that people would turn around and spit on their uniforms. I looked at my mom, and I said, "What the hell?" Well, I didn't say hell because my mom would slap me upside the head. I said, "Mom, what's wrong with these people? Why are they doing that?" Then my mom would just grab my hand and say, "Just move along." My mom wasn't right after losing Michael, but then she saw other families go through the same grief that she did. She knew she wasn't alone, but they had no support. They had no support groups like they do today. We all struggled with what happened to him, and boys were supposed to just suck it up, be a man, and move on. We didn't get a chance to grieve or even know how.

There was no support at all for the war. I make it a point, to this day, and I've been doing it for years, but more so after, we reburied Michael down in Arlington, that I'll go out of my way to welcome those guys home. I shake their hand and tell them, "Thank you for doing what you did." And a lot of these guys, they'd look at you in the eyes and say, "Wow, well, thanks for remembering." They don't know how to react, but they will say thank-you.

So it's my mission on this earth, to the day the Big Man takes me "home," to make sure veterans past and present get the honor they deserve.

How did Vietnam shape your life?

For Charlie, Peter, Stephen, Christopher, and me, it totally changed all our lives. I think that it made you appreciate what we have in this country despite the political turmoil, even in today's world. As a twelve-year-old, it was personal. It wasn't just Mike, but all the older guys I looked up to. They were doing what they were told to do and dying for this country. We were still playing ball, working, and going to school, trying to act like life was normal. It was surreal. I feel some guilt at not having served our country, and I'm hoping to be able to do something about that, but Charles has told me, "Our family has done enough." I do think the war changed this country forever. I think that the modern military has to appreciate and thank the Vietnam-era veteran. I think our modern military has a lot to be thankful for even though they're in two wars right now fighting. I feel it's because of their predecessors, in Vietnam, that they have what they have—the support, the love, and the backing of most of the American people. Our modern-day military is "the best" in part because of what the 'Nam vets brought to the table!

Advice to someone considering a military career

Go for it! I would not mind joining myself if they ever removed the age exception. I'd serve my country. I feel like I let my family down; I let myself down by not joining. I think it's so honorable. It is something that I'm sure changes your life forever, but it makes you appreciate what we have.

Those men all feel that they did not lose that war. The politicians, the people protesting back home, and the media brought down this country's efforts with the scandalous crap that they wrote and slanted every which way. War is hell as they say. I have a very, very high respect for the military. They're giving their time to protect their nation and its citizens. That was just brought up at the Navy League dinner honoring Colonel Barney Barnum, USMC (Ret.), and Medal of Honor recipient in 'Nam. A four-star general, General Mattis, was our guest speaker at the Navy League. He spoke quite a bit about the modern world right now. He did say that someday the draft will be reactivated. It shouldn't have been deactivated when Nixon pulled it. He said, "We're still waiting on it to be reactivated, but Congress will not act on it."

Current day

Michael isn't here to enjoy the present day, but I've thought so many times over the years what his life would have been like. He would have married Chrissy. I'm sure there would have been kids, and he would have had a happy life. Bill Stafford, the medic in his unit told me that he is here, married, and with children, because of Mike. I know he must have some survivor's guilt issues.

Going through everything our family went through and then moving Michael to his final resting place at Arlington, I think I can say we finally have found peace. I think my brothers and I feel like a weight has been lifted from our shoulders.

WALTER "JOE" MARM

Colonel (Ret.), United States Army
Semper Vigilans: *"Vigilant Always"*
First Battalion Seventh Cavalry Regiment First Cavalry Division
Home of Record: Washington, PA
Home of Residence: Fremont, NC
DOB: 20 November 1941
Interview at his home 29 June 2010
University of Duquesne
Citation Location: Ia Drang Valley Central Highlands South Vietnam
    14 November 1965

First Lieutenant Marm's official Medal of Honor citation reads:

> For conspicuous gallantry and intrepidity at the risk of life
> above and beyond the call of duty. As a platoon leader in the
> First Cavalry Division (Airmobile), First Lieutenant Marm
> demonstrated indomitable courage during a combat operation.
> His company was moving through the valley to relieve a friendly
> unit surrounded by an enemy force of estimated regimental size.
> First Lieutenant Marm led his platoon through withering fire
> until they were finally forced to take cover. Realizing that his
> platoon could not hold very long, and seeing four enemy soldiers
> moving into his position, he moved quickly under heavy fire and
> annihilated all 4. Then, seeing that his platoon was receiving
> intense fire from a concealed machine gun, he deliberately
> exposed himself to draw its fire. Thus locating its position, he
> attempted to destroy it with an antitank weapon. Although
> he inflicted casualties, the weapon did not silence the enemy
> fire. Quickly, disregarding the intense fire directed on him and
> his platoon, he charged thirty meters across open ground, and
> hurled grenades into the enemy position, killing some of the 8
> insurgents manning it. Although severely wounded, when his
> grenades were expended, armed with only a rifle, he continued
> the momentum of his assault on the position and killed the
> remainder of the enemy. First Lieutenant Marm's selfless actions
> reduced the fire on his platoon, broke the enemy assault, and
> rallied his unit to continue toward the accomplishment of this

mission. First Lieutenant Marm's gallantry on the battlefield and his extraordinary intrepidity at the risk of his life are in the highest traditions of the US Army and reflect great credit upon himself and the armed forces.

Without a sign, his sword the brave man draws, and asks no omen but his country's cause.

—*The Iliad* (Pope's translation)

Growing Up

I grew up in a small town called Washington, Pennsylvania, with a population of twenty-five thousand. I went to Immaculate Conception grade school and high school. My formative years were great. The only sport we had in my high school was basketball, but it was one of those sports that you have to practice a lot. I shot on a rifle team. We had a .22-caliber rifle. It was called Frazier Simplex. We used to go to the range once a week and shoot at nights, then do tournaments around the Pittsburgh and Pennsylvania areas. Every year, we'd go down to the capital of Harrisburg and shoot at one of the big matches down there. Our team was very good. Western Pennsylvania and West Virginia were noted for having very good shots. My dad didn't shoot rifles, but he was on the Pennsylvania State Police and shot on their pistol team and was a very good shot with a pistol. I never developed a lot of skills with a pistol even though we shot them in the Army. I didn't shoot them much with my dad; plus a .22-caliber bullet is a little bit cheaper than the .38-caliber pistol bullets that he used. I used to help him load his ammunition. We'd melt the lead, put the primer in the casing, put the powder in, and then put the wad in. It was kind of neat as I learned some new skills.

I graduated in 1959 and then went right into Duquesne University. I started out in pharmacy, but switched to business, and graduated in 1964. I shot on the rifle team for three years and ran cross-country my senior year. The rifle team was coached by the ROTC department. There was a young major in there, Major Lutholz who was one of our coaches. He said, "Marm, you're going to be drafted. Did you ever think about going into OCS (Officer Candidate School) spending time as an officer? Then when you get out you can use that on your résumé." I thought it sounded like a good idea so that's what I did. I enlisted and went through basic training; I enlisted five days after I graduated on 5 June 1964.

I went through basic and advanced training, AIT and then into OCS. It took me ten months to get my commission—19 April 1965. I proceeded to ranger school and was supposed to go to airborne school. Then I was to go down to my first assignment at Fort Jackson for basic training, possibly as an XO (executive officer), but that didn't happen. In Ranger School, they needed lieutenants for this unit that was forming up at Fort Benning. The 11th Air Assault had been testing the helicopters against 101st and 82nd Airborne. It proved very successful, so they were going to send it to Vietnam, and they changed the name and brought the colors of the First Cavalry Division back from Korea. The unit was now called the First Cavalry Division Airmobile. We had over four hundred helicopters in our unit. That was our main means of moving around in Vietnam, and it proved very successful. They needed lieutenants, and we didn't know much about Vietnam in Ranger School. We had a big formation, and they announced about forty names and said, "Your orders are now being changed. You're going to a new unit. You can make one phone call home tonight to tell your relatives not to pack their bags because your orders are changed to Fort Benning." That only lasted a month. We left Fort Benning one night in August and took a bus up to Charleston, South Carolina, and boarded a merchant marine ship. It took us about thirty days to get to Vietnam through the Panama Canal, up to California and across the Pacific. We went through a typhoon on the way. We did calisthenics, had classes, and shot our weapons off the fantail (stern area of the ship). We put a wooden target on a big cable so we could shoot at it to get some rifle practice on the trip over. We stayed busy those thirty days. When we got there, we went by helicopter up to our base camp. It was called An Khe and was located in the Central Highlands of South Vietnam. Our advanced party went over about a month before us and was kind of sorting out where everybody was going to go. They did some clearing, but it was our job to clear the base camp for four hundred helicopters and fifteen thousand soldiers. It took one entire brigade. We had three brigades, but it would take one brigade to provide perimeter defense around the division base camp.

I was assigned to General Custer's unit, the First Battalion Seventh Cavalry (listed as 1/7 for remainder of interview), which was commanded by Lieutenant Colonel Hal Moore. His commanding sergeant major was Basil Plumley who was an outstanding noncommissioned officer. We had great troops. Something that they're doing now is sending units over to Afghanistan and Iraq as a complete group. They didn't do that in Vietnam save for when the units first deployed. So we had a lot of esprit and camaraderie because they'd been training and working together for over a year in the test bays of the airmobile concept at Fort Benning and around that area. In my unit, I had a combination in the unit—draftees, volunteers, both in the enlisted ranks, and the junior NCO (noncommissioned officers) ranks. Like many of the Vietnam veterans that served later, I had a full composite of NCOs. All the NCOs that I was authorized, I had E-6 (sergeant) squad leaders, and E-5 team leaders. Two teams in a squad; so I had E-5s in each of those positions. I had three rifle squad leaders and a weapons squad leader for my E-6s, and I had an E-7 platoon sergeant. I was very fortunate.

Everyone was well trained, but everything was new. The M-16 (.223 caliber) was a new weapon. We weren't sure just how accurate that weapon was going to be, but it proved to be very successful. The M-60 (.30-caliber) machine gun was a great weapon. The M-79 grenade launcher was good. You just had to take care of it because of the humidity and all the dampness in Vietnam. All the weapons had to be cleaned daily.

Vietnam

We arrived in country in September, and we were doing local searches and patrolling in September and October. I carried just the M-16, but we weren't real sure of it. We went over and put all of our stuff in conex containers. Many of us including the chaplain had personal weapons. My dad gave me a .38 snub nose pistol that I carried underneath my fatigues. I also took over and gave my point man a sawed-off shotgun, twelve-gauge double barrel—sawed-off both stock and barrel. We didn't use it for long. There was an accident in our battalion with one of the personal weapons and Colonel Moore had all the personal weapons collected and stored away. The M-16, the .45 pistol, the M-79, and the M-60 were our main weapons. We didn't use any of the heavy .90 millimeter recoil rifles. We didn't have any. It was heavy. We used the (LAW) light antitank weapon. It was much easier to carry. We carried bayonets too. We had to fix bayonets in the Battle of Ia Drang (for the action to come).

The Battle of Ia Drang started on 14 November 1965 and was a three-day battle against three regiments of NVA. One of my sergeants was a medic in Korea. We didn't have a medic in my platoon, so he was the squad leader, and he carried the aid bag. He was busy taking care of his squad and taking care of the wounded. I was wounded on the first day of the battle. I was shot in the jaw. The bullet entered my left jaw, I think it was probably an AK-47, or a carbine, not sure what. It shattered my left jaw and exited out underneath my right jaw. I was a walking wounded. They patched me up with a first aid compress, and I walked back to the—it was probably 1700—center of the area where Colonel Moore's battalion CP (command post) was located. This is where all the wounded were being collected. They were bringing in ammunition and resupply. Bruce Crandall (awarded the Medal of Honor at Ia Drang), one of the lead helicopter pilots, Ed Freeman (also awarded the Medal of Honor due to actions in this battle) were bringing in water and ammunition and taking out the wounded. The medevacs weren't coming in because it was still a pretty hot LZ, and they didn't want to have any more helicopters crash and burn. So they were just being backhauled on the supply helicopter, which was a standard Huey that we used. It was the "jeep" of Vietnam. So I went back and kind of worked my way back to the States and recuperated in an Army hospital. They tried to put you close to your home town and Valley Forge was the closest Army hospital to the Philadelphia area. They closed it down after Korea and opened it back up for us. There were a couple of other Vietnam Ia Drang vets there. One of the company commanders lived in the Philadelphia area too—Bob Edwards. He recuperated there with me. He got shot pretty badly in the back, 15 November, and we recuperated together there.

I came back. I spent a night in the Philippines, a night in Presidio, San Francisco, and then flew to Fort Dix, then a ground transport from Fort Dix to Valley Forge. I first talked to my parents when I was in California. They gave me a pair of scissors because they had my mouth wired shut. They had gum bands on my bottom jaw—I didn't lose any teeth in the injury so they said, "hey, if you get nauseous and have to vomit."

The bullet came in on my left and exited on my right. Over the years, you can't see it as much. It missed the jugular by inches which probably would have killed me, but I didn't seem to lose a lot of blood. I was not getting any intravenous blood supply that I know of while I was still conscious. I'm not sure if I ever lost consciousness. I don't think I did, but maybe in the trauma center. Anyway, I don't remember them giving me any blood or anything.

I recall the general (then lieutenant colonel) asked for more medics to come in. Before he finished, he was commanding nine companies (almost regimental strength). In fact, the brigade commander (his CO) wanted to come in and take over, but Colonel Moore said he had it all under control. He respectively declined orders to get taken out during that battle or for the brigade commander to come in, but the medics were there too. Just in our battalion alone, we had 79 killed in action and 121 wounded. That's not counting the 2/7 (Second Battalion Seventh Regiment) that went in as well. When they were walking out, going toward the landing zone, they hit a large enemy force, and they took 151 KIA, 121 WIA, and 4 MIA the next day. It's called LZ Albany.

That's not in the movie and a lot of the Albany guys are upset—like Rick Rescorla who's on the cover of the book *We Were Soldiers Once and Young* and was an OCS classmate of mine and was killed on 9/11 at the south tower. There's a book about him called *Heart of a Soldier*. He's credited with saving over 2,500 people. He was head of security for Morgan Stanley in the south tower. He got everybody out and went back in to make sure the building was secure when it went down.

At Fort Benning, there's a statue of him similar to the cover of the book. I went down for the original dedication of that a few years ago. They have a new museum where they moved the statue. We're trying to get him the Presidential Medal of Freedom. It didn't happen under Bush, so now we're hoping to get it under the Obama administration. That would be a nice plus because of all the people that he saved. Initially, he said, "Everything's okay, stay in place." He'd been practicing fire drills for six years as head of security. People pooh-pooh fire drills, but he had his bullhorn, and he was singing. He was a very good combat leader too because he'd been in combat in South Africa and came to America and got his citizenship after being in the Army. He went to law school and rose through the ranks of corporate America.

He was completely calm that day. He was like that in combat also. He came in and helped us with his company. He was one of the first companies in and took Bob Edwards's place because on the morning of the second day, Bob Edwards's company suffered over 50 percent casualties. This was in the perimeter; the "lost" platoon that they couldn't get to. That lieutenant was another OCS classmate of mine named Herrick. Henry Herrick (*Vietnam Memorial Panel 03E Line 057*). A good guy. We went to Ranger School together. The buck sergeant that took over after Herrick, Ernie Savage, never lost another man, killed or wounded. This was after sustaining three heavy attacks. Savage was awarded the Distinguished Service Cross along with his medic Doc Lose. Now Doc Lose just died a few years ago, and Bob Edwards went to his funeral. He didn't come to many functions. The demons were still there.

Rescorla was one of those guys you would think would stay in and become a general, but he got out and went to law school. He stayed in the reserves, and he became a colonel in the JAG (Judge Advocate General) corps as a lawyer. Good guy. Our OCS class is filled with those guys. In terms of (who) went over to Vietnam, we had probably one of the highest decorated OCS (Officer Candidate School) classes. Class no. 465 was our class number. Every time we would sit down, we would say, "Six hundred classes since 1941 tried, but none will compare with 465." OCS started in 1941, and we were the six-hundredth class. That's kind of ingrained. Every time we would sit down, we had to say that, but we had a lot of guys that went right over to Vietnam.

We were getting together yearly in Washington DC. We haven't had a big reunion up in Washington, but we still have mini reunions around the country, primarily in Fort Benning and other places. Just for 1/7, the one in Washington DC was getting very, very big. Everybody was coming to it. The helicopter pilots and all the units that were involved in Ia Drang Valley came—everyone. My company Commander Tony Nadal is up in Virginia in Williamsburg. He's very well-spoken and taught at West Point. Every year we get together; we have a 1/7 meeting. Next year it'll be at Fort Benning; this year it was at Charleston, South Carolina. Last year General Moore and Sergeant Major Plumley were there. Sergeant major's 90 and the General's 88. They were both in Korea. In fact, Plumley was in WWII (he was airborne). The last reunion was the biggest one in Washington, and the man that directed the movie *We Were Soldiers* (Randall Wallace) was the master of ceremonies. He tried to make it as accurate as possible, but he did tell Joe Galloway and Hal Moore that he was doing a movie for Hollywood, not a documentary.

Mel Gibson did a good job playing General Moore. General Moore's wife is buried at Fort Benning. The cemetery's all filled up, but Sergeant Gell from A-company (*Vietnam Memorial Panel03E Line049*)—our radio operator for our company commander Tony Nadal—was killed in action, and his wife remarried and donated her spot to the Moores. Mrs. Moore died a few years ago; she's buried in her plot. General Moore will be buried there too. A lot of the guys are buried right there at Fort Benning. The general lives right across the border in Auburn, Alabama.

How did Vietnam shape your life?

I was in a total of thirty years, so this was early in my career. A Korean War Medal of Honor recipient named Scooter Burke, who retired as a colonel and spent a lot of time in Washington DC as head of Army legislative liaison for the House, made a comment, and it's very true. "It's harder to wear the medal than it is to earn it." In other words, we've had some recipients who have PTSD problems. There was one that robbed a 7/11 and was shot dead after he'd received the medal who was probably suffering from posttraumatic stress. Others have had alcohol and drug problems. I have a belief in God and deep religious faith that have helped me through the tough times plus a very tight, very good family both when growing up as well as with my kids and wife. It's kind of like being in the Army. It's a team effort. You can't do it by yourself. You need that support around you.

I had three sisters; one is still living. My mom is still living (*Mrs. Marm passed on Spring 2011*). I saw her last weekend in Washington. My daughter, Courtney, was married on 29 August 2009 at the Old Mill Inn (Media, Pennsylvania). My mom was present, and it was her ninety-fifth birthday that day. We sang "Happy Birthday" at my daughter's wedding. This August I'm going to go up there for her ninety-sixth. She lived down here for about eight years, and then when my boy was hurt in that racing accident, she moved up with my sister in Ohio.

No one hates war more than a warrior. I stayed in not because I loved being in combat but because I loved being with soldiers. I volunteered to go back. They don't send you back to the same theater that you received your medal in, but many Vietnam veterans did as I did. Medal of Honor recipients went back for a second tour. Barney Barnum went over again. I was a captain in the First Cavalry Division throughout 1969. It was a very, very long war, and it was tough. Just like the wars now in Afghanistan and Iraq, it's very tough on the family. I think we're doing a better job at keeping the family involved with all the family support programs we have now. We've learned from some of the things that we didn't do in previous actions. We were fighting a very, very tough enemy. The North Vietnamese were dedicated, and they were there for the long haul. I think had we continued to provide logistical support to the South Vietnamese, they could have held their own. When we cut that off, I think that hurt them. They didn't have the logistical, the "beans and bullets" to continue fighting the NVA. We trained them, and they were doing pretty good job on their own.

Advice to someone considering a military career

You have to go in like I did. I went and served because I would have been drafted. I liked being with soldiers. It's a very unique and special career. If you like it, do it. God bless you. You can start at the bottom in the military as a private and work your way up to command sergeant major, or you can start in as a lieutenant and work your way up to a general—stop anywhere in between. You can stay in for twenty years if you like it. I stayed in for thirty years and realized it's harder to get a civilian job when you stay in longer because you're a little bit older, but you get a little bit better retiree pay at thirty versus twenty. There are pluses and minuses for everything you do. We need a strong military. It's very important that we have soldiers, sailors, airmen, Marines, and Coast Guardsmen to fill the ranks. America's a great country. I've been around the world, been to many a third-world country, but America is great because of the people in it. We're a cross section of all nationalities, races, and religions. People still want to come here and be a part of America.

Current day

I retired from the Army in 1995 and moved south. My wife had been following me around for a number of years, so we decided to move back to her hometown. I have been happy everywhere I've been assigned, so I'm easy to please. My kids, they like the bright lights of Philadelphia and other cities. They aren't real happy with the quietness and the austerity of a small town of 1,400, but it's a great town. I learned some new skills. I learned how to farm and drive a tractor, how to give a pig a shot of penicillin—whatever he needs to get better. We have a finishing hog operation fifteen miles away, out in the country from the town of Fremont, and we raise six thousand finishing hogs over a sixteen—to twenty-week period. I started that right after I retired. I looked into going into Corporate America, but decided just to be out in the sun, kind of like being an infantry officer. I like being outside, plus my mother was living here with me. I was able to come and go as I pleased—come back and check on her. God works in strange and mysterious ways. If I had gone to Raleigh and worked there, it would have been a little bit tougher on my family situation. All the kids are gone now. It's just my wife, me, and my mother when she was here with us. My wife works for Congressman Jones in Greenville, just forty miles east of here. She does immigration casework. She used to do military casework when I first met her in DC. She was working for a famous senator, Jesse Helms. He was a legend in his own time. She did military casework when we met, but I never dated her until I went to Fort Benning and was battalion commander. I needed someone to take to the infantry ball, so I called her up and asked her if she'd come down and be my date; she agreed. We had a long-distance courtship there for a while. We were married, and she went to Philadelphia with me and gave her place up with Jesse Helms. We've been together ever since.

Medal of Honor Grove
Valley Forge, PA

Picture approved by the Friends of the Medal of Honor Grove

On 18 September 2010, I was asked by my friend, USNR Commander Kevin Potter (Ret.), to attend the funeral services of Special Forces Sergeant David Dolby. David passed away on 6 August 2010. President Johnson awarded the Medal of Honor to Dolby for his actions on 21 May 1966. The service was held at VFW 1564 in Phoenixville, Pennsylvania. His home of residence was Norristown, Pennsylvania. There were hundreds of veterans from all foreign wars (WWII to present) in attendance, along with family and friends. Both a Pennsylvania senator and congressman were asked to speak on David's behalf. It was quite a solemn day.

On the way home, I realized that the Medal of Honor Grove, conceived in 1942, was only a mile away from the VFW. The Grove is situated on the grounds of the Freedoms Foundation. The fifty two acres (one for each state including Puerto Rico and the District of Columbia) of the Medal of Honor Grove contains markers, by state, to honor every recipient of this Medal since the Civil War. Thanks to the collaboration of the Freedoms Foundation and the Friends of the Medal of Honor Grove, the stage is set to preserve and maintain the integrity and physical grounds of the area.

On 12 June 2011, a rededication of the grounds was held on the eastern boundary of the Grove. Along with representatives of both non-profit foundations, Vietnam Medal of Honor Recipients Walter "Joe" Marm and James E. Livingston were present to pay tribute to the new "alliance" of these foundations. Colonel Marm, US Army (Ret.) and Major General Livingston, USMC (Ret.) both spoke on this very hot and humid summer day. Over one hundred civilians and veterans of foreign wars were also in attendance.

Let me not forget to mention that literally thousands of Chester and Montgomery county residents, including students from area high schools and universities, have donated their time and efforts to assist in the continued upkeep of the Grove.

The Congressional Medal of Honor Museum

Pictures approved by The Congressional Medal of Honor Society

The Congressional Medal of Honor Museum is located on board the historic aircraft carrier USS *Yorktown* at Patriots Point in Mount Pleasant, South Carolina. It is home to the Congressional Medal of Honor Society, whose living members share the honor of wearing our nation's highest award for military valor. The society is one of the most unique and exclusive organizations in the United States.

The museum features exhibits to explain the origin and purpose of the medal and to tell the stories of those brave recipients who displayed remarkable courage. The Medal of Honor is still being awarded to this day, and the museum pays special tribute to the first Medal of Honor recipients from our current war, the War on Terrorism.

Closing Comments

This medal is not mine. It belongs to all those kids who never grew up to be grandfathers. I just hold it in trust.
—2nd Lt. George H. O'Brien, Jr. USMC
MOH recipient, Korean War, Died March 2005

It was very surreal for me interviewing Colonel Marm, knowing the background both of his actions and the battalion's movements on 14 November 1965 prior to driving to Fremont, North Carolina. In our discussion, Joe used some terms that were new to me like the "bullets and beans" comment to describe what the ARVN did *not* have to effectively engage the NVA (after we pulled out). To think a man of his caliber would take the time to speak to me about his life was the highest honor a career military man could bestow on this civilian. As we sat in his living room/den, adorned to the hilt in memorabilia, the conversation stirred emotions never experienced by me before. I was fortunate that evening of April 2010 to have investigated and called the colonel to request an interview. Now I have found a man that I not only respect as a career military officer but have established a friendship that will hopefully last for many years.

Upon speaking with Joe Crescenz about his older brother Michael that warm day in June 2010, I walked away knowing the effort to track him down was worth it. I remembered the *Inquirer* article covering Michael's re-internment from my family's cemetery to Washington DC. It was important to this work finding men who had served from the tri-state area. Joseph Martin Crescenz and I are now "connected" by a teenager who paid the ultimate sacrifice for his unit, his family, and his country. Both Joe and the colonel have left footprints in my heart. I visited Michael unbeknownst to Joe in August 2010 to pay my respects. May he continue to rest peacefully in his "home" at Arlington National Cemetery Section 59, Grave 3226.

CHAPTER FIVE
Five-Star Family

The Jamisons

Dedicated to William J. Jamison
Captain, United States Army
Alpha Company 227th Assault Helicopter Battalion
First Cavalry Division (Airmobile)
Website: www.williamjamison.com

Any helicopter pilot, inserted into an area to rescue injured or dying soldiers by way of a medevac, should have received at the very least a Bronze Star—each and every time. A unit citation does not do justice to this incredible feat of bravery.

—Carmelo Infantino

This eighteen-month voyage I undertook placed me in front of, or among, veterans who knew many helicopter pilots. There were four main "choppers" used in Vietnam. The UH-IH Iroquois was made by Bell. This was the workhorse of the US Army. Usually carrying a pilot, copilot, and two door gunners (one of which was the crew chief—he was totally responsible for the condition of the helicopter). When inserting troops, an additional squad could be airlifted in. So this "bird" carried roughly nine men. The Iroquois was also used for casualty extraction (see below). Another unit the Army used was the Boeing CH-47, popularly called the Chinook. This was a medium-weight helicopter capable of moving larger loads of troops, ordnance, guns, jeeps, and the like.

The Marine Corps used two helicopters. The CH-46 was also a medium lift unit similar to the Chinook. Boeing manufactured both models. This helicopter was used for troop and material insertions as well as medevac maneuvers. Heavily armed, it was a monster. The other big chopper was the CH-53 (formerly the HD-34) made by Sokorsky. This heavy-duty (thus, the old HD designation) also supported marine operations on the ground.

Both the medium and large-duty choppers are still in service. This heralds their original design from the '50s and '60s. As Doc I states in his quote above, these insertions and extractions were dangerous business. The enemy could see them coming from miles away. Because of this, there were over five thousand KIA pilots and crew who manned these helicopters.

Jamison Brothers
Glenside, PA
1964-1972

'Tis after death that we measure men.
—James Barron Hope

Introduction to the Interview

Glenside, Pennsylvania was the home of residence to the Jamison Family. Lawrence (Lonnie) and Margaret (Betty) Jamison were married at St. Luke's Church in Glenside and bore ten children—eight boys and two girls. Not unusual for a Catholic family in the 1940s and 1950s. The parents along with the other five siblings supported their brothers during their course of duty. Billy and Frank served in Southeast Asia while Lon (the oldest and the one interviewed below), Jack, and Jim were all stateside. Mr. Jamison passed away in 1981, and Betty joined her husband in 2002. Five of the Jamison boys served in the Army continuously from 1964 to 1972. Billy Jamison received four out of nine of the highest honors the US Army can bestow on a soldier. I actually went to the same high school (Bishop McDevitt High School) as several of the Jamisons. Since the boys were a few years older, their service to our country somehow got lost in the shuffle. Not anymore.

While having breakfast with my friend, Jim Hargadon, one morning in September 2010, a guy walked in to the restaurant where we were eating and looked my way. He looked familiar, with a very particular "strut" and in very good physical shape. I think we both knew at that point our paths had crossed before. After finishing my meal, I walked over to him. Jim had already told me who he was. When I identified myself, he immediately stood up and shook my hand. James Sullivan, who graduated with my brother George from BMHS in 1969, was one of the best point guards ever to come out of the Catholic League Northern Division. He married Katie, who was Billy's younger sister.

So we started reminiscing for a few minutes. Then he told me about his brother-in-law, Billy. Within a few weeks, the initial draft of this chapter was written and forwarded to Lon. Looking at the draft dates, the trail on where all the boys were stationed, it begs the question—did the government grant Jim, Lon, and Jack a reprieve since Frank and Billy were already in Southeast Asia? Lon believes Divine Providence should receive the credit.

Interview with Lon Jamison

I was drafted along with Jack, Frank, and Jimmy. I went down to Fort Jackson, South Carolina, for a week. They had an overflow there. It was July 1964. From there, we moved to Fort Gordon, Georgia. Fifty-two other draftees and I ended up in a company with a bunch of Southern National Guards and because of an overflow at Fort Gordon were assigned to an AIT Regiment for our basic training.

I was in basic training during the Gulf of Tonkin incident (August 1964). The Drill Instructors (DIs) made a lot of noise about how much cannon fodder would be coming from our ranks, but they were already building up significantly. The train that I was on from Thirtieth Street in Philadelphia started in Boston and just kept adding cars. It was 99 percent draftees or kids going into the service. When we got down to Fort Jackson, they give you twenty bucks and walk you to the barbershop. You paid the barber five bucks, and you had no hair left in seconds. After basic, I got transferred to Fort Knox. As usual, they couldn't figure out what the hell to do with me for a couple of months. Then I ended up working at what they called the separation and transfer point where they discharge people every day. That's what I worked on—a clerical job. I put a lot of time in down there because of what happened especially as things kicked up in 1965 and 1966. You would get shipments of guys coming back with less than three months, and they hit Fort Ord, California, and they'd get an overflow. They just couldn't handle it, and they'd ship them into Fort Knox. Those guys would arrive all hours of the day and night and often we would work around the clock to make sure they got out as quickly as possible. My service was from July 1964 to July 1966.

Jackie was drafted in October 1965. After basic, he was trained to be an Air Traffic Controller at Keesler AFB in Biloxi, Mississippi. During this time, he was married, and his wife, Kathy, moved south with him for the duration. After graduation, Jack was assigned as an air traffic controller at the Army Helicopter Pilot Training Center at Fort Rucker, Alabama.

Frankie went in from September 1968 to May 1970. After basic, Frank was sent to Engineering School at Fort Belvoir, Virginia. After that, he was assigned to the 528th Engineering Battalion and shipped to Thailand. This was located right on the Gulf of Siam and immediately adjacent to a major B-52 AFB. Frank and the 528th worked on building and maintaining the port and shipyard where all supply ships stopped before going on to Vietnam.

Jimmie was drafted in September 1969 and served on active duty until June 1971. After basic, he was sent to Combat Medic School at Fort Sam Houston, Texas. Upon completion, Jim was the only one in his battalion not sent to Vietnam. Rather, he was assigned to Martin Army Hospital, Physical Examination Center, at Fort Benning, Georgia. While there, he was selected to be the medic on a train carrying nerve gas for disposal at sea in concrete vaults. Jim had to check often to make sure the canaries and rabbits were alive and kicking. With the exception of threats by Lester Maddox to stop the train in Macon, Georgia, this one-week trip was fortunately uneventful.

That's a brief rundown on the four of us who were drafted. There were a lot of kids drafted back then from all over the country; many from Pennsylvania. There were quite a few from Pennsylvania (eight hundred KIA) that did not make it back. They are on the Wall in DC as well as the Wall in Philadelphia, Pennsylvania.

William Jamison

Bill volunteered for the Reserve Officers' Training Corps (ROTC) upon entering Temple University, Philadelphia, Pennsylvania. In May 1969, Bill graduated from Temple with a degree in Business Administration and simultaneously was commissioned a second lieutenant in the US Army. During his years at Temple and in the ROTC, Bill took flying lessons and earned his pilot's license on fixed wing aircraft.

On 5 July 1969, Bill entered active-duty military service and was sent immediately to Fort Benning, Georgia, where he successfully completed the

Infantry Officer Basic Course on 9 September 1969. He was then assigned to the United States Army Primary Helicopter School at Fort Wolters, Texas, where he completed the Officer Rotary Wing Aviator Course on 13 February 1970. Then Bill was sent to the United States Army Aviation School at Fort Rucker, Alabama, where he successfully completed the Officer Rotary Wing Aviator Course (Counter Insurgency) on 16 June 1970.

From 24 July 1970 through 22 July 1971, Bill served in Vietnam mostly with A Company, 227th Assault Helicopter Battalion, and First Cavalry Division Airmobile. The unit's call sign was "Chickenman." In early 1971, Bill was selected by the Battalion CO to be the Battalion Headquarters & Headquarters Company executive officer and, in March 1971, was made the commanding officer. Subsequently, Bill was again assigned to Alpha Company, 227th Assault Helicopter Battalion. This time with the 52nd ABC (Combat Aviation Battalion) he continued his pilot duties on combat, supply, and resupply, and medevac missions including missions in Laos and Cambodia and strictly "volunteer" missions.

Bill returned to the states and was again assigned to Fort Benning, Georgia, where his duties included evaluating recommendations for an All-Volunteer Army. Bill was discharged from active duty on 7 March 1972 with the rank of a captain.

For his service, he was awarded with the following:

*The Distinguished Flying Cross
*The Bronze Star
*The Air Medal
*The Army Commendation Medal
*Vietnam Service Medal
*Republic of Vietnam Campaign Medal
*National Defense Service Medal
*The Army Aviator Badge
*Two Overseas Bars

Billy's Letters Home While in Country
Letter dated 25 August 1969 to a brother—Fort Benning, GA:

You'll never get used to being away from home—no Jamison ever will. The Army won't make a man out of you. That's for you to do for yourself. The Hippies of the Now Generation are classic proof of this. That the Army will make a man out of you is a well-preserved myth . . . I can tell you this as a brother, however. Be moral—you'll find it pays big dividends in the long run both for yourself and for those who love you. This is what really counts—it is the basis of life. Life without morality is not worth living. If you can be moral, then you are a man.

Letter dated 3 August 1970—Lai Khe, Vietnam:

American Airlines got me into San Francisco on schedule and I got a bus to Travis AFB. I ran into a few of the guys I went to flight school with—and we took off from Travis with about 200 E-3's. We made stops in Anchorage, Alaska, and then Yokota, Japan before landing at Bien Hoa AFB . . . We officers found ourselves aboard an air-conditioned Army bus . . . to Long Binh . . . the replacement center for officers. On Monday (27 July) orders came down assigning me to the First Cavalry Division. They sent me down to Bien Hoa again . . . I spent some time in the Cav's in country jungle school . . . On Saturday morning (1 Aug), I boarded a Chinook for Phuoc Vinh where the Cav has its real headquarters . . . Saturday afternoon, I was assigned to the 227th Aviation Battalion (Assault Helicopter) . . . Late Saturday afternoon found me aboard a Huey and headed for Lai Khe . . . which is further west. I consider myself very fortunate now that I am a member of Alpha Company—227th Aviation Battalion (Assault Helicopter).

First Cavalry Division (Airmobile). The First Cav Division, in my opinion and many others, is the best, most decisive unit in the world. It has almost twenty-one thousand men and I don't know how many helicopters. It is daily rewriting the books of warfare by showing just what the airmobile division is capable of doing . . . Co. A of the 227th—is generally conceded to be the best company in the division. Believe me, I am happy and proud to be here . . . I was made a section leader for one of the company's two platoons. I live in a hooch (living quarters) with about six other officers . . . We are situated right in the middle of a rubber plantation. Yesterday—Sunday—I took my in country check ride and it really felt good to be back on the controls again. It was a pretty satisfying ride for my first in Vietnam as we medevaced four little Vietnamese kids from Lai Khe to Bien

Hoa. It made me feel that I was doing something worthwhile and it certainly resolved—for me anyway—most of the stateside arguments against our presence here. I am as far away from home as you can get . . . Be assured that I'm okay and that I will stay that way. I think I can do a job over here and I wouldn't feel right if I wasn't here now.

Letter dated 3 January 1971—Lai Khe, Vietnam:

Despite the truces on Christmas and New Year's, my company has been as busy as ever. We have done a great deal of flying over the course of the past ten days. Christmas Eve:

I was scheduled to fly the flare bird and spent the night in an on-call status . . . Christmas Day: The major saw to it that a bird was launched to get a couple of chaplains from Phuoc Vinh and we had Mass on Christmas night. In the afternoon, we hosted about seventy orphans from the neighboring village of Ben Cat at a Christmas party in the mess hall. This really proved to be the highlight of my Christmas—the food we served them and the little toys we gave them were probably the most meaningful gifts I ever gave to anyone. The differences in our languages proved to be no barrier at all. As they sang song after song for us in their own language, you could still recognize the unmistakable sounds of Silent Night, Noel, etc. The whole show was plain and simple and heartwarming. I spent New Year's Day flying around Loc Ninh in support of the ARVNs. Due to the truce, there were no offensive operations allowed—on our side anyway—so I spent a few hours flying a Vietnamese colonel around scouting landing zones to be used once the cease-fire ended. Yesterday, the second of the New Year, I picked up about forty "Chieu Hois"—people who have decided to surrender. They took advantage of the truce to walk into a log site that some grunts had set up on New Year's Day. We ferried them back to FSB (Fire Support Base) Green and then a Chinook took them to Song Be for relocation. They were mostly women and children and most of the kids were unclothed and suffering from malnutrition. They were really a sorry sight. One little girl out of this group was the most beautiful little girl I have ever seen. She was really cute despite the fact that she was scared to no end by her first ride on a helicopter . . . I'm happy . . . because I know that all those people that we hauled in yesterday will enjoy a much better life now that they will be getting a helping hand from America.

Family

I believe having any of your kids away when you come from a large, tight-knit family had to be very hard for my mother and father. Having many away at once—Jack and I overlapped; then Frank, Jimmy, and Billy overlapped as well. I think there were the typical worries any parent would have when their child goes away anywhere. I think their real heartache was with Bill in Vietnam. I believe they wrote to each other frequently, but having a child in Vietnam was probably extremely stressful for them or any other parents. Frank (who was in Thailand) has never talked about anything having to do with combat, so I think he was removed from that.

How did Vietnam shape your post war life?

I goofed around for a month after I came home and then I went right back to work with my former employer. I remained at this firm for sixteen years. Then moved to Rhode Island where I currently reside. To your question—our government and our people were absolutely correct going into Vietnam and trying to help the Vietnamese. I think it was the right thing to do, and I have been forever absolutely pissed off at the way this country allowed our soldiers to get vilified. Further, the way we abandoned the people of Vietnam, Laos, Cambodia, and Thailand. It was absolutely awful and one of the most disgraceful periods in this country's history. And at no time more so than in 1975 when our Congress refused President Ford's request for financial assistance—not military, not boots on the ground, just money—mandated by our promises to South Vietnam in the Peace Treaty that in the event North Vietnam invaded South Vietnam, we would provide adequate financial help. Our Congress, for nothing more than political reasons, refused to honor the word of the United States to another country in desperate need, and thus, who can forget the Fall of Saigon and all those poor people trying to escape certain death by clinging to our helicopters? How do those politicians sleep at night? To be candid with you, if you look at things, the last time this country declared war was WWII. Since then we've had a truce in Korea and kind of a half-assed peace agreement when Nixon was being impeached, negotiated by Kissinger to I think the country's detriment. And they pardoned all those draft dodgers that I thought was a horrific mistake.

You go from Vietnam where you ended up with a truce through to where we are today, and we haven't successfully prosecuted a war, in my opinion, since WWII. I don't think any of them have ended conclusively, and no other war has been declared which I think is an absolute disgrace and shows that you have a Congress loaded with a bunch of cowards. You have presidents that won't ask for war to be declared.

Fifty percent of the country today would not fight even if Al Qaeda was standing there pointing a gun at their wife. I'm very, very upset where the country's headed, and I think a lot of it has to do with what was fomented and allowed to exist during Vietnam.

I think the Vietnam War was won militarily and lost by a bunch of weak-kneed politicians and long-haired hippie bastards afraid of being drafted, who were egged on by a commie-infiltrated academia, many of whom are still there. What this country has to recognize is that if we are going to send troops to war—our young men and women—then they deserve the full and unequivocal support of this country and all our people. We must fight to win. We must stop being appeasers. We must not put our troops into positions where they cannot act to win, but place them where they can defend themselves and prosecute the war successfully. We must have military leaders who do not put their careers and pensions ahead of their constitutional duties—we already have that with too many politicians in our government at all levels.

I think Jack, Frank, and Jim would basically agree. If Bill were here, he would definitely be upset. I think he was devastated when Saigon was lost. I think he had formed a bond with many of the Vietnamese people with whom he came in contact, and I think he would have been heartbroken. I think the situation today would have made it even worse for him.

The night Billy went missing

Bill never married and did not have a family of his own. He was thirty-three when he disappeared on 27 March 1981 while living in Roselle Park near Elizabeth, New Jersey. He was vice president of a die-casting company in Kenilworth, New Jersey. What we know is that he left work at his normal time around 1800 and went to a restaurant for dinner. We're not sure whether he then went back to his apartment in Roselle Park. The next thing we know is that he met friends at the lounge in the Linden Lanes in Linden, New Jersey, around 2000 and then had something to eat at the St. George Diner, also in Linden, around 0100-0200. That was the last that anyone we know of saw him or heard from him. His company car has never been recovered.

The family would like to hear from anyone who has information on the whereabouts of Bill. His website (listed at the beginning of this chapter) has contact information.

Current Day

Frank is the owner and president of Jamison Masonry Restoration out of Oreland, Pennsylvania. I am retired with four children. Jackie is semi-retired and has three kids. Jim also has three as well and works with Jamison Masonry Restorations in historic restoration and preservation. We had a family get-together down at the shore this year. Not everybody made it, but I'd say more than half the family. Most of the family lives around the Philadelphia and New Jersey area, so they get together more frequently than, say, my family and I (Rhode Island) or Charlie, who lives north of San Diego with his family. Michael still lives in Glenside.

Advice to someone considering a military career

Well, I would say if you want to serve your country, I think the military's one of the best ways to do it. However, it is also one of the most hazardous ways to do it. I believe it has the potential to have the poorest reward financially (although the money and benefits today are not too shabby compared to what we were paid) and from an advancement perspective. In order to maximize your potential to the military, one truly needs to give the military academies a very serious look, and for personal gain, as well as evaluate what training will be most advantageous to a civilian employer. Not too many companies looking for gunners hanging out a helicopter door.

The Boys Who Served

Billy DOB 29/4/1947
Served as a helicopter pilot in Vietnam with Co. A, 227th Assault Helicopter Battalion of the First Cavalry and the Fifty-Second Aviation Battalion. Was XO and CO of the HHC of the First Cavalry in 1971. Was lead

investigator on two aircraft crashes and was commended for clearing the pilots in one instance by finding a single bullet hole in the speed governor (mechanism to control rotor speed). Finished active duty at Fort Benning and was discharged with the rank of captain.

Frank DOB 21/11/1948

He served with the 528th Engineers in Thailand, on the Gulf of Siam. All ships stopped here before proceeding to Vietnam. Frank was a specialist 4 (E-4) at time of separation from active duty.

Lon DOB 9/1/1943

Lon served at Fort Knox, Kentucky, at the US Army Armor Center in Charlie Company Special Troops. He was personnel and finance Specialist. Honorably discharged specialist 5 (E-5).

Jack DOB 17/11/1945

Jack was an air traffic controller for Helicopter Pilot Training in Fort Rucker, Alabama, and achieved the rank of Specialist 5 (E-5).

Jim (Melvin) DOB 19/6/1951

Jimmy trained at Fort Bragg, North Carolina. He was a specialist 4 (E-4) at the time of separation of duty. Jimmy was the only one in his battalion not assigned to immediate duty in Vietnam.

Closing Comments

To live in the hearts we leave behind, is never to have died.
—Thomas Campbell

While writing this section on 26 March 2011, I received a call from my brother, Peter, at 0900 who was having breakfast with our friend David Newns. It was almost six months to the day that I had met Jimmy Sullivan (Lon Jamison's brother-in-law). David was very friendly with the Jamison family. Another friend of the Jamison's, who walked in to have breakfast and after Peter and David mentioned the book, was immediately interested as he was friendly with the family as well.

The man who was interested was Jerry Hagarty, older brother of my friend Lou Hagarty. I was meeting them both at the Philadelphia Turf Club in a few hours.

Here is the catch—Jerry and I were having a cigarette outside the Turf Club. I met a vet (Herb) who was in the First Cavalry Division in 1970 for one tour. He made the exact same comments about combat that Homer Steedly mentioned in chapter 2 about combat—"95 percent boredom followed by hell on earth."

Another situation also blends in with Homer and Herb's statements while driving through North Carolina in June 2010. A gas station in Appalachia had only two pumping units. I was next to a man who had an impeccable-looking Harley Davidson in his trailer that was attached to a Chevy Blazer. I casually asked him how much he "rode." Responding to my question, he went on about his trips with buddies from time to time who were retired state troopers and police officers. He said it was always difficult to stay with them because they rode so fast. When I asked him if they were Vietnam vets, he said, "How did you guess that? These fellows tell me the only way they can relate back to their experiences in 'Nam and get the incredible 'high' of combat is to ride like the devil."

So quantum physics and intentionality at work here? Situations like these continue to happen to me since 23 December 2009.

CHAPTER SIX
Healers

Surgeons, Nurses, Medics, and Corpsmen

Dedicated to George Reed
Lance Corporal, United States Marine Corps
G Company, Second Battalion, Third Marine Regiment, Third
Marine Division

The military, which prided itself on the records it kept in Vietnam—counting the enemy number of weapons captured, for example—cannot to this day say with certainty how many women served. The Army that sent them never bothered to count them. The estimate most frequently given is that a total of 7,500 served in the military in Vietnam.

—Laura Palmer, *Shrapnel in the Heart*

Thousands of Americans moved to Canada in the '60s and '70s to avoid the draft. Of the conscientious objectors who stayed and intended not to be combatants, men choose the "healer" route so they could help those in need, but not be in the fray. So they thought.

A corpsman was a Navy-trained soldier who was assigned to a Marine Corps combat unit. On the ground, corpsmen were usually positioned in the middle of the squad when in country. If assigned to a chopper, they rarely, if ever, stepped foot on soil, serving the wounded and dying in the air en route to a carrier, an LPH (Landing Platform Helicopter), or a field hospital. Army medics were also stationed between the point man and the soldier in the rear, but these men (like the corpsmen) became rifleman first when their unit was engaged with the enemy. Doctors were assigned to combat units either in direct support (with medics as underlings) or in field hospitals (with both nurses and medics). Among them all, the healers were in dangerous roles. The enemy new, that if you took out a medic or corpsman, it was comparable to wounding or killing half a dozen or more men.

There are eight women whose names are carved into the black granite wall in DC. The impact of these nurses who served in Southeast Asia cannot be fully measured. My aim from the beginning was to publish an interview with a nurse who served in Vietnam. This goal was never achieved.

Introduction to the Interviews

Of all the veterans and people I met, the "healers"—those who were in the business of saving lives, were some of the most fascinating. After meeting then interviewing Carmelo, it was Steve Knuboff, Ed Gehringer, John Murphy, and Doctor Richard Odom. Army Medic Steve Knuboff decided not to release his interview. The written word of our dialogue was just too painful to read. However, on 3 May 2010 after our breakfast together in San Diego, he was gracious enough to allow me to use his quotes.

These "healers" collectively saved hundreds upon hundreds of lives. Be it in a field hospital behind the lines, in a medevac helicopter, or on the ground, all these specially trained personnel provided lifesaving treatment for their injured buddies and patients. DUSTOFFs (**D**istinguished **U**nwavering **S**ervice **T**o **O**ur **F**oreign **F**orces), were by far one of the most dangerous duties in the war. Marine, Air Force, or Army Huey's (Bell UH-IH-Iroquois helicopter) would be called in to rescue or pick up injured soldiers in the field. Depending on the source, it is estimated that over 40 percent of the eleven thousand plus helicopters that served in Vietnam were damaged or destroyed. At any given time, there may have been more Huey's on the ground and damaged than in the air or ready for service.

Doc I (Carmelo Infantino) was interesting when we met in Atlanta. He spent a lot of time sizing me up. Before agreeing to the subsequent five-hour interview on an unusual snow-bound February Southern day, he made it very clear; "I will not allow you to print or publish anything without my approval. No one, ever, will say anything that casts shadows or cinders on my fellow corpsmen, serviceman, and Vietnam veterans if I can intercede." On the receiving end of this, it appeared that Doc was ready to walk ten paces, turn, and fire. I didn't have a gun, and I was intimidated to say the least. That instance occurred exactly one year before I wrote this passage. Now, each and every time, before Carmelo hangs up from one of our countless phone calls, he says, "Love you, bro." I think I literally dodged a bullet.

Doc K (Steve Knuboff) was also very reluctant to complete an interview. I have dedicated the Afterword to Steve because of the countless issues he has resulting directly from his combat experience. One example: While Steve and his good friend, Nick Mihaescu, were meeting late in 2009, Steve vented to Nick. The Army company medic (each company had platoon medics as well) that replaced Steve in country was killed just a few days after Doc K's tour was over. His replacement received the Medal of Honor for his actions (PFC David Winder, *Vietnam Memorial Panel 10W Line 037*). Other unit members were also KIA in that engagement. Steve said to Nick, "I should have stayed. Maybe I could have saved all those guys." Nick's response was revealing, stating, "If you had stayed, we wouldn't be having this beer forty years later." Every time Steve and I liaise, either via e-mail or phone, I always tell him there are many of us who are praying for him.

Thanks to Hank and Barbara Cavalier (née Ansel—who I grew up with), Colonel Odom presented himself. Hank knew I was looking for surgeons who were in Vietnam and Richard Odom was his doctor for a stint. Living in San Francisco, it was yet another Pacific trip that required planning from three thousand miles away. Dr. Odom's interview is unique, particularly since he was involved in the initial insertion of the newly created First Cavalry Division in 1965. The war was heating up and the battle in the Ia Drang Valley became the first major American action against the North Vietnamese Regular Army. This was the same engagement that Colonel Marm received his Medal of Honor. *We Were Soldiers,* starring Mel Gibson, was the 2003 film that many vets say is the only true depiction of a ground battle in Vietnam up to that point. At six feet and six inches, Richard is the only veteran that I was able to see eye to eye.

Corpsman John Murphy was another Pacific vet resident. I actually found him online looking for psychiatrists for my initial PTSD section. His wife, Beth, directed me to her husband for the "healer" interviews. With the exception of my Atlanta connection friends in this book, John and I go back and forth as much as anyone. A current-day lawyer at sixty-three, he is going back to medical school to become a doctor. People ask me where I get my energy. That question needs to be posed to John as well.

Combat medic Ed "Dutch" Gehringer sadly was never able to confirm his interview copy. What a great guy. Born and raised in Kutztown, Pennsylvania. Ed lost quite a few friends while in Southeast Asia. Got his reverse "ticket to ride" after taking shrapnel in his head, back, neck, legs, and feet. Ed just retired, from all places, the United States Post Office as a letter carrier for thirty years! There are pieces of lead still in his feet and body. I'm not quite sure if Henry Shrapnel, the German inventor in 1784 of antipersonnel projectiles, ever would have dreamed Ed would spite his invention. God bless you Ed.

RICHARD ODOM

Colonel/Surgeon (Ret.), United States Army
Semper Vigilans: *"Vigilant Always"*
First Battalion Eighth Cavalry Regiment First Cavalry Division
Home of Record: Ahoskie, NC
Home of Residence: San Francisco, CA
DOB: 04 October 1937
Conducted on 27 May 2010
Met Richard 06 October 2010 in CA
Wake Forest University, Wake Forest Medical School

> *Thru this door pass the most deserving people in Vietnam—Our Patients.*
>
> **—Sign at Câm Mang Vỏ Khỏ;
> Ninety-Third Evacuation Hospital**

Growing Up

I was born in 1937 in a small rural town in Eastern North Carolina named Ahoskie. It was a town of about three thousand people, and I was raised on a dairy farm. During World War II, my father did not go to the military. He was considered a critical community person because of the dairy farm and delivering milk to the community. Therefore, he was not drafted. However, three of my uncles were drafted in WWII. One of them was a naval medical officer, and the other two an Army medical officer and Army enlisted man.

Growing up I was very interested in sports and fortunate to be a good student as well. Sports were my major interest when I was in high school, and I played football, basketball, and baseball. I received All State Honors in both football and basketball. During my senior year in high school, I played football in the North Carolina Shrine Bowl game. I was 6 foot 5 and ½ and weighed 175. I was playing against men from much larger schools, and I was from the smallest athletic division in North Carolina. As a result of that game, I recognized immediately that I was not going to spend four years in college playing against tackles who weighed 230 pounds and linebackers who weighed 215 pounds. I did not think I had the ability to survive four years of that type of contact. When I returned home from the game, I was determined to really concentrate on basketball. Fortunately, I received multiple football and basketball scholarships as well as a few academic scholarships. I made the decision to attend Wake Forest University where I received a four-year athletic scholarship. As I progressed through college, I applied to only one medical school, Wake Forest School of Medicine, as I did not think I could matriculate elsewhere if I were unacceptable to my undergraduate school, which I greatly appreciated and enjoyed. After medical school, I served an internship at the University of Florida from 1963 to 1964. In 1963 following Kennedy's assassination, President Johnson announced that he would build up our military as we were about to engage in combat in South Vietnam. I was drafted during my internship at the University of Florida, but finished that program in 1964 and reported to the United States Army in August 1964.

In view of the fact that I was born in a small county in North Carolina and the fact that doctors were being drafted, I knew that I was a prime candidate since there were only two physicians from my particular county. The other physician was a year senior to me, but he had more political connections, and I realized I was going to be selected by the draft. I attempted to enroll in the Berry Plan for the Navy, which would have deferred me throughout my residency training, but at that time, only 25 percent of physicians who applied were accepted. I was not accepted and received orders to report to Fort Sam Houston, Texas, following my internship for basic training for physicians. After I completed basic training, I was assigned to Fort Bliss, Texas, for one year. I then joined the First Cavalry Division at Fort Benning, Georgia, as a battalion surgeon for an Airborne Infantry Unit. The First of the Eighth Cavalry, the Fighting Mustangs. After arrival at Fort Benning, my second child was born at the military hospital on 21 July 1965. My unit deployed to South Vietnam, and we sailed from Savannah, Georgia, through the Panama Canal to the Republic of South Vietnam.

Vietnam

I learned a tremendous amount about medicine and what occurs during wars both good as well as bad. Unfortunately, a lot of people are killed unnecessarily from accidents. One major, an artillery officer, walked in front of an artillery gun and got hit with a shell, killing him instantly. A lieutenant colonel was hastily taking a flight in an observer helicopter, but he did not free up the runners at the base of the Huey, and it was caught under a root, turning over, the blade coming back through the bubble and killing him. The younger soldiers would not appropriately clear the foxholes of trees and bushes, and on at least one occasion, a hand grenade was thrown out, and it bounced back in the foxhole with fatal results. Such minor occurrences such as Jeep accidents occurred, faulty ammunition exiting the mortar tube, exploding just above the tube and injuring many soldiers. Hand grenades being poorly attached to the vest would fall off some of the soldiers preparing for combat, and numerous avoidable events happened in my particular battalion. Rarely, fragging (attacking a superior officer in one's chain of command with the intent to kill that officer with a fragmentation grenade—thus the name) would occur in our battalion. However, a second lieutenant, who went to school at Wake Forest, was intentionally shot by friendly fire during a mission. It was astonishing to see how many of our battalion members were injured and killed by avoidable accidents.

From a medical standpoint, I saw a large number of diseases that I never experienced while in the United States. Many of these diseases we heard about in medical school, but I never had any idea that I would actually experience so many tropical diseases such as malaria, scrub typhus, and sexually transmitted diseases. While we took prophylactic anti-malaria drugs, many of our soldiers would acquire malaria when we would go out on missions in certain parts of central Vietnam. Unfortunately, many cases of malaria were of the resistant type, and our drugs were not extremely effective. Some of the soldiers would develop severe complications, such as black water fever, which was occasionally fatal. Also, we would come back from field operations in areas that were heavily infested with mosquitoes, and my unit alone would have fifty to seventy-five cases a week. The number of sexually transmitted disease cases was so high that our military leaders did not want to report the high incidence. I realized that, even in the heat of battle, many of the prostitutes in our location would visit the men on the front line in their foxholes at night. In the town of An Khe, we set up a small secure area that we called Sin City so that the prostitutes could be gathered in one area. Fortunately, we were able to control these villages by examining the prostitutes on a regular basis. I became an expert in diagnosing and treating STDs.

In battalion, we had a medical unit that belonged to the headquarters company. There were approximately thirty to forty medics, and I was the head of that unit as a doctor. During combat operations, a company comprised of 160 to 180 men would go out on search and destroy missions, and the medics in my unit would be assigned to these companies for basic medical coverage. We made certain that there were enough medics for combat operations to provide the necessary support.

During my year in Vietnam, there were some major battles including the Ia Drang Valley engagement and in Bong Son Valley in which one of our units (First Battalion, Seventh Cavalry Regiment, First Cavalry Division) were inserted, then surrounded by 2,000 NVA regulars. It was a vicious battle as we were only able to get a small number of troops into the area. The airmobile group was the new cavalry arm of the Army and troops were inserted via helicopters. Our troops fought valiantly and, with less than 200 soldiers, they successfully fought off and killed more than 1,500 NVA. My unit was back up to the First of the Seventh Cavalry and it was an extremely harrowing experience. Even with the difficulty of search and destroy missions, and the time needed to rest and recover, morale was pretty good at the time. Most of our troopers were airborne infantry soldiers who were extremely loyal and dedicated. At that time, there was not a lot of marijuana or other drugs that were obvious to me.

In August 1965, as my first year of service was ending, and I was leaving the jungle on a Chinook helicopter, we took fire from below. A sergeant later pointed out to me that a bullet came through the helicopter, landing within twelve inches of my head. I felt very fortunate to get through this year without serious illness or injury.

Prior to being drafted and experiencing my first two years in the military, I knew that I wanted to train in dermatology, but because I was in Vietnam, I did not have the opportunity to interview for any of the training programs. So when I returned home after my two years of service was over, I did not have a permanent position. I was not particularly interested in working in the emergency room for a year in preparation for my training and the Army offered me a residency position in dermatology at any of the four programs training dermatologists. These were at Walter Reed, Brooke, and Fitzsimmons Army Medical Centers. At that point, I decided to remain in the Army for my training in dermatology if I could enter the program at Walter Reed Army Medical Center. Being a Southerner, I knew that institution had an outstanding reputation. I was aware that I would have a great clinical experience because of the influx of diseases from all over the world that would come through Walter Reed. The military pay at that time was reasonable especially for trainees in residency programs as compared to civilian programs, and I realized that I could incur a three-year obligation for the three years I trained at Walter Reed. Soon after arrival there, I made rank of major and had a wonderful and exciting experience during my time at this outstanding institution.

My military experience was exceptional and special because I had the opportunity to experience a broad scope of the medical field. The medical experience in Vietnam was unique because I saw so many tropical diseases, unusual types of injuries such as punji sticks, and illnesses among the indigenous populations as well as our soldiers. It was a good experience to take my medics into the villages of South Vietnam and hold sick call where we would see many different diseases in such a short period of time. I developed a special interest in infectious diseases as well as fungal infections that were widespread and extraordinary sexually transmitted diseases that are not often seen in the United States. The traumatic injuries and wounds that occurred during combat operations were also advanced and extremely serious and life-threatening. Fortunately, our medical evacuation system was so superior to WWII and Korea because we had helicopters for rapid evacuation from the field to our direct advanced medical companies. Many lives were saved because of this system. The medical experiences in Vietnam also piqued my interest in dermatology because of the skin diseases caused by bacteria, viruses, and fungi as well as coetaneous manifestations of some of the tropical diseases that were primarily systemic in nature. The experience was invaluable, and to this date, it has remained a valuable source of information and experience.

How did Vietnam shape your life?

I did not resist being drafted during the infancy of the Vietnam era. I was a Southerner, and many of my family members had been involved with WWII and Korea. Knowing someone had to provide medical services to our soldiers, I was willing and excited to be one of those individuals. Following my three years of training at Walter Reed, I was reassigned to the 130th Station Hospital in Heidelberg, Germany, where I was the chief of dermatology. I had a young corpsman who worked with me in the dermatology clinic, and during my first year, I saw thirty to fifty patients daily for a total of about ten thousand patients my first year. Soon after my arrival in Germany, my youngest daughter was born at the 130th Station Hospital, and she was diagnosed with sensor neural hearing loss (deafness) when she was six months old. I requested compassionate reassignment and after sixteen months in Heidelberg, I was reassigned to Letterman Army Medical Center, a major hospital in San Francisco. Here there was a residency training program in dermatology, and I was assigned as the assistant chief upon my arrival. Following the chief of dermatology resignation upon retirement, I became the head of the department. My sole job was to train military physicians in the specialty of dermatology. At Letterman, we had a number of residencies including internal medicine, psychiatry, pediatrics, dermatology, OB/GYN, ophthalmology, as well as other specialties. It was a major teaching hospital for the US Army. I had a wonderful experience there, and it was another great opportunity for me to become involved as an academic dermatologist. My daughter was able to participate in a federally funded program in Marin County. I commuted daily to the Presidio and felt truly fortunate since I was able to serve out my twenty years at Letterman. I was a Republican well into my sixties because my upbringing basically instilled in me a strong work ethic, and I was resentful of paying high taxes and supporting individuals who were less fortunate than I. After my experience in Vietnam, I thought to myself, *we made that mistake once, but I don't think we'll ever do that again as a country.*

I always enjoyed the many interactions with the wide variety of individuals in the military. I continued my athletic activities and especially enjoyed participating in all the opportunities that the military offered in team sports. Basketball was particularly a continuing pleasure of mine. I grew up in an extremely prejudicial environment, and as the years passed, my experiences in the Army taught me that everyone had something to offer and each one deserves respect. My years in Vietnam as well as many experiences I witnessed during my childhood years showed me the real value in trusting other people even though they are different from me in many ways. In Vietnam, we learned to depend on and support one another equally. In a life-and-death situation, we all bleed the same color blood, and each and every individual wants to return home to his or her loved ones. While living in Silver Spring, Maryland, Martin Luther King Jr. was assassinated. These were very uncomfortable and unsettling times in Washington DC. This event affected me deeply as I would have nightmares about racial issues no doubt stemming from my experience in childhood.

Nevertheless, all of my energy over the next fifteen years went into my job as a full-time teacher in the military. I was separated from my first wife in 1981 and remarried in 1983. My new wife actually had been a Vietnam professor, and she never thought she would marry a military man. She was a very liberal person, and for years, we had a number of conversations about conservatism; and fortunately, these discussions were provocative and always led to a lot of soul-searching on my part. It was very easy for me to see the difference between a boy from North Carolina and a girl from Marin County, California. I learned that wars are not initiated by military people, but rather by politicians. I felt that the politicians were weak and not capable of standing up for their constituents. I asked myself, "Who are the people who serve in wars and get killed or maimed or end up with PTSD? Who are the people who allow these wars to get started in the first place? Have they served in the military? Do their sons and daughters serve?" I understand from my own experiences that it is very important to have political connections, money, and friends in the right places.

The turning point in my life came when we invaded Iraq. I was so discouraged; all I could visualize was Vietnam all over again. I wanted our military forces to be successful, but it went on and on. I was also very discouraged knowing that companies like Halliburton were making obscene amounts of money. Stories about how much companies charged American soldiers for breakfast and lunch. It almost made me nauseous that American companies were profiting off the lives and money that our government was providing. It was unbelievable that our country would repeat the same mistakes forty years later. This made for a tremendous change in my behavior and feelings about our country. We have people who are neglected, and we don't support them, and we are even resentful about providing them health care. I became an avid Obama supporter.

Even though I would have preferred not to spend a year in combat, I did develop a great appreciation for the Vietnamese people and, particularly, the villagers among the Montagnard population. Several medics and I (when we were in base camp) would go out into these areas and see children and adults on a weekly basis. A number of my fellow soldiers would say, "Don't you realize you are probably treating VC who are our enemy?" I would respond, "Maybe so, but at least it is a service to people who never had service before."

I believe that our uniformed military are the most professional in the world. During Vietnam, however, the military was placed in a very compromising position. We had the capability of ending the conflict in weeks if the Air Force was allowed to bomb Haiphong Harbor. North Vietnam would have been rendered powerless. My understanding was that the United States was concerned about Russia and China entering the conflict. We sacrificed over fifty-eight thousand soldiers because of the limitations placed on the military.

I was transferred to the Presidio in 1971. There were many protests; it was at the height of the war. It was most unusual to be concerned about wearing a uniform because the population had a number of people who were more or less violently opposed to Vietnam. The war was blamed on the military, where, in truth, it was the politicians who controlled the events. The reason for many conflicts is financial, and as we see today, money remains the motivator. While I feel the entire war was a negative experience for the military, I felt positive about our troops and their professionalism while I was in Vietnam.

Advice to someone considering a military career

I'll tell you what I would tell any of my grandkids. First of all, I think it would be very important in your life if you did two years of voluntary service for your country. It doesn't have to be in the military. It could be in the Peace Corps or Indian health service—some other endeavor. This would give our young people a time to gain some important moments of maturation straight out of high school. It would help them decide a pathway for their future, be it academic or a trade or service. The military can teach certain skills and provide education in various fields, and the travel can be exceptional. My only hope is that if you choose the military path, you would not be subject to our politicians' whims. Each person has to choose for him/herself.

In recent years, I have developed beliefs that are more in line with Buddhism than any of my prior experiences with religions. The Buddhists believe in intelligence, compassion, and enlightenment rather than ignorance, greed, and anger. I would definitely want to live the remaining days of my life attempting to acquire intelligence, always expressing compassion, and striving for ultimate enlightenment.

Current day

My daughter was born deaf. I didn't know whether Agent Orange had anything to do with it. Plus, about a month ago, I read something about thyroid disease from dioxin; they studied that recently. I looked on the VA thing this morning about Agent Orange, and it's not yet listed as a disease. Where I was, we defoliated everything. I used to sit and watch the planes dropping and spraying it. I developed thyroid disease about fifteen years ago. I had it treated, and I take synthetic thyroid every day. I'm fine. I had Gray's disease, which they were talking about also.

My daughter, she's doing fine. She was educated through the public schools, went to the Liberal Arts School for the Deaf in Washington DC. She became a pharmacist. She can speak, do sign language, and read lips.

She just doesn't hear—hears very little. She has three children. They're all hearing. They're great kids.

I have two other daughters. One of them was born at Fort Benning when I was getting ready to go to Vietnam so I didn't see her the first year of her life. My oldest daughter was born when I was a senior in medical school. They're all living in San Rafael, which is just north of San Francisco. My first wife died of ovarian cancer about ten years ago.

My dermatology private practice is doing well. Originally this was started along with two previous friends and trainees in 2000. Since 2004, I developed my own private practice in Sonoma and work there to this day.

CARMELO INFANTINO (Doc I)

Navy Corpsman, United States Navy
Non Sibi Sed Patriae: *"Not self but country"*
Kilo Company Third Battalion First Marine Regiment First Marine Division
Home of Record: Fitchburg, MA
Home of Residence: Atlanta, GA
DOB: 20 March 1948
Interview conducted at McKendrick's Restaurant Atlanta, GA

> *In any moment of decision, the best thing you can do is the right
> thing, the next best thing is the wrong thing, and the worst thing
> you can do is nothing.*
> —Theodore Roosevelt

Growing Up

My name is Carmelo James Infantino. I was born in Fitchburg, Massachusetts
on 20 March 1948. Fitchburg was an industrial city of about 50,000 people.
I was the oldest of five children and my parents divorced when I was 10 years
old. I was from common stock, mixed nationalities. My neighborhood was
filled with blacks, Hispanics, Puerto Ricans, Hawaiians, Asians, Germans,
Irish, Scottish, Italians—a real melting pot of souls. I was a good student
in grammar school. The teachers would send notes home to my parents
saying, "Carmelo is a very intelligent child. He is first to finish his tests
with 100 percent. If there was any way that he could be placed in a private
school, it would be best for his education." Money was not available for
private school, so public school would have to do. When I took a test, it was
always on this premise – I looked at a question and I answered it. I would
not look back or correct an answer because I knew life would not allow such
things; to go back in time and to change everything was impossible.

When I was in high school, 10ᵗʰ grade, I quit. School was boring and
the students had their own little groups. There were the jocks, the rich, the
poor, the neighborhood gangs, socialites, musical groups, etc. What led to
my quitting school and joining the Navy was this.

In high school, I had a friend. His name was Brian Hascal. He was
physically challenged, walked horribly, and his speech was slurred. The
bullying jocks would tease and harass him regularly. One day they harassed
him to tears. I stood up and got between him and the bullies and I shamed

them by saying, "If your mother and your grandmothers were here, you would not act this way." I did this with many of the other students present and I knew most of the other students agreed with what I said. The bullies knew it too and they didn't like it. So, in the bathroom one day, three bullies picked me up and were going to push my head into the toilet. I was a very small framed person, 120 pounds, but very strong. I could go up a rope hand over hand which very few people could do. But I fought back against the three of them. I hurt them, they let me go, and they went to the principal and they complained that I was the aggressor. I got in trouble for doing the right thing. They harassed me by knocking books out of my hands in the hallways, tearing up my notebooks, messed with my lockers, my gym gear in sports, and one day I had had enough and I just brought my books down to the office and said, "I'm sorry, but I won't be coming here any more."

I went home and told my mom. I got a job at one of the plastic manufacturing plants for about a month or so and then at the Andel Shoe Factory putting soles on boots. I was also a short order cook. Then I worked at a place carting around pieces of material for women to sew. I wanted out of this boredom and to see the world. My father was in the Navy in WWII and so were all of my uncles on my mother's side except for one, Uncle Sage. He was Army and in both Normandy and North Africa. My reasoning was to join the Navy, see the world, have a GI Bill for education, and finish my military obligation.

Enlistment

I joined on 2 December 1965 on a kiddie cruise. If you joined before your 18th birthday, they would discharge you the day before your 21st birthday. Boot Camp was in the Great Lakes and so was the Navy Corps School. My first duty station was Chelsea Naval Hospital in Boston, MA. Several months later, I was sent to the Marines at Fort Montford, NC near Camp Lejeune (pronounced "Luh-jern" USMC Lt. General John Lejeune was born in Louisiana) for field training and weapons use, obstacles courses with live ammo, explosions, living in the woods, doing mock battles, advanced medical training, tracheostomies, and emergency medicine for combat related wounds.

My next assignment was with the 6th Marines at Camp Lejeune. I got my orders from 'Nam several months later in late May. I had 30 days of leave and I arrived in Vietnam on 2 July 1967. A C-130 brought us from the Philippines into Da Nang. Heat, humidity, and the smell of Vietnam-the fish odor which was detected with every breath. Diesel fuel was always in the background as an aroma. I smell it to this day. I was assigned to the Headquarters and Supply Company, 3rd Battalion, 1st Marine Regiment, 1st Marine Division. After a week of quiet time to myself and firing hundreds of rounds of the M-16, I was assigned to Kilo Company, 1st Platoon. My name was Doc I from then on.

Vietnam

Our battalion covered the area just south of Da Nang, about 10 miles from the coast. We would go out as a platoon-sized unit in places that were called the Riviera because they were by the ocean, the bridge position, and other areas with similar names. Permanent base camps that we would run squad-sized patrols around the clock. There were two corpsmen assigned to each platoon which was made up of three squads. When any patrol went out, a corpsman went with them. This meant that corpsmen were out in the bush fifty per cent more than the Marines on patrols. When we were not platoon-sized, we were operating as a company, battalion-sized, for operations such as Operation Swift in September 1967.

The enemy at that time was the Viet Cong, lots of snipers, booby traps, small ambushes, no major engagements, but Marines getting shot up in booby traps really started to take its toll. The worst casualty I treated, when we were still south of Da Nang, was on a lineman soldier. We were out on Operation Swift, or Shelbyville, and we were working with some other units on a long, stretched out line sweeping. We were sweeping in a long line through open country and to my left, less than 75 feet, one of the soldiers tripped the booby trap, a "Bouncing Betty". This device pops straight up off the ground, about three or four feet, and then explodes out and it throws shrapnel in a 360 degree circle. The Bouncing Betty popped up at his hip level inches from him and it blew his hips and his legs away. It cut him in half. It also took his left arm off leaving a six inch stub at the shoulder. Blinded his eyes and the flash burn burned his face. I crossed the distance in less than 10 seconds to find his internal organs fully exposed with the flap of abdominal skin still attached to him. The Bouncing Betty literally cut him at the hips. I used all my hemostats to cut off his bleeding. I had to go up inside his abdominal cavity to clamp off . . . it hit his femoral arteries to his legs. I called for everybody's canteens to wash off the debris and covered his organs with my largest bandages to hold his intestines in. I applied a tourniquet to his stump on his left arm. He never lost consciousness. He was asking me, "How bad is it Doc?" I kept telling

him, "Hang in there! We got a chopper coming." A laid back kid from
God knows where in America, cut in half, still alive in a country on the
other side of the world. He was conscious when I put him on the chopper
and I watched him fly away to where a whole team of doctors, nurses, and
medical personnel were waiting for him should he land and still alive. Very,
very sad.

Another incident occurred when I had saved the company senior
corpsman and he doesn't even know it to this day. Here's what happened.

Stories

Kilo's 1ˢᵗ Platoon was at the bridge position. We had been there a week or
two. A platoon from Lima Company was relieving us. With them they
brought hot chow in metal containers. Fresh ham was in one canister and
the other was boxed and contained boned boiled turkey from the number
10 sized cans. Lima's Platoon was greedy, kept the ham, and gave us the
boned turkey. After eating, we, the 1ˢᵗ Platoon, started to walk back to the
Battalion. We had walked out to the bridge position from Battalion and
we were walking back. We left at dusk and walked for hours and we could
see the lights from the Battalion, one more hill to go, when we got a call
on the radio that Lima's 1ˢᵗ Platoon was sick with food poisoning from the
ham they ate. Our orders were to return to the bridge position and do the
patrols they were scheduled to do. We turned around and force marched
back to the bridge. On our arrival, which was early in the morning, all
but two of Lima's Platoon was on the ground sick as dogs. I was already
tired from patrols the day before and we had a new corpsman from Rhode
Island. He was short and pudgy and the heat in the late August made him
sweat as heavy as anybody I ever saw in 'Nam. I took compassion on him
and I would take the patrols that would be in the morning, during the
day and early evenings. He would take the nights when it was coolest.
Arriving at dawn, I went out with a squad on an eight hour patrol, came
back in, and went out with another squad for eight hours more to save
Doc S from the heat. Doc S took the night patrol and I stayed with Lima's
men through the night. When morning came, I went out on another eight
hour patrol. When I returned to the bridge position, Lieutenant Kenney ,
the lieutenant commander, told me, "Doc, get some sleep in my bunker."
I had been up for two and a half days. Lieutenant Kenney had the only
bunker at the bridge position. I went to sleep on a fold-out cot which was
unbelievable. I wasn't going to have to sleep on the ground. The cot had

an inflatable mattress; amazing! This was the Ritz. I never had it so good in the bush. They called the inflatable mattress a "rubber whore". While I'm sleeping, the senior corpsman came from battalion out on a trip to access the situation. I was never told he had come or gone. After a few days, Lima's boys were back in the saddle doing the patrols and we marched back to battalion. Just back to battalion, I was hungry. I was walking between the hooches heading for the chow hall. The hooches were large tents on flat —. I see the company corpsman walking toward me between the hooches. At about 150 feet away, I hear him yelling obscenities, "You mother fucker. Goddamn asshole. You piece of shit." I'm looking over my shoulder to see who he's yelling at and I don't see anybody. I look back at him walking very fast towards me and he stops a foot in front of my face and continues with, "You fucking piece of shit. How dare you sleep your fucking ass off on a rubber whore while your men are lying on the ground dying! Get your fucking head out of your ass." While he's rattling off these endearing lines, I thought this was some form of indoctrination into some inner circle or something like that. I never said a word, knowing that I gave and did more than anybody. I was awake longer; did more patrols than anybody. Yet, I stood and I watched him as he did a 180 and walked away still swearing. On the steps of one of the hooches, 25 feet to my left, sat two of my men from the 1st Platoon. After hearing it all and watching the senior corpsman walk away, they approached me and said, "Don't worry Doc. He won't see the morning light." I said, "No." The other says, "He's an asshole and he deserves it." These men had seen me to into the open to tend to a wounded Marine. I was a hero to them and they were not going to let this asshole get away with insulting their corpsman. It took five to ten minutes to get them to stop threatening him and to promise me on their honor as Marines and on their mother's soul that they would not harm him or have anyone else harm him in any way. I had them promise and it holds to this day. I've been to five reunions with my battle buds waiting for him to show up so I could tell him, "I saved your life." Another amusing incident.

On 2 November 1967, the 3rd Battalion 1st Marines received orders to be the next Battalion Landing Team. On 2 December 1967, the 3rd Battalion 1st Marines were loaded onto the USS *Valley Forge* LPH, an old WWII aircraft carrier. We went to the Philippines for extra training, worked with the Forward Observers for the Navy, beefed up the battalion, squads, and the choppers loaded onto the USS *Valley Forge*. There were seven operating rooms below deck. There were LST's which were supply ships to hold the tanks and Amtrak's. All the supplies were self contained fully loaded battalion. We used our own choppers for transport or supplies, the medivac. Medical staff in the operating rooms back on board the ship were there for us because all the wounded would be brought back to the ship first. We would be used as a wild card extensively. We were in the Philippines for about 10 days and served in Vietnam to stall eight major operations starting on 21 December to the 24th 1967. I was on the ship for Christmas day and went back to the bush 26 December until I left the DMZ in June 1968. We were at a village called Lam Son during the Tet Offensive in 1968. We were sweeping our line as a battalion-sized unit around 31 January and Kilo Company was left at Lam Son as what I figured to be a rear guard and the rest of the battalion moved on. We set up just outside of a village. There was a finger-shaped piece of land which was extended out into an open area. It appeared to be where the playground was for the kids. It was about 270 degrees of open area around that perimeter which was an exposed area. The other 90 percent butted up to the village itself. We were three days and two nights in the same place. My hole was less than 25 feet from the command post. I heard Captain John Regal, the Company Commander on the radio the morning of 1 February asking the battalion that he be able to move our position to a more defensible position because S-1, S-2 intelligence reported that large enemy forces were in the area. Battalion said, "No. Hold your position." Later that afternoon, Regal requested again to move our position and was told the same thing. "Hold your position." Shortly after that last "Hold your position," Captain Regal took the three platoon leaders and they went for a walk. The Captain had found a more defensible position about a hundred yards out from the village and maybe 200 yards parallel to the face of it. But it was completely dark. The word came down to backup. We were moving out. "Don't make a sound." I thought we were going to catch up with the battalion. We returned to the quiet, very quiet, no noise and when we moved out, we walked only a short distance and set up behind a hedgerow that was facing the village. The hedgerow was about three feet high and six feet across the top with six to eight feet sized little tiny trees, like little Christmas trees, as a windbreaker. The ground was hard-packed clay and my hole was no more than six to eight inches deep. I was about 20 feet behind the hedgerow. Captain Regal would put out listening posts at about 25 yards between us, the hedgerow and the village. Around 0200 on 2 February, the 803rd NVA Regiment attacked our whole position with a 15 to 20 minute artillery and mortar barrage. Then they overran it. We could hear the grenades going off as they swept by the holes. RPGs (Rocket Propelled

Grenades) hitting the old holes that we were in earlier that day. When they discovered we were gone, it took them about two hours to find us. One of the listening posts reported they had heard movement just outside of their hole. The captain called the listening posts back behind the hedgerow and had everybody on our line ready to rock and roll. We called for an 81 millimeter illumination round and when it lit up the area, between us and the village, the ground was covered with hundreds of NVA crawling toward our position. Some were within five to ten yards of us. All hell broke loose. The NVA had artillery and mortars raining down directly on our position with the village tree line throwing everything at us; .51 caliber machine guns, small machine guns, AK-47s. Our 105 cannons were out of range and we called for the Navy ships to shoot across inland. They were shooting maximum range and the accuracy was off. It was so off that it had actually killed the Forward Observer and a Lieutenant and his Radioman, they decapitated Corporal Moses Arnold (*Vietnam Memorial Panel 36E Line 065*), and a badly wounded Mark McNalty. Navy guns after that were used at a greater distance in the tree lines hundreds of yards away.

We called in the 155 ARVN gun. We called them in for support, but they couldn't be used for accuracy because they were shooting at maximum range also. It was used along the tree lines with the Navy guns. Our 81 mortars were our only effective guns. David Martin, who I refer to as my hero, was one of the 81 squad leaders. 81s had full guns going non-stop for five hours and we were calling them as close as 25 yards from our position. Corporal Martin had told me afterwards that the empty plastic tubes that carried the 81s were stacked six feet high around the firing pits. That is why I firmly believe that David Martin and his men saved Kilo Company from being overrun. The Company had 25 Forward Observers for every possible form of support such as naval guns, Army artillery, ARVN artillery, air support, and Marine guns. After five hours of fighting, the enemy backed off leaving 200 dead lying in the open. Death trails were everywhere back in the village. The NVA were like the Marines; never wanting to leave anybody behind. The NVA could not remove the dead and wounded out in front of our lines because it was so open. Anybody's attempt would certainly end in their death. Kilo lost 44 men during the battle and the Navy lieutenant and his radioman left us with about 99 men. The Battalion 3/1 suffered 455 casualties in one six-week period from late January to early March 1968.

After that battle, I was burned out from fighting and refused to carry a weapon. This last battle left me washed out. I didn't want to fight the enemy or life itself anymore.

I left Kilo Company somewhere on the DMZ in June; my time to rotate home. On 28 June 1968, I flew out of Vietnam on a commercial airliner. I feared being shot down on takeoff and once we cleared the mainland and were over the open water, I still felt the booby trap on the plane could blow us out of the sky. About an hour or two later, I finally started to relax. I really believed I was going home.

Home

Upon arriving in the good old USA, I landed in San Francisco, CA. Stepping off the plane and walking through the waiting area down towards the terminal hallway, I saw the length of the terminal, six foot deep on the left side wall as far as the terminal was long stood a lot of people, young hippie types; college students. As I walked by them, they called me every name in the book from baby killer, mother raper, village burner. Some were spitting. As I walked and listened to them, my mind said, "If you were where I was, you would do what I did if you wanted to live." I changed out of my uniform and into civilian clothes.

I arrived home to a family gathering in my honor; 50 to 75 family members with some friends mixed in. They had made a huge cake which they divided into three sections. On the left section, it said, "Happy Birthday" for the one that I had missed. On the right side, it said, "Merry Christmas" and "Happy New Year." In the middle of the cake was a large waving American flag with the words "Happy Fourth of July" and "Welcome Home." I didn't feel comfortable with the party that I had walked into. My buds were still in 'Nam and I shouldn't enjoy myself until they all come home.

I walked up to the top of the hill and sat down on the car. My mother came to me a short time later and asked me if I was alright. I told her, "No." My friends were still on the DMZ and I was here and it didn't feel right. I should be with them and they should be with me. Neither was going to happen. I could not see the great American dream after my return. I saw America interfering with other people's dreams and lives.

How did Vietnam shape your life

3.4 million Vietnamese died during our stay; mostly women and children. We killed more civilians than combatants. We defoliated over 10 percent of Vietnam's vegetation with Agent Orange, a defoliant so toxic that still leaves the world with birth defects. They, the Vietnamese, still have over 200,000 missing in action. Yes, 200,000 people remain unaccounted for. We devastated villages that had stood for thousands of years. All gone. Nothing stands up to 500 and 750 pound bombs from the B-52s and the bomber jets. Thousands of bullets were fired for every dead combatant. We dropped more ordnance from the sky than all of WWII times two on a country no bigger than the state of New Mexico.

The war, in my opinion, was avoidable. John F. Kennedy wanted all men home by 31 December 1965. They killed him for that. He let the intelligence community from the Eisenhower administration run the show until October 1963. He had made it clear to Congress that 1,000 men would come home before 31 December 1963 and the rest home by 31 December 1965. This number slashed the CIA into 10,000 pieces and took away the income tax from the oil barons. They killed him six weeks later. Three weeks before his assassination, South Vietnam's president and his brother were killed in Vietnam. With Johnson now at the helm, the war escaladed into what we call the Vietnam War.

Advice to someone considering a military career

Advice for anyone seeking military service at this time—DON'T, unless you can assure yourself that the war you may fight in is truly called for. To go to war to later find out it not be justifiable is a devastating blow to one's own sense of morality and nobility. I, for one, have felt used and abandoned by my country's leaders and military. No matter how many support groups I attended upon my return, they all failed to help me relive and sort through the different and ever changing reasons of why the Vietnam War ever happened. To be a hero in war, your friends are dead. Some maimed for life and some come home to commit suicide. Don't wish to be a hero. The cost is too high a price to pay.

In conclusion, it is not the biggest, baddest moments of our life that define us. It is the bestest, mostest, goodest ones that lead us home as heroes. Share those moments with the world and live them to the fullest. War brings out the worst that men can do to one another. The opposite comes out the best that we can do for one another. From a child's mind, remember your bestest, mostest, goodest and you go do that. Your own, in service, Doc Infantino.

JOHN MURPHY

Navy Corpsman, United States Navy
Non Sibi Sed Patriae: *"Not self but country"*
First Battalion Ninth Marine Regiment Third Marine Division
Home of Record: New Bedford, MA
Home of Residence: Issaquah, WA
DOB: 14 August 1947
Interview conducted via phone
East Stroudsburg University

> *I went to Vietnam in January 2011 and the main thing I got out of it is
> the realization that the combat experience is forever. There is no escape,
> and if we can get that and accept it, I think things are better for us.*
> —Lt. John Gulick, Navy SEAL

Growing Up

I lived in New Bedford, Massachusetts, in the typical two-parent household
with two brothers. My dad was a textile engineer when that industry was
big in the northeast. Our family was mostly Irish with a little German
and some French Canadian. My grandfather was French Canadian and a
trained architect, but his main vocation was a carpenter and house builder.
He built about fifty homes in the New Bedford area and was very proud
of his work. I attended a parochial school, Sacred Heart School and was an
altar boy. Part of our daily activity was to attend the Mass every morning.
Nuns still terrify me.

Then in fourth grade, my dad's textile company moved to the south,
and we moved to upstate New York where my dad worked for the Borden
chemical company. The town was named Bainbridge, just north of
Binghamton, New York. I graduated from high school there. It was a small
school so you do all the sports. I played baseball, football, and wrestling.
Since it was a farming community during the summer, most of the kids
worked on farms picking bales of hay, working with the animals, and
shoveling a lot of cow manure. Hard work gave me a great work ethic.

My dad was born, raised, and graduated high school in Philly. He then
went in the Navy. After his service, he attended night school where he
received an engineering degree. My mom grew up in New Bedford. She
went to school at New Bedford High School. She then became a legal

secretary. When we moved from New Bedford to Bainbridge, she worked at the high school in the guidance office as a secretary.

My dad thought the service was a good thing for him, and a lot of kids went into the Navy, Army, and Marines out of high school. It was wartime, so I could understand his feelings, but it was also an eye opener for him. My dad was an aviation mechanics machinist mate in WWII. He was on the USS *Bennington* and just turned ninety. His era of warriors is dying out.

When I was booted out of college, his comment was, "You're not living here, you're not working at the chemical company, so you need to go figure out what you're going to do." The Navy seemed like a good thing to do because that's what he did, and he enjoyed it. My other two brothers went in the military as well. My middle brother went into the Navy, and my younger brother went into the Army. We were three years apart. I am the oldest.

I graduated from high school in 1966, and I went to East Stroudsburg State Teachers College (PA) for 3 years as a physical education major and played football. Academically I wasn't all that interested, so after three years of a great time, the dean of Academics said I would probably do better somewhere else. So that year (1969), I worked as a lifeguard in the Poconos Mountains; and during that summer, my friend, Obie, and I enlisted in the military under the 120-day delay program. Obie went to the Marines, and I went to the Navy. During that summer, we went to a few concerts in New Jersey; and in August 1969, I went to this concert in upstate New York. The music was great, and the conditions were horrible, but I had a great time. It was not until a few years later that I realized that this was Woodstock, the greatest concert ever for my generation. The concert in August was actually on the week of my birthday. I hung around my hometown for a few days after that concert, and then I went into the Navy the day after Labor Day on 2 September. My dad, a Navy veteran himself, drove me to the airport, and his parting words were, "Don't bring home one of those slant eyed bastards." The war in the Pacific was hard on his generation, and he, to this day, has never forgotten his time in combat.

So the culmination of my college career for three years included a physical education major, football player, beer drinker, and woman chaser. All in all, I had a great time, and it was the beginning of a great adventure.

I joined the Navy under some sort of a guaranteed entry into a program of your choice—a great recruiting ploy. I originally was assigned under this program to the underwater demolition team (UDT) guarantee program as I thought it would be really cool and as a college jock, I thought this would be a piece of cake. That was the reason they sent me to San Diego, because the UDT training center was right there on Coronado Island. After several weeks in boot camp, there was a selection process for the UDT program, so I went over to the office and took the physical evaluation and found out that I couldn't even get into the program because I was color blind. This was an automatic exclusion for me. Being color blind is a lifetime condition that the recruiter knew, but it was wartime, and I was a young stud, so he said I was good to go. So my military career plans changed in the first early part of boot camp, and I decided to become a corpsman. The Navy said I would make a great clerk or in some other administrative position, but the sound of being a clerk in the Navy didn't sound all that exciting. Admiral maybe—but definitely not a clerk.

After boot camp, I went to Balboa Naval Hospital in San Diego for Hospital Corpsman Training. We were there probably ten to fifteen weeks. It didn't seem like it was that long. Then I got stationed at Bremerton Naval Hospital in Washington State. We took care of a lot of combat injured Marines that came back for recovery. My whole hospital ward, which I was one of the ward supervisors, took care of dirty surgery and open wounds. All the guys that came back were Marines, and they were basically all blown up with multiple injuries. The process for these guys was, after they got rotated out of Vietnam, they went to Japan, then flown to McChord Air Force base in Tacoma (WA) where we would go and pick them up. Then they stayed at the hospital until recovery from their wounds well enough to go home and got hooked into the VA system. Some returned to the corps but a lot got discharged. I was at the hospital for about two years. During my time there, I did some on the job training in dermatology and general medicine.

In 1972, I got orders to report to the Marine Corps and attended the Field Medical Service School in Oceanside, California, for several weeks to learn the Marine Corps way of field medicine. I was then assigned to 1/9 of the Third Marine Division garrisoned at Camp Schwab on Okinawa.

I was assigned to Battalion Landing Team 1/9 (BLT), and their function was to storm the beaches, a carryover from WWII and Korea, but what we actually did was to float out on the South China Sea on a couple of LPHs (landing platform helicopter ships) and wait until the shit hit the fan on land, and we would helicopter in to save the day. That never happened, but we were ready to kick some ass if called upon.

One day we mounted up, left Camp Schwab, and went to White Beach and boarded a LPH named the USS *Inchon*. Later, our BLT was transferred to the USS *Iwo Jima*. They were both LPHs. We would sail around the South China Sea and the doctors and corpsmen would fly in country and do MEDCAP missions. Those were humanitarian missions where we would go in country with the doctors and dentists and treat some of the Vietnamese, and then at night we would fly back to the ship. We also did some Search and Rescue for the B-52s when they got shot down and landed near our area of operation, and we worked with some Force Recon who was assigned to the LPH as well. The helicopters would fly them into god only knows where in the dead of night to drop them off, and pick them up several days later. I was there, in '72 to '73 and that was the beginning of the end of the war. So my combat experience with the Marines was a little over ten months. On the LPH, they had a helicopter squadron HMM164, which I got TDY orders to replace another hospital corpsman ready to rotate back to the "world." He was afraid he was going to be shot down, so we traded places. On ship, I was bored, and all we saw from the ship was Vietnam. I had never flown in a helicopter before, so I figured what the hell. So we TDY'd (temporary duty), and he went and took my position at the company, and I went with the helicopter squadron, and we flew all over the place for several months; then we came back to Okinawa.

We did the insertions with the Marine Force Recon guys. We didn't hang out. We just dropped them off. They would jump out of the helicopter, and we would head back to the ship. We were lucky, and on the ship, we had a hot cot and nice meals and showers. I wasn't a ground pounder. As I said earlier, there were a few B-52s that went down, so we did search and rescue. That was all on the water and we never went on land to do search and rescue. By the time '73 rolled around, most of my involvement was in the medial battalion, the aid station. They called it B Medical Company.

Vietnam

Vietnam was a beautiful country from the air. We did a lot of flying as I did TDY with another corpsman. We flew the CH-46s which have the big double rotors. The difference between the 46 and the 47 (used solely by the Army) is basically just the design. I found out later that the 46s were designed for the LPH due to rotor configuration and weight. They were bigger, but basically look the same. All the stuff we see flying around today looks exactly like the ones that I flew in Vietnam. I'm sure that they upgraded the avionics. Every time a helicopter flies over, I always look up just to confirm what I am hearing. The military helicopters had a distinctive sound unlike the civilian helicopters. Living in the northwest and close to military bases, there are a lot of CH-46s and 47s (Chinook) flying around with occasional Hueys. You don't see those much anymore. The Black Hawk is the helicopter of choice. The CHs carried about twenty to twenty-five Marines and the crew. You had your pilot, copilot—you had your gunner and me.

On the LPH, we did have some civilians onboard, and most of those guys were engineers and weapons systems guys. I'm sure there were a few CIA, but we didn't really deal with them.

My general impression of the time I was there was I didn't get shot, but got shot at. I did spend a lot of time at sea with no amphibious landings—the kind of one of those ready action forces if there was a problem. We continued to turn the operations over to the Vietnamese, and the Americans were getting ready to withdraw as peace talks progressed. We were still bombing and mining the harbors, but the attitude was to get the hell out before they kill more Americans. They were trying to wind the war down, and our response was to stay out of harm's way. We stayed out at sea all the time except when occasionally we would go in.

I wasn't engaged in much ground combat. I was older when I went into service at the ripe old age of twenty-two. So most of the units I was stationed with, I was the old guy. A lot of the Marines there were during the era of you either go to jail or the Marines—we had a lot of disciplinary issues. When we were on the ship, we had a race riot one night. They had a lot of racial tension going on that ship, and we treated a lot of injured Marines and sailors that night. We did make one "landing" and stormed the bars in Singapore for R&R for a week and then returned to Okinawa.

I was an E3 when I was in boot camp due to my college time, then ended up at the end of my tour as an E5 Hospital Corpsman (HM2). My expectations were given to me by my brother who went in the Navy before me. He went in right after high school and had been in for about a year, and he said, "You want to be a recruit chief petty officer (RCPO) when you go into boot camp because then you're the boss." Also, he said, "Just keep your mouth shut, especially in boot camp." Boot camp is just a passage in time for getting people ready for that sort of discipline that is expected of you when you are in service. When I went into corpsman school, it was a lot more relaxed. It was more of a vocational training. They trained you as an LPN (licensed practical nurse). We worked in San Diego in Balboa Naval Hospital. One of my patients was Lt. Robert Frishman who was one of the first released POWs / Navy pilot. He was pretty screwed up. He was telling some stories that were pretty horrible about the torture. We were there to basically learn our corpsman skills. Then I got stationed at

Bremerton (WA), so I was stateside for two years. You got a job, you didn't get paid a lot of money, but life was good. My stateside experience was much like a college town. There were a lot of other people just like you. You work with nurses and doctors. It was fairly enjoyable.

When I got stationed in the Marines, the expectation was that Doc could do nothing wrong. The moniker Doc was an earned title. Not all corpsman were Doc to the Marines as some of the corpsmen were dopes and did not deserve that honor. The Marines took very good care of you while you were with them.

We all looked the same. We all wore the same marine cammies. When we got dressed in our dress uniforms, we wore our Navy blues or whites, depending on the event or the season. There were exceptions with a few chief petty officers who wore the marine green. They were Marines through and through. The Navy chief corpsman assigned to the Marines was in the Marines forever.

You could reenlist at the end of your tour, and you could extend your tour in the Marine Corps. You could spend your whole time in the Navy stationed with the Marines, but ordinarily, what you would do is you would rotate to sea duty. As a corpsman, my sea duty would have been with the Marines.

It was interesting returning to the "world" or the land of the big PX. We came out of Vietnam on our float and steamed back to Okinawa. After we collected our gear at Camp Schwab, we reported to Kadena AFB, were "processed," and got on an airplane with our cammies on and our duffle bag. Everything else we shipped back home. Over there you buy a lot of stereo equipment and "stuff." From Kadena AFB, we flew into Hawaii, then San Francisco. We landed in San Francisco and got thrown in the brig that night because we got in a fight with civilians, hippies, or "fucking hippies" as we called them. We had a big brawl. There were probably twenty-five to thirty of us, mostly Marines and corpsman, and the Navy guys were originally going to Long Beach and spend ten days there so we could get processed out of the service. It was great. We thought it was hilarious for us. We got spit on, got called baby killers, so we kicked ass. The next day, we all got on a bus and got shipped down to Long Beach Naval Station.

While at Long Beach, we got assigned picking up garbage, cigarette butts and doing administrative chores. When they were done processing us, I got out in August 1973.

How did Vietnam shape your life?

I joined the fire department after the Navy. My plans were to go back to school in Washington. I liked the state because of my experience in Bremerton, so I moved back to Olympia (WA) for a period of time. I stayed with my former commanding officer and his family from Bremerton, Dr. Jim Gallent. During this time, I worked at St. Peter's hospital as an emergency room technician. I was going to go back to finish my undergraduate work and to be a teacher.

One night, I had a patient come in from the fire department who said, "Hey, we're starting this paramedic division with the fire department. You seemed like you'd have the experience being a Vietnam vet and being a corpsman." So I applied to the department and got hired. This happened before the letter from the University of Washington arrived indicating that I was accepted to finish my undergraduate degree and then go be a teacher.

When I got into the fire department, I went directly into paramedic training. I was a paramedic firefighter. I think that my Vietnam experience shaped my public service desire. I really liked the excitement of the fire department. I liked being a paramedic. Then I did that for a couple years and then I had an opportunity to go to physician's assistant school in the MEDEX program at the University of Utah. The MEDEX concept started out at Duke University in the late sixties to recycling corpsmen back into the civilian life providing medical care to underserved areas of the United States. I went to MEDEX in Utah in 1976 and left the fire department to attend this program. I was married at that time and the MEDEX program at that time was a six-month program. They were looking for independent duty corpsmen to attend this program, and after the six-month program, you were assigned to a preceptor and worked with a doctor for the remainder of this program. The total time was for about one year. Then you would go work in these rural communities and become the doctor for a lot of these communities.

After this program was completed, we came back up to Washington because we wanted to have another child, and we liked the medical care in Olympia. I rejoined the fire department as a paramedic firefighter in another department and worked as a physician's assistant for group health, which is a HMO. I worked in their emergency room. I moved through the ranks of the fire department in several different departments and retired as a deputy fire chief after thirty-two years of service.

In my travels, I run into a lot of Vietnam vets. There is a guy who I work out with in Issaquah (WA) who was an officer in the Force Recon Third

Marines. There is another interesting guy, Colonel Bruce F. Meyers, living in Issaquah (WA). He's a lawyer as well and lives about ten miles away from me. He and others started the Force Recon (Marines) after the Korean war. He started working with the Army at Fort Benning developing the Special Forces branch because some of the stuff that happened could have been done better in WWII. He told me that he was actually in law school and he didn't want to graduate because they wanted to put him in JAG (Judge Advocate General), and he didn't want to do that. He is quite an interesting person. Bruce was in Korea and in Vietnam in addition to WWII.

Regarding the war, honestly John, I think the words to use are—it was fucked up. I really didn't have any political awareness. I grew up when Eisenhower was the president and Kennedy was elected. It just seemed like when you were over there, we were not well-organized. Being on the float, we just didn't get the sense that there was a mission to accomplish. It was just like a police action.

My dad lived in the McCarthy era, where he would come home at night and say that during most of the McCarthy hearings, they were asking him at work to report if there were Communists working in his factory. We weren't all that sophisticated, and it was hard to fathom that sort of witch hunt for that particular group of individuals that didn't look any different than us. That was the feeling growing up. They had a "good war" in WWII, which my dad was in and galvanized the country. Then there a kind of "mediocre war," which my dad was not in, but was relatively short-lived in Korea.

Then we entered the Vietnam War to prevent the domino theory of preventing the Communists from taking over Southeast Asia. I never realized that during the Eisenhower era, we were supporting this conflict and supporting the government in their action against the Communists.

We put our flag down in Vietnam, but when you were there, you just didn't have a sense of mission. When I got out and really studied the war, it was more screwed up than ever. We try to prop up this false government, and when you take a look at Vietnam today, it's doing not too bad. They still have poverty, they still have urban development, they still have cities, and they have people with money. They don't live relatively long, but they live a lot longer than they used to. So the question is, "Did we make a difference?" To be honest with you, I don't think we made a difference.

Advice to someone considering a military career

Go for it. A few reasons . . . You cannot find any other place, except maybe as a policeman or firefighter, to gain these life experiences that puts that kind of camaraderie and group focus together. This will not only benefit you but builds a kind of unit cohesion and team building. You cannot find that in a regular civilian or corporate industry. You get the chance to be educated in whatever disciplines you have an interest in. Medicine, law, police, fire suppression, or any other interest you have.

When you get in and stay for a period of time, you can get any kind of education you want when you get out through the GI Bill. I remember when I got out of the Navy in 1973 I made $411.40 a month net, and I had more money than I knew what to do with. I was cutting a fat hog then. I was happy, and I didn't have any overhead. The pay is much better now as are the benefits.

I think the life experiences these individuals get in the military can't be found anywhere else. I know that today we are in a war, but in Vietnam, there were a couple million guys who went over there and not many of them were in actual combat. Many were in support. They were behind the fighting lines or floating out at sea doing support working in Japan or in Okinawa and other countries. Outside of the United States, you get to live and experience the kind of life of the country that you're in, which I believe is invaluable.

I think in today's economy, you can't beat the deal you get when you go into the military. I try to impress upon my girls, if you're not going to do anything you should go into the Air Force. Why? Because of all the places I traveled in Southeast Asia, the Air Force had the best bases, the best food, the best gyms, the best lodging. The uniforms are kind of goofy, but they had good technology. I had a friend in high school in the Air Force and was stationed in Thailand. They were flying air support and a whole bunch of other goofy things, mostly secret stuff. He said he never got shot at; he lived like a king. He had no money and said it was just a great experience. My brother was a radar man on a Navy destroyer escort (DE) for four years. When he got out of the Navy, and for years afterward, he walked from side to side because of the ships roll. No kidding.

All in all, my Vietnam experience was one of my many life experiences. I was not in hot combat, but was in a combat zone and fully prepared to engage the enemy. I respect those who went before me and who have come after me. We live in a dangerous world, and at times, we are called to serve this great nation. Take the opportunity to live and experience a different side of life and grab this military experience if you have a chance. You will be a better person for it.

Current day

I worked as a physician's assistant, and I worked for the fire department. I achieved my educational goals, and I ended up getting my bachelors degree and a master's degree in education. I did a lot of teaching in trauma, medicine, infectious disease—that sort of thing. I worked a lot with nurse's physicians, paramedics, and trauma training. Then I went to law school in 1998 and attended night school at Seattle University. During this time, I didn't practice medicine as a PA because you can't do both. You really have to focus on the law school part. After graduation from law school, I had a small private practice and retired out of the fire department in 2007.

I've since been a part-time associate at a local law firm that does probate, estate planning, and medical malpractice. I do all of the review in the medical malpractice cases based on my background in medicine. Then I have a small law practice, mostly focusing on the fire departments, keeping them up on education and out legal jams. For example, ensuring the fire chiefs stayed out of trouble and labor negotiations.

I've renewed my PA license because I am returning to the practice of medicine. As my medical practice is focused on emergency and urgent care, I would also like to be eligible to go on some medical missions to disaster areas—like to Haiti, or Chile—and do some disaster medicine.

I have two daughters from my first marriage and have two grandchildren. My second wife had three daughters as well so I am surrounded by women—not necessarily a bad thing. I am healthy with a few hip replacement parts, but continue to be productive and relevant.

Closing Comments

A deep man believes that the evil eye can wither, that the heart's blessing can **heal**, *and that love can overcome all odds.*
—Ralph Waldo Emerson

Imagine twenty years of formal education, then being on the receiving end of a phone call, stating, "You're in the Army now." This thought ricocheted around my brain while listening to Dr. Odom. Knowing also that his battalion was in a reserve role during the Battle of Ia Drang Valley (colonels' Marm and Odom were both in the First Cavalry Division in 1965), I hung on every word. Here is a man who exuded professionalism, even while his residency was cut short for the war effort. Following our May 2010 talk, we keep in touch regularly. While I write this passage, I am just two feet away from his family's 2010 Christmas picture. It makes me want to fly back to San Francisco to experience the magnificent weather, since all eighteen family members in the picture are in summer garb.

Doc I: To be clear, Marines referred to their corpsmen as "Doc." I stared at my laptop for quite some time assessing how to proceed with this section. We are joined at the "hip" because it was Hip Biker who introduced Carmelo Infantino to me. Doc I has the tendency to ramble on at times—eloquently, mind you. The subject matter is not the issue, but when he was describing certain engagements with both the VC and NVA, I was listening, but also looking into his eyes. I believe that my subliminal was working in reverse. There was a type of transference that I never felt before. I'm pretty sure that I will never forget it. His interview, and all these interviews, will continue to affect me forever.

John K. Murphy: He actually tried to talk me out of the interview, undercutting his value to the book even before I started the tape, but finally, John spoke. I listened. No regrets. For a corpsman who was always in the air, doing his duty out of a helicopter, John had a keen sense of what was happening with the grunts and fellow corpsman on the ground. I have never met him in person, but once I do, the open circuit that has developed via e-mail and phone between John, his wife, Beth, and I will be closed. And I will be a better man as a result of shaking their hands.

It saddens me greatly that an interview was never included here among the nursing corps. Please honor them by visiting the Women's Memorial in Washington DC. It is located due south of the Vietnam Memorial. Sculpted by Glenna Goodacre, handcarved out of Carnelaian red granite from Minnesota and dedicated in 1993, this serves as a testament to those eight women who perished while saving the living.

CHAPTER SEVEN
ARVN and NVA/VC

Army of the Republic of Vietnam

Friend

Dedicated to Thong Nguyen
Army of the Republic of Vietnam
1st Battalion 501st Regiment
101st Airborne

*If the Americans do not want to support us anymore, let them go, get
out! Let them forget their humanitarian promises!*
—President Thieu, April 1975

It was difficult to obtain approval from many of our American soldiers to
participate in these interviews. For the South Vietnamese, couple this with
the fear of potential sanction and retribution by the current Vietnamese
government. That is why so many ARVN soldiers, even after initially
agreeing to the interview, bowed out. A high ranking officer who actually
sat in on the Paris peace talks, South Vietnamese Marines and sailors, and
a few combat soldiers. These men who now make their home in the United
States weren't even open to using an alias. Many of these former soldiers
live in the eastern corridor between Maryland and Virginia.

They were caught in the proverbial crossfire of a civil war. Vietnam was
a country torn apart by religious beliefs, which also bred political beliefs.

They are all good people, but the horror of war became their backyard. As James Fenton stated in 1985,

> *Saigon was an addicted city and we were the drug: the corruption of children, the mutilation of young men, the prostitution of women, the humiliation of the old, the division of the family, the division of the country—it had all been done in our name . . . The French city . . . had represented the opium stage of the addiction. With the Americans had begun the heroin phase.*

The ARVN soldiers were sometimes shed a cautious eye by the Americans. They were with us in many battles, or should I say, we were by their side. Their general officers collaborated with ours in strategy and tactics. With the collapse of Saigon inevitable, many committed suicide rather than be captured by the NVA in 1975. Colonel Ho Ngoc Can was captured after a failed suicide attempt and executed subsequent to a kangaroo court. The following South Vietnamese generals committed suicide on 30 April 1975 while Saigon was falling. Some of these officers called their families immediately before their final action.

Brigadier General Le Van Hung
General Pham Van Phu
Brigadier General Le Nguyen Vy
Brigadier General Tran Van Hai
Major General Nguyen Khoa Nam

Many Vietnamese felt we abandoned them in 1973 following the peace talks and the POW release beginning February 1973. Thousands of ARVN soldiers took off their uniforms and boots and scattered them all over the streets of South Vietnamese cities to avoid capture once the North broke out en masse toward Saigon. The political leaders of South Vietnam also felt betrayed by us. Nixon privately promised President Nguyen Van Thieu in January 1973 he would "respond with full force" if the NVA broke the cease-fire. Since the bulk of our fighting force was removed by 1973, and Nixon by this time was under tremendous pressure at home for his own antics (Watergate), he did nothing. This sealed the fate of the South Vietnamese. Admiral Zumwalt, the Chief of Naval Operations, said, "*We prevailed upon Vietnamese President Thieu to accept a very bad truce. This truce permitted the enemy to remain in South Vietnam in exchange for something that was good for the United States and that was the total removal of our forces."* These "agreements" were never conveyed to our Congress. Finally, President Thieu, knowing the end was near, finally immigrated to Taiwan and then took up residence in England just before the Fall of Saigon.

The Army of the Republic of Vietnam suffered over 200,000 killed in action. The price of freedom in Vietnam was indeed costly.

NVA AND VC

North Vietnamese and the Viet Cong

Foe

**Dedicated to Hoang Ngoc Dam and his family
Combat Medic 559th Command Group
Peoples Army of North Vietnam**

*"You never beat us on the battlefield," I told my North Vietnamese
counterpart during negotiations in Hanoi a week before the fall
of Saigon. He pondered that remark a moment and then replied,
"That may be so, but it is also irrelevant."*
                                        —*General Frederick C. Weyand*

The American servicemen and women were imperiled by three distinct
groups of "foes."

The first was the VC. The South Vietnamese who comprised this
segment were farmers and villagers whose sole purpose was to unseat the
current governmental regime (of the '50s, '60s and '70s) in Saigon. They
were well-armed, blended in with the regular population, wore the same
black "pajamas" and white hats of the indigent nonviolent villagers, and gave
our troops a difficult time through the Second Tet Offensive spring 1968.
After this major Communist offensive, the VC was virtually wiped out as
a fighting unit. The next group were also VC, but did not blend in with
the denizen. Rather, they were hardcore soldiers who wore uniforms and
were well organized into units similar to any formalized military hierarchy.
Finally, the third group was the PAVN (Peoples Army of Vietnam), or
NVA as designated by the Americans. These guys were trained, fighting
soldiers. Not always up to the standard of the American marine or US
Army rifleman, but tough nevertheless.

Introduction to the Interview

This interview is with retired captain Homer R. Steedly Jr. USA at his
home in Hendersonville, North Carolina. The book *Wandering Souls* by his
friend Wayne Karlin (Vietnam veteran USMC) is a moving and emotional
novel about NVA Medic Hoang Ngoc Dam in Pleiku Province that begins

19 March 1969. It then follows the chain of events subsequent to Homer finding Dam's personal belongings (2005), which he had sent back (while still in country) to the States for his mom's safekeeping. The story touches your inner being, from start to finish, with captivating dialogue.

I purposely did not explain how I met Homer in *chapter 2*. It was 28 February 2010 while I was interviewing combat medic Ed "Dutch" Gehringer in Kutztown, Pennsylvania. He kept talking about a website detailing his company's actions in Vietnam. After finishing his story, he and his wife, Ingrid, pulled up a website. Upon probing him on some issues and dates, he mentioned that his former CO was noted in the site. He mentioned that this man lived in North Carolina. After the due diligence via phone and e-mail, Homer's interviews were completed just one month to the day later. Not only was I able to have Homer tell me Dam's story, but I watched the video portraying the burial of Dam in his village.

There were many villages in the North that supplied the Communists with fresh troops. Over two hundred young men from his small village of Thai Giang died as soldiers in the war. They did their duty no different than the American soldiers did theirs. Few of their remains have ever been found.

A tradition within Buddhism is that upon birth, the umbilical cord is buried in the soil of the village. This is one way that all people are "connected" in a particular village within Vietnam from birth. This is traditional within the tens of thousands of tiny hamlets that dot the country. By Homer burying Dam's remains, and my association with Homer, I am now also connected to the Dam family.

One does not ask of one who suffers: What is your country and what is your religion? One merely says: You suffer, that is enough for me.
—Louis Pasteur

Dam's Story by Homer R. Steedly Jr.

During my first tour in Vietnam, just before I went back to base camp and took over headquarters' company, I was on a patrol with our company as XO (executive officer). I led a detached platoon that patrolled the ridgeline along the Mang Yang Pass. This is a very ambush-prone area that transported between Pleiku to Qui Nhon by the ocean. On 19 March 1969, while I was on that ridgeline, I encountered a young Vietnamese medic. He rounded the trail as we were taking a break on the side of the trail. He saw me, and I saw him, and we both reached for our weapons. I had my weapon already level, so I just hollered at him to stop. He continued to bring his weapon around and before he could get it leveled on me, I went ahead and shot him. I just put a three-round burst through his chest and killed him with my AR-15.

Well, as I was preparing my website years later, I asked my mom if she kept my letters from Vietnam. Part of what she gave me back was a little bundle of things I had taken off this medic that I had killed. The documents—they're incredible. There are three books, one of which looked like a handwritten copy of an algebra textbook. It went from algebra all the way into calculus. He was using it to either educate himself or train other troops. Another was a booklet of medical drawings and medical text where he had hand copied some medical textbook from somewhere. They were beautiful three-color pen and ink drawings of physical anatomy, vein structures, muscle structures, and so forth. He was using that as a reference for himself, but also to teach others. At the time, he had been promoted to surgical assistant in one of the field hospitals out in the jungle. I had taken all these documents. He had personal letters—some were his, some were from other people. We assumed they were from people he attended to who had died and that he had taken the letters to give back to the family. He had a driver's license, which I thought was his driver's license. I had already been damaged by then, and I couldn't recognize faces anymore, so I didn't realize the face didn't match up with the face of the guy I shot. It turned out the driver's license was from someone that they thought had died. He knew the gentleman, so he was taking the driver's license back down south to get it to the village where the man lived.

Let me digress now. At some point in time, we met on the jungle trail. He died and I didn't. I forgot about it for forty years. I didn't have a memory of it at all, and then these letters and that bundle of documents came in the mail from Mom. As soon as I opened the book and saw the medical drawings, I remembered everything. My first reaction upon opening the bundle was sadness. This was obviously a very gifted, very caring, and very intelligent individual. He was very young. Of course, he was probably twenty-one or twenty-two, but being Vietnamese and being so short of stature and so fair of skin, he looked much younger than that to me. He looked like a babe, a teen, and I just thought of the terrible waste. If only I had known he was a medic or if I had met him six months later when I was not terrified. This was my first face-to-face encounter; I had shot people before, but at a distance. Six months later, I would have shot him in the leg or something, or taken him prisoner because that would have been the intelligent thing to do. To get intelligence from him about the unit and the people in the area, but I was just so terrified at that point that I just reacted instinctively. I think if we had only met six months later I would not have killed him, and the world would not have lost this wonderful human being.

In that moment, I don't remember what he said. I had yelled at him. One of the deficits of my education in the military was that they didn't teach me Vietnamese. I didn't know the language and I couldn't communicate with the enemy. The only thing I knew to say was, "Chieu Hoi," which I thought was surrender. Actually, what it really means is "open arms." Those words were written on all the pamphlets that they threw out to the North Vietnamese telling them "open arms, give up, come over to our side, and we'll forgive you and bring you back into the fold." Well, that probably confused him a little bit, although open arms should have also indicated, "Get rid of your weapon." If he had been a combat soldier, if he had been someone who was familiar with combat, he would have known better than to try bringing the weapon around against me when I already had mine leveled on him. But he wasn't a combatant; he just carried the weapon, and literally, this weapon was brand new. It was an SKS semiautomatic carbine with the folding bayonet on the front. It was so new that it still had the storage grease, the cosmoline, on it. The thing I remember about him—we're in the Central Highlands jungle in red clay mud. Everyone is covered with this mud. You can't walk through it. It's ankle deep. You can't possibly stay clean out there, and here this guy comes around the trail. He's got a light khaki uniform, pith helmet, and he's absolutely spotless! He had just come down from the North on his way to a new unit. He had been up north where he had gone every year for the last five years to receive commendations for his exemplary performance. He had just gotten another award in the surgical field, in the field hospitals out in the jungles. The Chinese advisors had given all the troops new uniforms. Now he was coming back down there with a new uniform and a brand-new, clean rifle. When I first saw him, it was so hot I wasn't sure that I wasn't hallucinating because it's not possible to be that clean; it was surreal.

Let me digress again. I have found out since then that he joined the Army out of his village. He actually joined before he was required to, simply out of a sense of duty and a sense of wanting to prove himself. He'd been in the political youth groups. He would get up in a tree in the afternoon and yell out the political news of the day with a little paper megaphone he'd made. He did all kinds of work with the youth political groups in the village there. He went to war before he really needed to. When he left, he said, "I'll either come back a hero or I'll come back with daisies on my chest." Meaning I'll either die or I'll come back a hero. He intended to serve his country honorably.

I found that out when I went back to Vietnam. One of the people present when I first got to their family home was his niece Thi. When I came into the family home, there was a Buddhist altar. On it was the other son who had died in the war and Dam's picture with his mother and father's picture because they were dead. I came up to put a bowl of fruit on the altar as an offering and there was a young lady on the side. She was just wailing, screaming, crying and writhing around. She had a hideous grimace on her face and I found out later that this was the niece. She was the most deeply affected by my returning to Vietnam to help locate his remains. She was a young girl when Dam left. When she was young, she had eczema so bad she was just covered with scabs. Most of the family members didn't want to touch her and he was the only one that would. He would bathe and clean her wounds. There was a deep connection. That was the kind of person he was. That's why he actually went into the medical corps. Dam wanted to learn more about how to help people and eventually wanted to come back and go to school to become a doctor. This was a very political, active young man in the village community. It was a tight knit village community in North Vietnam about fifty miles outside of Hanoi in the mountains.

Dam had married just before he left for war as was customary for soldiers. They would marry their sweetheart and usually give the wife a child before leaving. Well, his wife was so shy, so terribly shy, and he was too. They didn't consummate the marriage—just couldn't do it in that short amount of time. So about his second or third year in country, down south during the war, he got a leave and went back home. He didn't get all the way home, but he got close enough to where she could have come to visit him as most of the wives of the soldiers did. His father offered to escort her because single woman can't just move freely around in the community, but she declined to go; she was too embarrassed. She was going to go there and everybody in the world would know that they were going to make love. She just couldn't handle the embarrassment of that. She didn't go and to this day she regrets that deeply.

They had no children, and she never saw him again. The family is really, to this day, very upset with her for not doing her part. She regrets it too, but that's just life. They're rice farmers, and literally, the last mile to the village you're driving on a dyke between rice paddies on either side of the road. If you meet somebody, one of you has to back up. There are water buffalo out there plowing the rice. As you're coming down from the actual village itself, there's a graveyard on the left. It's a raised area with rice paddies all around it. Then you go down and the road and village are on the right, and again it's a little high spot there. Everybody's there with these adobe courtyards that separate the family groups and so forth.

The homes are either concrete or concrete blocks, I suspect, because of the rain. They have rain 80 percent of the year so whatever they build has to be able to withstand the moisture. The family had a beautiful little compound with a little fishpond that's fed by a stream. There were papaya trees, bananas—pretty much self-sustaining. Well, like I said I had forgotten about the man completely for forty years, and then when I got the documents, I thought that they probably didn't know what happened to him because we left his body there. We had a situation where we had to get down the ridgeline in a very short period of time, clear it, and then meet a helicopter to get pulled back out again. We were having difficulty just marching. It was about 105 degrees with 90 percent to 100 percent humidity in the mornings. We were having trouble just walking, much less try to carry someone. We couldn't carry the body so we took the documents and weapon, which I did not turn in. We left Dam where he was killed and some of the local villagers who also use that trail found the body and buried it.

They had no way to know who it was so they buried him. Later, a military team from the area got his body, another body that was in the same grave with him, and three other bodies from another gravesite. They took them to the local military cemetery. Now here are five people and nobody knows the identity of any of them. When I saw the documents again, I decided it would be nice if I could get this to the family. By then, I had realized from the Internet that the Vietnamese have nearly 220,000 that are still missing. They went to war and just disappeared. Nobody really knows what happened to them and Dam was one of those. In their village, there were a couple hundred like that; they went to war and nobody knows what happened to them. So I thought, well, if I can get this document back, at least they would know he died—when, and where, and how. That he died trying to do his duty. It would be nice to have something tangible since they're Buddhist, and they really worship their ancestors so much, but I didn't have any idea how to do it. I decided, well, I'll scan a couple of the images and put them on the website. Maybe someone, somewhere, will recognize something and get in touch with me. No one did. One of my friends on the web, Tom Lacombe, wrote a book called *Light Ruck*, which was about his tour of duty in the Fourth Division. He knew Wayne Karlin, a professor and writer who works at the College of Southern Maryland. Sergeant Karlin was a marine door-gunner on both CH-53 Sea Knight and HD-34 helicopters during Vietnam. Professor Karlin goes back and forth to Vietnam helping Vietnamese writers get published here in America and also getting information from Vietnam to include in his books about Vietnam. He's been back and forth at least once or twice a year for several years and has many contacts over there. I explained to him that I was trying to get in touch with somebody to return these documents; he said he would call his journalist friend and see if she knew anybody. She went to the website, saw the documents, saw the story, and was just blown away by it. She decided to print the story with the pictures in her newspaper *Education Times*. She did and the family contacted her overnight saying they wanted to get the documents. I made arrangements to get them back, but I didn't feel comfortable mailing them. I was afraid they'd get lost, so the best way was to take them over myself.

This was only about two years after I started dealing with my memories of Vietnam though and I really wasn't ready to go back. I don't think I could have handled it then.

It was 2005, and Wayne was going back in about six months to meet with some of his writer friends to discuss a book they were working on. I threw the proposition out: could you just take these and give them back? The reporter had gone to the village and spoken to the family once she found out about them. Well, he was reluctant at first. Eventually he realized I just simply was not going to go. I mean, think about it. I'm going back to a country where I was the invading foreign Army to a family whose son I killed. I just couldn't even imagine doing that.

Wayne agreed to take the documents back. He thought that he would get there, drive the fifty miles out to the village, and he'd just give it to the brother and turn around and drive. That is not what happened. When he got to the village, the whole village had turned out. That mile-long road was just lined with villagers wearing white mourning Buddhist headbands. Wayne stopped by the political offices like you always have to when you go into the village, and they explained that there would be a ceremony in the village meeting hall. From that, after the speeches and the presentation of the documents to the family, they would go to the family home. They would have a meal and discuss things. It turned out to be quite a cathartic experience for Wayne—a lot of his ghosts I think got eaten up during that process. Eventually, Wayne wound up writing a book called *Wandering Souls*. He titled it *Wandering Souls* because in the Buddhist tradition, if a person dies away from the family village and the body is not returned, they think the body is lost—wandering, trying to find its way back home. As they were driving into the village, they were throwing green and orange paper out the window. This is the traditional Buddhist way of leading the spirit back home. They would follow the little paper that was thrown out the window. Wayne wrote the book *Wandering Souls* because that's about what was actually happening. The soul had been wandering, safely stored in my mom's attic for forty years, and was now returning back to the village. With the documents, they read my account of the incident; they read my descriptions of where I was. They started contacting military leaders in that region and the local veterans in that region. There were some people who remembered the incident. I didn't know it at the time, but there was a group of eleven other soldiers behind Dam. We could have had a major firefight real quick, except that they were supply soldiers. They were just basically moving things up and down the trail; they weren't really combat soldiers. As soon as I shot Dam, the others left the area because they were instructed not to engage. They weren't combatant type soldiers. I didn't know that there were eleven people behind him. I really would have been scared then, sure enough.

They didn't expect to meet anyone on the trail. They were literally just ditty bopping down the trail. He had his rifle slung on his shoulder. He had no intention of bumping into anyone. That's what our job was, to do exactly that. Catch them off guard; disrupt the flow of supplies down the trail. Anyway, we get back and about a year later, Wayne comes up with this idea that he's taking a political group back, and they have the funds to include me in the group. By then, I had e-mailed back and forth to the family and realized that they were really sincere in their desire to meet me and totally forgiving of what happened. They understood that, in combat, these things happen; their people did the same thing to us. They were very forgiving and open about it and really wanted to meet me to express their gratitude for returning the documents. They had also found out where the body had been taken to by then, and they thought they could identify the grave that Dam was in.

In Vietnam, they believe in spiritualists. They had talked to a fortune-teller, someone similar to Sylvia Browne here in the States; someone with a track record of finding things. Maybe ten or fifteen years earlier they had talked to her about Dam and she had told them that Dam had gone to

America, but he would return in triumph. She hit the nail on the head, but the villagers thought she meant Dam had defected and was a traitor.

There was a little bit of shame for the family in the village because there was a traitor in the family. When they found out that he had died a martyr, the prestige of the family immediately returned. Also, not knowing whether Dam had lived or died, the oldest surviving brother could not become head of the family until it was confirmed that he was dead. All kinds of things were hanging in the balance. Wayne finally convinced me to go even though the political thing didn't go through. Finally, in May 2008, I just decided we had saved up enough money by then, and I would pay my own way and go. We went and met the family. My wife didn't go; she wasn't feeling well at the time.

When I went back and met with the family, his niece, Thi, was doing something called channeling. She was channeling Dam's spirit. She was saying things and sometimes my interpreter said, "I don't know what she's saying. She's speaking in tongues." Being from the South, I have seen people occasionally lose control at a funeral and begin speaking in tongues. I was familiar with what was going on and once I realized what she was doing, I was no longer fearful. I was standing about two feet from her and she's wailing and gnashing her teeth. She's babbling this nonsense and crying out. I expected her to grab me and claw my eyes out any second. Then I realized what was really going on and I relaxed a little bit. Anyway, they contacted the psychic again. She didn't know anything about their unsuccessful trip to the military cemetery two years before. They were very careful not to tell her anything because they wanted whatever they got from her to be from her, not reading into what they said. She told them basically that he was in a military cemetery just outside of Pleiku. She said that there were maybe eleven rows of graves and eleven graves in each row. He's the third grave in from the woods. She said, "When you dig up the grave, you'll find a blue porcelain bowl and a red raincoat." She told them his was the third grave, seventh row. Of course, Wayne and I are looking like, "Right!"

We were afraid we were going to get there, they were going to dig up a grave, and it was not going to be the right grave. There would be a big stink because we dug up somebody else's grave; they're very sensitive about graves in Vietnam. I was supposed to go to the graveyard with them. They supposedly had clearance, but once we got there, the military officials supervising said they did not want Americans in that graveyard. Having Americans there would be like an insult to the dead. They also said they were afraid I might be a spy, which kind of cracked me up. I couldn't go so his sister and brother went. They spent the entire day, that night, and most of the next day trying to get permission. Normally, you're supposed to dig up the grave after dark, but somehow, they got special permission to go ahead and dig up the grave anyway. Well, I found out later they probably did not have permission. They just went in and dug it up anyway, which has caused a big stink since then. It's strange—the story in Vietnam is now one of total admiration for what I've done and for the whole story of Dam's martyrdom. There's even a play in Hanoi now based on this little adventure I had. On the other side, there are thousands of comments about grave robbers and stuff like this.

So his brother and sister went and dug up the grave. When they dug up the grave, they found just a couple of bone fragments, but they found one little shard of pottery with blue markings on it and the fabric that the bones were wrapped in was a red canvas fabric. It was spooky, and the grave had not been disturbed. When they dug up the bodies to bring them back to the military cemetery, they just dug down until they found a few bones, enough to identify how many individuals were in the grave. They just brought some fragments. They didn't bring them all back.

We got the remains, and they came back to the hotel. We met in the parking lot, and they're holding this showerhead box. It's a box a showerhead came in from the store and it's very small; it's maybe eighteen by six by ten inches. The remains are in the showerhead box. I was a little puzzled about that, but in Vietnam there's a big taboo about moving dead remains. It can only be done under certain circumstances, by someone licensed to do that, and transported in a particular kind of vehicle. You definitely can't just take remains on public transportation, but the only way we had to get back to Hanoi was a nineteen-hour train ride. They had disguised the remains in the showerhead box, and when they showed them to me, the box had the red star flag draped over it as a sign on honor. They put it back in the vehicle just as though it were any other showerhead box. I met them at the hotel in Pleiku, and we had to drive back to Qui Nhon. We had to go through the Mang Yang Pass and then followed the train along the coast back up to Hanoi. As we're driving through, they asked if we could stop in the Pass because that's where the action had occurred and where I had killed him. I said, "Sure, it is okay with me." They wanted to have a little ceremony on the side of the road consecrating his remains and giving thanks for having his remains back. They asked if I knew where I met Dam. I told them, "No, it's been too long." I told them to just pull off wherever they felt comfortable pulling off. We're within one hundred yards of being out of the Pass and into the valley on the other side when they finally found a place. From the front edge of that little area, you can look right down into the valley and it's a beautiful view. They set up this big TV crew there because they were doing a documentary. They set up a big commercial camera on this ninety-pound steel tripod; it was a huge tripod. Meanwhile, the brother and sister are setting the box up. They have the flag on top of it and set it up on top of a briefcase. They were getting ready to light some incense and have a little ceremony there when all of a sudden a gust of wind comes up and blows over the ninety-pound tripod. It destroys the camera. I mean just breaks it, destroys it. *And there's no wind at all! This one gust comes out of nowhere.*

So we got ready and Jessica Phillips, the girl who was doing the NPR interview and audio recordings had this digital recorder, but she's fiddling with it because it's not working. The batteries were dead, but she just put the batteries in. We had stopped the day before and picked up a dozen new batteries. She got a dozen and I got a dozen for my camera. She went through three separate sets of batteries. They're all dead. I gave her the batteries out of my camera, and they worked; all my batteries were good. All hers were dead. We both got them out of the same bin at the same time. Go figure. So the TV crew used her camera to film the documentary and then took it back to Saigon with them and transferred it. While we're waiting to do the little ceremony, and they're working all these details out, I was walking around. I felt a little bit disoriented. It was really, really quite emotional. I was looking around, and everything I saw look extremely familiar. Especially that view across the valley. It looked really familiar like I'd seen it before. I turn around; I was looking at the ridgeline. It's a five-thousand-foot ridgeline and we're maybe twenty thousand feet from the top.

I looked up, and there's the tree. When we got there on the original patrol, we were supposed to come up the end of the ridgeline and walk the whole ridge. We couldn't get up the end of the ridgeline because it was too steep. The red clay was too slick. We had to walk up the Mang Yang Pass road about three quarters of a mile and then go up the ridgeline. Well, when we came up on the first plateau of the road coming up the ridgeline, there's this concrete reinforcing on the side of the road. They'd just paved the side of the hill, and the concrete was keeping it from collapsing. There were stairs in the center of it. It is 100 degrees, and everybody's just about passed out from coming up that grade. I told them to take a break, and I went running up the steps to see if we can get up the ridgeline there. It's still too steep, and I almost passed out going up the steps because I took it too fast, and the heat got to me. I literally had to kneel down a couple times on the way up because the heat was so bad. I got back down and caught my breath for a few minutes. We walked about three quarters of a mile, and we could see far enough down the road to realize it wasn't getting any better. We had to go up the ridgeline here. I figured we needed to go back and check that front part of the ridgeline. I looked up, and it's double canopy trees on the top of the ridgeline, low stuff 6-8 feet tall and then 90-100 foot trees. There's this one tree 120-130 feet tall, way above anything else on the ridgeline in triple canopy.

I told everybody we'd aim for that tree, because when we get up there, we'd be able to see that tree. We could go back down the ridgeline, and when we came back, we'd know where we're starting our new territory; so we did. It was hard, but we finally got up there. We carefully went back down the ridgeline and saw indications it had been used recently, but not in the last twenty-four hours. We started coming back the other way moving pretty fast because we just walked that area, so we figure it's safe. We're just ditty bopping down the trail. I didn't have any security out on the sides or anything. We stopped at that tree, and I walked up. There's a curve maybe forty to fifty feet away in the trail, and it started zigzagging again. I walked up until the point man and the slack man were maybe twenty feet in front of me. I turned around to talk to the medic there because I always use my medic to determine how hard I had been pushing my troops. I could tell by the way they're able to catch their breath whether they're too flushed or not. I was talking to him, and then I turned around and was going to walk up and talk to the point man. I was going to tell him to be careful and slow down because this is fresh territory. Just as I turned around, not fifteen feet past the point man, Dam came around the trail. That's when I wound up shooting Dam. The tree was the marker.

I was standing there waiting for the ceremony, and I looked up and saw the tree. All of a sudden, the view of the valley made sense. I remembered the concrete, and it all just came together all at once. It's so shocking that we would inadvertently stop at that exact point that I really couldn't believe it. I was in disbelief. I didn't say anything to anybody because I was not sure I was not just making this up in my head. I went through the ceremony and got back in the car. I was real quiet on the ride back. Wayne thought it was just the emotions of the experience. He didn't realize that I was processing a mile a minute. I was trying to remember all of the details, and it all started coming back very clearly. That night, I stayed in the hotel, but I didn't get any sleep at all. I kept playing it over in my mind. I finally realized that it had to be. There can't be another tree like that, sitting on a ridgeline like that. Not on the pass. It just had to be that exact point. Take that, the audio, the camera blowing over, and the batteries.

All the coincidences so far; it's just like, whoa. There's something spooky going on here. Maybe there's something about this wandering soul thing, sure enough. On the train, I was sitting there with that thousand yard stare because my mind was working. My eyes were not connected anymore. Wayne looked over to me and asked if I was all right. I said, "You're not going to believe this" and then I told him. I told him what I'd seen and what I remembered. Wayne's jaw dropped. He said that he didn't believe this. He said, "I can't put this in a book, nobody would believe this!" But that's what actually happened. When we got back to town, the family took the remains on to the village cemetery. Then they got the village set up for the ceremony the next day. We arrived about 0600 that morning and had to wait outside the courtyard to the village. The TV crew was doing filming and the political officers had stuff to go through with them. By the time I finally got into the courtyard, it's around 0930, and everybody's drenched in sweat.

The village courtyard, the large meeting area, now has this really big tent. It's a huge tent, maybe one hundred feet long and fifty feet wide. This is where they're going to have the ceremony. The casket was centered there, and there's a military band playing with traditional Vietnamese instruments.

There's a military general sitting up front with a microphone making announcements. I could see all this off to the right as I went into the family house. Again, I had a basket of fruit to put on the altar. As I went in, the niece, Thi Dam, was scary. She looked like a wild animal in the throes of rabies. Her teeth were bared; her head was tilted back at a strange angle. She's gurgling and struggling with the girls that were holding her. It's really spooky. I thought she was going to have a heart attack or something the way she was reacting. She was just completely losing it. We then got escorted by the other sister and the brother over to the funeral tent, which was open on the side. The whole village of about 1,500 people was there. It's a mob scene. We came down the center aisle, and the extended family was on the right, kneeling down. Then there's the speaker's podium with the military and the casket. It's only a little box about three feet long, a foot and a half wide, and about three feet tall. It is solid concrete covered with red glazed tiles and was extremely heavy.

They seat us down right in front of the family in these little blue plastic chairs that were made for Vietnamese, and that my butt wouldn't fit into. So Wayne, Jessica, my interpreter, tour guide Doug, and I were all kneeling down there. We sat there for probably two, two and a half hours. It's sweltering hot. We had not been intelligent enough to bring a hat, but I had a bottle of water with me. You go through that really quickly. By the time the ceremony was over, we were probably on the verge of dehydration already. Most of us had a headache by then from dehydration. Anyway, we're sitting there about two hours, and every five or six minutes, someone would come up and stand at the end of the tent. Then the military announcer, the general, would announce family so-and-so and the family would come up. One of the family members would take an envelope and put it in a basket. This is an offering to the family to help pay for the funeral. Then they would all light incense. There were six very old veterans in uniform, three on each side of the casket. Of course, there were so many incense sticks in this sand bowl in front of the casket that by the end of the ceremony, I was beginning to feel sorry for the guy on the right because the smoke was blowing his way. He was about to get asphyxiated from it; he was getting woozy from so much incense smoke coming his way, but true military type, he never flinched. At one point, I talked to Dam's youngest brother who was the one who spoke to us the most. I said, "You know, this guy's getting asphyxiated by the smoke." He said they couldn't do anything about that and it wouldn't be much longer. This went on for two hours. Just toward the end of it, the family got up and paid their respects also. The oldest surviving brother had not spoken very much and was very stiff; I recognized him as suffering from posttraumatic stress. He had that withdrawn personality. He came over and grabbed me by the arm and lifted me up. I couldn't figure out what he wanted me to do; we'd already put the incense up ourselves. Now he's pulling me up and the pallbearers were getting ready to move out to the graveyard. He's pulling me and I couldn't figure out why. I finally got my interpreter and I asked, "What's going on?" He said, "He wants you to be a pallbearer. He wants you to." He walked over, pushed one of the guards away and put me on the left front of the casket. Well, there's a slight problem there. I'm tall. Taller than they are, which means I'd got to bend over to be able to keep the casket level. It's a very heavy casket, weighing 250-300 pounds at least.

It's dead weight, and we'd got these little sticks to carry it on. Not only that, but I've got long legs too. It took me a few seconds of tippy-toeing to realize that the poor guy behind me was kicking my heels with every step he takes. I figure we're going to fall down and make complete fools of ourselves. Finally, I realize my arms are long enough that I can step out and walk outside their line of walk. We walk out very slowly down past the family house and past the courtyard out onto the road. There's this covered cart with glass sides and carved handles on the front carved like dragons that you pull it by. This is the funeral cart. It was really hard, but we managed to get the casket into the funeral cart. I stepped back, and the six soldiers take their positions—one on each side of the front; one right at the front wheel and another at the rear wheel. They push the cart along to the graveyard, which is about half a mile up the dirt road. The whole way was lined with villagers, and there were villagers streaming out behind us. The military band was in front now, and the family altar had been put on a little dirge right in front of the casket to be carried on the shoulders of another group. The youngest surviving brother grabbed me and brought me up to put me on the left front. The older brother took Wayne Karlin and moved him up to the front also; now, we're both holding onto this dragon's neck handle. We began slowly, and it took forever to get to the graveyard. About halfway there, the heat finally got to us, and I almost passed out. I actually got the "swimming dots" in my eyes because the heat was getting to me, and I was dehydrated. One of the villagers, an elderly woman, probably in her seventies at least, came up to me and gave me a bottle of water. I stepped off just long enough to swig some water, which really helped. About that time, one of the veterans who were in uniform came up to me and gave me the boonie hat off his head. I was getting the royal treatment.

I was thinking, these people are in the middle of this great grieving process and they're so concerned about me. It really shows you the quality of these people. We got to the graveyard and, in on the left, were the regular family graves. On the right, all the graves were red, tiled gravestones. There were about 200 of them. I asked Wayne, and he said they were the martyrs' graves. That's where the veterans were buried. He said there were only about a dozen of those 200 that actually had bodies in them. The rest of them just had markers because they didn't know what happened to them. They went to war and disappeared. We were filling a grave that used to be empty, and that means 150 or so families in the village were getting a little bit of closure from this process too. They still have loved ones that are missing; their souls are still wandering.

We went through the ceremony. We had brought this big floral wreath, and Dam's older brother gave a little speech. We set the wreath down, and then the veterans from the village set a wreath down. Another group, I think the family, set a wreath down. Then they lowered the casket into the grave. That was really difficult because all they had to lower it down with was some communications wire.

It's thin enough to cut your hand right off! That's what happened, they almost lost it. It was almost more than they could do. They could only have one person on each end, and there's four people trying to hold 250 to 300 pounds going into the ground. They almost upended it several times, but they finally managed to get it in—superhuman strength. The moment gave them the adrenaline to do it was all I can figure. They finally got it in there, and then there's a prayer. We're ready to close the grave, and the older brother grabbed me and brought me over. I was at the foot of the grave, and he brought me around to the front, and he reached down to the ground. He grabbed a clot of dirt, and he gave it to me. He motioned, and I realized he wanted me to be the first one to throw the dirt into the grave.

I lost it several times, which was not totally out of character for me. I was sitting here with a handful of dirt, thinking, *I'm a farmer. I'm a farmer's son and here's a farmer's son. He probably has held the same dirt in his hands.* I crumbled it up, and dropped it into the grave, wiped my hands, and stepped back. They got Wayne Karlin, who had brought the documents back the first time, and had him do the same thing. Then the family members put dirt in the grave, and they quickly closed the grave up. There was another prayer, and then we presented incense again. We walked back away from the grave, and the group started separating to go back to the village. The TV crew did a couple of interviews with Wayne and me, and that was it. We went back to the village, and by that time, the people were all gathered. It's tradition that they had a feast, so the family had eighteen or twenty tables set out and just covered with food. Everybody's sitting around eating. The family had one side of the table, and they had saved seats on the other side of the table for Wayne, Jessica, my interpreter, and me. Now it was time to eat.

It turned out I like Vietnamese food a lot. We're sitting there, and the niece who had been out of it the whole time I'd known her came around the table, sat next to me, and just had her hands all over me. She's talking to me the whole time; just won't shut up. She's so thankful and so grateful and wanted to meet my mother. For the rest of the hour and a half that we were there, she was just talking a mile a minute. She was just so affectionate and so grateful, but eventually, we did manage to get back out.

We went to visit the rehabilitation center to see the journalist who had published the original newspaper article. I got to the education center of the rehabilitation center, and for part of her rehabilitation program, she had a set of little exercises they went through. They're little group building exercises and were the same exercises I trained on at Fort Benning as an officer candidate. It's the same exercise. Same setups. There's the wall with the ladder that you couldn't get across by yourself. You had to work as a team to figure out how to get across. Same exercises! I was looking and asked where did she get the idea for these things? These are what I used. She said, "One of the Marine Corps gunnery sergeants at the US Embassy helped me get these plans and get it set up." Talk about coincidences, you know!

Feelings subsequent to coming back to the States after Dam's burial

My wife and my friends can attest to this more than I can. John, the conversations you and I have had the last couple of days would not have happened before that trip. I was much more reserved. You would have gotten monosyllabic responses as you get from many posttraumatic stress victims. You get answers to direct questions and no volunteering of information. You have to drag things out of us. I was very much like that; very quiet, very reticent. After I got back from my trip to Vietnam, and the returning, and the meeting of the family, it's like a burden had been lifted off my spirit; I felt happier. I could feel joy again. If you haven't felt joy for so many years, for forty years, you don't know what you're missing. That's what I keep telling my veteran friends. You don't realize what you're missing. If you could just get in touch with the ability to actually enjoy and feel pleasure again, and to be open and to let your emotions gush . . .

When I came back, I was a different person; I wanted to engage people. It really opened me up. I can't be specific about what changed. My attitude for life has changed in a very positive, very upbeat, very wonderful way. I regret that it took me forty years to get to the point where I could get back to where I am. I'm back now. I'm probably very close to what I was before I went to Vietnam. A little bit changed still, but at least, I've gotten the joy part of my life back again which had been missing for so long.

Closing Comments

The quality of mercy is not strain'd, It droppeth as the gentle rain from heaven. Upon the place beneath. It is twice blest: It blesseth him that gives and him that takes.
—William Shakespeare

Thanks to Ed "Dutch" Gehringer and Professor Wayne Karlin, Homer, his wife, Tibby, and I are joined together forever. Next to Hip and Carmelo, I have been with the Steedlys more than anyone else. Knowing what I know now, and listening to how he "met" Huang Ngoc Dam from thirty feet away on 19 March 1969, the uncovering of the papers at home after all those years. Then watching the video of the arrival of Wayne initially in Vietnam in 2006, Homer's trip two years later coupled with the burial of Huang Ngoc Dam makes me understand better how all these events have shaped the captain's life.

As I write these closing notes, my mind went to the similarities and differences between the US soldier and the North Vietnamese "grunt." The NVA soldier believed that a unified Vietnam was best for the indigents, both in the North and South. Although Communists, it was the nationalistic fervor that drove these men. Conversely, the American GI initially believed, overall, that they were helping free a country (the South) from Communist rule.

The South was populated by those who truly believed that a free government was best for the people. However, greed and self-interest swayed many to show us faces that contradicted each other. Thus, the mistrust among the American soldiers toward the ARVN. In their defense, the VC were so ruthless in their quest to overcome the government in the South that they threatened both villagers and soldiers (through their families) to attain the overthrow of the seated politicians. Farmers by day and combatants at night, the Viet Cong played both ends. It was only after the Second Tet Offensive in 1968 that the VC were virtually eliminated as a fighting force.

Aside from all that, you have to marvel at the noncombatant Vietnamese people, and how they handled the constant presence of bullets and bombs, while doing back-breaking daily work. Their rice paddies became battle zones. Their countryside was scourged by friend and foe. None of us in this country since the Civil War have ever experienced anything of the sort. We should all take a moment to ponder the old Hippocratic "rule" of nolitangere cordus (don't touch the heart). The act of touching a human heart was thought to be taboo by doctors until Dr. Blalock from Johns Hopkins performed the first blue-baby operations in the 1940s. Reverse this postulate as Dr. Blalock did and touch the hearts of the Vietnamese population today by showing our deepest sympathies.

CHAPTER EIGHT
Women and Children

The Displaced

Dedicated to the estimated 1 million Vietnamese
who made it to the United States, and over 3.5 million
North and South Vietnamese who are no
longer on this earth.

*Picture of Phan Thi Kim Phuc. Nine years old, naked with her brothers.
Taken 8 June 1972 by Nick Ut, Associated Press*

Cam Lo Village

Oh, Cam Lo. With your roadside beggars and starving eyes. / How long must you suffer? Your homes of brush have rotted, and your air smells from filth. / Your nights bring you torture and your days bring you shells. / Oh, when will you rest? When will both armies go home? When will you live again?

—A poem for the Vietnamese people
by Paul Ferraro, Sergeant, USMC

The "people from the South," as the Chinese called the Vietnamese, were subjected to the horrors of war for many years before and after US involvement. Stuck in the middle between politics and religious beliefs, they suffered unimaginable pain and suffering. Add to this the poisoning of their food supply (by Agent Orange), and terror by day and night, these rice-paddy farmers and their families paid a heavy toll.

Introduction to the Interviews

The following people are from all walks of life. Bettye Beverly lived in Vietnam while her husband worked for the US government. She had a bird's-eye view from 1970 until April 1975. She and her husband saved twenty-three Vietnamese from being forced to stay in country and from the retribution of the Viet Cong and NVA.

After a dinner meeting with Joe Beverly, president of an Atlanta payroll processing company, he asked about the book. Realizing the scope, he recommended speaking to his aunt, Bettye, who lived in Richmond. Joe was one of the first to request a book signing, and we have had numerous dialogues since that cold February day in Atlanta. What he neglected to tell me was that his aunt, a woman of eighty-six years young, could have been mistaken for the Queen of England! Women with more charm and grace on this earth are in strict minority.

While Bettye, Nguyet (Bettye's daughter), and I were having lunch at a Richmond Vietnamese restaurant in May 2010, a young woman walked over to me. Again, being a loud Philadelphian and excited eating such delicious food for the very first time, I apologized for my tone. She said, "I overheard you speaking about your book and would like to be interviewed." She was smartly dressed, a true professional, but after she told of being a refugee from Vietnam, I said, "Miss, you can't be a day older than my daughters." Responding, she said, "I am forty-two years old." I was amazed at her youthful features. We scheduled an interview while I was already planning a trip for Richmond in June.

Lucy (*last name removed by author*) had another amazing story, very difficult to read emotionally, let alone be in her presence while she tells her tale as a young girl captured by Thai pirates. Separated from her parents in 1980 while attempting to leave Southeast Asia via Thailand, it truly is a frighteningly real story. Lucy's goal someday is to write her memoirs. As of this writing, I have forwarded her numerous American contacts whose goal is to assist Vietnamese writers obtaining publication.

Unfortunately, Lucy decided against publishing her interview. Revisiting her childhood may have been too much to bear on paper. I am honored to have known her; a total stranger telling me her story, up to that point, reserved only for Vietnamese friends and family.

Nguyet was born in Vietnam, then adopted by Bettye after she escaped the country in 1975. As Paul Ferraro wrote in one of his many poems, these victims almost had their "hope murdered" had it not been for the angels on their shoulders.

Finally, Tran Minh (not her real name) lived in country until 2000, emigrating to the United States. She had some very intuitive comments while we spoke. She characterized Vietnam post-1975 to "building a new house after it had been torn down." She also spoke of Vietnam leadership considering changing the name of Ho Chi Minh City *back* to Saigon. A lovely woman, fate again reared its head, finding Tran Minh after a maze of phone calls to various people. We met in a Chinese restaurant in Virginia, the day after Lucy's interview. After many months, she finally sent me her interview approval, but fearing reprisal from the current Vietnamese government, Tran Minh requested my using any name but her own.

A key ingredient to Tran Minh's interview was our discussion on rationing following the Fall of Saigon. All Vietnamese had to accept rations on food. The country did not have the ability to provide the necessary provisions due to the war and the conditions of the country, so each person was allotted 9 kilograms of food per month. Converted, this means *2/3 a pound of food per day*. Rice was in addition to the food rations, but there were sand and stones in the rice; each person received a handful of rice per month. Clothing—each person was given 2 square meters of fabric per month. The material was terrible and living conditions very bad. Many people died due to starvation.

BETTYE SIEVERS BEVERLY

Widow of Paul B. Beverly
CIA Chief of Translation Saigon 1970-1975
Paul DOB: 28 February 1925
Interview conducted in Richmond, VA in Bettye's home on 15 May 2010

If you find it in your heart to care for somebody else, you will have
succeeded.

—Maya Angelou

Bettye Sievers Beverly was married to Paul Beverly for over fifty years. A retired Iwo Jima Marine, Army officer in Korea, and government employee in Saigon from 1970 through 1975, Paul passed away in 2004. This chapter is also in memory of him for helping save the lives of many Vietnamese folks.

Growing Up

I was born in Texas, and when I was somewhere around three years old, my parents moved to Iowa. We only stayed there a very short time and then we moved to Illinois. My father came from a family of nine children and was a mechanic at that time. Finally, when I was about seven years old, we settled in Waukegan, Illinois. I had a normal, happy childhood. I was an only child and had lots of relatives around.

I did well in school—not the smartest, but in the upper 10 percent. I graduated from high school in 1942. I immediately started at Lake Forest College, which was near my home, so I commuted. I graduated from college in 1945 and worked for the transportation office at Fort Sheridan, Illinois, setting up troop moves for fifty or more men.

After getting divorced in 1947, I started working for the Red Cross. Some of the women there got sent to Europe, and they wrote back; it sounded like a lot of fun. So after I put in for it, I traveled to Osaka, Japan.

Being an only child, you can imagine how my parents felt. They didn't like the idea at all, but I still look back and wonder how I ever did it. I went to Washington and had my orientation. They put me on a train with a Red Cross person. We got on a military transport and went into Yokohama, Japan on 8 May 1949. After a week or so there, I got sent to an Army hospital which was the second largest military hospital in Japan.

Overseas

On 23 December 1949, we were having our Christmas party over in the officer's club when three military men walked in. There was a nurse who took these three young men around and introduced them to women. Paul was one of them, and he was introduced to me. From then on we were a twosome. We decided in March 1950 that we would get married, but he was military and he had to have permission to marry me. He put in for it in May, and we thought surely the permission would be back by September, so we placed our wedding plans in motion.

He didn't have to go to Korea, but all of them were saying, "Oh, it'll just be three or four days. We should be back in a week." When they got over there, the twenty-fourth division was just chewed to pieces. Within two weeks, the twenty-fifth division was gone. I saw the American women left behind. Almost all of them had someone to look after the children; someone to do all of the housework. They were pretty frightened about their husbands being in Korea.

Paul did not get home in September for the wedding, but completely unexpected, on 23 December, he did get to come back to Japan. That was a Saturday night, so believe me, it was a mad rush trying to get everything done. He only had ten days, and of course, we wanted to get married as soon as we could. We couldn't get married in Japan on Sunday because the Japanese office was not open, and you had to get married according to the laws of Japan.

After that, we went back to the States to Waukegan, Illinois, where my parents were. We went back because of my mother's health. We stayed there until 1962 and then we went to France. My husband was selling to non-appropriated fund activities, and when de Gaulle took France out of NATO, they started moving the troops out. This left my husband with no job really, so he started looking around for something else. That's when he started working for the CIA in 1964. In 1965, they came through looking for people to go to Vietnam, so he went in January 1966. I had a really good job as the secretary to a major general of military assistance, so I stayed there. Our headquarters moved from there to Stuttgart; I made the move, and then in November 1967, I left. Paul was due to come home at the end of January from Vietnam, so I went earlier in November in order to spend some time with my folks. He came back, and we spent about a year in the Washington area while he went to language school. He went to Vietnamese language school, so of course, they wanted him to go back to Vietnam, but wives could not go to Vietnam.

I got a job in security; it was a pretty dull job, but at any rate, I was in Vietnam. My husband had a house with plenty of room. I arrived at the house to find a Montagnard family, one of the men who had worked for Paul when he was up in Buon Ma Thuot. Very soon thereafter, someone came in and told Paul that his housekeeper was at the gate. Somebody had broken into our place. They had taken Nguyet (Bettye's adopted Vietnamese daughter) by her pony tail and pulled her back in. They closed the gate, then took things like TV, camera, jewelry, and anything of that sort that was there. Then they went out and got in a taxi. I don't know whether they hit Nguyet, but they hit me. They tied her up, and they put something over her eyes so she couldn't see. She didn't know Paul's name, so she went out and found a Vietnamese military patrol because she couldn't get her hands untied, but she got the scarf off her eyes.

She found them, and she got a picture of my husband. They took her down to the gate at the US Embassy, and she handed them the picture. Right away they knew who Paul was, so they went and got him. That was one of the first big things that happened. So soon after that, we moved to an apartment. It wasn't as nice in some ways, but we managed. At any rate, they had guards on the gates. This all happened after the Tet Offensive in 1968.

I eventually found a better job working in logistics. The embassy was in Saigon, and the logistics office was out near Tan Son Nhut airport. At that time, almost anywhere you wanted to go, you had to fly. There was about a fifteen-mile radius around Saigon where we could go. There was a big Army base at Bien Hoa, and we could drive there, but there wasn't anything to do once we got there.

The road was very much like interstates for those fifteen miles. We did what we could do in Saigon in the way of sightseeing. There was a French restaurant not too far out of Saigon. We used to go there and eat. You spent your time either going to someone's house for dinner or having someone to your place for dinner. We used to go to the movies. About every six months, we would take some leave and go to Bangkok or Hong Kong. Once, we went to Penang which is on the sea. It was a beautiful spot. Hong Kong was interesting. There was lots of shopping, and there were some beautiful places in Hong Kong. Every two years we got home leave for thirty days.

When I first went to Saigon, there were convoys of trucks going through all the time. Almost all the houses were sandbagged. There were walls around most of the houses anyway. Everything was dirty. There had been trees on the main street of Saigon and they had cut these down for wood during the war. In 1973, when they pulled the troops out, there was a big change. The Vietnamese actually had some hope then that things were going to be all right. They started painting their places and trying to make them look better. Two hours (drive) from Saigon was the port of Vung Tau, but on the opposite side, it was kind of a peninsula. On the opposite side of it was the China Sea. We went down and found an old French hotel. It was in an area where a lot of the French had lived. When the French left, they took the roofs off their houses so that the planes wouldn't bomb them. They would be able to see everything in the house. At this old French hotel, the restaurant was up on the roof, which was true of many Vietnamese places. They would have it up on the roof, open on the sides and a roof over it. It was run by an ex-GI and his girlfriend who was a wonderful cook. He had some experience with entertainment things; his father had booked circuses and carnivals and things like that for towns. We fixed up a place down there and went down every weekend. When others saw how interesting that was, they came down to. There was always a big crowd of us down there on the weekends. This American who ran it would have an orchestra every weekend and he would put on a show. He could play the flugelhorn, and he could also ride a unicycle. We had some really crazy times. A lot of the embassy people came down there.

Most of the wives in Saigon had someone to take care of the house and do the cooking. In many ways, life was a very peculiar sensation. You'd go to work and go out to dinner, go to the movies, entertain yourself in the daytime; and at night, you could go up on the roof and see the fire from the guns. If you went down into Saigon, the people who were out doing the fighting were in the bars. Of course, that wasn't true of all the places where they were fighting, but it was true for the ones close to Saigon.

Leaving South Vietnam

Things really got better after 1973, and the Vietnamese had some hope that they would get a more normal life, and the fighting would stop. However, in December 1974, the North Vietnamese started more fighting. They came in to Buon Ma Thuot; they went into Da Nang. Da Nang fell; I think it was January 1975. When Da Nang fell, everybody knew that was pretty much the end. Everybody but the Vietnamese; they kept hoping that the Americans would really support them with ammunition and parts as they had promised to do when the Accords of 1973 were signed. There was a very bad situation when they evacuated Da Nang. All the Vietnamese wanted to get out of Da Nang. Some of them hung on the under carriage of some of the planes and, of course, dropped off. In Saigon, they started planning for the evacuation. That was a big problem because there wasn't that much military in Saigon after 1973, but there were a lot of American contractors who had their wives with them. There were also a lot of them who were married to Vietnamese. It was a real job to figure out how they were going to get all the people out. They gave people special ID cards, and they gave them special cards for the employees. They gave them locations where there would be helicopter pads and where they would go in case of an evacuation. They said that whenever the ARVN radio started playing "I'm Dreaming of a White Christmas," they were to go to some of those spots. Household goods were a big problem. In 1970, you could only take six hundred pounds, but by the time we were getting ready to leave Saigon, people had been authorized to bring a lot more. However you couldn't get orders to ship your household goods until you had orders for a new assignment. Of course, people didn't have new orders. We had some French friends who ran a transport company; they'd take anything anywhere. We asked them if they could pack our household goods and they said yes. They would pack them for us, but we'd have to again get them back.

Things that we sent to be shipped were just things that we had collected during our time there. We were only sending things that we felt we could not replace. Any of the things like a camera, a TV, records, or any of that sort, we didn't try to take.

After we got everything packed, we still had quite a few things left so then we started mailing things. In April 1975, my husband's office told him that we should leave the country. We could go get commercial tickets, and we did. At the same time, we decided to try and bring some of the Vietnamese out with us. We drove out to Tan Son Nhut and looked at the operation and found out exactly what was being done. We came home and picked out I think twelve people that we would take out. This would have been maybe on a Saturday. We decided that we would leave the next Tuesday. We didn't call any of these people to tell them or go to see them and tell them until Monday because we didn't want them telling a lot of people.

Almost all of the people that we were planning to take had access to Tan Son Nhut. You had to have a pass to get on to this airbase and most of them had it, but Nguyet and her son didn't. Also, the sister of someone else that we were taking did not have a pass. We decided that I would go out on the bus from the embassy, and my husband would go out to Tan Son Nhut and be there to meet the people that we were taking. We packed all day Sunday and Monday. I got a truck from logistics, and they took all my things to the APO for me, and I mailed them. Then I came home and packed some more, and we went down to the APO to take those things, and there was a big notice that the office had closed as of noon and would not be opening again. You could leave your boxes in the hallway, and they would get them out. I felt like it didn't make any difference, and I might as well leave them since there was a chance that they would get out.

Nguyet, her son, the other woman, and I went down and waited for the bus to Tan Son Nhut. We were there maybe shortly after seven. No bus came. People really started building up, and I was wondering how we would ever manage to get on the bus because there were so many people. Someone came from logistics and asked if I needed some help. I said, "Well, we've been waiting for the bus, but it hasn't come." They said they would go on in and do their business and see when they came out. I kept wondering where my husband was and why he hadn't come. It was somewhere around 0900. The people from logistics came out, and we got in the car with them. On the way out, we saw my husband coming in, and he saw us so he turned around and followed us. We got to the traffic circle close to the airport and close to the office where logistics was. The logistics people had said we'll take you to logistics and see if we can get a closed truck or something so that we can put the Vietnamese in the truck and you in the front and we'll try and get them in that way. When we got there, there were no trucks. Everything was out somewhere else, so finally, they decided they'd just take a sedan and maybe they'd let us in. We got out there, and they wouldn't let us in. We parked close to the entrance because I knew that my husband would turn up eventually and find us. I had a car and driver, but my car and driver had been used to pick up people. Paul had my car and driver sitting inside. When his driver saw that we didn't get in, she went and got him. Paul gave his driver some money and told the drivers to go back and bribe the guards. They did and we got on to Tan Son Nhut. This was on 19 April 1975.

After we got out to Tan Son Nhut with all these people, it became apparent that you could also get people out who were of military age. At the time we had started making this list, they had said not to try taking any military age people out. It became obvious that they were getting out so the general sent for his two sons. The sister of the wife of the general had two sons, and she sent for them. I took about ten of the group and got us all signed up. About three planes an hour were leaving. They would get to Clark Field (Philippines) and land, get refueled, and turn around to go back to Vietnam. It was a three-hour flight from Tan Son Nhut to Clark—it depended on where you lived. You didn't realize that you were not in Saigon. It was like leaving Washington DC and going to Bethesda; it was a solid city.

At the airport, they said they didn't know what time we would get out. They finally brought a camouflage net and put it over the tennis courts and that gave us a little break from the heat. Several times my husband and I went and got something to drink and brought something back for the people there. All the time I kept thinking, this seems like a movie that you saw during the war when they were on a train trying to get out of some place, and it never seemed to happen. This just went on and on. Finally, about 1830 that night, they called our flight. They had what used to be a theater, and next to the theater was a little garden with a trellis for roses or something. They had a couple of Air Force officers and maybe some enlisted men there. As you went in, I just had to tell them my name and how many people I had with me. The Vietnamese and others had been told they could bring one suitcase. You could check your suitcase, and they even gave you a check for it. They got up and announced that from this point on we were under the protection of the US Air Force, and I must say it was a very good thing to hear. There were lots of Vietnamese around, but they were ones who were trying to get out. So then we had to wait a little while longer. They said there would be one more checkpoint, and Vietnamese guards would get on the bus and any Vietnamese that they wanted to take off they could if they wanted to. We were a little bit concerned about that. Finally, the bus came, and we got on. We passed the checkpoint with no problem and got to the plane. They had airmen standing elbow to elbow all around the plane. It was a C-130 and had a camouflage net down at the rear and had the baggage behind that camouflage net. There were at the most twenty seats. By the time I got onboard, the Vietnamese were already sitting in there. I was the only American woman on the plane; can't remember how many men from the United States. It wasn't a plane that could take off and go straight up, but it sure went as straight up as it could go for a plane that size.

There were doors on each side, I've forgotten the name for them, but where they close the bottom and leave the top open. They had airmen with guns and rocket launchers in case we were attacked. If they launch those, they'd put out heat. The rockets that they would have been trying to hit us with would have been heat seeking and hopefully would have followed that. None of that happened. We had an uneventful flight to Clark Field.

On our way Home

This is still the nineteenth. It was a day that went on forever, especially when you're standing in the sun. When we arrived in Clark Field, the waiting room was filled. They had taken over a big hangar and had a reception area set up. Then there was an area that you had to go through giving them lots of pertinent information. They unloaded us and left us on the tarmac. Then we went in and from then on, I must say they did a marvelous job. The wives of the officers and enlisted men took over volunteering, and they had Pampers for the children, drinks, formula, and milk—anything that they might need because they knew that everybody had been out in the sun and that they were probably dehydrated. They did that and then the next area was ready. There must have been about twelve or thirteen desks. I had to stop at every desk and give my name and ID number of all the people with me. To do that at twelve different desks took quite a while. We finally got through that, and they took us to what had been a cafeteria and served us breakfast. They were doing this because they knew people hadn't anything to eat and hadn't had much to drink. Then they took us to a big gym where there were already a lot of people in there. I've forgotten just how many of us were on that C-130. As long as there were cots, you used a cot. When they ran out of cots, they had blankets or something on the floor. There was one set of bathrooms for men and one for women. There were maybe five stalls in the women's; there were around 350 people in that room so that was not a very good thing. I went to sleep, and the next thing I knew, the overhead lights went on. The very first thing that I knew I would be doing was looking for an emergency flight back to the States. The night before I left, my mother had called and said my father was in the hospital. I needed to go home. I told the people with me where I would be and left to go and see if I could find my husband. When he got in, he had gone through this long row of tables and had asked if anybody had seen me. Of course, everybody remembered the American woman with a bunch of Vietnamese. They told him where I was supposed to be put for lodging, but when he got there, I wasn't there. The first thing he did was go to where the emergency flight would be because he knew that's where I would be going. It was in a theater and when I looked up the aisle, there he was. I was never so glad to see him. I went up, and they were telling me when they thought they could get me out and got it all set up. We went back to talk to the Vietnamese, and somebody had called a meeting at 1300 of all the sponsors so my husband was going to that.

They kept getting me on flights and telling me for sure this time it was going and it wouldn't go. Finally, we found out what the problem was and why none of them were going. It was because they had changed the operation to Guam, and they were trying to move everybody from Clark Field to Guam. After a flight was scheduled to go and was cancelled, they decided that they'd have to get me transportation into Manila. They got a driver, and we left there about 2200. There was a Pan Am flight that was supposed to be leaving at 1330, and we weren't sure at all whether we would make it. Well, we got there, and I got out, rushed in, got to the Pam Am desk, and there was no one at the desk. I waited around and waited around. Finally, someone showed up. They said the plane hadn't come in yet, and they didn't know when it was coming in, but they would take my ticket. Well, when I pulled out my ticket, it turned out that, in the rush, I had pulled out Paul's ticket. I had Paul's ticket, and I didn't have mine. Pan Am would not take that. I had to call the embassy in Manila and get CIA. They said they would get money and send it out to me. They did, but of course, it took a long time, and I was on pins and needles thinking that plane would come in. It didn't come in, and they finally got there with the money.

When I had come in to Clark Field, I had not gone through immigration, but I had to go through immigration to get on the plane. I had to go over and explain all this to the Philippine immigration officer. He was pretty sarcastic, but he finally let me go through. Finally, the plane came in at about 1530. And what do you think! It was the plane that was bringing all the employees from Clark Field to Guam. If I had just stayed in Clark Field, I could have gotten on the plane down there.

I flew on to San Francisco and then took a commercial flight from San Francisco to Tampa. My father was still in the hospital. It turned out he didn't die then, but he died in October of lung cancer. The others took the bus and the Vietnamese handed this shaving kit to Paul; that's where all their gold was. There was $20,000 worth. That's something that I never understood. When you told American people that they brought gold with them, they seemed to resent the fact that they had $20,000 worth of gold. I would have thought that they would have rejoiced that they had enough money to take care of themselves; the government didn't have to take care of them. The afternoon that Nguyet came in, we drove her to Sarasota to my aunt's house. She went into the kitchen and started helping to fix supper. She is very good about no matter where she goes, she can go into somebody's kitchen and take over.

TRAN MINH NGUYET

Home of Record: Saigon, South Vietnam
Home of Residence: Lorton, VA
DOB: 13 February 1954
Conducted at her adopted mother's home Richmond, VA 15 May 2010

> *I remember once, while passing by the garbage dump near the village of Di An, seeing babies—three, four, five years old, crawling around the dump, like rats, seeking food. They had no one. No families—they were all dead. All they had was that moment and a garage dump. Human Rats! Never forget it. I am very sorry now that I remembered it.*
>
> —Hip Biker

Growing Up

I was born in Saigon (Gia Dinh Province) to a poor family 13 February 1954. My father had so many "girlfriends" (not called wives), so I grew up with my grandmom, aunt, and other family members since my mom was so embarrassed and upset. My father never really lived with us. When I was ten, I found all this out. I also had two younger sisters. We lived in Saigon together until 1968 when my (future) adoptive mom had me working in her home.

It was a very poor family with no money for education. My real mom got sick, so I had to go to school so I could get a job. I needed to provide for my family since my dad was not around. We lived in a small town within Saigon. My mom got better and then I met my adoptive father (Paul Beverly) who hired me to cook. This is before my adoptive mom (Bettye Sievers Beverly) came from Korea to live with Paul. I did not live there (yet). I worked from 0900 to 1900. I was not in school anymore. I took the bus home every night.

I lived in Gia Dinh Province from 1954 until 23 April 1975, the week before Saigon fell. My adoptive father got me out along with my son and quite a few other Vietnamese because of his position at the embassy.

It was very sad growing up. I know some families grew up very happy with a mother and father at home. These people had education. I feel very empty. Some families had their father leave and they had to grow up differently. Some Vietnamese people do care about their children and some don't. The multiple wife issue caused some fathers to stay with certain women and abandon the others. My father did not support us, which made my mother very angry. My mom needed him. In the United States, you have child support. They don't have that in Vietnam. Some of my extended family (my natural dad's other wives' children—my half-sister) moved to Texas, but I have not been in contact with them because I am still angry. They get more care and treatment than we did. By this time (back in the United States), my dad had money, and the kids received education and he provided for them, not us.

My dad did not go into the ARVN. He worked for security with the United States and the South Vietnamese Army when people tried to cross the borders between Vietnam, Laos, Cambodia, and Thailand.

To the United States

When I left Vietnam I came with my son who was nine months old. This was in April 1975. His name was Ha Minh Dai. When he became sixteen, he took the American name of David Beverly. So his full name became Ha Minh Dai David Beverly.

We flew into the Philippines at Clark AFB and stayed for about a week. After that, we flew to San Francisco.

My Family in Vietnam

I had to leave my birth parents and sisters in Saigon. After I left in 1975, about five years later, I reached out to my mom and received a letter. I was not working at this point, just living with my new family in America. My adoptive father gave me some money to send back to my family. This was after I received the letter. Then, in 1992, I finally had the opportunity to go back to Vietnam to see my family for the first time in seventeen years. We all broke down and cried. My mom said that when she received the first letter, she felt better knowing that I was still alive. She also said it was so hard for all those years because there was no one to provide for the family. They were desperate. By this time, they had no money.

My mom said that the letters that we exchanged helped her keep going. She would always hope that I was still alive although she was never sure. She said it was very hard for everyone. One day, my sister told me (before I sent the $100) that my mom said, "If we don't hear from your sister soon, we will buy some good food [they had been eating horribly for many years] and put some poison in the food and die together." When they finally received the money, my mom was so happy she bought good food. They were all around the table ready to eat, but my younger sisters would not eat the food. My mom said, "Why don't you eat?" They said they thought the food had been poisoned. They said, "We don't want to die," but my grandmother said the food was not poisoned, that it was all okay.

The $100 would give them good food for a long time since they were living on just an allocation of $2 a day for the family combined. Buying a small fish is one thing, but buying a large fish is actually cheaper, which means it would last longer and be healthier for them. She was very careful with the money. By this time, my sister was working so they had a little cushion. Instead of buying a cheap vegetable, they could buy bigger and better.

They were at the end prior to the money being sent. They would have all died of starvation. The thought of not knowing if I was alive or dead gave them nothing to live for. This is why we all cried so much when we were finally reunited.

Transition to American Life

By the time I got settled, my new parents taught me the culture. My husband came out to the United States, and my husband and I lived with my American family in Middleburg, Virginia. In 1978, my father and mother purchased a home in Alexandria, and we all lived there. My daughter was born in 1979, and not long after, my husband and I separated. My children and I continued to live with my adoptive parents. With the kids still being young, my new parents gave me a lot of support in our home in Virginia. My ex-husband and I have a pretty good relationship now, but he was always very dominant and always telling me what to do. He has remarried twice since our marriage. All were Vietnamese women.

My son is now thirty-four years old and works in security. My daughter Thi Minh Chau has two kids. She is a secretary at Fair Oaks Hospital and lives in Woodbridge, Virginia.

How would you describe your whole life experience?

I am so glad I'm here for the future of my children, but I am sad that I left most of my family behind.

Anything you would do differently?

Right now I just want to be happy with my family and my grandkids. My son's daughter lives with me, along with my daughter's two kids. On the weekend, her kids stay with their mother in Woodbridge.

I have a happy home. (*Author asks Nguyet if she can sleep at night*). Sometimes I do, but sometimes I have nightmares. Like today—you coming here brought out some bad memories. Not so much from the war, but why some people have the good life, good family, and some had to struggle so much like we did, then leave their country.

TRAN MINH

Home of Record: Saigon, South Vietnam
Home of Residence: not recorded by her request
DOB: 29 May 1964
Interview conducted in Virginia

> *This is the first time I had seen starving people—I had come to*
> *Dong Ha for supplies once. We had some trash we had taken over to*
> *a garbage dump there. Old people, little kids, women were fighting*
> *for some slop from the mess hall at Dong Ha. We came back and*
> *swapped some of our gear and supplies for food that we could take*
> *back to these folks. There was a fence-line that separated the people*
> *from us along the road. We had all these cans of food that we*
> *ended-up throwing over the fence to them: Cases and cases of food. It*
> *was quite a sight. I will never forget the look in their eyes.*
>
> —Scene captured live and viewed via film
> by the author before this chapter was written
> Sergeant Paul Ferraro, USMC,
> Second Battalion Ninth Marines Regiment
> Third Marine Division

Growing Up

When I grew up . . . I look back at the history, and I think in my mind, maybe they want what the Communist talk to people about. They want to make everybody the same. That's when they started to control the country. They took everything. They come back together. They want to make everyone okay. The rich people and the poor people have the same, but in reality, it's different—completely different. When you want to do something, when you plan, it looks easy; but when you start to do it, it's difficult because something will happen. You never know.

Before 1975, when I was a child, I went to school and studied. The education was completely different. For example, when you were from class 1 to class 5 before 1975, they taught you a lot of things about Vietnamese history—when our people first came to the country. They let you know about the history and about establishing the country. At least they taught the basic things they thought all Vietnamese should know. After 1975, it changed. They started to teach the kids about the Communist party. The problem is, when you're growing up, they'll ask about the history; when did you establish, some general idea, but these kids today don't know. In place of that, you will learn about the model of the military history when you grow up. That's the difference.

The second thing I remember before 1975 is in South Vietnam. You could move wherever you wanted. You could move to Saigon, to another province. No need to report to the police. But after 1975, they controlled you. They controlled you and your family. Currently, it's okay. Before I left, that way had changed. They allow you to move now, but when you go to a new location, you have to fill out an application stating your political party and your own location because you have to be absent for a while. Because of business or, say, a new job.

There was a community officer there we had to talk to. When you went to the new location, you had to report to the new location (manager) that you will be there for how long. After a year, you can apply for another year no problem. You can move for business or for studying. He had to know everything. The problem is, sometimes the rule in the countryside is (different) than in the city.

I'll give you an example. If you stay next to the heat, it will be hotter. Because it is hot, that's why you must be careful and not let the heat burn you. When you live far away from the heat, the heat does not affect you. So you do whatever you want. The rules are the same. If you live in the city, because the city a big place, the rules (are) very strict. Far away in the countryside, nobody is controlling except the man who is at the top of the village, the chairman. He can bend the rule, because if you complain, you have to go far away to the city to complain.

In Communism, the person who has the highest power is the general secretary. Before that, they had the person who had the full power, control of the country. For everything, to contact outside or to control the economy inside, it should be the general secretary. Right now, the chair is the prime minister. Right now the prime minister controls the country. They don't want to lose again to the republicans. They had to try to do everything they could to keep their achievement.

Embargo

There was an embargo on Vietnam for about twenty years. The American government finally lifted the embargo. President Clinton cancelled it on the birthday of the Vietnamese Communist party. Because America is a very big country, they (can) affect most of the countries. When they banned the flow of goods to Vietnam, lots of countries were affected directly. This helped promote the black market trade. This means the Vietnamese were paying too much money for certain things.

Russia had to help Vietnam. The Soviets had to assist my country, and a lot of food and medicine (was) sent to the Vietnam people by the Russians. Even people who were sent to Russia to study were people who have very good background about the Communist party.

Thanks a lot to Mr. Nguyen. He died I think a couple years ago. He had become the general secretary of Saigon. He's the one who came from the North, but he's the one who had the open mind.

Family

My family was a big family. I had ten siblings. I'm the youngest one. My father, if he was alive, would be 102 now. He passed away in 1992 in Vietnam, and at that time, he was 84 years old. My family emigrated prior to me coming over here. Chung came to the United States first. Then my other brother came here after Chung in 1986. He stayed in Singapore for almost a year until came here.

I came here in 2000 by myself. I came with a travel visa to the US Consulate. When I came here with the travel visa, luckily Mr. Clinton before he reached the second term (end), he signed a bill that allowed the people to come here even if their visa expired if they have family here. They allowed me to stay. My brother who was a sponsor for my mom came here first. My mom did not get the US citizenship at that time, so my brother cosigned.

She passed away six years ago in 2004. When she passed away, she was in Vietnam. We are very big family, and my mom said she tried her hardest to push all of us to school. That's what she wanted. I am the youngest one, and that's why in 1975, when the government changed, most of my sisters and brothers grew up. They were old enough to go out to work, and they wanted me stay with my brother, my father, and my mom.

Right now, I still have three sisters who live in Vietnam as well as two brothers. I'm the youngest, so I lived with my parents in the hard times; living conditions were tough when we changed governments. Luckily, I have a good memory and read a lot.

At the time, my parents were old, and they had the thing about the living for the family. They have no time to teach me. I watched myself, and I read books. My mother worked. My father, he got sick. He was a tailor before, but after he got the surgery, the doctors said he couldn't sit. After a year, he lost most of his customers, and he stopped working. After that, everything was put on my mom's shoulders; she worked.

I went to a college in Vietnam. I studied accounting. Right now, I don't know the name of it; they changed it. It was Financial Economy College or something like that. That is in Ho Chi Minh City—Ho Chi Minh City University of Economics. At that time, when you wanted to go to the university, it was very hard. You have to try and take this test. Not like here. Here they check your GED. If your GED looks good, you can go to a university. Over there, you have to take an exam. You have to make a résumé. In the résumé, you have to list those in your family who served in the government before 1975. You also need to be level three or level four. That means if you want to get inside university, your score had to be very high. Families who served the military or government; they hurt the student. The score for them would be lower, less. If they wanted to enter the university, they would have to try and study very hard. If your father was in the government before 1975 and you want to enter the university, you had to take the exam and your score had to be twenty.

I worked for ten years in accounting. Luckily for me, after I graduated, I worked for a Taiwanese company, a Vietnamese company, and a German company. The last one I worked for was an American company. Before I came here, I started as a financial analyst. After that, I moved. When I worked with the German company, I worked on quality control to check the quality of merchandise—check items. I did the quality check when the merchandise was on the assembly line. It was good—I signed to approve, and they stocked. Otherwise, I had to haul the whole amount, and they had to remake it. After that, I worked as an assistant for the financial director at a Hong Kong firm. The last position I had was the office manager for an American moving company. Luckily, I don't have to work for the government.

I don't have any children. I got married in 2001, and my marriage ended soon after. He was Vietnamese. When we married, it was good. My ex-husband never seemed to want to talk and he didn't call me either. Even right now, he doesn't know where I am; I don't know where he lives either. I knew, when I was in Oregon, he lived with another woman who was the owner of a nail salon. That was the last information I knew about him.

I went to Portland after I left Vietnam. After a year, I moved from Portland to Miami, Florida, by myself. I drove for a week across the country by myself. I remember I left Oregon on a Tuesday afternoon and drove all the way to Miami, Florida. The following Monday, I arrived Miami.

Now, I work for Lens Crafters Vision Center. I make the glasses. I am a lab person. I travel a lot.

Vietnam

People who have bad memories about the time they lived in Vietnam and could not stand for it, they had to leave. If they are lucky, they left (to come over) here. They still had a bad memory about the time they lived there; it's not fair.

Every time you go (leave the country), you pay by boat—it's not free. A lot of people they go free because they knew that you had the boat. That boat may be free tonight; they had to watch it. They made you stay in the boat somewhere next to the river. They hid themselves there. The boat left at night because they had to always watch it, and they jumped inside the boat. At that time, people could not push them out because they might scream, make a big noise. Police might come. That's why they had to let those people leave with them. Some people left free in those ways. All they had to do; I have people over there, you take me there, and my people will pay money. They will help you come to America because you had the boat, no money, but you want to live over there. It was difficult for you to come inside. That's why somebody has bad memories trying to leave again. They couldn't stand for that. They try many ways to escape Vietnam and the very, very hot living conditions. When they came here, they were lucky. They stay here and they still have the bad memories about the time they lived in Vietnam. When they begin to talk about Vietnam, they don't think about the good times.

For me, I came from very hard living. I give the best opinion about Vietnamese right now. Right now, at least everybody in the country, everything is under Vietnamese control. Vietnam as a country is a union. At least we still have the name that people know it by.

Opinion about America's involvement

I believe that American government did the right thing because they wanted to try to help, but the problem belonged to the Vietnamese government before 1975. They lied to the American government quite a lot. They took advantage of a lot over there and of the Vietnamese people before 1975.

Do you think that the South Vietnamese military were capable of fighting North Vietnamese on their own?

I am not a politician, but I just have one idea about people. You have some problem. Before somebody helps you, you have to help yourself first. Now, the Vietnamese government before 1975; they wanted the American government to help them. That's a good thing, but they have to try to help themselves first. I know the story I'll tell you will be a shock. When the American government sent stuff, merchandise, everything, weapons, food, and medicine to Vietnam to help them for the Vietnam War, everything would blow up in the truck. Big truck and a whole line up of truck(s) ride to the warehouse.

Sometimes, not only one time, I believe that. They don't know what kind of merchandise was inside. Everything was in boxes, and they pay—whole truckload I pay you ten thousand, four thousand to five thousand. If you opened it, sometimes you got merchandise, sometimes clothes, or some kind of medicine. Sometimes you know what's inside: weapons. Guns—new guns. They ended up in the hands the Viet Cong. What did they do? They scare people. People want them in jail. They fought everything.

How can those Vietnamese Communists get American weapons? Brand new weapons? Because someone got through in the river system and the Vietnamese spy, they knew that. They come to their side, and the same people move there together. American guns; these weapons kill American troops.

Did you know that a lot of people who had high positions in the Vietnamese military before 1975 had more than one wife? Here you say they're friends, but in Vietnam, when a woman lives with a man, a husband and wife, consider it wife. Even if it's not marriage, no marriage certificate, based on the culture they're still husband and wife. There's second wife, third wife, even. They have many kids. How can the payment, the salary of the soldier cover for that? Simple—corruption. A corruption that said you can take two, three wives—many children. Only children had good living conditions. One of my sister's friends, after 1975, her father went to the camp jail because he broke the commandment. After that, after he got out of jail, he lived in the countryside with his second wife. The first wife and children lived in the city; he didn't care. With the money before 1975, how could they do that? Simple; by paying off the soldier, enough to take care of a big family.

Describe the war

If I describe it from my own life, it's a sad thing that shouldn't have happened. If the war never happened, not a lot of American soldiers would have died in Vietnam. I talk about the American soldier. Second thing, the Vietnamese people have to spend more time to make whole the country. Many things happen. In the Vietnam War, a lot of Vietnamese people died too. After the war, Vietnam became a whole country and the whole country had to live under hard living conditions; especially the spouse for many years. It then led to the situation of a lot of people trying to escape to find the good land, the Holy Land. A lot of them died in the sea—died horrible deaths.

Current day

Right now I work at the optical lab for Lens Crafters. I have worked there for almost six years. I live in Atlanta. I am trying to look for a condo for myself.

Closing Comments

Sympathy is the path to understanding.
—Morgan Meyers, *class of 2015*
College of Southern Maryland

The first question some readers may have is why is Mrs. Beverly, an American woman, in this chapter? Simple—both she and her husband, Paul, saved twenty-three Vietnamese souls. She and Paul were also "displaced." Upon my arrival and walking around her Richmond home, it probably took me an hour to peruse all the pictures, books, and medals of her late husband. When I hear of an Iwo Jima survivor (one out of three Marines who landed—*almost twenty-five thousand*—were casualties of a total (ground) force of over seventy five thousand), my senses accelerate to high gear. Once we began the interview, it was truly remarkable that an eighty-six-year-old woman would have such impeccable memory with the insight to boot. Subsequent to our interview, I have visited Bettye to drop off material she so graciously lent me for the book. I promised Mrs. Beverly that I will always stay in touch. To date, my word is still good to go. Bettye turned eighty-seven years young on 21 February 2011. I called her to wish her the best that day.

After inhaling my first Vietnamese meal, I interviewed Nguyet. No sooner than we started our discussion, she began crying. Nguyet's own version of post traumatic stress disorder slammed her hard. It was very difficult to maintain my composure as well. Thinking in reverse, what if *I* was standing on the tarmac in Philadelphia International Airport, desperately waiting to get the heck out of my hometown (with my family still here) as enemy troops were bearing down on the city—you get the analogy.

The past came alive and engulfed Nguyet. Her emotions stirred mine. Although difficult to understand (I had to transcribe my own work due to the language barrier), I listened intently to obtain accuracy. She cried through most of the interview.

Tran Minh (not her real name)—what a heartfelt conversation and lunch we had. One of the more "up" women I have ever met; this demeanor to a total stranger. I was referred to Minh by another Vietnamese woman with whom I crossed paths with. Minh began our interview explaining what it was like growing up after the French were tossed out of Vietnam (1954) and the subsequent conflict that she lived through while living in Saigon. She spoke candidly about how hard it was. You could tell by her comments listed earlier that she held our government in high regard for assisting the "new" Vietnam by killing the embargo that was in effect for twenty years. Since she lived in country until 2000, who better would know than an inhabitant of the country all those years? What impacted me were her candid remarks about rationing. It is no wonder so many Vietnamese went starving due to these outrageous and unrealistic quotas. A handful of rice per person *per month*! My mother always used to say "clean your plate—people are starving in other countries." I think I was around twelve when she said this—or 1965 in Vietnam. The Marines had already landed around my birthday, and the future of Minh's country was unfolding before her eyes.

CHAPTER NINE
Prisoner of War

The Lost and Imprisoned

Dedicated to Paul E. Galanti
Lieutenant, United States Navy
Navy Light Jet Attack Squadron
VA-216, USS *Hancock*
Prisoner of War: June 1966—February 1973

*There's no such thing as a bad day when there's a doorknob on the
inside of the door.*
—Paul E. Galanti, *USN (Ret.), ex-POW*

Saturday, 7 May 2011. I was standing in the center of Wickham Park in
Melbourne, Florida. The Vietnam Memorial Moving Wall solemnly stood
in the center of this huge field. It is literally a massive replica of the Vietnam

Memorial in DC. Each Wall and Panel perfectly mirrors the 58,267 names carved in that DC granite structure. Trust me, it is quite a view. Allen Lloyd and R. O. Martin, both 101st Airborne from Vietnam, had taken me to this event. There were thousands of people milling around at noon on this beautiful spring afternoon. A woman told me it takes almost a week to assemble the pieces with machinery, a boatload of volunteer workers and veterans from all over the country.

While speaking to vets who manned various booths at the event, one man told me that no fewer than five Vietnam ex-prisoners of war resided in the immediate area. It renewed my zeal since I was already deep into the hunt to dedicate the POW chapter to a man who lived through incarceration. Because of both an e-mail and phone call a few weeks prior, and as fate has driven this work, I "found" Commander Paul Galanti shortly after returning home from visiting the Moving Wall. This chapter is dedicated to him. On 19 May 2011, Paul and I had lunch in Richmond, Virginia, after walking the Virginia War Memorial, and visiting the new Paul and Phyllis Galanti Education Center.

By the spring of 1970, more than 350 US pilots had been downed in North Vietnam and were being held prisoner. Exposed to horrid conditions and frequent torture, most American prisoners of war were never allowed to contact the outside world. In May 1970, reconnaissance photographs revealed the existence of two prison camps west of Hanoi. At Son Tay, one photograph identified a large *K*—a code for "come get us"—drawn in the dirt. All those who were unaccounted for were initially MIA (missing in action). In many cases like Colonel Myron Donald, whose interview follows, it was over two years before the military and families knew flyers and soldiers were in captivity. If there was no "body in hand," then you were MIA. One of the main reasons the "guests" were so strong and sometimes so belligerent to their captors was reinforcement of Dean Rusk's (Secretary of State in 1964) statement that "appeasement only makes the aggressor more aggressive." In addition, officers, both commissioned and non-commissioned, as well as draftees and enlisted men, are sworn by a code of conduct to "resist by all means available" when captured.

John Wayne wore the POW bracelet of Capt. Stephen P Hanson (*Vietnam Memorial Panel 21E Line 46*), a young soldier who sent a picture of himself to his wife and son with the caption of "Me as John Wayne." Hanson, a marine, was shot down over Laos and never returned home, but Wayne stayed in contact with his family.

Introduction to the Interview

Myron Donald is now retired. His story in many ways typifies the "flyboys" and servicemen who were captives of an unrelenting enemy. The Vietnamese said the Geneva Convention did not apply in the Hanoi Hilton or in the other prisons that the over seven hundred captives resided in because it was not a "just" war, and in Colonel Donald's case, because he was not shot down over the United States! The physical torture to these POWs was unrelenting. The effects on their emotional and psychological souls' were, to many, unbearable.

Thanks to Commander Caldwell (*see chapter 3*), I read Navy Lieutenant Commander John M. McGrath's book, *Prisoner of War: Six Years in Hanoi*. This work of just 114 pages graphically portrays, in Commander McGrath's own hand, the environment where these prisoners lived, the conditions under which they suffered, and the treatment that they encountered. Forewarned is forearmed; these graphic depictions of the NVA "methods" to break the prisoners are difficult to observe, but necessary to understand.

As to Myron's MOS (military occupational specialty)—in order to become an aviator in the Air Force, there were several paths. Any graduate of the academies, ROTC, MROTC, or college were able to compete to be entry level as a second lieutenant all the way to a general officer. In the Navy, rank upon graduation was an ensign and path that could lead to an admiral. These were dangerous positions in Southeast Asia—I say that because we flew missions out of Thailand as well as South Vietnam to support ground troops or bomb key positions in the North. Large bombers as well as surveillance missions were flown out of islands east of Asia (Guam). Take the F-4 Phantom aircraft that Myron flew. This plane had two pilots—the weapons operator, or GIB (guy in back) and the FUF (fucker up front). Both men could fly the plane. As of March 2008, the plane had its fiftieth birthday. McDonnell Aircraft, which became McDonnell Douglas, produced many versions of this plane for the military over the course of time. The planes flown in Vietnam were the Phantom 4D, 4C, and 4E.

The biggest threats to any Navy, Marine, or Air Force pilot in South Vietnam were ground-based fire systems. However, as the bombing moved to North Vietnam and Hanoi, their main nemeses were Russian and Chinese surface-to-air missiles (SAMs), anti-aircraft (AAA) systems, and the infamous Russian MiG-21 plane. During the entire war, over ten thousand US pilots and crew members (fixed, swept, and rotary wing aircraft) were killed, wounded, captured, or missing. Please **remember** these figures when you read Myron's story. For over five years, he bore a number, not a name.

MYRON DONALD

Lt. Colonel (Ret.), United States Air Force
Semper Fortis: *"Always Courageous"*
497th Tactical Fighter Squadron 8th Tactical Fighter Wing
Home of Record: Moravia, NY
Home of Residence: Tucson, AZ
DOB: 20 May 1943
Stationed at Ubon, Thailand
Shot Down on 23 February 1968 in North Vietnam
Interview conducted at Lt. Colonel Donald's home 2 May 2010
Release Date from Captivity: 05 March 1973
US Air Force Academy

> *What lies behind us and what lies before us are tiny matters compared to what lies within us.*
>
> —Ralph Waldo Emerson

Growing Up

There's kind of a history in this country of soldiers coming from farms. It may be that has changed now since so few people live on farms anymore, but I grew up on a corner of my grandfather's farm that my father had bought from him for $1. As a teenager I also worked on a neighbor's farm.

My dad was a carpenter and my mother was a housewife. My folks first lived in a town called Moravia, which is a town of three thousand people. It is a farming community on the south end of Owasco Lake in central New York. When I was in elementary school, we moved onto that corner of my grandfather's farm and into a house my father and mother were building themselves.

Some traits we learn, but I also think there must be some traits that we are born with. My parents used to tell a story about when I was really little. They had a harness and a line going up to a clothes line so I could move up and down, but not go into the street. I just sat there and howled until they let me go. I never even tested the limits. I just knew I didn't want to be restricted. I think that was an early symptom of an independent streak.

Many people might think it odd then that I went into the military. I think most people don't realize that, in many ways, you have more freedom in the military than in civilian life. I think I was just born with a certain energy or restlessness or curiosity or whatever it is that drives a lot of people. I don't really remember the early years too much, but I know I was always bucking authority when the rules seemed silly.

I played basketball, baseball, and football in high school. I wrote the sports section for our hometown newspaper. I was president of the student council, and on the National Honor Council, but some teachers thought I was too rebellious for that. I was a problem, but also a top student. The school had the same conflict as my parents. Neither knew exactly how to handle me. When I was about ten and in Cub Scouts and with more arrow points than anybody else, my mother took me to the Red Feather, a predecessor of the United Way, to find out why I was such a little shit. She just couldn't handle me very well when I was that age, and she was pregnant with my first brother.

At the Red Feather, a woman gave me an IQ interview in a basement room with no windows. One of the questions was, "Which way is west?" I was thinking, *You ding a ling! I'm in the basement. I can't see out the windows so I don't know which way west is.* That set my mood, and I didn't do very well on the IQ test. They concluded that I was so pissed off so much of the time because I was below normal intelligence. That is, I was smart enough to know I wasn't too sharp, but sharp enough to realize it and resent it. On the other hand, while they were talking to my mother, they left me in this little room with toys. So I built this ray gun out of Tinker Toys. They just couldn't quite reconcile the ray gun with below average intelligence. I've since learned how useless IQ tests are, but they are still fun to take. I've always had that streak of "Don't tell me how to do stuff!" Another streak is to question the conventional wisdom.

Growing up in the country, my two brothers and I roamed pretty freely. We have a sister, but she was much younger and so wasn't part of these early expeditions. We'd tell Mom sort of where we were going, and we'd just take off for the whole day. Some days we'd go to Grandpa's woods. We'd go into the woods with an ax and build a camp or whatever struck us. My grandfather lived a few hundred yards right up the road. We'd get the feathers from his chickens and stick them into corncobs and make these darts. They'd spin when you threw them if you had the feathers from the same side of the chicken. And we'd build forts up in the hay loft. We had tunnels and all kinds of little rooms. Luckily, they didn't collapse and smother us.

My dad had a single-shot .22 rifle. I'd hunt woodchucks. I didn't get many. I learned to shoot in the military. I think Dad never taught me how to do stuff. I just saw him do it. I remember him and my mother tearing down a maintenance barn for the wood to use to build our house. Dad's tools were always around. We built race cars in the basement and powered one of them with a lawnmower engine. We drilled holes in the basement floor, which was dirt, to make a well. Dad would bring home lead pipe from old plumbing and we'd melt it in the furnace and make lead balls for bolos and to weight submarine models and all kinds of stuff.

My sons can do all kinds of stuff too. I don't recall them ever saying, "We don't know how to do it," and I hardly ever said, "This is how you do it." They just assume they can figure it out. They can fix their own cars and houses, but now they're ahead of me with their ability to manipulate the computers in their cars and wire their houses for all kinds of electronic gadgets.

I think a lot of our ability is simply not thinking we can't do it. I fall down on that sometimes when it comes to some computer stuff. When I don't know how to do something, I call one of my sons, but if I remember to try, I can usually stumble to what I need.

We did have some chores. We had to dig up the potatoes in the fall. Well, it's a problem with an end, which is a useful thing. I didn't get enough scholarships to pay everything, and my dad was working one Saturday near where the senator from my area gave a civil service exam, which he used for appointing men to the service academies. I didn't want to go to a service academy. Didn't want that military discipline crap, but a friend of mine took it and said those are the things you do well in. So I took it. About a week later, I got a call from the senator. He said, "You can go to West Point or the Air Force Academy because the number one guy wanted to go to Annapolis." I left graduation early because New York graduates late and got on a plane to Denver and went to the Air Force Academy. Of course, they met you at the gate, and instead of being the president of student council, they see you as pond scum. It was quite an experience. I was in shock for a week, but the first night there, we're looking out at the Air Gardens, and it was clear and crisp and blue, and the gardens were just gorgeous. I knew I didn't want to go the Army because I had been to West Point, and it was gray and drab and overcast. Looking back, I think part of it was simply that I didn't like the green uniform. Blue uniforms just felt right.

I don't mind being alone at all. I'm not lonely as some people are if there are not people around. I think part of the farmer mentality, because I worked for other farmers, is you got to fix it yourself. You got to get up when the hay is ready, and you got to get up and milk the cows on your own hook. Nobody makes you do that stuff.

High school had been easy. I just read the book, and that was it. I didn't have to do anything, but at the academy, they had study time, and you had to be in a room. They had to account for where you were. That's probably the only reason I got through college because if I'd been in a regular school with no outside discipline, I don't know where I'd be. Well, I think I would have been gone within a year because when you get to college, it's a whole step up. High school, you can be the big MFWIC (motherfucker who's in charge), and in college, everybody's a MFWIC.

I sort of think of stress like that in military school and being a prisoner of war. Whatever you were when you started, you're more of it afterward. I sort of think that's what happened. I really can't think of it and know who changed drastically because of their prison experience. I think they just became more whatever they were before. That's my personal experience.

From the Air Force, it's very sterile. You fly over, then you drop bombs, and never see who you hit. You go home in your clean flight suit to a hooch and air conditioning. I really don't think I had any thoughts on the South Vietnamese versus the North and the "enemy." I think that's one of the reasons warfare uses younger people. First of all, they don't really have any significant views. I just accepted that because I was a US person and a US troop, so if the United States asked me to do something, it was for the country.

In country

When I went to Southeast Asia, I was twenty-four. I got there in the fall of 1967. I don't know how many real political views you can have at that stage in your life because even going to a military school, you don't hear a lot of political talk. All this anti-war stuff didn't really happen until shortly before I left for Southeast Asia. When I was in training in the Air Force, there were three or four people standing out at the gate, but I never saw them. All the real anti-war things started after I was in Southeast Asia. I had already been shot down by then, but for me, it was in many ways an antiseptic war. I guess that's often the case for pilots. You don't see them. You go over them at twenty-five thousand feet at five hundred miles an hour. You take off from your base. You do your thing. You come back, you land. You take a shower, you go to the chow hall, and you go to the movies whatever the hell it is. For us, it's not weeks on end in the bush. We're in air conditioned hooch's with house boys. You mentioned "Air Farce" (some ground troops called the USAF pilots this) and part of that is an inter-service problem. It's the reason why we need more joint activities because I got called in on a couple missions in support of Army guys on the ground and they'd pick the target and we would see it and make a pass and then it took us five miles and about a minute and half to turn around. Then you got to find the target again. If you're in the bushes, your world is twenty feet. Our world is five miles per hour. An F-4 is just not a good ground support airplane for that kind of stuff. That's why the A-10 (Warthog-tank buster) is such a superb airplane. That's why the Army has its armed helicopters because they can provide close support. Plus, the Army uses their helicopters often as mobile artillery. They don't really use them as aircraft. They just use them as a way to move guns quickly from here to there. They might hide behind a tree, pop up, launch a missile, and go hide behind the tree. They almost think an F-4 can stop in the air and wait for them to get their shit together.

We don't even have bombs that small. The Marine Corps carries 250 pounders. We were dropping napalm in the North, which was the dumbest thing you could do because you're low, and you get the shit shot out of you. Robin Olds (brigadier general) is the guy that stopped that, but the way we dropped napalm when we practiced it is, I forget now whether you went in at 100 or 200 feet. The bomb site would not be secure enough without resting on the nose cone of the airplane. The way you dropped it is you went along, and as the target went under the toes, you dropped it off. This was surprisingly accurate, and it flows very quickly, and it stays behind you. Iron bombs stayed right under you. That's why you can't drop them below say 2,500 feet because your own shrapnel hits you. You've probably seen the movies where the bombers open their doors and you see the bombs all the way down. That's because the bomb has the same forward speed as you do. It just drops and stays with you.

I almost felt like there wasn't any real strategy. My mission was really different than day guys. I flew nights. The other three squadrons at my base were day missions north of the DMZ and primarily around Hanoi. I flew in Laos almost exclusively up until the last couple of flights. We would often take off and have no target. We would go up and contact this C-130, which is the Airborne Command Post. We didn't have a flight plan at takeoff. We knew when we contacted the Airborne Command Post that they would give us one.

A Forward Air Controller (FAC) was a guy that was flying low and slow. It was normally a daytime thing. He was just up there hovering and suppose somebody would say, "Okay, I see something over here." Then he would send somebody over to check it out. All the flights at night would report what they saw, and he would send someone back. Then we had sensors along the Ho Chi Minh trail, so they'd pick up something, and they'd send us over there to bomb the trail or find trucks or whatever the hell it was. When you're going to war, you don't think of, especially when you're the guy flying it, you don't think of the cost of it. It was like a $3 million airplane, but it was just a way to get us over there. We'd go out with a full load of ammo and most of the nights we'd empty it. That's a 1,100 round clip at $5.50, and it took us 11 seconds to empty the gun. If we ever found any trucks, we would just go down and hose down the side of the road because they might hear us and pull off to the side in the bushes.

The criteria for guns and fighters are that you have to have six seconds worth of ammo, but because we had a pod, there was no internal gun. We had eleven seconds worth. Then the F-4s C, D, and E models have an internal gun. The reason for that was, in the 1950s and 1960s when that plane was built, we never thought there'd be dogfights, and everything was going to be done by missiles. So much of the Cold War was perceived as stopping a Soviet mass aircraft attack. That's why we had missiles. The trouble in Southeast Asia is most everybody in front of us, was us.

Even after we crossed over into the North, sometimes the MiGs came out. One day, I was flying a mission in Laos and the EC-121 was the flying radar ship called the *Bandit*, and they sent us in to get them. We were on them and hot and then they started turning, and you could see they were two Navy F-8s. Now what they were doing in Laos, I had no idea, but the Navy didn't squawk their IFFs (identification friend or foe) because they didn't want to give away their position.

If it was north of demilitarized zone, essentially, we were trying to bomb them into not supporting the South. In the first raid into the North, we bombed their power plants. We blew up their storage area the first day. After that, there wasn't anything for us to hit. We tried to take down the Paul Doumer Bridge (now called the Long Bien Bridge), which was heavily defended. We lost forty airplanes trying to knock that down before we finally got the SAM missiles that took it down on the first flight. What the Vietnamese did after we blew up their POL area is, they put all their stuff in fifty-five-gallon drums and spaced it out all along all the highways about every ten or twenty feet or whatever. So now what do you attack? I think there is basically a fundamental problem when people perceive you as the invader and then defending your nation against invaders. We were perceived as supporting the South Vietnamese against the invading North. That's how our view of it was.

Release from captivity

5 March 1973. At various points through those five years, something would happen. When I got shot down in February 1968 and Johnson called the truce a week later or thereabouts, I thought, *Oh, I'll be out of here in a month*, you know? Well, two years later, they're still arguing around the shape of the table. I kind of figured I was going to be a little longer than that. The Vietnamese thought they had won the war essentially, and so I really wasn't mistreated much those first two years. Then it just kept going on and on and on. Then Nixon started the bombing of the North with B-52s in 1972. They moved a bunch of us up to Cao Bang, which was ten or fifteen kilometers away from China, because I think they thought the United States was going to physically invade the North.

I was in the Hanoi Hilton first and then I went to another camp also in Hanoi called the Plantation. Then I was moved from there to Son Tay (Prison), and we were moved out of there just like a month before the raid (Son Toy Prison Raid by Special Forces 21 November 1970). Otherwise, I would have been rescued, which would have been a thrill. Then we went to a new camp they had been built in response to all the public pressure for poor treatment of prisoners. We were only in there a month because it was also exposed. When they raided Son Tay, they moved us out of the new camp into another section of the Hanoi Hilton.

When Nixon started the B-52 raids, we were in Hanoi, and the bombs knocked down some of the ceilings. I mean talk about amazing how those things came over. Then the F-111s came over just whistling like crazy. You'd hear the gunfire, then you'd hear the airplane because there's always about this far ahead of the flack . . . screaming over the city. Blew up an NVA gun right outside the camp. It was pretty exciting. When the B-52s started coming and tearing up Hanoi, they moved a group of us, not all of us but quite a few of us, up to Cao Bang in a little place we called Dog Patch. We were essentially out of the war, any news, or anything for a couple of years. Then they moved us and an interesting thing happened on the trip. We're tied up in the back of these Soviet trucks, and that's the worst beating I got was from rolling around in the truck with no—*makes noise*—over the potholes. We stopped in the middle of some truck parks that had been bombed by F-105s and the big bomb craters are there.

So I'm hoping Nixon doesn't call off the troops this week! We made it to Cao Bang, and then at one time, they just moved us all back to Hanoi. We were there a couple days, and they read the Paris Peace accord to us, which includes our release. We said, "Oh, bullshit!" We'd been through this. Quite often, especially with Mid-East and other countries, they'd make the agreement. Then they start to carry it out, and then they say, "Well, you haven't done this or the other thing" in an attempt to get more out of you. They always reneged sort of halfway through the bargain. These events would happen when we were in the camps and "Oh, that's a good sign. We'll be out of here soon." Well, after we'd been up and down on that four, five times a year . . . Like one day we got corn, said, "Oh that's a good sign!" Well, most countries corn is animal food. It's only Americans that think it's a good deal. So when they read this thing, I said, "Yeah okay. We'll see when it happens." Then one day, we went in this room and got all these crappy clothes to wear. You know jackets and pants and shoes and shit, and we picked stuff. Then they released us in groups. We thought one group would go, and there'd be this "violated the treaty" crap, and we'd go right back to the same old crap, but they didn't, and they just kept moving through the line. I was in the third group—in the third part of the third group. We went out to Gia Lam Airport (their international airport), and they would only let three C-141s land at a time. You needed three for the group, so they would be out there somewhere, and one would come in and taxi, and he'd drop the door. I could smell the flight nurses perfume all the way across the ramp because I'd smelled North Vietnamese camp for all those years. Connie Evans was the flight nurse on my flight. I was in seventh heaven. So we got in, and they went through their little ceremony shit, and we got in the airplane, buttoned up, and took off. Finally, we cleared the Vietnamese airspace.

They never did prevent us from shaving or taking a bath. It just wasn't very frequent. If there's water, they used it. If there's no water, they don't. If it's winter, it gets to be like 70 degrees. They think it's cold. They'd put on sweaters. They don't wash until the spring. We'd go to the showers and come back steaming off. They thought we were the craziest people in the world. We got to wash pretty frequently. At one point, I weighed 120 pounds and was bleeding from every orifice. I had colitis. They didn't know what it was. They thought maybe it was amoebic dysentery. The other reason why I weighed that much was we'd all been . . . I was in isolation for six months and then I had one roommate for two and half years and then a group of eight. After the Son Tay raid, they moved us into Hanoi, and they couldn't keep us isolated anymore, so we were able to distribute the food better.

Home

When we got to Clark Air Force Base after our release, they first had to de-worm us, because everyone has worms in Southeast Asia. Second, was to get us a uniform, but the main thing was, they didn't know what they had on their hands. We'd never had anybody who were prisoners for so long. I believe the (American) WWII pilots might have been two years, two and a half tops. British were longer. July 1943 was Sicily, but we were in Kasserine Pass in 1942. Then they brought Patton in. We'd been flying missions. I would say two, two and a half years—1942 to 1944. A lot of those camps were liberated once we started crossing the Rhine, but the Americans were treated differently . . . and pilots especially. Aircrews were treated quite well. In World War I, you'd capture the guy and take him to the mess hall. It was honor among fellow pilots.

First, we were debriefed for whatever they could find out about who else might still be there. Psychiatrists came around; questions like can you count backward and that sort of thing. It was very minimal, really. After that, you just went back to your job. The hardest thing was, I don't think they know what they had. There's a story, which I don't know is true, that they asked some guy to come up with what we might be like, and the only similar population he had access to, was the US criminal population. We'd always thought we'd be homosexual and suspicious and unable to make decisions. You can imagine telling that to your wife who you meet in a major Air Force base, and she hasn't seen you for six years, and the first thing a guy wants to do is go to a motel. She's thinking, *I don't know if I want to be alone with this nutcase.*

The Navy was better, in that they treated many of their physical problems. The Air Force; we had so many pilots during the war that we didn't need pilots. If you had some physical problem, you didn't fly again, but the Navy was much more willing to work with their flyers. One guy had done something, I don't know what he had cut, but they transferred this tendon to his thumb so he could fly again. Air Force didn't do any of that. The Navy, a guy named Bob Mitchell, started a program where he obtained a control group to match up with Navy pilots when they got back. That's still an ongoing program. It's called the Robert E. Mitchell Foundation, located in Pensacola. It looks more at the physical problems although some aspects of the psychological. His control group was even to the type of airplane they flew. It's still going on. I mean his control group is incredibly detailed.

I think pilots are more willing to talk for a number of reasons than the ground guys. One is, like I said, we're really kind of distant from the combat and killing. Second, the part that they didn't look at is, you take the physical and mental traits of pilots, we are supposed to be the top 2 percent in the country (military). I read a book in high school that was called *The Twenty-One Who Stayed*. It was the guys (POWs) who stayed behind in North Korea, nineteen of them were from broken homes. Sixteen couldn't . . . it was just a whole different group of people than the pilots.

I think some of it probably comes from World War II when we had the draft, and these huge numbers of people going in, and the attitude was, you went in and you did your time and left. Even after I'd been in the Air Force for about fifteen years, I'd go home and "Oh, going to make a career out of it, huh?" because career guys are those dogs over there we didn't want anything to do with. You know the sign, "Sailors and dogs keep off the grass" and that kind of stuff. The professional military started just before we did away with the draft somewhere in the 1970s. It was a draft Army up until somewhere around that time period. Today's armed forces are different. Today every single enlisted man is either high school or GED. If you're not at war, the military's the biggest educator in the country. We have remedial classes for people that can't read or write. Not all enlisted guys get to stay in. They have to reapply, and we don't take most of them. This goes for officer corps as well. When I was in, just about every second lieutenant made first lieutenant unless you're a total fuck up. Then 95 percent made captain. From that point on, half the captains made major. Half the majors made lieutenant colonel and you couldn't stay to retirement if you didn't make lieutenant colonel. That's what it used to be.

If you want to be a sergeant, you almost always have to have a college degree. It just works that way. They all have master degrees when you get to that rank. For officers, you have to be a college graduate to be an officer. If you want to get past major, you probably have one master if not two. Generals have the equivalent of a PhD almost universally. If you start at 95 percent and you pick half of them to make major and half of them you're already down to like 18 percent. Of all the lieutenant colonels available, they only pick a few hundred to make full colonel. Of all the colonels, numbering in the thousands, they only pick fifty to make brigadier general. So, the armed forces are by far the best educated, smartest, most disciplined segment of American society. We don't keep the cats and dogs. The judge no longer says, "Go to jail or go in the Army." The Air Force doesn't even have jails because if they're that bad, we don't want them, and we kick them out. Send them back to the society they came from. It's a different deal.

It is often because of the politics that run the armed forces (that they've made these strategic mistakes). President Johnson and Robert McNamara picked my personal targets at lunch. Remember the famous von Clausewitz line, "War is the extension of politics by other means." I mean, that was never so true. Not that we did much politicking in Vietnam in 1964, but you know that's really part of the problem.

Describe the war

In our case, we had a worldview that the Communists were taking over and nobody bothered to look that Ho Chi Minh was really a nationalist who turned to Russia because nobody else would help him. It's really Nixon who turned that around. Well, you think of him, he's the first guy that recognized that Communism was failing on its own hook. The worldview from the end of World War II up through Vietnam was . . . East Block fell, China fell, Chile; I guess it fell. There was this notion that the Communists, if we don't stop them here, will take over South Vietnam, will take over Laos and Cambodia and Thailand. That was our worldview. Opposing Communism was the biggest part of it. When you asked what my opinion was, that's what I took the war to be. The North looked to me like they were being militant about taking over the South. We still look at that now. What happens is that the people who have spent their careers studying war know this stuff. The folks who tell us what to do, often don't. Like Shinseki (general) said when we invaded Iraq, "We've got to have troops on the ground." Eventually, he was forced to retire because Rumsfeld wanted this mobile elite miniature force. The first time I saw those people raiding and looting the town, I said, "We're in deep shit because we didn't control the population the moment we took over." It's not the armed forces. Although admittedly, we have some stupid people despite all this. It's what we're told to do. We could see Soviet MiGs in Haiphong Harbor that we could not attack until they took them to the airfield (and) put them together, and once they were off the ground, we could shoot at them. We couldn't bomb Haiphong Harbor where the MiGs were. We were just scared to death of that. It's unbelievable how much ordnance was dropped. Almost 2 billion pounds of bombs. More ordnance was dropped on North Vietnam than all of World War II.

I don't think anybody ever put together the pieces of what combat does to troops. Even today in the armed forces, if you think you have a problem, you don't go see the base psychologist. You go to somebody outside, so it doesn't get back to the base. It was the same thing when I was flying. If you had some little problem, and you thought the flight surgeon might say, "Well, you're grounded," we wouldn't go to him. I just don't think there was much awareness of what combat does to people. Up until recently, the VA wouldn't even talk to people unless you'd been in combat for up to thirty days. Now studies show that three days are enough. But it is not just combat that can cause PTSD.

If you're on ground, you may be out on patrol for a week, and you sleep with your feet touching the other guys so you can kick him and wake him up. You don't know. Right around the corner, there's one of those punji sticks or this thing flies through the air or an ambush or claymores (M-18 antipersonnel mines). They sneak up at night, turn the claymores around, then they attack, and they blow you up or naked women would come up with hand grenades locked behind their fingers.

Stories

I was pretty screwed up for the first week or so. The days are all the same except there were some Vietnamese who did go to church. They'd put on their church clothes, and you'd know it was Sunday. Some guys started out with a rope with a knot in it, but pretty soon, it just got out of hand after two thousand knots. You can't really keep track with that shit. It took me like two years to figure out which day of the week I got shot down. Even before, I only knew it was Sunday because that's the day they put out the anti malaria pills in the mess hall. The days were all the same.

I thought of going to a motel for a few days to just think. I couldn't do it. Just get away from everything and just think about. When you have all this time in prison, you review your life and think about all this stuff. That's what my brother thinks. He goes out there fishing and says, "It doesn't even matter if I catch anything. I just sit out there and think." I can't do that. I know I can always go to shore.

I knew this from survival school at the academy. We lived out in the mountains for a week. They said, "When we come back, we're going to the chow hall. Don't overeat." Well, we didn't think we did, but still probably about three quarters of the guys just puked over the wall. We knew this. I knew this. I was careful. I still overdid it.

After we'd been designing stuff in our heads for three years without anything, the gooks gave us some paper. It got in the way. We didn't know what to do with it. It's an artificial boundary, but you don't recognize it. You draw a line, and you need some more space. You've either got to add more paper or erase the line. Once you draw a line, it becomes a line. It's a thing of its own, you know, but if it's in your head, there are no outer dimensions. You could put on as many rooms as you want. If you don't like it, there you can move it over there. It's very flexible when you're doing it in your head. One of my friends designed a whole house. We're all in this mode for a while of wanting to be in someplace with one entrance so you can defend it so he designed a bomb shelter with different sections and there would be the country and the town. He designed it all and put feet and inches and decided to be done so he just changed it to metric. Then, one day, we collected all these cigarette wrappers for about three weeks and saved up some rice. He just put it on the papers. We cut it out, folded it up, glued it, built it all together, and had the real model.

It was probably within a year or so that I went through the whole appeals process and was turned away. I had colitis before I went over, but they didn't know what it was. Then when it got bad, I did not go to the flight surgeon. It really intensified in prison to the point where they had to do something about it. Colitis is one of the most debilitating things because you have no control over your bowels. You spend your life checking out where the closest bathroom is and hoping nobody's in it when you have to go. At that time, they looked at colitis as being debilitating for flying because you might get one of these attacks when you're in the middle of something critical, and now they've reversed that. Guys that actually have a colonoscopy can fly.

Aviation is very conservative with changes. They don't allow people to fly if they've had LASIK surgery even now because they're afraid they don't know what's going to happen to their eyeball under G-forces. Plus, the other part of it is, if you have a few slots and all the applicants, you pick the guys who have all these good traits. There's no reason the pick someone with a problem and then have to deal with it. It's the reason Joe Namath didn't get drafted. He was up for the draft, and they turned him down. Quarterback for the NY Jets for crying out loud. The Army says, "We can't afford to keep his knees going." You've got all these able-bodied guys. During the war, they'd train all these pilots, and then the war is over, and they got all these guys with problems. That's part of it. I had come back expecting to be able to fly again, because I was promoted while in prison.

The Air Force considered everybody a fighter pilot no matter what they flew. That has changed, but you had to be qualified to all types. There were only a few specific airplane types that had certain limitations. I was the highest sitting height you could be and be a pilot in the Air Force. The SR-71 (Stealth Blackbird), for example, I couldn't fly that because the cockpit's too small.

You need the A-10 (Warthog) for close air support against armor. You need helicopter gunships. You need guys that are willing to go out on two-man patrols for a month. Part of the problem is not the technology, but our unwillingness to commit men.

One night, I was flying a mission into Laos, which is the truck crossroads. Half the weather comes in from the Gulf, so Vietnam get's flooded. Then everything comes in through Laos. Then half the year, the wind would shift, and Laos would be flooded, and Vietnam would be dry. One of the quirks of the war, your hundred mission count was only over Vietnam, it didn't count over Laos. So half the year, most of your missions didn't count. Guys in the South flew for a year. We'd fly one hundred missions over the North, which might mean you'd fly two hundred missions, but only half of them counted.

Shortly after I got shot down, there's an initial interrogator, a guy who sort of spoke English. He was trying to figure out how the villagers treated me, which was actually quite nice relatively speaking. This was a pretty remote section where I went down. This guy wanted to find out if the villagers had beaten me because guys who went down in areas that were heavily bombed quite often were beat up by the villagers. The Army would have to come in and keep the villagers off them—obviously an interesting little dynamic here. I was sitting on this little stool, and he said, "Did anybody blow you?" I said, "Well, not recently." He said, "That's kind of hopeful." He didn't get it.

Vietnam was an individual engagement war. We weren't guys trained as a unit, went on a ship, fought the war as a unit, and came back on a ship. In

Vietnam, you went over as an individual on an airliner with stewardesses and landed at Tan Son Nhut and went to the replacement hut. You didn't even know what unit you were going to be connected to. This is ground troops. You might get a week or two days or whatever the hell they needed in Tan Son Nhut before you joined your unit. Sometimes if they're under heavy shit, you'd go from there by helicopter right into the middle of the firefight. Then you do this shit. You're on the ground, you're burning your shit in a barrel, you get beer flown in once in a while, and then your year is up. Helicopter comes in. You go to Tan Son Nhut Airport. You're on a plane with a stewardess, and twenty-four hours later, you're in San Francisco. There's no unit action primarily. We went over, and came back, as individuals.

Our relationships are probably like guys in World War II who were in units the whole time because we were a group. I have some long-term friends as much as I had friends. One of the odd traits of the military is you might not see somebody for ten years, and then you see them and it's like you never left. You just don't worry about keeping up relationships because you know when you see them it'll be just where you left it.

I went to my reunion a few years ago, and the program included how many people died. Half of them on one side of the program were killed in an Air Force crash, or shot down in Vietnam. The other side of the program list included heart attack victims, cancer, and the like. There's such a split between the two pages. Some died young flying airplanes, and the others by disease, and I am suffering ravishes of old age. I've got a lot of dead classmates.

When I finally went to the VA, he said, "You have a flight or flee thing. In normal circumstances, the threat goes away and you come off it, but after you've been under that for a year, two years, a month, three days, whatever it is, it becomes . . . what you do." The reason for this annex is it broke that cycle. It allowed me to back off from always being on the edge and ready to go, so I wasn't always ready to fight or run. Then you could sort of see it building up. Apparently, I was lucky that was all it took for me.

When you're in (ground) combat and the guy next to you gets blown away and his blood and brains are all over you—that's got to be a lot different from my case where guys would take off and just didn't come back. We didn't see them, generally. Some guys saw their wingman, but generally, we didn't see that. They just didn't come back. In some cases, they go out by themselves. Nobody knows what happens to them. They just don't come back. We don't know if they hit a hill or what.

One of the things I think you should say in favor of the military is we put five hundred thousand guys a year through in Vietnam, and this thing about the crazed Vietnam vet going out and shooting up some place, that has got to be so small. The postal workers, the disgruntled office employees, they do far more. I think it's amazing that you send millions of guys through that shit, and they don't come back blown away. Most everybody I know did two or three tours.

The hard part is going to be getting these guys (soldiers in Iraq and Afghanistan) to admit they have a problem. I didn't think I had a problem for twenty years until I damn near killed somebody.

In my room, the bunks were in the middle. You had this great big cement pad in the center outside, and you know it sloped a little, and you slept like that. What it meant was the outside was the only place you could move. We would walk you know in one direction and then we would go, "About face" and go the other way because there wasn't enough room to go counter each other.

I only had a roommate for two and a half years and that was it. We had one guy who came into our room at Son Tay for six months or so and then they had this raid and then they moved us into this other camp where there were eight or ten of us. After the raid (Son Tay Raid 21 November 1970), when they moved us all back, this room had like forty or fifty. So it was better, but on the other hand, there was so little room and so many people you were just ready to deck somebody once in a while. It was just too damn crowded . . . for me anyway.

This was a French prison to keep the Vietnamese in. They had the eyebolts and stuff for where the French used to shackle the Vietnamese to those concrete beds. This is one of the few legacies the French left; the prisons and a broken ice cream machine.

Everyone was on a corner, and there was a hallway between us and then another room over there, so to communicate with those guys, we'd stand up on the bed and signal through the window to another guy over there in that room. Let's see. It starts out A, B, C, D, E, F, G, H, I, J, K, L, M, N, O, P—and you'd be doing this thing to the guy over there. He'd tell the guy down here which we called the amoeba system, and he would remember whatever verbatim, and he would take it down to the wall down here. This guy would use the tap code to send it to the next room. So we could send the messages completely around the camp in a matter of minutes.

We were in a town called Cao Bang, which is fairly close to China and we were taken back into Hanoi. The trip back was much looser. I don't remember if we were even tied up or anything like we were on the way up. We got back to Hanoi to the heart of the camp we'd been in before. There were holes dug through the floor, like bomb shelters, churches and such. There was nobody there that we knew. There were some signs left over from somebody else. I think those were Army guys captured in a raid, but I don't know that for a fact. Then, one day, they called us out into the courtyard and read that there was a peace accord to us which was the section about returning us home.

How did Vietnam shape your post war life?

When I got home, they treated my colitis. They couldn't miss it. First guy wanted to take my colon out because it was really advanced. I said, "I'd rather try anything else." Another guy said, "Let's do sulfasalazine," which is really what brought it under control. After I retired, the VA was doing the colonoscopies because with colitis, you have a higher chance of cancer. They found some polyps and took about half of my descending colon. Between the sulfasalazine and that, it's been great.

There were two kids born after I got back that were affected by the war. They'd do something that would kind of bug me, nothing would happen, and then I'd just go flippin' nuts. There's no prediction. They could say, "Dad, Dad, Dad, Dad, Dad." And I'd go, "Aaaaah." It's just being on the edge all the time. I don't have flashbacks to Vietnam. I have flashbacks to stupid stuff like 'Nam, but it has nothing to do with 'Nam. Noises will make me jump, that kind of thing. I like to sit with my back . . . so I can see.

Feelings about release

I think everybody held those expectations in check because we'd seen so many things before that we considered a good sign and turned out to be nothing. There was probably less excitement than there had been way back when we thought something was going to happen, but that was four and five years before we were actually released. Once out of their airspace, that is when everybody cheered. Then we felt we were truly away.

I don't recall any ambassadors. There were other military. There was of course the flight crew and flight nurses. Probably a couple of doctors, I don't know about that, but there weren't very many. There was a civilian guy, a guy that showed up for Laos just before our release claim. He was CIA, and some civilian was in the airplane to take him. I think he was actually a kind of fraud. The guy had landed in South Vietnam and got somebody to fly him, and then he was captured and came to camp. He was kind of a strange duck. I think that was the only civilian I recall who was in the exchange group.

We went to Clark Air Force Base in the Philippines. Everybody went through there. The thing that surprised me is, we got in there pretty late at night, and we were the ninth airplane. This had been going on for several months. There were still a slew of people from Clark Air Force Base out there to meet us and cheer us on and all that stuff. Then we went to the hospital and had a meal. That's when I passed out from eating too much, that first breakfast back.

I think it was about a week we were in the Philippines at Clark Air Force Base. The Filipinos that worked on the base gave us all manicures and pedicures. The only pedicure I've ever had. They either made us or found us all uniforms, and they had them all fit. Custom altered. A little bit of a debriefing, a medical checkup, and a deworming. I think they were generally looking to see if we were real nutcases or not.

There was a guy I roomed with up at Cao Bang, John Fredrick, who died of typhoid fever while we were up there, just a few weeks before we were released. He was a Marine Corps gunnery sergeant who had been in WWII and fought through the Pacific. He was in China with Chiang Kai-shek's troops and was flying with the Navy. The Drut, I think it's called. It was kind of a crappy radar plane, and he got hit. The cockpit was on fire, and he didn't wear gloves, which burned his hands all to crap. They grew together, and the Vietnamese just used scissors to cut them apart. His hands were all crippled up. He was probably in his fifties, late forties.

Reunion

From there we went to different places. I went to Mather Air Force Base in California. I think it was the closest place to my ex-wife. The Air Force approved her and my son up to Mather and we met there.

It was kind of weird. Of course I knew who I was, but it was different for her. I didn't feel like I'd been away that long, although there must have been some changes. She was a little nervous. I think all the wives were. They'd run a study because we'd never had anybody who had been in prison that long. So the US population thought we'd be suspicious, homosexual, and unable to make decisions. You can imagine. A woman hasn't seen her husband in five to eight years and he wants to go out someplace to a motel and screw. Must be a little nerve wracking for some of the women I would think. We were there for a few days, and the Air Force flew my parents out from New York to California. That was pretty cool.

At Mather, we still had some time on our own. There was a taxi driver there at first who spoke Spanish. Since I'd learned the language in prison camp, he made himself our personal taxi driver for that time we were in California. We went up into town a few places. I had a bunch of these bracelets people had given me. People would come up and say, "Where did you get all those bracelets?" I'd say, "They're all mine." Most of the people didn't believe it. It's kind of like meeting a Hollywood star. You don't think you ever will, but people came up and talked to me, gave me bracelets if they had some or talked about the bracelet they wore, for whomever they wore it. I have two hundred or three hundred now. I have talked to quite a few people. Actually, when I got back, I got a bunch of letters and stuff, and I answered all of those and some of the people I actually went and met on my own. It was kind of an interesting time.

When we got back, they gave us a bunch of choices. One of which was going back to school. I had the choice of the University of Arizona or Notre Dame. They both had outstanding English departments, and since my ex-wife was living here in Tucson already, we just stayed here. I didn't have to be anywhere from March 1973 until August. We had what they called medical leave or recuperative leave. So Susan, Lance, and I bought an open ticket to Asia and went back for three or four months. We got flights. We started in the Philippines and went to Hong Kong, then Thailand and Burma. My high school classmate was stationed in Taiwan, so we went there and stayed with him for a couple of weeks. We just didn't have anything to do, so we went on this big tour of Asia.

Relationship with ex-wife

We were married before I was captured. When I went to California, then to Southeast Asia, she went back to New York to live with her parents and finish up her degree. During that time, her father had retired and moved to upper Michigan, and she was ready to get out of their house. She moved to Tucson because we had been here before and liked it. Then she was here when I got back, so we stayed together. I think it was two years later we decided it was okay, and we had the next son, Rhett. Two years later, we had another one, Sean. I was here in Tucson for seven years, and then from there, we went to Germany, and that's when we broke up. When we came back from Germany, I went to New York, and she came back here to Tucson.

We separated when we came back from Germany, but the law was if you're married for twenty years, she could get her own medical rights through the military. We'd been married for twenty years, so we did that and divorced shortly after I retired. She remarried within a year, so it didn't matter anyway. I see her once in a while—usually something for one of the kids. It's kind of guarded still. It took us a long, long time to get over that. It's only probably the past five years that she's even agreed to be in the same place I am.

The GI Bill was changing. So every year that I stayed on active duty, or every month, I lost a month of the old GI Bill. I decided to retire and come out here and use whatever I could of the GI Bill. I went back to the University of Arizona and obtained my MBA. Then I started on a marketing degree; but one, the bill ran out, and secondly, it just didn't seem to be going anywhere. I started looking for a job, and I couldn't find one. I applied for three hundred jobs, with only three interviews and no jobs. That's when I became a carpenter just to get through. Ten years went by after the divorce where it was a very difficult time financially. Between dividing up my retirement and paying child support, I didn't have much money left at the end of the month.

Current Day

After we separated and I went to New York, I was a free guy. I was in public relations, so I was out a lot doing talks and taking people on tours. It really was a very pleasant part of my life for three years. Once I retired, I received half of my base pay, not the extras you get for housing and food, and all that stuff. So my income went way down. Then the court started giving her part of my retirement plus child support. I went from making a fair amount of money to living hand to mouth for about ten years. Eventually, I had to file bankruptcy to get out from under all the debt I was carrying. That was a difficult time to struggle by for that time period.

For the five and a half years of internment, my pay went to my wife. The Navy and the Air Force handled it differently, but before you go to combat, you have to fill out this thing on how you want your pay to be handled. In my case, it went to my ex-wife—to my wife. She actually is a very frugal person so when I got back, I had about $40,000 that she'd saved up. Then Nixon worked the deal through Social Security, some kind of a thing for the family—well, we got five bucks a day from that. There was no extra pay for being a prisoner of war. You normally get your pay in allowances, just as if you were not in prison. The extra money we received was through Social Security.

Any retired military person can fly space available. It's much more difficult now because of the use of airplanes to go to Afghanistan and stuff. There used to be a lot more flights here and there. I went to Australia on a military hop after I retired. You can go anywhere that the planes are going. It is just a matter of being able to get on a military plane. There are, as far as I know, no benefits that get you on commercial airliners.

Advice to someone considering a military career

I think it has many, many benefits. I grew up poor without a lot of prospects. It really is an avenue to advance. You can go see places, get training that's not available anywhere else. It's a wonderful camaraderie among people in the armed forces. You learn a lot of discipline. When we're not at war, we're in school. The armed forces are by far the biggest educator of anyone in the country with all the programs and such. There's always that risk that, especially if you're a pilot, you're going into combat. Then you very well may get killed. That's a bigger thing for Army and Marine Corps. That's what their job is. So there's that risk. It's a wonderful institution. It's based on merit. There's very little social status that has anything to do with anything. It's just how well you do. The benefit to officers is that it instantly puts you in the higher levels of society, which I am sure I never fully understood when I went in. Because you're an officer, you're accepted into higher levels of society that you didn't ever get into on your own. The other thing that happens is you get responsibilities at a much younger age than you ever would in the civilian world. If you're an engineer of any sort, very shortly, you'll be in charge of a lot of people and major projects, where if you're an engineer in civilian world, you spend most of your early career drawing blueprints for somebody else. I was flying a three and a half-million-dollar airplane when I was twenty-four years old.

For my engineering degree, they taught basic sciences. It was more of a Liberal Arts program with all the various aspects. I had aerodynamics, thermodynamics, fluid mechanics, regular physics, nuclear physics, eight semesters of mathematics. Rounding me out was economics, history, law, and literature. The difference between arts and sciences is the science degree requires a language. At the Air Force Academy at the time, it was almost half and half between what you would call the liberal arts and sciences. We all had to have a language. I think it's a wonderful opportunity. It's one of those things, there's a risk involved. I think, compared to, say, Vietnam, the armed forces get a lot of respect that a lot of other places don't have.

I think it was pretty much Vietnam where the population just gave the service folks no respect and generally did not appreciate what they went through. I have not heard Korean War guys say that. I think Korea came so soon after World War II that there was this carryover respect from what the servicemen had done in World War II. In addition, there was the view that we were defending against Communism. There was so much anti-war sentiment against the Vietnam War, and of course, the people in uniforms are the ones identifiable. There are a lot of people who thought they should be a draft dodger or go to Canada or somehow resist it. Those of us who didn't were looked at as being complacent. There was a thing with the families to go around and talk to groups about trying to drum up support for the prisoners of war, better treatment, and so on. At one of the talks, somebody told my ex-wife that they thought I got what I deserved for having gone to war in Vietnam. There were guys calling up the families of people who were in Vietnam telling them that their brother, husband had been killed when they hadn't been. I don't really have an appreciation for the level of opposition to the war because it was just building up when I left. By the time I got back, it had pretty much died. I can only say what other people told me about what was really going on here. I don't see that going on now with Iraq and Afghanistan. I think people really do now separate the armed forces from the political aspect of it.

Andersonville National Historic Site
Andersonville, GA

Pictures by John Siegfried

The Andersonville National Historic Site is managed by the National Park Service. Andersonville contains three main features. The National POW Museum founded in 1998, the original grounds of the Civil War Union Prisoner of War camp, and the National Cemetery. Congress stated in the authorizing legislation that this park's purpose is "to provide an understanding of the overall prisoner of war story of the Civil War, to interpret the role of prisoner of war camps in history, to commemorate the sacrifice of Americans who lost their lives in such camps, and to preserve the monuments located within the site." As you drive onto the grounds, you initially perceive the entrance of a resort—a spectacular entry. Once you approach the cemetery area, you see the results of the painstaking and ongoing manicure of the grounds.

There is not one cemetery in the country that I have seen, including Arlington, which is more beautiful, serene, and solemn. The trip is a must-do. My second trip included folks from Georgia, Pennsylvania, and Arizona who had heard the stories and wanted to go. Buried in the cemetery are not only the almost thirteen thousand Union soldiers who expired here during the Civil War but many other servicemen, women, and their family members from our armed forces over the years.

The POW Museum was designed to capture many aspects, one of which was the Spartan conditions outside, as well as inside various POW camps throughout the course of time. As you walk through the building, you come away with a feeling of astonishment and understanding of how men treat other men.

Exiting the museum and moving southeast toward the actual Civil War encampment site, there is a beautiful stone walkway that has a stream running through it. Continuing to walk away from the museum, the observer now enters the area where almost forty thousand Union soldiers were imprisoned at the height of the war (1864). There were twenty-foot-high wood "stakes" that surrounded the camp. The only protection against the natural elements were the clothes and belongings the prisoners had on their backs.

Closing Comments

There were 766 POWs captured and interned by the North Vietnamese from 1965 thru 1973. As of March 1973, 114 had died in captivity.

—Lt. Mike McGrath, USN.
Ex-POW. Historian DPMO

The bracelet on the front cover of this book changed my life. Colonel Donald graciously allowed me to place it there. I pray for deceased family and friends every day, never forgetting to "talk" to my deceased mother-in-law, Marlene Tinari, about what that errant box in my basement did for me. Myron, Carol Garrard, Rhett Donald (Myron's son), and I all sat comfortably in Rhett's home while the colonel spoke about his life that Sunday in Arizona. More often than not, when I reach out to Mr. Donald, he is packing for, arriving from, or planning another trip. He truly has seen the world. Those 1,835 days in captivity may have been the springboard for all the travel. I never asked him and probably never will. Some things are just better left alone. Only those in chains, compliments of the North Vietnamese in Vietnam, will really ever know how the imprisonment affected their future actions.

When he was speaking about what the NVA did to him, I was thinking back on Commander John "Mike" McGrath's book *Prisoner of War: Six*

Years in Hanoi. McGrath goes into great detail about "the ropes," whereby the interrogators would tie the Americans up in morbid fashion. Mr. McGrath pictorially, as well as descriptively, portrayed this in his work. I also quickly remembered a piece where Admiral James Stockdale spoke about his imprisonment in Hanoi as well. This highly decorated Medal of Honor recipient pretty much stated that no one alive could beat "the ropes." It was only a matter of how long you could withstand this utter torture.

While I am writing this paragraph, it suddenly dawned on me that the date was 22 February. Because of the international dateline, it was actually the twenty-third in Vietnam, the same day forty-three years earlier, that Colonel Donald's Phantom Jet was shot down. Einstein said that "Coincidence is God's way of remaining anonymous." This is yet another "twist" that I simply cannot dismiss.

Commander Galanti and I met exactly 473 days after I first shook the colonel's hand in Arizona. As fate would again rear its head, I realized that the pictures folks took of us at his Education Center included the exact same outfit I wore with my initial picture of Myron and me in Tucson. My intention is to visit Paul again before summer's end 2011. The hour tour that we did of the beautiful, spanking-new Paul and Phyllis Galanti Education Center was not nearly enough time to absorb the atmosphere and contents of the building. The Virginia War Memorial in Richmond, Virginia, that occupies the same ground as the Education Center is a destination that I highly recommend.

CHAPTER TEN
Missing in Action

Those Who Never Returned

Dedicated to Walter Alan Cichon
Staff Sergeant, United States Army
Alpha Co. Third Battalion Eighth Infantry Fourth Division

There ain't no grave/Can hold my body down
There ain't no grave/Can hold my body down
When I hear that trumpet sound/I'm gonna rise right out of the
    ground
Ain't no grave/Can hold my body down.

—Claude Ely

Over the millennia of military history, warfare has always included
combatants who were listed as missing or unaccounted for. This would be

determined by execution of a "muster," or roll call, whereby a designated soldier or officer *after* a battle would shout out names of all those who were originally present *prior* to a battle. The potential reasons why a unit member was unaccounted for are many. Desertion, killed, wounded and not attended too initially, held prisoner, or empathy and change to the other side.

This information would eventually be communicated to the next of kin where proof of status (or status listed as missing) was confirmed. In Vietnam, due to the types of sorties (missions) our aviators flew, many of pilots were "alone" without a specific attack squadron. So if they were shot down, their status was only known due to lack of arrival back to base. This assuming no radio contact was made prior. In these cases they were either missing, missing, a POW, or KIA.

The operations of ground combat units in far smaller numbers than most wars in the past (largest engagements in Vietnam were typically battalion strength, or 400 to 500 men at most) meant that the likelihood of "missing" status could be far greater. A battalion was comprised of about four companies, say 100 to 125 per company. When a much smaller size force (like a squad, platoon or company) went into the field, which was more the rule than the exception with an Army and Marine unit, the possibility increased dramatically. There just wasn't enough "boots on the ground" to determine exactly what happened to a man when they missed muster call.

By the time all combat troops in Vietnam arrived home in the spring of 1973, there were 2,646 servicemen and women including civilians that were "unaccounted for."

On 7 April 2001, in Central Vietnam, a helicopter carrying seven Americans and nine Vietnamese crashed, killing all on board—members of a joint team searching for missing Americans in Vietnam. The Americans were from the Joint Task Force-Full Accounting and the Army's Central Identification Laboratory—Hawaii. The Vietnamese included the helicopter crew and the Vietnamese military personnel who work with Americans in the joint MIA recovery effort. The Americans and most of the Vietnamese killed in this crash *were not even alive during the war*. Tragically, the Vietnam War continues to take the lives of our young men.

Introduction to the Interviews

In June 2010, my wife and I met Lou Taranto, a retired NJ State trooper and marine, at a benefit dinner for the Marine Corps Law Enforcement Foundation. Mr. Taranto served after Korea and before Vietnam. Lou said he had a friend, and former colleague and state trooper, whose brother was shot down and originally missing in action in Vietnam. Lou gave me his card and a challenge coin for the Marine Corps Law Enforcement Foundation. A challenge coin is a small coin or medallion bearing an organization's insignia or emblem. It is carried by the organization's members to prove membership when challenged and to enhance morale. All of the Armed Forces, as well as each "branch" of these services, have a challenge coin. I already had randomly contacted the New Jersey Vietnam Veteran Memorial Foundation (NJVVMF). Upon speaking to Lynn Duane at the NJVVMF, we found families from Jersey who had siblings, nephews, and sons who were MIA. My brain being deep-fried from all the travel to date, I literally forgot about the discussion with Lou.

Lynn was of great assistance. She not only mailed over one hundred personalized letters from her Foundation, but called people she knew concerning my book, and the importance of paying homage to these MIAs and their families. Subsequently, the inbound calls hit my cell phone. This started the process of discussion, follow-up, review, and ultimate meetings with three families. Including Colonel Donald, only the MIAs have their pictures included in this work. My gut said this was the best testament due to their unfortunate statuses.

Lou Taranto's *friend* turned out to be Larry Pollin, whose brother George was shot down in 1967. Missing for over twenty-three years, George's remains were finally repatriated to the United States and buried in Arlington National Cemetery.

I met Barbara Pollin Greger and her brother Larry on 12 July 2010 to talk about their sibling, Major George Pollin. It was truly a solemn interview. Trinkets and plaques along with family heirlooms graced Larry's home in Lavallette, New Jersey. In addition, memorabilia that they bestowed on me (Larry insisted on my taking an entire album of pictures and documents) was quite moving—the material had never left his home in over forty years. All the government documents, from the initial "We regret to inform you" note from the USAF, to the specialists in the military, were granted to me. Anthropologists, MPD (missing persons division) officers, DIA (Defense Intelligence Agency) agents, as well as a host of other personnel were, and still are, involved with the MIAs. The Vietnamese government contacted our State Department regarding remains found. This led to the determination that they belonged to Major Pollin. Larry actually handed me a picture of his brother's skeleton laid out on a grid. Because DNA testing was not improved until years later, coroners had to go purely on dental records.

After George was identified, the family coordinated with funeral director, Tim Ryan, the government, and other folks to set the stage for burial in Arlington National Cemetery. The procession from Lavallette, New Jersey to DC spanned for miles. Thanks to the efforts of Tom King (King Tours of Lambertville, New Jersey), all the buses were donated to the family for George's final resting place. Tom was one of George's best "motor head" friends from their younger days. Larry and Tom see each other every year and always end up speaking about George. Finally, Larry asked me to include in this work two other best friends of George: Joe Burelli from Lavallette Grammar School and Ted Ham.

What was so interesting, and karma-esque, was that Larry Pollin called Lynn Duane (from one of the letters she mailed to him) around the same time Lou had told him about my quest. Within hours after speaking to Lynn a second time, my associate, Margaret, received a call from Larry at our business. Neither Lynn nor I connected the dots until a week later.

Larry always thought from the beginning that our meeting was beyond the normal circumstantial chain of events. His gut told him this was unusual. Further, after our interview, I was driving home from my third 2010 visit to the Vietnam Memorial in early August. Somewhere in Maryland, I received an e-mail from the publisher stating they wanted to pursue the book. Being the hyper guy that I am, my mind started racing. Who do I call first? Do I keep it close to the vest? What the heck should I do? Calming down, I decided to call just a few folks. Larry was one of them. Retired now from the New Jersey State Police, he answered his cell. He works part-time for Tim Ryan, and they just happened to be at Arlington National Cemetery. Here is where the plot thickens. He was literally standing at his brother's grave marker when I called him with the news of the book. He was astonished.

It gets better. A few weeks later, I dropped off all of George's material. Sending UPS, FedEx, or USPS was just not an option. Those delivery boys are all good, but I couldn't take the chance of misplacement or loss. Just a few days before, and shortly after Larry was in Arlington, he received a letter from an old friend. She included George's MIA bracelet she had worn for years. The woman thought it best that Larry should have it. Again, Larry reiterated the chain of events, saying there were higher powers at work here. Colonel Donald obviously feels the same way.

Richard Kelly called me on my cell subsequent to one of Lynn's letters. He was Major Harold (Billy) Kroske's uncle and a veteran as well. On one of the most beautiful summer days in all of 2010, I drove to Eatontown, New

Jersey, to Richard's home. While we were talking about his nephew, his wife, Johanna, made us lunch. If anyone ever says Jersey tomatoes are not the best in the country, they are mistaken. I eagerly ate the most delicious tuna fish sandwich ever. Sorry Mom—yours were great, but Johanna's was better.

Mr. and Mrs. Kelly also allowed me to part with very personal information about Billy. With the same affirmation relative to Major Pollin's history and personal effects, I delivered the papers back to the Kelly's in person.

Captain Norman Berg's son was shot down in South Vietnam while the war was still raging in February 1971. Norman was a WWII Navy man. He provided information to me prior to my New York City train ride in July 2010. Again, Lynn was of great help, as it was her letter to Norman that drove him to contact me. Meeting Captain Berg's wife Diane, I again was a guest for lunch, compliments of Diane.

For a veteran of that horrific war and being born in 1920, Norman was in amazing shape for a ninety-year-old man. At first glance, he doesn't look a day over late seventies. Goes to the gym daily; sharp as a tack mentally. I thoroughly enjoyed our two-hour meeting.

My appetite for New York City now has an added flavor. The next time I head north and stop at Penn Station, my journey will be interrupted to knock on their door in Manhattan. Also, thanks to Mr. Taranto, I carry the MCLEF challenge coin everywhere I go.

A final note before you read one of the most important parts of this book. The last known remains to be recovered from Vietnam (22 December 2010) and identified (11 February 2011) as of 24 March 2011 were those of Lieutenant Commander William P Egan USN. *Remember* the Egan family when you think you have lost something important to you. LCDR Egan's family lost William for almost sixteen thousand days, a lifetime for many people. Fort Worth, Texas, lost a true naval aviator. Say a prayer the next time your travels take you to the Vietnam Memorial at *Panel 07E Line 008.*

GEORGE PHILLIP BERG

Warrant Officer George P. Berg, U.S. Army Helicopter Pilot.
Born: July, 1946. Appointed as a Warrant Officer and Pilot, April 1970.
Assigned to a unit in Vietnam, May 1970. Listed as MIA, February 1971.
Listed as MIA, Killed in Action, Remains Not Returned, April 1971.

Chief Warrant Officer, United States Army
Semper Vigilans: *"Vigilant Always"*
Alpha Co. 101st Aviation Battalion 101st Aviation Group
101st Airborne Division
Home of Record: Belford, NJ
DOB: 16 July 1946
KIA/MIA: 18 February 1971
Remains not recovered as of 19 July 2010
Status (in 1973): KIA/Body Not Recovered
Thua Thien Province, South Vietnam
Conducted in Captain Norman Berg's home Manhattan, NYC on
    19 July 2010
Vietnam Memorial Panel 05W Line 114

Let us continue to remember *the 1,689 Americans listed by the Defense POW/MIA Missing Personnel Office (DPMO) as missing and unaccounted for from the Vietnam War.*
—Philadelphia Vietnam Veterans Memorial Society
And JPAC (Joint POW/MIA Accounting Command)

Captain Norman Berg USNR (Ret.) speaking about his son

Growing Up

I graduated from high school in 1938 in Bremerton, Washington. I was just an average guy, not very popular, but I did have a girlfriend, Jean Devaney, who was very popular. We fell in love while we were in high school. I left Bremerton for college, University of Washington in Seattle. We stayed in contact with each other, and I came home on the weekend, but had a hard time keeping my grades up. I wanted to marry her; I wanted her to be my wife. I loved her, and she loved me. Then the situation changed considerably in Europe when the war was really expanding, and we began to look at the draft, and I find myself eligible for the draft. I was twenty years old, and I was flunking out of college. I decided to enter the military.

Entering the Service

I had a chance to look at the Navy who then offered an opportunity for me to go and learn to become an aviator. I thought to myself, *Well, I can leave college, learn to become a naval officer, marry Jean, and start a life.* We weren't at war yet, this was March 1941, and my family finally agreed to it. I signed up for flight training. Jean really thought I was leaving her. I talked to her, "Just be quiet, go date fellas, go do what you want to do, but when I get my wings, I want to get married." So I went to flight training, had to solo in ten hours, and I managed to solo in just eight. If you didn't do it, you stayed in the Navy as a sailor. I made it.

I was in a biplane, yellow peril, and open cockpit. I did seven hours with an instructor, and one day, he said, "Let's fly up here." So I did, and he got out and said, "Okay, take it around. Fly it around the field and make a landing." I took off, flew around the field, came back in, picked up the pilot, and went back. Within a month, I was on my way to Corpus Christi, Texas. I started flight training there, had some problems with the navigation and passing the examination for the flying, but I finally made it.

I was on my way to success. It was December 1941, and I had a weekend off, so I headed into Corpus Christi, met some buddies down there, had a few drinks, did a little dancing with some of the girls, and got to bed at two in the morning. Got up the next morning on Sunday 7 December, and all of a sudden, my life changed. I came downstairs from the hotel room with a pretty good hangover, and there were people listening to the radio, and I was wondering, "What's going on?" They looked at me and said, "Look, Cadet, you'd better get back to the base. The Japanese just bombed Hawaii." Talk about a change in your life. I was excited basically, "By golly, look at this! This is good. I'm going to get a chance to fly against an enemy. I'm going to be in a war!" This was a reaction of nearly everyone I knew there. This was really what we wanted to happen, but we'd never admitted it to anybody.

Service in the United States Navy

I graduated from flight training, went back to Bremerton, and Jean and I were married. We honeymooned in New York City. From then on, I was flying. In December 1942, I deployed in a torpedo plane squadron to the Pacific. Our first child, Don, was born in 1943. I came home after the first cruise, and I left again for another cruise in the Pacific. My second child, Norma Jean, was born in October of 1944. I never saw my wife give birth to our two children. In 1945, I left the Navy, the war was over, and went back to college. Then our third child, George, was born in 1946. So there I was with three children and in college to boot. Jean worked at home typing labels for a company. We were living there in Seattle, Washington. Boeing was there, but they weren't building big airplanes. I was in the University of Washington and running a fruit stand on my time off. My wife was working at home, raising the three kids. I got back in the Navy as a weekend warrior, going out on weekends. I joined the reserves, and I ended up as the commanding officer of a squadron there; had a squadron of nine torpedo planes and meeting once a month. Same planes as I flew in WWII, and I flew one weekend a month, getting four days pay for it.

That was a TBF, which was a torpedo bomber built by Grumman. TB was bomber and F was Grumman. Our life was a struggle, but then I had an opportunity to come back on active duty again, and I did. I spent the next twenty years in the Navy and raised the children. At this point, I was a lieutenant commander, and then I got an assignment to a carrier squadron in San Diego. I reported for duty and was assigned as executive officer to an all-weather night carrier outfit, and I served there for about two and a half years.

We were on a jeep carrier, one of those small little carriers. We were an antisubmarine outfit. We were training to fly twenty-four hours a day around the clock, day and night, hunting for subs. My commanding officer was an Annapolis graduate, and I had two or three more Annapolis guys in the squadron. I was the XO, second in command, and had a wonderful experience. We did the whole show and didn't lose an airplane or a pilot. The commanding officer is basically the responsible person, but I had the responsibility of seeing to it that the pilots were trained. I had five or six department heads who reported to me, and I worked closely with them.

We had a staff of about 275 enlisted people. It was a big command and a difficult job. We were going to operate at night. In WWII we had no trained night pilots at all. The only time we had pilots at night was an attack by the Japanese Navy fleet following the Marianna's Turkey Shoot. The pilots launched at 1600 hours to attack the Japanese carriers. As a result, our pilots had to fly back at night. Some pilots did not make it back to our carriers, ran out of fuel, and crashed in the ocean. In my outfit, only three of them got back on board and one of them crashed in the water alongside the carrier, and we saved the three crew members, but night flying didn't start until the Korean War. We began to fly at night and did some submarine work because we were watching the Russian submarines in Korea. Now that was an experience and a half because we were on a slow jeep carrier. We were flying old WWII-era planes. One airplane had a huge radar under it on the belly and another plane had a small attack radar, and we flew in pairs. I was flying the big one. If I got a contact from a possible submarine from my big radar, I could vector the other plane out after it. Sometimes at 0200, you're doing this and the rain is coming down, and it's kind of crazy because what are you going to do when you get there? Nothing.

At the beginning of WWII, we had no radar at all. We didn't even have high-frequency radio when I first went out there. By the end of the war, we had pretty good radar. I had good communications to the carrier, because the first cruise I was on, we had no radar, and we searched for 150 miles out looking for submarines. Fly out 150 miles, turn left for 60 miles, and then start back to the carrier. Meanwhile, the carrier moved. Now this is dead-reckoning navigation (flying by the stars), and I have no radar and no radio contact. I can't call—radio silence. All I have is a device for Morse code and a little lever, and I can use that to fly back to the carrier. Night experience was unique. When I finished my assignment with the Navy squadron, I was promoted to commander and reported in the Reserve Aviation Program in Columbus, Ohio. From there, I went to New Orleans to the reserve base there. I was down there two years, had a wonderful time there. We had quarters on the base and a delightful time in New Orleans. Then I was ordered back to Seattle.

I had quarters in New Orleans. I had quarters for my family there, and we drove to Seattle for duty. I was the third senior officer on the base there by then, and we had beautiful quarters there on the base, and I remained in Seattle until I was promoted to captain. I was there about four years. I retired in 1965, so it might have been 1960 when I was passed over the first time for captain, made it for the second time, which was a big surprise; and from there, I went to admiral staff, and I was responsible for all recruiting for pilots for the flight programs. I had people working with colleges and recruiting potential aviators; I headed that program. Then I was promoted to commanding officer of the Naval Air Reserve Station at Lakehurst, New Jersey. By this time, my oldest son, Don, had quit college and gone off on his own in the Navy. He was in the Navy—enlisted man as a reservist—and went on active duty. He was nineteen or twenty. My daughter got married, and my youngest son was still living at home.

George, he was a wonderful boy. He was a fine athlete, state champion in cross-country running. He was about five feet and six inches. I'm five feet and ten inches, but George was a fine athlete, outstanding athlete. Not an outstanding student, but a good pilot. After he graduated from high school, we shipped him out to prep school, and he went off to college. Then he called me from college and said, "Dad, I want to go in the Army. I got a chance to become a pilot. I want to do that." I said, "Talk to your mother." Jean said, "Well, George, if that's what you want to do, you know what you're getting into." We went down to George's college and saw him sign up.

My wife understood it. She liked the military very much. She was a very fine Navy wife. Being a Navy wife is a very special exercise. She was the president of the wives club in some of the bases. She was very active in Chicago among the admiral staff teaching kids how to bowl. She was a good bowler, and she went to the nationals. She was a very active woman that loved the military, enjoyed it. I don't think she was ever unhappy about it until we lost George. It was a hard thing for her to adjust to. We went down for George's graduation, pinned his wings on to him.

Missing

George Phillip Berg was named after my wife's grandfather. Two of the people I wrote about in my book, *Regret to Inform You,* had their remains recovered. One was from just outside of Milford, Pennsylvania. His name is Edwin Pearce (*Vietnam Memorial Panel 02W Line 02).* The other was an Annapolis guy. His name is Mike Newell (*Vietnam Memorial Panel 13E Line 045)* from Ellenville, New York. I interviewed their families as part of the book.

One of these boys' brothers has made two trips over to Vietnam. When the doorbell rang on my birthday, 17 February 1971, I answered the door. There was a colonel and chaplain from the Army. I knew immediately that this was not good news. They told us George was missing. Jean (my first wife) and I sat down and cried together. She went away in George's room for about three to four days. I was working with the Boy Scouts. After a week went by, one morning, Jean said, "Come and sit down with me." I did, and she said, "Norm, I was down at the church the other day and I saw that picture of the statue of Mary, and I know it was not our fault, it was not your fault this happened. You can't blame yourself for this, and you've got to accept this." It took me another twenty years to finally celebrate a birthday.

I put my arms around her and said, "Darling, I know you understand. We're both terribly proud of George, of what he was doing. He was doing what he wanted to do, what he felt he should do, and we can't let that run our lives forever." She said, "I know that, I'm going to find something to do." So she went to work for the Boy Scouts of America as a secretary, and I started going on with my work. That's about all we could do.

George's Childhood

We were moving around. George started school in Spokane, then San Diego, Columbus (OH), New Orleans and finally Seattle. My older children did very well, but George just did not get along in school. He loved the athletics and loved the girls, but he didn't give a bit about school. He was able to pass, but marginally. He was a fine athlete. He was a state champion in track and cross-country—New Jersey State Champion.

The junior college was over in Pennsylvania, but he was a leader in school, a natural leader. People responded to him because he was a very outgoing guy. Girls—boy did he have girls. I remember he had a date before he had a driver's license, and he said, "Dad, would you mind driving us to the movie house?" So I get in the car, he'd get in the backseat, we'd drive to where she was, and he'd go in to get her and put her in the backseat. Then I'd drive them to the theater; that was the kind of guy he was, just a wonderful young boy. He was just himself; and he did what he wanted to do.

He got along with his brother and sister. Two boys that lived together until they got older; then they had to have a room of their own, but he was always on the outside. The oldest boy, Don, was very self-important. He wasn't a kid that could deal with people. He didn't like to be around people; he liked to be alone. He liked to build model airplanes; he loved model airplanes.

Family

Don was in the Navy. He was a first-class petty officer after six years of service. We had a falling out in college. When I got orders to go to Chicago, he was in junior college in Bremerton. He wanted to stay there. He had a car, and I didn't let him bring his car back, so he had to come back and start school in a college close by us. It was a mistake. I shouldn't have done that. He was nineteen or twenty years old then. He lasted about six months in that school, came home, and said, "Dad, I'm through with this. I'm done. You can go to hell as far as I'm concerned." Then he left. I think I saw him maybe three times the rest of his life; then he came back out of the Navy and stayed in Seattle. He did not want to come back to where we were. He died in 1984 at age forty-two of alcoholism. I was in Europe when we got the message. He had one son, and we're very close with his son now, very close. Don and I just never got along together. I wanted him to be a naval aviator. He didn't want to be a naval aviator, and I would try to force him to be one. I did a lot of things that I shouldn't have done, looking back on it now.

My daughter married. They have two children, and she and her husband both worked. She went to work in a shoe factory in the Carolinas'. She worked at LL Bean as director of Quality Control for a global retailer. She's in her late sixties. She's retired now. They live in North Carolina, two sons, and she has four grandchildren. She's about an hour and a half drive to the ocean where she is. We stay in contact. In fact, they're going to stop by and see us next month. They're both retired now.

Don's wife is still alive. She's a grandmother now. She took care of her son after they divorced. Don was on his own now, and she took care of their child. Don, my grandson, joined the Army. Must have been about twenty years ago, I guess. I remember I got a telephone call that said, "Grandpa, what's an article twenty-one?" I said, "Who did you hit?" He said, "I got in an argument with my sergeant and I hit him." I said, "What's going to happen?" He said, "I'm not going to be a policeman. They offered me a job in northern Virginia and I think I'm going to take it." So he went out to Virginia and got involved in the boat side of the Army. The Army has more boats than the Navy, a huge number of boats.

He found a mentor . . . a very fine leader, an older man, a warrant officer, probably a W-4. He took him under his wing, and next thing you know, Don was as happy as he could be. He was single at that time, and he worked his way through it now. He's had tours in Kuwait and Tasmania on a boat over there. He also has two lovely children. He's now a W-5, which is top of the heap. Just two guys made it this year, he was one of them. It equals an E-7 (sergeant first class), and he was just the damndest kid I'd ever seen. He was nothing until the Army got a hold of him, and he fell in love with it.

We're in touch with him on a regular basis. Eventually, Jean and I had ten years in Europe together working for the Boy Scouts of America. After we got the word on George, I was promoted and went to the national staff for the Boy Scouts of America and became the national director of sea scouting. I traveled all over America meeting guys. I was on the national staff as national director of sea scouting and then became the assistant director of exploring for the national office. Then I had a chance to go to Europe, so I grabbed it, and we went to Europe. We had scouting in every place where we had a military operation. We had scouting going in Turkey, Spain, Italy, Greece, England, and Germany. I retired when I was sixty-five years old in the mid-1980s.

I was never a Navy captain. I was a naval aviator who happened to be a captain. There's a big difference in that, so I didn't look at a career in civilian life as a Navy captain. I'm not that kind of a guy. Then the Boy Scouts came along, and I said, "Boy"—I thought to myself and Jean did too— "that'd be a lot of fun." I knew some of them because I worked with some of them, so Jean and I went to Europe. Jean went back to work again as a secretary and she worked in the Girl Scouts in the office, and I worked at the other end of the building. We spent ten years over there, and when I retired, we were having a meeting. All the volunteers were all Army generals. Our scouting president was an assistant general of Europe. My boss announced to the generals that Norman is retiring, and the head of the military in

Europe stood up and said, "Mr. Berg, would you please stand up?" So I got up, and he said, "You know, I understand you've spent a little time in the service . . . about twenty-six years and retired as a captain, and spent twenty years in the Boy Scouts of America. I'm going to ask every officer here to stand up and salute you for the job you've done for America." Every general in that room, and there were about twelve of them. They were our key volunteers in transforming the scouting. If I wanted something done, I could pick up the phone and call the general and say, "General, Norm here. I need somebody to take care of this problem," and he'd say, "We'll take care of it, Norm, don't worry about it." So there I stood with these generals standing up.

Jean and I came back to the states, got a motor home, and we did a lot of traveling around the country. When George died, I bought eighteen acres of land up in this place called Peenpack Trail in Huguenot, New York. It was just a little old town of about eight thousand people. It's an old Indian trail that goes back about eighty-five miles north and west of New York City.

I bought this property and built a cabin there. Jean and I moved back in to the cabin, and we were living there when Jean died. She died twenty years ago. She was seventy. She had some real medical problems including heart issues over the years and battled them all. She died in her sleep. Diane and Steve were our next-door neighbors, and Diane (Di) lost her husband three weeks before I lost Jean. The night Jean died Di was with us having dinner. It was Jean's birthday, and she had cooked a very special dinner—one of her specialties—fried chicken with all the trimmings and a special strawberry dessert with balsamic vinegar dressing. We invited Di over because she had just lost her husband and that night Jean died, so we found ourselves alone and we married a year later. We've been married for about nineteen years now and are looking forward to a good future.

Service in the United States Army

I mentioned earlier that George was a very independent young man. He did what he wanted to do. I remember one time we hoped his sister would help him with some of his reading problems, and he refused to cooperate with her. He felt he had no need to do it, but he was a pleasant kid. Everybody enjoyed his company. He was the smallest guy, but the fastest runner on the football team. He loved athletics. He was very proud of his decision to learn to fly. Part of it was because I know he admired me. He was very obvious about that, but when I pinned his wings on to him, he said, "Dad, I have one just like yours now." His mother and I we were able to adjust to this, mainly because we knew that there were inherent dangers flying airplanes.

I never got a report back on him on how many missions he flew. Through his letters, I did hear from him while he was training in the Army. He wasn't able to talk about much, but he was strictly a rescue guy. I would not think he'd do as much flying as if he was flying in combat. When he went out, he had to rescue someone.

His commanding officer said he was an excellent pilot, but he was so independent. "I'd get upset with him because he would do something I wouldn't want him to do. It was nothing serious, but he wouldn't follow orders, he wanted to do it his way." The only time I knew his location was during flight training, He would come back home to us, then back to his training. I was out of the Navy by this time with the Boy Scouts during the Vietnam conflict, and I didn't believe in that war as a person. I thought it was dead wrong what was happening over there. We were making a terrible mistake, but I saw George in there rescuing people. He wasn't killing anybody, and I had a different attitude altogether about what he was doing. I don't believe in what's going on right now (current wars).

People's reaction to war

The reaction here in America to the Vietnam conflict was pretty horrible. America was dead set against that war. As a military guy, I understood what he was facing. So many people not having military backgrounds whose sons were killed didn't understand how that could happen. I got shot down in WWII. The airplane got smashed in the water, and I floated around for a while until I got picked up. I got shot up pretty well at times, but only one time got shot down. Every time I went out, you had to keep that in mind. I remember someone dreamed up an idea laying mines in Bougainville Harbor, which was three hundred miles from Guadalcanal. I flew four missions up there at night alone and dropped the mines and flew back again at night. We lost five to six planes every time we flew.

We were flying down there, just didn't know if you were going to make it back or not. So when a disaster hits your family, you've always lived with that thought. That it could happen to me . . . it happened to me. It's just part of the military you live with.

Describe the war

I was very pleased that he was selected to be a rescue pilot rather than a combat pilot. I was out of the Navy by then and I'd felt like a lot of the American public. We wasted time over there. We were fighting an enemy that we're not going to win against, but my son was there because he wanted to help people. I saw a little different point of view. The people we rescued were able to come over here and find someplace else to live and survive. The South Vietnamese were going to be killed if they stayed there. I know we had a large influx of Vietnamese into the country, but I never thought much about it.

Advice to someone considering a military career

I'd say go to the Navy. I certainly wouldn't recommend today's infantry (Army), for the kid who's just barely out of high school and has no college education. He's going to end up in the infantry if he goes into the Army. In the Army, you're facing death, but if you've got some college behind you and some experience, you can almost be what you want in the Air Force or Navy. My grandson got into the Army, but he was running boats, and that was very safe.

I'm very proud of my son, George. He was doing what he wanted to do, and he was trying to save lives. He was well thought of by his commanding officer. I had dinner with him and two other officers who knew George. They were pleased to have known him, and he was a good soldier.

GEORGE JOHN POLLIN

MAJOR GEORGE J. POLLIN

FEB. 5, 1942 - APRIL 29, 1967

Major Pollin will be interred with full military honors at Arlington National Cemetery at 10:45 a.m. on January 14, 1991.

Major Pollin is the recipient of the Silver Star, Air Medal, 7th Award, and the Purple Heart. (2)
Distinguished Flying Cross

JANUARY 12, 1991

Maj George J. Pollin
USAF 4/29/67 NVN

Major, United States Air Force
Semper Fortis: *"Always Courageous"*
389th Tactical Air Command Fighter Squadron
366th Tactical Fighter Wing 7th Air Force
Home of Record: Lavallette, NJ
DOB: 05 February 1942
Shot Down: 29 April 1967
North Vietnam
Missing in Action
Repatriated: 13 September 1990
Interned: Arlington National Cemetery Section 60, Grave 4666
Vietnam Memorial Panel 18E Line 116
Interview conducted in Lavallette, NJ in Larry Pollin's home on
    12 July 2010

> *From time to time, the tree of liberty must be watered with the blood
> of tyrants and patriots.*
>
> —Thomas Jefferson

Growing Up

My brother was older than me by a couple years; very gentle guy, physically strong, handsome, great car mechanic. Built hot rods, helped me build a few. I'd blow them up, he fixed them for me. He was born with this gift. We all worked at gas stations in town. Bud Speaker took my brother for his first plane ride at a very early age. (Bud was the lead on the casket.) My brother was psyched about flying. He said, "I want to be a pilot someday." He wanted to be in medicine. He changed his career path after graduating from Lavallette Grammar School—we all went there. He went on to Point Beach High School, four years, very intelligent guy, smart. Nine varsity letters, football, baseball, track, honor society, and he talked first about going into the Navy. They refused him because he had flatfeet, so the Air Force grabbed him, and he couldn't wait to get in. He went to OCS, received his commission, and was accepted into flight school, which he finished in fifty-five weeks.

At graduation, he was voted by his peers as outstanding pilot in his class. He said, "Flight school was like taking final exams in chemistry fifty-five weeks in a row. One mess up, there's the door, no second chances. You fail one part of that training, you washed out." George was a chemical engineer with a great mental ability. When George graduated Monmouth University, he had the highest degree in his class in chemistry. He was a mathematical, chemical genius—very, very intelligent. Everything he touched was done right, from building a hot rod to flying an aircraft. His original orders were to go to Germany, which pleased my mother to no end because Vietnam was hot and heavy.

He left here around 2 January 1967, but while he had a month off before he went overseas, he had his orders changed to go to Vietnam. He said, "This is what I've been trained to do." I don't know what it costs to train a pilot. It was tens of thousands of dollars, I guess. George said, "What am I going to do in Germany, fly mail? I'm going to go over there and win the war."

I can't imagine what training was like to get through. He came out number one in his class in flight training out of around forty pilots, and at the time, this phantom jet was the state of the art plane. He liked speed. My brother had a corvette, built hot rods, and it was done right and faster than the other guy. He was just one of those types of guys. (*Barbara and Larry now showing pictures of George.*)

He was pumping gas, working his way through college. The family had no money, and he was on his own as far as education. He started working there when he was fourteen or fifteen, and he became a mechanic. He needed the money to pay for education, and it was there that he met Sue Johnson. They started dating and finally got engaged while George was in the Air Force. He wanted to get married before he went to Vietnam, and Sue said, "No, if anything happens, your mother should be the recipient of everything." But Sue waited over twenty years for George to return until she was forty years old. He was missing for eleven years, and during that time, his vacation time approved, his pay, his promotions—Mom got all that. At that time, there was a bank in Arizona that would open accounts for POWs and MIAs, and if you had the money sent there, they'd pay 10 percent interest, which was astronomical back then. That was a lot of interest, so my mother had everything sent to Arizona in case he came home. He'd have that to get started with. This went on for eleven years. He got paid for eleven years; then the government reviewed all the MIA cases and the ones that looked really hopeless. They changed his status to KIA, and they issued my mother a death certificate, which ended his pay. And my mother was able to collect his life insurance.

George was fifteen when my father passed away, so George became the man of the house. At that time, you had to be eighteen to pump gas, unless you were a member of the family that owned the gas station; and seeing how he was big for his age, Bud let him pump gas. He said, "If anyone comes in and asks what your age is, tell him your name is Speaker." He worked many hours there, and in his spare time, he cleaned fishing boats in Brielle. He worked on a head boat during the day and pumped gas at night. He was very energetic. He had his sights set on something and got it done. The people still alive in this town remember George. They always speak very highly of him.

Circumstances surrounding George missing in action

George's aircraft was lost on a Saturday afternoon. The United States Air Force knocked on my mother's door at 0605 Sunday morning, the next morning. It's their policy; they go immediately. His official date of death is 29 April 1967. It was a twenty-four-hour difference between Vietnam and state side. My poor mother called me up. Three people knocked on her door. They did her first because she was a widow. It was a chaplain, a captain, and a pilot from McGuire Air Force Base. It was a blue Air Force car. As I recall, it's still a big blur to me; they spent half a day with my mom. I was married, and was expecting my third child any minute.

She saw the hat in the window, the captain's hat. She knew right away. I don't know that my mother knew the process, but as soon as she opened the door, my sister said there were a couple lights on top of the door. It was a solid door. She saw the airman's hat, and she knew what they were there for. They spent a lot of time with us answering questions. They knew he ejected out of the plane, but to this day, they don't know which one and told my mother that he was flying with Loren Torkelson from North Dakota. Two weeks later, they reenacted Loren's capture and took a picture of him. His picture was in a newspaper in Thailand of him being captured. As soon as he hit the ground, he blacked out. It was in a paper in Thailand, but he was still in Vietnam. So when he hit the ground and came to, they took all his clothes off, took his gun, and blindfolded him. He said he thought he saw an ejection seat over to the left, but everything happened in seconds and the civilian militia marched him through the streets and threw tomatoes and whatever else at him. He basically said, "I knew my war was over for a long time." Loren told me he was kept in solitary confinement for the first three years. He never talked to another American, and once he was added to a little bigger general population in some camps, they kept moving him.

He kept asking about George, "Has anybody seen this man?" He tried to correspond with captured fliers.

The picture of Loren was very good, and his family identified that was definitely, positively Loren Torkelson. His family was lucky enough to get some letters back and forth from him. He was one of the luckier POWs if you can call him lucky, but a lot of the men wouldn't divulge they had them. At this time, no one knew if George was dead. We had hope. He had a parachute on, so hopefully, he got out. We had hope he'd got out as time progressed. My mother went to the Paris Peace Talks with my brother's girlfriend, and they were basically ignored. They were just out there, respectfully well dressed trying to find something out about her son. They spent at least a week out there in 1971.

I had very small children then. My mother came home very disappointed. Now when they notified the Torkelson family, they never told Mrs. Torkelson that Loren was flying with my brother. They never told her anything; and while my mother, Sue, and her parents were in this big auditorium for this meeting, this lady came walking up the aisle. They all had name tags. This one lady with a nametag came up, and her name was Mrs. Torkelson. Well, it's a very unusual name, maybe not out there. So Mr. Johnson, Sue's father, stepped up and asked, "Excuse me, are you Loren's mother?" She said, "Yes," and he said, "Well, we're George's family." She said, "Have we met?" She passed away not too long ago, and Loren passed away about five years ago of natural causes, probably due to that war. His name should be put on the wall.

Loren Torkelson

The treatment was horrible: horrendous. To keep his sanity while in solitary confinement, he always wanted to have a horse ranch in Montana, so that was his plan. If he got out, which he did, to complete his twenty years. He got his law degree, went into law practice, and bought his horse farm in Billings, Montana. They had racehorses, and he was in Lexington, Kentucky, picking out a horse when he had a heart attack and died. He was in his late fifties. He spent a week with me, one visit; and then another time, he came back we went to Saratoga, New York. We went to the races with him, along with his law partner, and we had a great time together.

He didn't have much longevity. When he came home, after they checked him out at the hospital, we watched him get off the plane on television. We were watching the POWs getting off (the C-141) and he said that he didn't know until the last minute, until he got off the bus, that he was going home. He said the last couple weeks as a POW, the food got a little better. They were trying to fatten them up a little to make them look good because they were political capital. An interesting note Loren told me: When they had a feeling it might be coming to an end, they would put them out in the yard a little more to get a little color on their face so they looked healthier, so to counter this all the POWs walked around with their heads down. He was a very humble guy, very quiet, a man of few words. It was a pleasure to meet him.

After they got him up on his feet and halfway healthy, they interrogated him on this whole mess. They were flying in the six o'clock position and got hit in the back end, which was where George sat, and he told them to eject. They lost communication; he got out. According to the condition of the remains, everything on the left side was fractured, so they're assuming that his seat did get out; but it malfunctioned, and he was in the seat when it hit the ground. They were going about two hundred miles per hour. One question I did ask Loren was, "How many parachute jumps did you make prior to your chute downing?" He said, "I just hit the button and prayed it'd work and it worked." There was no pilot training as far as parachutes.

Remains

The Air Force told us that the North Vietnamese treated the POWs as trophies. The family had the pleasure of getting a full set of remains back. These remains and the dental records were reviewed by the Navy, Air Force, and the Army, independent of each other; and they had come to the same conclusion that these remains belonged to George. The whole thing went to the presidential review board, and they had to review all this and come to the same conclusion. Then they packed everything up and sent a forensics expert (William R. Maples Ph.D. Diplomatic American Board of Forensic Anthropology) with all this stuff and he flew from Florida to Philadelphia, came here, opened everything up and said, "This is yours to look at and review." We had Tim Ryan here, the undertaker, but the dental records were . . . thank God they had his teeth. Some of the other boxes had bits and pieces I don't know if they've even been identified yet. When you're in the military, there's one primary next of kin. When my mother passed away, I became that person because I was the oldest. His remains came home in September 1990, and I got the call 4 December 1990 at work from Randolph Air Force Base where all their casualty records are kept.

This is in Texas. When this Southern gentleman with a real Southern accent called me at work and said, "We have your brother's remains, they are at Hickam Air Force Base," where all the forensic work is done. That's where the central mortuary service is for all the services. They went on to tell us they have sets of remains they'll never identify. They have them, but they just don't know who they are. They have Korean remains also, but they'll never be identified. Our family was lucky to get closure after twenty-four years.

My mother passed away November 1981. She was sixty-nine years old. This probably killed my mother in the literal sense of the word, it just devastated her. My mother also buried my sister, when she died in year 1, but she had closure with her.

Loren said to me in so many words; I don't want to misquote him, but basically, it was, "George might have been the lucky one, not me," which means he may have known at the time George was killed instantly, but Loren had to endure what he went through for his six years internment.

Growing up as a kid down here, there were maybe five hundred all-year-round residents, and people knew and heard about Vietnam, but it really hit home when this town lost two men within a month. George was at the end of April while Donald Skinner, a kid I went to high school with, was at the end of May. Skinner was in the US Army and died of wounds. He was a PFC. George was 29 April and Donald was 27 May 1967. He is on both Walls (New Jersey Memorial and DC Memorial).

This fellow in Texas said, "When do you want the remains?" We looked at each other and wondered what are we waiting for? What do we do now? We thought we would know what to do, but we never thought the phone call would come that day. After 4 December, after I got the call, the forensic expert came from Florida with all this paperwork and the picture with the dental records. We hadn't done anything for Christmas yet, so I said let's get Christmas done and then we'll concentrate on George's funeral because that took a lot of planning. Tim Ryan, the funeral director who I work for now, grabbed me by the shoulder. We went into the back room, and he said, "That's your brother, that's him. I know what x-rays look like, that's him."

They said they would pay for one escort to fly to Travis AFB in California, which was the port of entry on the West Coast, so I'm thinking, *It's got to be Loren.* So Tim called Loren who was retired, and he said, "Absolutely, I flew his last flight with him." His remains came from Hawaii to California and then Loren went to California. At midnight, we picked them up and brought them to Lavallette.

Wake

At his wake, Sue, his fiancée, waited until his status was changed from MIA to killed, which was eleven years. My mother encouraged her, saying, "Sue, if you want to go out, we'll understand," and she said, "No." When he was changed to KIA, then she started to . . . she met Dick, whom she married. She was our history teacher at Red Bank High School. She took a deferred retirement, and she married Dick. He was also a teacher at Bloomfield High School. He taught shop. He retired, and they moved to Florida (where her parents resided) for the winter. Her father was a retired chemist from DuPont. They all came up, and Sue had a single red rose on the casket. My mother would spend every Sunday afternoon at the Johnson house, every Sunday she had dinner with her family, without fail, every Sunday. I don't think they missed one within all those years. They loved George. My mother was half-Danish and half-German. George looked like my mother—blond hair, blue eyes. Sue's father was blond hair and very light, and George looked just like her father. He had a tremendous amount of respect for my brother because Bill was a chemist as well. He was one of the founders of Teflon. The guy was a genius, and he knew my brother was a chemical genius. They would talk Greek to each other. They just melded like that and to have this guy marrying his daughter . . . Sue was an only child. The Johnson's were just a lovely family. She's up here in Lavallette now with Dick.

We've kept in touch with each other all these years. We do Christmas cards, and I see Sue during the course of the summer, and she always gives me a big hug. She sees George in me, I swear.

George was not Catholic, but we held the wake at the Catholic Church because it was the biggest building in town, and it was filled to capacity. People came from everywhere. They didn't know the Pollins', but they heard about this man and came.

The only disappointment I have with George's homecoming, if you will, Loren had arranged to have an F-4 fly right up over the church when they were bringing him out, and the weather was terrible, they said they couldn't do it. The weather was foggy. There was snow, ice—they were going to fly right over Route 35, right over the church. That was the only thing I was disappointed in. However, in Arlington, they did the missing man protocol. He had the same situation that Kennedy had, except for the horse with the stirrups that went backward. It's all in the pictures.

Four days after his wake here, Lavallette hired two buses, so everybody in town who knew George, my mother, and all of us went to Arlington. A representative at the cemetery said, "We'll have cookies and coffee and whatnot for you at the reception." They're expecting fifteen or twenty people and two busloads of people come, plus the people who drove down there. There were more than two hundred people! Literally the whole town took the day off to go there. The bus left at 0400. The ironic thing is, as they were burying him in Arlington, they were signing the papers for the Gulf War at the White House on the same day.

One of George's lifelong buddies, Joey Borrelli, took a bag of sand from Long Way and sprinkled the casket with sand from the beach in Lavallette. Joe served in the Navy during Vietnam on both the USS *Randolph* and USS *Enterprise*. On these carriers, he was a mechanic for an air squadron. Joe shows up with a big white plaster bucket and all of his buddies, right from the top of our street on the beach. Another friend, Rich Burke, was there as well. Rich served in the Army in Vietnam as well. Along with Tom King, who provided the buses, these were his best buds. They were all his "motor head" friends.

Larry ended the conversation, stating, "John, I'm impressed with you taking the time on George's circumstances because people don't forget men like my brother and they shouldn't."

HAROLD WILLIAM KROSKE JR.

Major, United States Army
Semper Vigilans: *"Vigilant Always"*
Recon Team Hammer
Military Assistance Command Vietnam
Studies and Observations Group (SOG)
Fifth Special Forces Group
Home of Record: Trenton, NJ
DOB: 30 July 1947
Date of Loss: 11 February 1969
Bu Dop, Cambodia
MIA: 18 February 1968
Presumptive Finding of Death: 08 January 1979
Remains have not been repatriated
Vietnam Memorial Panel 32W Line 013
Conducted on 16 August 2010 in Tilton Falls, NJ at the home of his
    Uncle Richard Kelly

*Grave digger—when you dig my grave; could you make it shallow?—so
I can feel the rain.*

—Dave Matthews

Growing Up

A story: Billy was probably four years old. We were sitting in the living room, and I saw the French doors on the little parlor start to open. There he was with his Indian bonnet on. He shot and hit me right in the head with the rubber tipped (arrow). It was kind of awkward because I'm ready to kill him, and my sister of course wouldn't let anybody do anything like that to her Billy. So I had to sit tight. My oldest brother was a New Jersey State Trooper. Surprisingly, Billy was the first grandchild.

Billy was captain of his football team in high school. He was the quarterback. They didn't win a game all year. When he was eighteen, he decided to enlist in the Army. The military school was in North Carolina. It was a transient type of existence. He was in and he was out. I was very surprised, first when he went in the military they assigned him to military police. His father was a police officer in Trenton where he was raised. He joined the Rangers, went to OCS (Officer Candidate School), and was off to Vietnam. Because of our careers, I didn't see Billy except when we had a family function. I knew he was in the military. He did come home between tours-only recreational leave—and then he went back . . . for his last raid in 1968.

Entering the Special Forces

Billy was always a free spirit. I always wondered about that as a matter of fact. He hadn't been too successful, and as I said, he had been the captain of the football team, quarterback, but he didn't win any games. Not that that was his fault, but when he went in OCS, he was home. We had a little party for him before he went away. He and I were close. Despite the fact he almost took my eye out with an arrow that one time when he was four! You know the military. I took him aside, and I said, "Billy, I bet you $100 you don't make it." My sister found out about it, and she was furious. His father looked at her and said, "This is probably a safe bet."

In country experience

Quite frankly, I have so much documentation that I find it's redundant. They did send these notices to me about the search in Cambodia; certain alerts that might have some information, but it doesn't pan out. There're always survivors. A lot of them, probably, circumstances are switched, and it could be that, I wouldn't call them deserters, but found themselves in a situation where they could live with the Vietnamese.

Bill had many close friends. As far as his love life, I know he had a girlfriend in the States. I do have some material from his personal files that they sent me, and there is a letter in there that was never sent to the young lady. It told her, right when you get this letter, I will be dead. There was no question in my mind that Billy was ready to die. If you read that fellow's story, he basically says that Billy had, not a death wish, but a death desire. He was just fed up with it. I just think he packed it in. One of the things he mentions is when Billy came in to see him the night before he gave his buddy a bottle of Chivas Regal, saying, "I won't need this bottle anymore."

How did Vietnam shape your life relative to Billy not coming home?

Having had military experience myself, you have a certain dedication to the service. I think it angered me that we didn't do more over there, but I didn't trust the Vietnamese government. Why? There was no action taken on the behalf of the MIAs initially. Many of these governments we support now, we get involved, and they always seem to put somebody in power that we elected. You didn't know what to believe.

One of the problems is that it is hard for a civilian to know how tough discipline is in the military unless you go through it. The individuals are not structural thinkers anymore. Perfect example—go to a graduation and you say to the individual, "Are you going on to school?" "Uh, I don't know. Well, it's hard to say." "What would you like to do?" "I don't know." When you're out of high school, you should have some idea. Then maybe they think, I'll just go into the military. It's a great learning experience. God forbid that you get into a situation like Iraq or something, but it's a great experience.

The family really missed Billy—grieved for him—but there were no real bad situations for people. I was amazed at how well his father and mother took it. It was sad. We had a Mass, and the military chaplain attended. They proceeded to play TAPS in church.

Describe the war

Disastrous: What did we get out of it? Who benefited aside from North Vietnamese?

Advice to someone considering a military career

I think a lot depends on the individual that's considering it. If he's just considering it because he doesn't know what else to do, it's hard to judge. If he has an ambition to be a career man, that's another type of person. If it's an escape it's not a good path to get away. There's a lot of discipline involved.

Closing Comments

In thy faint slumbers I by thee have watch'd. And heard thee murmur tales of iron wars.

—Shakespeare, Henry IV

Major George Pollin, USAF. When I reviewed all the letters, pictures, government documents, and finally his skeletal remains, I looked up at Larry. A picture would have been worth a lot. How do you respond to something like this? You don't. I had to just take it all in. My eyes immediately went to the picture of George on the table.

Imagining George's mother, not knowing when he died must have been very sad. They were reunited in 1990 when his "wandering soul" was placed to rest in Arlington National Cemetery.

I mentioned earlier the earnest lunch with Diane and Norman Berg. His son's bracelet was ordered shortly after our interview. All the bracelets that I have possessed, and subsequently given away for people to wear, have been ordered through Lynn Duane. I wore George Berg's MIA aluminum wristband for quite some time. Sometimes, I wear both a black KIA bracelet (James Amendola) and another MIA (Walter Cichon). Both these men are from New Jersey.

Richard Kelly exposed me to his nephew, and the forces around this book brought me to Joanna and Richard. Harold "Billy" Kroske may have been like every Special Forces soldier I have met to date, regardless of theater or time period. But war apparently does things to a person; things we civilians will never understand. According to Mr. Kelly, Major Kroske may have had a premonition of his death. Certainly, this could explain his actions that evening on 11 February 1969. Billy may have been at a breaking point: Admiral Stockdale claims everyman has one. I pray that Major Harold Kroske sleeps with the angels.

CHAPTER ELEVEN
The Things They Carried In:
The Things They Carried Out

Weapons/Rations/Senses/Memories
Exposure/Nightmares/Friends/Other "Things"

Dedicated to Joseph Daly
Corporal, United States Army
C Battery, Second Battalion, Thirteenth Artillery Regiment
2 Field Force

Vietnam is the gift that never stops giving. There is no cure for PTSD as it stays with you. PTSD is a physiological disorder. Further, herbicide exposure continues to raise its head in terms of diabetes, leukemia, and different types of heart problems. New cases that arrive in my office suffer from hand tremors. Regarding PTSD and Agent Orange exposure, it is never over. It is very sad.
—Dr. Howard Cohen

Originally, the pieces of this chapter were spread into various sections of the book. The more thought given to the importance of the following components, I decided to blend these topics mutually exclusive of other sections.

In order to be a combatant, a man needs to carry a weapon in the field. He also "carries" his character, training, soul, psyche, and his duty to God and country. His sensory attributes will also serve him, as well as any firearm known to man, for it is his senses that enable him to hear, smell, see, and ultimately detect the enemy.

Our sensory and receptor systems act in conjunction with our brain. In Vietnam, when a soldier's senses detected heat, sulfur, smoke and small arms fire, these sensory receptors fired information to the brain, which in turn caused a mechanical physical reaction by the body. This response would mimic the classic "fight or flight" reaction-return fire or haul ass out of there.

Including the tremendous weight of their combat gear, men carried food, water, medical supplies, and a host of other items totaling, in many cases, a load that exceeded their actual body mass. However, you can never underestimate the power of the human spirit. In combat, the veterans have told me of countless situations where all normal bodily needs were preempted by the sheer involuntary need to stay alive.

Family, friends, sweethearts, wives, and children all were hopeful that their servicemen and women could withstand their 365 days in Vietnam and arrive back on domestic soil unscathed. The men were clean shaven, had one clean uniform, and a mission. Their loved ones waited for them, and the soldiers wrote tons of letters home. The nurses arrived with their impeccable looking "scrubs."

The weapons and munitions they carried were a rifle, a gun and up to a dozen magazines, each of which held twenty rounds of ammunition. Grenades, additional ammunition for their machine gun (if the squad had a weapons team) due to its rate of fire. "Sharing" the load of the .81 mm mortar, that when broken down before battle, including the base plate, mortar tube, and actual mortar rounds, weighed well over fifty pounds combined. The list rambles on . . .

What They Carried in

The willingness with which our young people are likely to serve in any war, no matter how justified, is directly proportional to how they perceive the veterans of earlier wars were treated and appreciated.

—George Washington

US Weapons of the Vietnam War

US ground forces across all services utilized (in most cases) the same equipment for small arms as well as assault firepower. The **M-16A1** fired a 5.56 MM round which was much smaller than the various versions of the **AK-47** the NVA and VC used. When early problems with the weapon were identified (jamming), then corrected, it became a respected assault rifle. Some men loaded one round *less* than a full clip (twenty rounds), or expended the first round prior to engagement, which helped reduce or eliminate jamming. In many cases it was not the actual round that failed, but the casing of the bullet that got stuck in the ejector mechanism. A Special Forces operator told me it was the actual gunpowder that caused the problem.

In the late 1950s, ArmaLite, a small arms manufacturing company in Illinois, developed the now famous **AR-15.** After its introduction in Southeast Asia in 1963, by 1969 it became the standard rifle carried by all US troops.

The **CAR-15**, called the Colt Commando, was a much shorter version of the M-16. It was used by Special Forces and some ground officers. The **M-72** light antitank weapon (LAW) was a light and waterproof weapon used for bunker busting. The **M-79** was made by Craft Apple Works. It was called the "blooper" by the Marines, and the "thumper" by the Army. Initially introduced to the Army in 1961, it was designed as a close support weapon for infantry units. Operator held only a hand-gun as a side arm. It was a single shot, shoulder fired barrel weapon. The 40 mm grenade it launched was accurate within 300 meters. The **M-67** 90 MM Recoilless Rifle was a heavy, 35lb single shot weapon, accurate and deadly up to 400 yards, but could be fired out to a distance over one mile. The rate of fire was limited due to the tremendous heat build-up so, after 5 rounds were fired, the M-67 needed to cool for at least 15 minutes. *Each round was almost 10lbs!* The **M-26** fragmentation grenade was also used; the Marines commonly utilized this ordnance in the northern part of South Vietnam, which was called I Corps area.

Both officers and NCOs holstered the **M-1911A1**, which was a .45 automatic pistol. Some soldiers originally carried their own personal weapons into combat. This was partially due to comfort level—mainly due to their knowledge that the "stopping power" of the .45-caliber was greater than the M-16. Others carried a .38 caliber special, a gun that many police officers liked due to its stopping power. My accuracy and comfort level with the various .45-caliber handguns I fired, including the M-1911A1, was far less than the rifles I had the opportunity to shoulder and fire.

The **M-60** general purpose machine gun (GPMG) was a 7.62 MM weapon that was the main firepower of an infantry-rifle section. Its range could yield a distance of over 500 yards. The M-60 was an air-cooled, belt-fed, gas-operated unit that could be "stood" on two different types of "pods." The machine also provided protective cover for vehicles and helicopters. In most cases it was manned by two soldiers. The combined weight of the gun and ammunition was over 80 pounds. Add the plate and mounting system, and you are over 120 pounds.

The **M2** Browning .50-caliber machine gun was designed toward the end of World War I by John Browning. It is very similar in design to Browning's earlier **M1919** (BMG), which chambered the .30-06 cartridge. The M2 uses the larger and more powerful .50 BMG cartridge, which was named for the gun itself. The M2 has been referred to as "Ma Deuce," or "the fifty," in reference to its caliber. It is effective against infantry, unarmored or lightly-armored vehicles, boats, light fortifications, and low-flying aircraft. The Browning .50-caliber machine gun has been used extensively as a vehicle weapon, for aircraft armament and ground use by the United States for almost one hundred years. It is the primary heavy machine gun of NATO countries and has been used by many other countries as well. With the exception of the .45 ACP M1911 pistol, the M2 has been in use longer than any other small arm in the US inventory.

The **M-40** was a Vietnam War era sniper rifle. The Marine Corps decided they needed a standard sniper rifle. After testing several possibilities, they ordered 700 Remington Model 40 rifles and gave them the **M40** designation. Most had a Redfield 3-9 power Accu-Range variable scope mounted. With time, certain weaknesses, primarily warping of the all-wood stock, became apparent. The M-40 was a deadly weapon in the hands of an expert. The record in distance in Vietnam for a confirmed kill with the M-40 was over two thousand yards.

Possibly one of the most terrifying and demoralizing infantry weapons ever produced is the **M2-2** portable flamethrower. As the introduction to the 1944 Australian Army training pamphlet for flamethrowers states: "Flame has a powerful psychological effect in that humans instinctively withdraw from it, even when their morale is good. In addition, it is a casualty producing and lethal agent." This device had three tanks—one of pure "jellied" gasoline, one with the accelerant (phosphorous), and the last with napalm (naphtha and palm oil). Together they weighed over eighty pounds. It saw limited use in Vietnam due to the terrain affecting the ability to carry such a load long distances. A little known fact—the Germans are regularly thought to have invented this device, but the credit actually goes back to the Byzantines from the seventh century!

Food

C ration, or type c ration, was an individual canned, precooked, or prepared wet ration. It was intended to be issued to US military land forces when fresh food (A ration) or packaged unprepared food (B ration) prepared in mess halls or field kitchens was impractical or not available and when a survival ration (K ration or D ration) was insufficient. Development began in 1938 with the first rations being field-tested in 1940 and wide-scale adoption following suit. After World War II, cost concerns later caused the C ration to be standardized for field issue regardless of environmental suitability or weight limitations.

The C ration was replaced in 1958 with the Meal Combat Individual (MCI). Although officially a new ration, the MCI was derived from, and very similar to, the original C ration. In fact, the MCI continued to be called C rations by American troops throughout its service life (1958-1980). These rations were canned, wet-combat rations. This "field-food" weighed heavily, literally, on the soldiers, in and out of the can. Some soldiers would actually toss their full daily rations, but keep one can, so their load(s) would be lighter. Introduced during Vietnam, the MRE (Meal Ready to Eat) ultimately replaced the MCI. These new rations were dehydrated, light, and only needed water to prepare.

What They Carried Out

Some of us came back home cold, reckless and without feeling. We were different from other people and suffered a silent loneliness.
    —Tony Lazzarini: *Highest Traditions: Memories of War*

Our men and women carried the stress of a year (of combat, support or medical duty), or one tour of duty, when in country. The flashback of firefights, the constant procession of casualties from DUSTOFFS, the care of the wounded and dying in field hospitals, incoming artillery and mortar rounds, and the never-to-be-forgotten sound of the AK-47 in full automatic position. Five-hundred-pound bombs meant for the enemy dropping ever so close to US lines. Long hair, purple hearts, memories of friends and unit members lost they would never forget. Nightmares that would occupy some of them every evening, a never ending stream of past action, to be carried to the grave. Malaria and countless skin diseases complements of the jungle. The impact of napalm, and the affects of Agent Orange that doctors, to this day, have yet to identify some of the cancers laden on the backs, and DNA, of the surgeons, nurses and soldiers.

A noncombatant cannot, and will not, ever understand what it is like to see a wounded man, or a friend or unit member who is KIA, or the enemy in either condition. This has haunted me due to my interest in military history at a very young age. Read until the cows come home, research ad nauseam, but the picture will never match the reality of a combat moment.

DIOXIN

If it stinks put a lid on it.
—Old Japanese Proverb

The figurative, as well as the actual practicality of this quote, is pretty scary. Dioxin was an herbicide that was manufactured by Monsanto Corporation and Dow Chemical along with other manufacturers and used in the countryside of Vietnam by the US Air Force. A defoliant by nature, it was part of the largest ecological experiment of all time. Most of the usage was exclusive to South Vietnam. Carl Sagan, the notable astrophysicist who introduced many people to black holes and the stars, said, "Extraordinary claims require extraordinary evidence." Relative to dioxin, there was no published evidence. No one really knew the danger of this menace that would affect our forces in the field for their lifetime and, ultimately, generations to come. However, this was one of the most toxic herbicides ever manufactured. Anyone who came in contact with dioxin from production through distribution in the jungles of Vietnam was totally unaware of its future impact. No masks, gloves, or skin protections. All the civilians and servicemen who produced, labored, loaded, unloaded, then reloaded onto vehicles and planes this incredibly toxic "agent" just followed orders. The "might" of dioxin, once finally sprayed on the countryside while both friend and foe were on the ground, was determined in the future by various doctors and professionals who collectively stated that scores of diseases and cancers are still unidentified. Of the eighteen predetermined diseases that the VA approves (as of November 2010) for anyone who served in Southeast Asia, dioxin is considered the culprit. Many of the interviewees have these cancers, or know of friends and unit members who are sick or have passed on due to this deadly agent. Now the VA needs only proof from a doctor to treat anyone exposed to dioxin. Extraordinary, don't you think? No other substance has been studied with such great detail as with dioxin exposure. It is unknown to this day how many VA cases are actually attributable to the herbicide mixture known as Agent Orange.

According to a recent Associated Press-GFK Poll, 82 percent of the Vietnamese living currently in this country surveyed said the United States should be doing more to help the Vietnamese people suffering with these illnesses. The birth rates in Vietnam continue to produce alarming numbers of children born with defects. Whether this be physical—missing an arm or having twisted limbs, or mental—the rates of defects are overwhelming. In 2006, President Bush worked with Congress to earmark $9 million to address environmental cleanup in Vietnam. As of May 2010, Vietnamese officials state only $6 million has been allocated. I would call this a proverbial work *not* in progress. My friend, Pat Knapp, sent me an article on the ravages of dioxin on the current Vietnamese population in Southeast Asia. His comment, "What did these people do to deserve this?"

To this day, the Vietnamese population struggles with the aftermath and the legacy of Agent Orange. Children born without limbs, or too many limbs, can't speak, can't walk, or are unable to do things a normal youngster can do.

Some of the villagers in Cam Tuyen remember watching US planes dump dioxin several times a day over their village in Quang Tri Province. They used to fish in the nearby streams and lakes where the deadly spray ended up. Tran Van Tram and his wife, Tran Thi Dan, who live in Cam Tuyen village, now spend virtually all their time caring for their children ravaged by the by-product of these dumps.

Closing Comments

Soldiers' Heart. Shell Shock. Battle Fatigue. Post-Traumatic Stress Disorder. Ever since the Civil War, the symptoms are all the same. All soldiers who have not perished during their respective conflicts have to bear the burden of warfare forever.

—JAS

Fear and terror happen when all a person's senses collapse into one during combat. I have tried to share, and ease, the burden of all the men and women represented in this book, but the survivor's guilt, and all the ingredients from Vietnam that are tucked away in the dark closets of their minds may never be totally removed.

Of the over 58,000 American deaths incurred in Vietnam, almost 32 percent (18,518) were the result of small arms fire. Most of these KIAs were the product of close combat action. What is very sad, no different than in the Korean War, is that there were many countries that had soldiers fight alongside our forces that do not receive the recognition they deserve. South Korean (4,407), Philippine (1,000), Thai (1,351), and Australian (520) servicemen were KIA during the war in Vietnam.

EPILOGUE
The Long Road "Home"

Proposed Legislation making 29 March
"Vietnam Veterans Day"

Dedicated to Douglas R. White
Private First Class, United States Army
Alpha Company, Second Battalion, Twenty-Seventh Regiment
Twenty-Fifth Division

If you are able, save for them a place inside of you and save one backward glance when you are leaving for the places they can no longer go. Be not ashamed to say you loved them, though you may or may not have always. Take what they have taught you with their dying and keep it with your own. And in that time when men decide and feel safe to call the war insane, take one moment to embrace those gentle heroes you left behind.

—Major Michael Davis O'Donnell
1 January 1970
Dak To, Vietnam
Listed as KIA February 7, 1978
Vietnam Memorial Panel 12E Line40

319

General George S. Patton said, "Compared to war, all other forms of human endeavor shrink to insignificance." "Shrink" is the operative word here, because when I spoke to all these folks, they implied that although Patton was correct in his statement from the physical equation, the damage laden on the backs of these men and women psychologically are only known to themselves, their families, friends, and counselors.

This book is the "right thing" relative to giving our Vietnam vets the respect they deserve, and the honor that we didn't bestow as a country forty years ago. We need not agree with a conflict or theater of any war, but I believe it is our responsibility, and duty, to support the men and women who are assigned to fight.

30 March is a day that the US Senate wishes to proclaim as "Welcome Home Vietnam Veterans Day." The challenge with this day is that it represents when the NVA launched their "Easter Offensive" across the DMZ in 1972. Further, on the exact same day three years later, one hundred thousand ARVN soldiers surrendered when Da Nang fell. This was a direct violation of the Paris peace talks when the North Vietnamese invaded the South.

The day with dignity and honor to establish recognition of the Vietnam Veterans and their families sacrifice and service is best identified with the official withdrawal of all combat troops from Vietnam ordered by President Nixon 29 March 1973. It was also the day and month in 1974 that under the urging of Congress, President Nixon and the politicians recognized the sacrifice and contributions of those who served in Vietnam and their families and declared it as "Vietnam Veterans Day." A group called Equal Honor for All, located in Cleveland, Ohio, has petitioned incumbent Senator Richard Burr 17 March 2011 to reinstate 29 March as "Vietnam Veterans Day." Thanks to Rimantas Ray Saikus (Vietnam vet 173rd Airborne Brigade) and his organization, we may have official deference to a day that honors all of our Vietnam veterans.

The participants in the book came from all walks of life. Farmhands, laborers, parochial and public school kids, college or one of the military academies—you name it. After their respective "engagements," many were married (then divorced), became professionals in law, industry and education, mastered a trade, pursued sales careers, finished college, or continued their career in the military. Some became authors.

Many of the soldiers and nurses have real, serious issues. Some so challenging that I offered professional help at my expense. I actually spoke to three Vietnam Navy nurses, one of which completed her interview then pulled it. If you know someone who is a veteran or currently serving, any service, in or out of uniform, show respect. Shake their hand and say thank-you. Buy them a cup of coffee. Take them to dinner. Pick up their tab. They have helped keep us free by placing their lives on the line. It was dangerous and fearful business for many. When you go to work, think about the fact that a second lieutenant dropped in a hot landing zone in Vietnam had a life expectancy of less than twenty minutes. Anyone who experienced combat and claims they were not scared, according to virtually everyone I met, is either not telling the truth or dead. As a British WWII pilot said in an interview, *"Fear is—you not only can feel it—you can taste it. I suppose it tastes like dry suds. Fear itself comes from the back of your neck to the top of your head. You can feel it every time because these people are very good at their business—and they are trying to kill you."* Regardless of your views on war, government or politics, these veterans placed their lives in harm's way at some point in their career. An old anonymous adage: "I cried when I had no shoes, until I saw someone who had no feet." Meeting these veterans has taught me not to complain about trivial issues. In Vietnam alone, there were over 10,000 amputations due to injury in the field. In Vietnam, 304,000 US personnel were injured in direct or indirect action. Almost 75,000 suffered serious injuries. Try your normal routine when your thumb hurts or you have a sprained ankle. Then think about the quotation above. It certainly places our menial civilian afflictions into perspective.

As of December 2009, there are over 3 million veterans of foreign wars receiving care at one of the VA's 155 medical centers or hospitals in the country. This number includes everyone from Iraq and Afghanistan through WWII. Of the over 3.4 million serviceman and women who served in Southeast Asia, less than one million remain on this earth. More Korean and WWII soldiers are alive now than Vietnam vets. In addition to death by (dioxin) exposure, wounds, or other natural causes, the Vietnam number continues to be reduced nationally, via suicide alone, by 18 people daily. This equates to over 6,500 annually.

For many of these folks, the transition from military to civilian life was a difficult and uneasy process. Many didn't speak of their experience; they walked through the valley of death and were changed for life. They were supposed to migrate back into the very society who vilified them. They felt helpless; they felt guilty of being on American soil while their buddies' bodies were scattered in the wind or in pine boxes. As Joe Galloway and Lieutenant General Hal Moore stated in their book *We Were Soldiers Once and Young*: "These soldiers (in the Ia Drang Valley November 1965) killed, died, and wept for each other."

To the over 58,000 brothers and sisters who never returned. These military heroes gave up all their tomorrows' so we could have ours. May they all rest in a peace that was not achieved during their brief stay on this carbon orb named Mother Earth. We all need to continue to . . . *remember*.

AFTERWORD

How This Project Affected My Life

Dedicated to Steven Knuboff
Company Medic, Specialist 4 United States Army
Alpha Company, Third Battalion, First Infantry Regiment
Eleventh Infantry Brigade Americal Division

*We are connected and that's something nobody can take from us. You
coulda had me locked up, but you didn't. That's proof that there's
something deep inside. There's a part that they can't get to. And it's
deep inside of us. And that's where the truth is.*
 —Character Ben Marco from the movie
 The Manchurian Candidate

All the research, travel, phone calls, interviews, writing, and long hours hit
my family like a ton of bricks. Where I saw fulfillment, they saw risk. The
mission that I undertook laid siege to everything at home. I pushed myself
to the brink. However, justification was simple. As my friends Lou Hagarty
and Chuck Whicker said, it was my "lifelong dream." I had to tell the story
about these men and women.

I spoke to many folks at the various veteran medical centers around the
country, offering my services before the book was finished. Through this, the
project continues to impact my life, as I remain involved with people who
need our support. The DSM 1V, the Diagnostic and Statistical Manual of

Medical Disorders, is published by the American Psychiatric Association. It lists common language and standard criteria for the classification of mental disorders. Many of these men and women at the VA centers are products of "man's inhumanity to man."

I grew up in the suburbs smelling flowers while walking to high school. We would play sports, then study at night. Juxtapose this with what the American soldier was going through; the constant pungency of gunpowder and nitroglycerin: jungle rot. Humidity and temperatures so high, that by midmorning, a soldier would be dripping wet and would remain soaked for the entire day; then freeze at night if they were in the Central Highlands. Leeches, biting ants, and python snakes: disease. Not to mention an unseen enemy lurking in the brush. What a dichotomy. Now throw in an American public spitting on and spiting vets arriving back on our soil. These men and women were not Ronin, but just the opposite. They were doing what their country asked of them—it doesn't matter if they were drafted or enlisted. No wonder many returning soldiers chose to wear street clothes upon arrival on US soil. Goethe's statement "There is nothing more frightening than active ignorance" holds true here. I pray this book helps others understand that many civilians, including myself, are unaware of the trepidation, tragedy, and trauma these Vietnam veterans (and all veterans) experienced and continue to experience today.

I was also influenced by the profound dedication among the folks interviewed. They all exhibited camaraderie and outright love of their unit members at the highest level. Your buddy had your back; and you had his. My friend Pat Durkin said it best: "Vietnam veterans are honorable folks." Of all the books that were perused and read to learn as much about the war as possible, many were works by the interviewees, as well as in country forces like Tim O'Brien. These eyewitness accounts affected me deeply. Mr. O'Brien's *The Things They Carried* delves into the psyche of the foot soldier. Here is one of the great excerpts from the book: *"War is hell, but that is not the half of it, because war is also mystery and terror and adventure and courage and discovery and holiness and pity and despair and longing and love. War is nasty; war is fun. War is thrilling; war is drudgery; War makes you a man; war makes you dead."* One of those interviewed also said, "Heaven and earth must exist because it was sheer hell in Vietnam." If you buy into this, and all the interviews I did support the view, then the true essence of war involves tremendous highs, followed by equally chilling lows. One of my postulates about the war is that many Vietnam veterans drive motorcycles, possibly to relive that experience or "high" that comes with the spirited ride.

"All that is necessary for evil to succeed is for good men to do nothing." So I beg the question: Was our going to war in Vietnam honorable and with merit? If we (good men) did nothing to control the Viet Cong and the NVA from taking over South Vietnam, then would evil succeed? Remember that South Vietnamese President Diem caused much of the malaise before the fighting increased. Yet over one million Vietnamese migrated to the South after the French were defeated in 1954. Although Buddhism was and still is the predominant religion, Communism, to the Buddhists as well as significant Catholic population in the South, was not an option. This book will not point blame, but you must factor in what many Vietnamese have said over the years, and reiterated to me, that we got them out and saved many lives. Collateral damage is a given in warfare. Many died in country because friend and foe were mixed together. The soldiers still knew they had a job to do. Politicians order the military to send their people into harm's way. Then soldiers do as they are ordered. Then the public vilifies the soldier doing his duty. What profits a society to act so hypocritically? It would certainly be interesting if I could ask the famous English statesman Edmund Burke (1729-1797) his opinion about his quote above relative to Vietnam today.

All that being said, it was the interaction and interviews with the folks listed here that moved me the most. Hip Biker warned me early on that "War changes your DNA." He was indeed prescient. According to the professionals, so does Agent Orange. These interviews opened my eyes to the point that although I did not get emotional *during* the interview, it certainly affected me afterward. Why? Mainly because it seemed the person experienced a "soul cleansing" during the interview. The tape was stopped many times. I went through tons of handkerchiefs with the ladies, and quite a few with the men.

The Vietnam Memorial in DC demanded multiple visits for me to capture the solemnity of the grounds. During my visits, I gained the most by just sitting and watching. In June 2010, there were school kids on road trips prior to their summer vacation. There were the families of veterans who slowly approached the Panels where their loved ones are listed by Line number. Others were just visitors and tourists who may have seen the Memorial for the very first time. The in country veterans, who pay homage to their buddies no longer here, transform this 1981 structure to their version of the Wailing Wall in Jerusalem. This is indeed hallowed ground for them.

Endless drives and long flights, countless expressways; if I had never written a single sentence, these trips alone validated that we live in a beautiful country, and justified the work. A travel website that lists the ten best North American road trip destinations includes eight in the contiguous United States. Of these, my "wheels" took me through five of these eight road systems. Tucson to San Diego was incredible as the scenery changed dramatically. I passed landscapes with virtually no cactus, followed by cacti of every height at twenty-foot intervals. Mountains that had no definition, looking like ice cream scoops that had melted unevenly on all sides: or Play-Doh from a youngster's hands. Until sunset, the range following the road to San Diego was breathtaking. Darkness limited its full effect on the driver. The following day in San Diego, I drove over the bridge to Coronado to see Stockdale Naval Base and where SEAL Team 1 trains. The bridge seemed at least five hundred feet above the bay with full view of the USS *Midway* on the starboard side. There was the drive up the coast to San Francisco. Most everyone who lives in California is aware of the view from the coastline inland, to Route 101, then north. Continuing through Mill Valley, the southern end of Napa wine country is mountainous, layered for hundreds of miles with vineyards.

The East Coast had scenery that rivaled Arizona and California as well. Drive down the Blue Ridge, Shenandoah, and Appalachian Mountain ranges and you will be spellbound. Five-hundred miles on Route 81 makes it difficult to keep your eyes on the highway. On either side of the interstate lay towering mountains that stretch from Carlisle, Pennsylvania, through Maryland, West Virginia, Virginia, Tennessee, South Carolina, and Hendersonville, North Carolina where Captain Steedly resides. Glaciers caused the eastern part of the country to be flat until you hit the western side of the Carolinas, then north to Pennsylvania. Some of the oldest mountain ranges and rivers on earth exist here. Then you have the Savannah River Basin overlooked by these mountains at 4,400 feet elevation where the foreground is over 100 miles in the distance. I had to stop counting the "out of control truck ramp" signs due to the altitude and gradient of the road system. I was lucky to have made this trip in March, June, September, and October to witness how the landscape changed with each season, never missing the opportunity to meet Tibby and Homer Steedly. While driving through Delaware and the Maryland Eastern Shore area, the Watershed of the Chesapeake leads to the Chesapeake Bay Bridge-Tunnel, a true modern day engineering marvel. The 26-mile run over and under the Bay connects Maryland and Virginia.

But the most beautiful and breathtaking of all were the automobile rides around Salt Lake City, through to Denver, then south to Grand Canyon country. The Rockies cast shadows so massive they engulfed both the land and the mountains themselves. These ranges were also immense in Utah. At 4,500 feet elevation, the towering heights moved skyward for an additional two miles. Cumulus clouds kissed the peaks of these natural wonders. At sunset, the sun radiated through these same clouds for a spectacular view. The corpuscular rays were unmatched by anything I had seen before. The Wasatch Mountains run south along the lake in Salt Lake City for many miles. This range includes the highest peaks in Utah. In the north, Mount Timpanogos peaks at 11,749 feet. King's Peak, the tallest in Utah, is over 13,000 feet. Robert Redford's Sundance Resort is on the north side of Mount Timpanogos. A biker who was visiting the state approached a man at a gas station (where I was fueling) and stated, "You people have no idea what you take for granted here."

I really don't know how to close this section. Maybe it should be called "How war will *continue* to affect my life." As I mentioned earlier, Sgt. David Dolby, US Army Medal of Honor Recipient, was interned (following cremation in August) on 13 December 2010 at Arlington National Cemetery. They played TAPS. The affect of this song, on almost everyone who hears it, is chilling. TAPS is unique to our armed forces and was first heard during the Civil War. The song is now played at all military funerals, services, and memorials where wreaths are placed around or on graves. When I was growing up and playing "Army" with my friends, the winner always sang TAPS. We sure didn't understand the significance at the time. But I know it now.

Doc K was one of the first interviews I conducted. He is one of the many souls who continue to suffer from the effects of the war. There have been countless studies on PTSD and percentages related to combatants from Vietnam. The sociologists, scientists, and the military simply do not agree on rates of post traumatic stress disorder. Some say as high as 20 percent; others say closer to one in ten. However, when measured against overall troops that were "boots on the ground," both are significant. Steve, after reviewing his taped transcript and reading the written word, respectively pulled his discussion from the book. Reading his depiction; therefore reliving the war, stirred up many demons. He left Vietnam due to his tour as a combat medic being up and a few days later, his replacement received posthumously the Medal of Honor. Couple this with some of his friends who were KIA in that battle, his survivor guilt remains. However, he was kind enough to allow me to include his quotes within the book, including the following:

> *John—I want to thank you for your kind and thoughtful message from last week. Needless to say, I'm humbled and honored for your consideration to dedicate the Afterword of your book to me. In the heat of battle, one thinks of two things—watching over his brothers and hoping you don't become a casualty yourself. As one ages, the clarity of life can become clouded with the burdens of grief and guilt and that, in my case, if only I could somehow go into a time machine, to alter some of the events of the period. I guess in a (sic) way, today, mentally, I find myself tortured with my failures to complete my missions on several occasions, by not being there to assist all my brothers enough to give them continued life, with my medical abilities. 40 years later, I'm paying that price. For you to take the time to honor those from combat is the highest honor for one to undertake. The love of a brother in combat has no equal—it transcends the love of family, wives, and all others; a bond that never loses meaning or importance. I thank you for your care and devotion to tell a soldier's story.*

There are many Doc Ks out there who can't sleep at night, victimized by what they did to the enemy, or weren't able to do, for their comrades. Vets who are 100 percent disabled with maybe not a scratch from battle but whose psyches are forever scarred, which prevents them from performing a job. Some vets were completely incapable of maintaining a relationship with another person. We, as a society, should do for the vets what they do for each other. Melanie Lucot was one of my initial editors and transcribers. I asked her for an opinion after transcribing these stories. Here is what she said, "Listening to these interviews has been an interesting experience for me since I've never found history very appealing. I would forget what I learned in school not long after taking the test. All I can remember about the Vietnam War is what happened during the Tet Offensive(s). Hearing these people's stories made my high school lessons come back to life and grab my attention. I was captivated by what the people experienced and endured. It also made me realize more fully the differing opinions on the war. I am now more grateful to those who serve our country currently and have served in the past."

Being grateful and showing respect at a VFW or an American Legion Post is another way we can pay homage to our veterans. On Memorial Day 2010, I spoke with Vietnam vet PFC Bruce Kooi USMC. That day, there was a ceremony at the Fort Washington Post in PA. Families and friends along with a Marine Color Guard and vets from all foreign wars were in attendance. Bruce said to me, "Take all this in now, John. In twenty years, who is going to attend these services on our major holidays? Most of my Vietnam brethren will be gone. Who will continue to carry the flag for us?" Because of his concern, my thoughts went directly to all of us civilians, paraphrasing the famous line in *Julius Caesar*: "*If you have tears, prepare to shed them now.*"

We all need to walk into the lives of a serviceman or woman and bequeath to them respect and admiration as they have already given to their country, which is all of us. Hope can be a very powerful emotion. Virtually all the interviewees expressed gratitude to me for taking on this project. "It was by chance we met . . . By choice we became friends." My friends' collective hope is that others, who didn't serve, obtain a deeper understanding of veterans' experiences. So I end the book with my final quote by Lt. George M. Jones, USAF, 1981-1985:

Those of us who've never gone, don't always understand
The sacrifices that you made, protecting hearth and land.
We take for granted our freedom, and forget to count the cost
To those who protect that freedom from war and holocaust.
So this simple poem is a thank you, to tell you someone cares
And that you are ***remembered***
In our hearts and in our prayers.

ACKNOWLEDGMENTS

Dedicated to Larry "Two-Step" Brown
Staff Sergeant, United States Marine Corps
Second Battalion Ninth Marine Regiment Ninth Marine Division

Thanks to my wife, Donna, and daughters, Heather and Allie. These past two years affected them deeply since I was unable to perform my familial duties to the best of my ability. My associate Margaret Brooks for her painful attention to research and detail. Margaret is one of the main reasons this book made it to press. Her research, coordination of the interviews, diligence, copy edit, and proof work were invaluable.

Thanks to airman Hip and Navy corpsman Carmelo Infantino. These fellas kept me on track, showering me with information. To this day, I shudder and stand tall as an American knowing what many servicemen and women incurred during their tours. A great deal of thanks goes to Colonel Jon Hoffmann (Ret.) USMCR, deputy chief historian, secretary of defense, who was of great service following our meeting in June 2010. To Sedgwick Tourison (Vietnam vet Army intelligence) and his wife, Ping, who after many visits and phone calls assisted me greatly in the introduction (Vietnam section) as well as explaining the culture of the Vietnamese people. Wick truly is one of the most intelligent men I have ever met, and his wife one of the prettiest women in Maryland. Thanks also to Coach Patrick Knapp Jr. and Bob Hogan: they are my lifelong friends and gave me constant input and suggestions as well—trust me, I needed the help. Thanks to my favorite high school teacher, James Lill, who grew many a gray hair having me as a student. His patience in English class, coupled with additional hours after school, greatly assisted me. Chris Nelson, whose guidance through most of 2011 forced me to continue to streamline the book to its present state. Further, I need to thank Gayle Konig for her counsel and editing assistance. In addition, thanks to all the folks at Xlibris Publishing for their guidance and support. Finally, I owe the world to my mother-in-law, Marlene Boehm-Tinari, for if she had not come back from the grave on 23 December 2009 to align me with Colonel Donald, this book would never have happened.

The following are the individual names of those interviewed or who in some way helped shape this book. I am indebted to everyone.

MEDAL OF HONOR RECIPIENTS: John Cavaiani, Mike Thornton, Brian Thacker, Walter "Joe" Marm, Fred Ferguson, H.C. Barney Barnum, Tom Norris, William D. Morgan (*Vietnam Memorial Panel 31W Line 054*)

EX-POWs: Myron Donald (**Vietnam**), Paul Galanti (**Vietnam**), James Alexander Kelley Jr. (**WWII**), Jon Cavaiani (**Vietnam**)

MIA's FAMILY MEMBERS: Norman Berg, Larry Pollin, Barbara Pollin Greger, Erin Miller, Richard Kelly, Johanna Kelly, Diane Borst Berg, Joseph Cichon

ARMY: Nick Mihaescu, Homer Steedly, Lon Jamison, Jim Schlegel, Alan Rappoport, Sam Holt, Ken Gurbisz, Tony Lazzarini, Douglas White, Bill Stout, Steve Zalewski, James Baskin, George Shuler, Ed Gehringer, John Sweeney, Robert Beaumont, Tom Reilly, John Sears, Stephen Kraus, Bill Stafford

NAVY: James Caldwell, Michael Roesner, Bob Hogan, Fred Peterson, Kevin Potter, Karen Matt Hunter, Tom Simko, Gary Ward, Chuck Geiter, Drew Amici

AIR FORCE: Mike McAllister, Hip Biker (pen name), Brian Shul, Michael Uson, Bill Crean, Don Solt, Tony Boyle, Ray Miller

MARINES: Bruce Kooi, John Lang, Bill Selko, Dave "Smilie" Martin, Dennis Frank, Paul Ferraro, Wayne Karlin, Dick Hrebik, Loran Eldred,

Jerry Lieberman, Tom McWilliams, Chuck Moffet, Dave Lynch, Martin Lynch, Ken Wilkins, James Cutri, Larry (Two-Step) Brown, Michael Tinari, Charlie Crescenz, Chuck Cummings, John Church, Bruce Meyers, Doug Kitselman, Dennis Worman, Dennis Whalen, Jay Morgan, Jack Meyer, Ray Quesnel, Jim Scroggs, Joseph Rieher

COAST GUARD: Paul Scotti, Gary Sherman, Michael Brostrom

SEALs: John Gulick

SPECIAL FORCES: Jim Baldwin, Buddy Rhoades, Thom Nicholson, Tom Yaegel, John Rawley, Tom Kelly

AIRBORNE: George Fallon, Lou Mossa, Walter Stock, Allen Lloyd, Eugene Simonson, R. O. Martin, R. Ray Saikus, Greg Davis, Bill Guarnere

AIR CAVALRY: Tito Rivera, James Meador

INTELLIGENCE: Sedgwick Tourison **(USA)**, Jack Cummings **(USA)**, Bob Poore **(USAF)**

ORGANIZATIONS: American Legion Post 148, American Legion Post 129, American Legion Post 10, North Penn Post 676 VFW, Rolling Thunder, Patriot Guard, American Legion Post 482

HEALERS: Dr. Richard Odom, Carmelo Infantino, Ed "Dutch" Gehringer, John Murphy, Steve Knuboff, Ken Brawn, Kathleen Fennell

EXPERTS IN PSYCHOLOGY AND PSYCHIATRY: Howard Cohen, PhD, Beth Murphy, PhD, Roger K. Pitman, MD. Kernan Manion, MD

SOUTH VIETNAMESE: Nguyet Beverly, Ping Tourison, Tra Minh (pen name)

NORTH VIETNAMESE: Huang Ngoc Dam and his family

COATESVILLE MEDICAL CENTER: Jeanie Smith, Lisa Wilson

MEMORIAL BRACELETS: Bob Casey

TRANSCRIBERS: Tara Nocero, Lynne Duane, Melanie Lucot, Kelly Lucot, Lynne Lucot, Jacky Urbas, Ashley Kraus, Amber Gallagher, Gayle Konig

SPECIAL FOLKS: Barbara McMurray, Barbara Cunningham, Hank Cavalier, Jay Horwath, Richard Decker, Elise Nash, Jann Kitselman, Mary Ferraro, Emily Schwarz, Marion Wagner Evans, Tibby Steedly, Matt Hagarty, Barbara Loftus, Bettye Beverly, Joe Beverly, Carol and John Garrard, Kay Eldred, Joe Crescenz, Cory Etchberger, Bob Owens, Eileen Owens, Joseph Cichon, Jason Saylor, Dick Williams, Al Herbold, Jay Heisler, Edward Colimore, Ted Silary

FRIENDS AND FAMILY: Peter Siegfried, Denise Torelli, Dan Durkin, Tom Cavanaugh, Karen Risch, Barb Cavalier, John Brown, Teresa Fallon, Pat Durkin, Lou Hagarty, Bernadette Rowan, Patrick Burke, Mike Tierney, Maggie Knapp, Bernadette Naab, Mike Kilgannon, Jim Hargadon, Beth Burke, Chuck "Dollar" Whicker, Kathy Smith, Kathy Tierney, Bernadette Durkin, Chuck Myslinsky, Bob Sweeney, Patrick Knapp Jr., Dottie and Bobby Pennypacker, Frank Kelble, Chuck Myslinsky, Mike Appleby, Bob Sweeney, Bill Torelli, Ed McCauley, Paul Flexner

NEW JERSEY VIETNAM VETERANS MEMORIAL FOUNDATION: Lynn Duane, Katie Henry

PHILADELPHIA VIETNAM VETERANS MEMORIAL SOCIETY: Bill Crean, Steve Zalewski, Leonard Law

IMAGINATIVE REPRESENTATIONS OF THE VIETNAM WAR. LASALLE UNIVERSITY CONNELLY LIBRARY: John Baky

WEST CHESTER UNIVERSITY: Dr. Robert Kodosky

MARINE CORPS LAW ENFORCEMENT FOUNDATION: Jack Cummings, James Kallstrom, Mike DiFrancesco, Lisa Spengler

VETERANS-FOR-CHANGE: Jim Davis

NORTH CAROLINA VIETNAM VETERANS BRIDGE BACK FOUNDATION: Bob Matthews, Joe Harsch, Bill Dixon

MEDAL OF HONOR SOCIETY: Victoria Kueck, Carol Capregi, Nicholas B. Kehoe

ATLANTA VIETNAM VETERANS BUSINESS ASSOCIATION: Pat Gartland, Don Pardue, Hamilton Henson, Alan Gravel, John Sours, Brian Johnstone, Bernie Kean, "Mac" McNair

MILITARY WRITERS SOCIETY OF AMERICA: Terry L. Gould

WILLIAM TENNENT HIGH SCHOOL: Eileen Porozok, Fred DiChiara

VIETNAM WAR COMMEMORATION: Richard D. Williams, Philip Bigler

VIETNAM AND ALL VETERANS OF BREVARD. Greg Welch, Ralph Earrusso

MEDAL OF HONOR GROVE: Deb Woolson

UNITED STATES VETERANS ART PROGRAM: Kimo Williams

SONS OF THE AMERICAN LEGION: Ron Cloos

BIBLIOGRAPHY

1 in 8 returning soldiers suffers from PTSD. (30 June 2004). *MSNBC*. Retrieved from http://www.msnbc.msn.com/id/5334479/

173rd Airborne Brigade. *Weapons of the Vietnam War.* Retrieved from http://www.173rdairborne.com/weapons.htm

American Patriot Online. http://www.americanpatriotonline.com

American Psychiatric Association, Diagnostic and Statistical Manual of Mental Disorders, 4th Edition.

Army and Navy Academy. (2005/2008). *About the School and Academic Program.* Retrieved from http://www.ArmyandNavyacademy.org/

Army of the Republic of Vietnam (ARVN). Retrieved from http://www.vietnamwar.net/ARVN.htm

Bates, Carol. *History of the POW/MIA bracelets.* Retrieved from www.miafacts.org/bracelets

Battlefield: Vietnam. *PBS.* Retrieved from http://www.pbs.org/battlefieldvietnam/index.html

Berg, Norman E. (1999). *Regret to Inform You: Experiences of Families Who Lost a Family Member in Vietnam.* Central Point, OR: Hellgate Press/PSI Research.

Bird, Thomas & Couturié, Bill (Director). (1987). *Dear America: Letters Home from Vietnam*. United States: Couturié Company.

Bradley, James P. (2000). *Flags of Our Fathers*. New York, NY: Bantam Books.

Brigham, Robert K. (2006). ARVN: *Life and Death in the South Vietnamese Army*. University Press of Kansas. Retrieved from http://www.au.af.mil/au/ssq/bookreviews/brigham.pdf

Buckingham, William A. (1982). *Operation Ranch Hand: The USAF and Herbicides in SEA*, 1961-1971. Office of Air Force History, United States Air Force.

Buddhist Temples. *History of Buddhism*. Retrieved from http://www.buddhist—temples.com/history-of-buddhism.html

Burkett, BG, & Whitley, Glenna. (1998). *Stolen Valor: How the Vietnam Generation Was Robbed of its Heroes and its History*. Dallas, TX: Verity Press, Inc.

Casualties: U. S. Navy and Marine Corps Personnel Killed and Wounded in Wars, Conflicts, Terrorist Acts, and Other Hostile Incidents. (7 August 2006). Naval Historical Center, Department of the Navy. Retrieved from http://www.history.Navy.mil/faqs/faq56-1.htm (Lists all wars/deaths of Navy/Marines)

Chapter 3-6, Army Regulation 600-8-22 (Military Awards) dated 25 February 1995.

Clausewitz, Carl von. (1968).*On War*. Edited with introduction by Anatol Rapoport. London: Penguin Books.

Coco, Gregory A. (1998). *A Strange and Blighted Land: Gettysburg, The Aftermath of a Battle*. Gettysburg, PA: Thomas Publications.

Code of Conduct. Retrieved from legalassistance.af.law.mil/content

Collier, Peter. (2003). *Medal of Honor: Portraits of Valor* [With DVD]. New York, NY: Artisan Books.

Congressional Medal of Honor Society. (3 August 2009). *Medal of Honor Recipients Vietnam (A-L)*. Retrieved from http://www.history.Army. mil/html/moh/vietnam-a-l.html

Congressional Medal of Honor Society. (3 August 2009). *Medal of Honor Recipients Vietnam (M-Z)*. Retrieved from http://www.history.Army. mil/html/moh/vietnam-m-z.html

Congressional Medal of Honor Society. (21 September 2009). *Medal of Honor Statistics*. Retrieved from http://www.history.Army.mil/html/ moh/mohstats.html

Congressional Medal of Honor Society. *The Medal.* Retrieved from http://www.cmohs.org/

Corbett, John. (2004). *West Dickens Avenue: A Marine at Khe Sanh.* New York, NY: The Random House Publishing Group.

Cordesman, Anthony H., & Burke, Arleigh A. (6 August 2008). *US Casualties: The Trends in Iraq and Afghanistan.* Retrieved from http:// csis.org/files/media/csis/pubs/080808_war_casualties.pdf

Current Statistics. (28 January 2010). Retrieved from http://www. aiipowmia.com/stats.html

Defense Prisoner of War/Missing Personnel Office. (22 February 2010). *US Accounted—For from the Vietnam War.* Retrieved from http:// www.dtic.mil/dpmo/pmsea/accounted/pmsea_acc_p_name.pdf

Defense Prisoner of War/Missing Personnel Office. (18 June 2009). *US Prisoners of War who escaped captivity during the Vietnam War.* Retrieved from http://www.dtic.mil/dpmo/pmsea/pmsea_escapee.pdf

Defense Prisoner of War/Missing Personnel Office. (22 February 2010). *US Unaccounted-For from the Vietnam War.* Retrieved from http:// www.dtic.mil/dpmo/pmsea/unaccounted/pmsea_una_p_name.pdf

Department of Army Pamphlet 381-10, Weapons and Equipment Recognition Guide Southeast Asia, March 1969.

Digger History. *Weapons*. Retrieved from www.diggerhistory.info/pages.weapons.

DPMO PMSEA Database. *All POW Returnees/Escapees*. Retrieved from http://www.nampows.org/no.stats

Duncan, Davis Douglas. (1970). *War without Heroes*. New York, NY: Harper & Row.

Dunham, George R. (Major USMC), & Quinlan, David A. (Colonel USMC). US Marines in Vietnam: The Bitter End 1973-1975, Headquarters USMC, Washington DC (1990).

DUSTOFF Association History. Retrieved from http://www.dustoff.org/history/history.htm

ECPI College of Technology. *Home and Why ECPI*. Retrieved from http://www.militarydegrees.net/index.cfm

Ferraro, Paul A. *Cam Lo*. Forest City News.

Ferraro, Paul A. *Cupfuls; Poems 1968 to 1983*. Published by Paul A. Ferraro.

Finkel, David. (2009). *The Good Soldiers*. New York, NY: Sarah Crichton Books.

Flitton, Dave (Producer) & Hodgson, Mat (Director). (26 March 2007). *Battleground Vietnam: War in the Jungle*. Episode 8. United States: Madacy Entertainment.

Frequently Asked Questions (FAQ). Department of Defense. Retrieved from http://www.defenselink.mil/faq/pis/med_of_honor.html.

Frisbee, John L. (September 1991.) "The Mayaguez Incident." Air Force Magazine. Vol. 74, No. 9.

Galloway, Joseph L. and Moore, Lt. General Harold G. (1992). *We Were Soldiers Once and Young*. New York, NY: Random House.

Gardner, Amanda. (23 August 2007). *Battle Continues Over Vietnam PTSD Numbers*. Retrieved from http://health.usnews.com/usnews/health/healthday/070823/battle-continues-over—vietnam-ptsd-numbers.htm

Gascoigne, Bamber. *"History of Buddhism."* HistoryWorld. From 2001, ongoing. Retrieved from http://www.historyworld.net/wrldhis/ PlainTextHistories.asp?historyid=ab77

General Accounting Office Statistics as of 2005.

Global Security. (27 April 2005). *US Military Operations:* Casualty Breakdown. Retrieved from http://www.globalsecurity.org/military/ops/casualties.htm

Grant, Ulysses S. (1999). *Personal Memoirs of Ulysses S. Grant.* Old Saybrook, CT: William S. Konecky Associates.

Grossman, Lt. Col. Dave. (2009). *On Killing.* New York, NY: Back Bay Books.

Hal-3 Seawolf. (3April 2010). *US Navy Helicopter Attack (Light) Squadron Three Seawolves, Vietnam 1966-1972.* Retrieved from www.seawolf.org

Hampson, Rick. (28 May 2010). *"Afghanistan: America's Longest War."* USA Today.

Historical Records of the United States Coast Guard. Washington DC.

Hoffman, Lt. Col. Jon T. (2002). *Chesty.* New York, NY: Random House.

Home of Heroes. *Recipients of the Medal of Honor.* Retrieved from http://www.homeofheroes.com/moh/war/1_a_main.html

Hovis, Bobbi. Station Hospital: Saigon. Naval Institute Press.

Hrebik, Dick. (2010). *Corps Vet.* Palatine, IL: Windy City Publishing.

Hunter, Ric. (April 2000). *"The Last Battle of Vietnam."* Flight Journal. Vol. 5, No. 2.

Interview with Colonel Nicholson regarding AO (areas of operation) in Southeast Asia.

Jones, Lt. George M. USAF 1981-1985 *Janlynn Leaflet no. 900 21.*

J. W. Place. (1998). *John Wayne-Patriot. The Bracelet.* Retrieved from http://www.jwplace.com/bracelet.html

Karlin, Wayne. (2009). *Wandering Souls.* New York, NY: Nation Books.

Karnow, Stanley. (1983). *Vietnam: A History.* New York, NY: The Viking Press.

Kirban, Salem. (1974). *Goodbye, Mr. President.* Huntington Valley, PA: Salem Kirban, Inc.

Kissinger, Henry A. "*Years of Renewal.*" Chapter 18. ("Anatomy of a Crisis: The Mayaguez").

Klotter, Jule. A History of Monsato. *The Light Party.* Retrieved from http://www.lightparty.com/Health/HistoryOfMonsanto.html

Kolko, Gabriel. (1994). *Anatomy of a War.* New York, NY: The New Press.

Lazzarini, Tony. (2003). *Highest Traditions: Memories of War.* Larkspur, CA: Voyager Publishing.

Leland, Anne, & Oboroceanu, Mari-Jana. (15 September 2009). *American War and Military Operations: List and Statistics.* Retrieved from http://www.fas.org/sgp/crs/natsec/RL32492.pdf

Luttrell, Marcus. (2007). *Lone Survivor.* New York, NY: Little, Brown & Company.

Mandra, Irene. (25 January 2010). *The Prisoner of War Issue.* POW Network. Retrieved from http://www.pownetwork.org/statistics.htm#top (bits of information regarding casualties and such)

Mangold, Tom, & Penycate, John. (1985). *The Tunnels of Cu Chi.* New York, NY: Random House.

Martin, Dave. (2008). *Crazy Asian War.* Bloomington, IN: Xlibris Corporation.

Martin, RO (yet to be published) *Spirit of the Warrior.*

McGrath, John. (1975). *Prisoner of War: Six Years in Hanoi.* Annapolis, MD: Naval Institute Press.

Meyers, Bruce F. (2000). *Fortune Favors the Brave.* Annapolis, MD: Naval Institute Press.

Military Channel. *Weaponology.* Season 1: Weapons. 2007. Episode 11: Fire Weapons.

Military Factory. (2010). *American Vietnam War Casualty Statistics.* Retrieved from http://www.militaryfactory.com/vietnam/casualties.asp#3

Military Spot. *Military Rank.* Sun Key Publishing. Retrieved from http://www.militaryspot.com/resources/item/military_rank/

Moïse, Edwin E. (6 November 1998). *The Vietnam Wars, Section 8: The Tet Offensive and its Aftermath.* Retrieved from http://www.clemson.edu/caah/history/FacultyPages/EdMoise/viet8.htm

Murphy, Edward F. (2007). *Dak To: America's Sky Soldiers in South Vietnam's Central Highlands.* New York, NY: Presidio Press.

Murphy, Edward F. (1987). *Vietnam Medal of Honor Heroes.* New York, NY: Presidio Press.

NAM-POWs Corporation. (31 December 2001). *Nam-POW List.* Retrieved from http://www.nampows.org/nampowslist.html

National Park Service. Retrieved from www.nps.gov

Navadel, George D. *A Rifle Company's Tale.*

Navy SEALs. BUD/S (Basic Underwater Demolition / SEAL)—Naval Special Warfare Center. Retrieved from http://www.sealchallenge.Navy.mil/seal/buds.aspx

Navy SEALs. Introduction to Naval Special Warfare. Retrieved from http://www.sealchallenge.Navy.mil/seal/introduction.aspx

Navy SEALs. SEAL Team Missions. Retrieved from http://www.sealchallenge.Navy.mil/seal/missions.aspx

Navy Seawolves. *Early History.* Retrieved from http://www.seawolf.org/history/hal3_history.asp

Nicholson, Col. Thom. (1999). *15 Months in SOG: A Warrior's Tour.* New York, NY: Presidio Press.

O'Brien, Tim. (1990). *The Things They Carried.* Boston, MA: Houghton Mifflin.

Olive-Drab. (22May 2008). *Vietnam War: Weapons & Equipment.* Retrieved from http://www.olive-drab.com/od_history_vietnam_weapons_equipment.php

Ordaz, Rigo. (2002-2005). *The Battle of Tam Quan.* Retrieved from http://www.ichiban1.org/html/news_pages/news_36.htm

Patriots Point: Home of the USS *Yorktown. Medal of Honor Museum.* Retrieved from http://www.patriotspoint.org/exhibits/medal_honor/

Patterson, Gerard A. (1997). *Debris of Battle: The Wounded of Gettysburg.* Mechanicsburg, PA: Stackpole Books.

Phan Thanh, Nguyen. *America's Bitter End in Vietnam.*

POW Network. *Index of Names.* Retrieved from http://www.pownetwork.org/bios.htm

Rotter, Andrew J. (1999). *The Causes of the Vietnam War. Modern American Poetry.* Retrieved from http://www.english.illinois.edu/MAPS/vietnam/causes.htm

Roush, Gary. *Helicopter Losses in Vietnam.* Pentagon sources.

Rudin, Scott (Producer) & Demme, Jonathan (Director). (2004). *The Manchurian Candidate.* United States: Paramount Pictures.

Rudin, Scott (Producer) & Friedkin, William (Director). (2000). *Rules of Engagement.* United States: Paramount Pictures.

Rummell, RJ (1997). *Table 6.1A Vietnam Democide: Estimates, Sources & Calculations. Line83.* Retrieved from http://www.hawaii.edu/powerkills/SOD.TAB6.1A.GIF

Ryscamp, Rix & Reay, Paul. Instructional shooting demonstration(s) with author in Salt Lake City, UT.

Schmidt, Arne L., & Lemley, Jim, & Wallace, Randall. (1 March 2002). *We Were Soldiers* [Motion Picture]. United States: Icon Productions.

Scientific Psychic. *Anatomy and Structure of Human Sense Organs.* Retrieved from http://www.scientificpsychic.com/workbook/ chapter2.htm

Scotti, Paul C. (2000). *Coast Guard Action in Vietnam: Stories of Those Who Served.* Central Point, OR: Hellgate Press.

Segal, Dave. (May 2010). "Please Don't Cry." Star Bulletin. Tour 365. For soldiers going home. 1970 summer Issue MACV.

Sherman's Travel. (29 May 2011). Philadelphia Inquirer. Retrieved from www.shermanstravel.com.

Simkin, John. The Vietnam War. *Spartacus Educational.* Retrieved from http://www.spartacus.schoolnet.co.uk/VietnamWar.htm

Slade, Stuart. (20 June 1999). *Analysis of the Battle of Dong Hoi.* Retrieved from http://www.navweaps.com/index_tech/tech-025.htm

Smith, Gary R. (1996). *Master Chief (Diary of a Navy SEAL).* New York, NY: Ballantine Books.

Special Forces Association. (2010). *A Brief History of US Army Special Forces.* Retrieved from http://www.specialforcesassociation.org/ sf_history.php

Special Forces Group Flashes & Army Rank Insignia. (2 March 2009). Retrieved from http://www.pamplin.net/Special-Forces_9/group-insig.htm

Stanton, Shelby. *Vietnam Order of Battle.* ISBN 0-89193-700-5. Retrieved from http://books.google.com/books

Statistical information about casualties of the Vietnam War. (December 1998). *The National Archives.* Retrieved from http://www.archives. gov/research/vietnam-war/casualty-statistics.html#branch

Stubbe, Chaplain Ray William. (2005). *Battalion of Kings*. Khe Sanh Veterans, Inc.

Summers, Harry G. (1995).*Historical Atlas of the Vietnam War*. New York, NY: Houghton Mifflin Company.

Tagg, Larry. (1998). *The Generals of Gettysburg: The Leaders of America's Greatest Battle*. Savas Publishing.

Tet Offensive of 1968—A Simpler Version. (23 August 2004). *Tet Offensive*. Retrieved from http://www.1stcavmedic.com/tet_offensive_of_1968.htm

The Legacy of Agent Orange. (July 2000). Retrieved from http://www. heureka.clara.net/gaia/orange.htm

Time-Life Books: The Civil War series. 1987. *Civil War Statistics*. Retrieved from http://www.phil.muni.cz/~vndrzl/amstudies/civilwar_stats.htm

Tonsetic, Robert L. (2007). *Days of Valor*. Drexel Hill, PA: Casemate Publishing.

Toperczer, Dr. Istvan. (1998). *Air War over North Viet Nam: The Vietnamese People's Air Force 1949-1977*. Carrollton, TX: Squadron/ Signal Publications.

Tourison, Sedgwick. (2006). *B5-T8 in 48 QXD*. Ray William Stubbe.

Tourison, Sedgwick. (1997). *Project Alpha*. New York, NY: St. Martin's Paperbacks.

Tourison, Sedgwick. (1991). *Talking with Victor Charlie*. Raleigh, NC: Ivy Books.

United States Department of Defense. *The United States Military Enlisted Rank Insignia*. Retrieved from http://www.defense.gov/specials/insignias/enlisted.html

USASOC. *A Brief History of Special Operations Forces*. Retrieved from http://www.soc.mil/sofinfo/history.html

USA Today. (6 October 2010). *"Does First Amendment Protect protests at military funerals."* Publisher David Hunke.

US Military Casualties in Southeast Asia. (31 March 1997). The Wall-USA. Retrieved from http://www.thewall-usa.com/summary.asp

US Navy Seals. (17 September 2009). *The Navy SEAL* Insignia. Retrieved from http://information.usNavyseals.com/2009/09/ the-Navy-seal-insignia.html

Veterans' Diseases Associated with Agent Orange Exposure. United States Department of Veterans Affairs. Retrieved from http://www. publichealth.va.gov/exposures/agentorange/diseases.asp#veterans

Vietnam. *The North Vietnamese Army (NVA) and the Viet Cong (VC): "Charlie."* Retrieved from http://www.diggerhistory.info/ pages-enemy/vietnam.htm

Vietnam-Era Unaccounted for Statistical Report. (4 December 2009). Retrieved from http://www.dtic.mil/dpmo/pmsea/Stats2009/Stats20091209.pdf

Vietnam Glossary. Vietnam Era Educational Center, a part of the New Jersey Vietnam Veterans' Memorial Foundation. Retrieved from http://www.orlok.com/hair/holding/links/vietglossary.html

Vietnam Veterans Webring, Schlatter, Joe, Colonel US Army (Ret.) Defense Intelligence Agency POW/MIA Affairs.

Vietnam Virtual Wall. www.virtualwall.org

Vietnam War. (2009). *Battles and Facts.* Retrieved from http://www. vietnam-war.info/battles/

Vietnam War. (2009). *Vietnam War Weapons.* Retrieved from http://www. vietnam-war.info/weapons/

Vietnam Women's Memorial Foundation. (2010). Retrieved from http:// www.vietnamwomensmemorial.org/vwmf.php

Wetterhahn, Ralph. (2002). *"The Last Battle: The Mayaguez Incident and the End of The Vietnam War."* Plume Publishers.

Wilson, Captain Barbara A. (1996). *Vietnam Southeast Asia.* Retrieved from http://userpages.aug.com/captbarb/femvetsnam.html

Women in Vietnam. (16 January 2009). Retrieved from http://www.illyria.com/vnwomen.htm

APPENDIX: DEDICATIONS

Rowland Joseph Adamoli
Corporal, United States Marine Corps
Company A, First Amtrak Battalion Third Marine Division
Home of Record: Philadelphia, Pennsylvania
DOB: 18 May 1940
KIA: 18 August 1965
Body Recovered
Quang Tin, South Vietnam
Panel 02E Line 053

David Charles Brostrom
Lieutenant (LTJG) United States Coast Guard
USCG Point Welcome
Division-12 TF 115 United States Naval Forces Vietnam
Home of Record: Los Altos, CA
DOB: 9 August 1941
KIA: 11 August, 1966
Body Recovered
DMZ: @17th Parallel
Panel 09E Line 126

Larry "Two-Step" Brown
Staff Sergeant, United States Marine Corps
Second Battalion Ninth Marine Regiment Ninth Marine Division
Home of Record: Cincinnati, OH
Home of Residence: Surprise, AZ
DOB: 23 September 1946

Injuries: Multiple shrapnel wounds, Traumatic Brain Injury. 100 percent disabled PTSD; many diseases through exposure.

Walter Alan Cichon
Staff Sergeant, United States Army
Alpha Company Third Battalion Eighth Infantry Regiment Fourth Infantry Division
Farmingdale, New Jersey
DOB: 28 August 1946
Date of Loss: 30 March 1968
Missing as of 5 June 2011
Panel 47E Line 009

Michael John Cutri
Lance Corporal, United States Marine Corps
Second Battalion, Third Marine Regiment, Third Marine Division
Home of Record: Syracuse, NY
DOB: 29 June 1949
KIA: 28 May 1968
Body Recovered
South Vietnam
Panel 64W Line 007

Joseph Francis Daly
Corporal, United States Army
C Battery Second Battalion, Thirteenth Artillery Regiment, 2 Field Force
Home of Record: Philadelphia, Pennsylvania
DOB: 02 September 1945
KIA: 23 April 1967
Body Recovered
South Vietnam
Panel 18E Line 074

Hoang Ngoc Dam and his family
Combat Medic 559th Command Group
Peoples Army of North Vietnam
Pleiku Province, Central Highlands, South Vietnam
Home of Residence: Village of Thai Giang; Province of Thai Binh
KIA: 19 March 1969

George Fallon
Charlie Co. 2nd Battalion 1st Brigade 327th Hawk Recon
101st Airborne Division
Home of Record: Jersey City, NJ
Home of Residence: Waterford, NJ
DOB: 04 June 1947
PTSD. Various dioxin-related diseases.

Richard Loy Etchberger
United States Air Force
Chief Master Sergeant.
1043rd Radio Squadron
Home of Record: Hamburg, Pa
DOB: 5 March 1933
Date of Loss: 11 March 1968
Country of Loss: Laos
Panel 44E Line 015

William J. Jamison
Captain, United States Army
Company A, 227th Assault Helicopter Battalion / 1st Cavalry Division (airmobile).
Home of Record: Glenside, PA
DOB: 29 April 1947
Missing as of 27 March 1981
Bishop McDevitt High School
Temple University ROTC
Website: www.williamjamison.com

Steven Knuboff
Company Medic, Specialist 4 United States Army
Alpha Company Third Battalion Fist Infantry Regiment
11th Infantry Brigade Americal Div.
Home of Record: Queens, NY
Home of Residence: San Diego, CA
DOB: 29 November 1948
PTSD. Various dioxin-related diseases
Website: www.hill4-11.org

Charles Lindewald Jr.
Master Sergeant, United States Army
Company C Fifth Special Forces Group United States Army
Home of Record: La Porte, IN
DOB: 30 July 1938
KIA/MIA: 06 February 1968, Presumption of Death: 24 January 1974
Lang Vei, Vietnam
Repatriated: 15 January 2004
Panel 38E Line 005

Thong Nguyen
Military Assist and Command Vietnam
101st Airborne United States Army
1st Battalion 501st Regiment 2nd Battalion 501st
Interpreter
Home of Residence: North Vietnam
Immigrated to South Vietnam to assist the Americans

George Joseph Reed Jr.
Lance Corporal, United States Marine Corps
G Company Second Battalion, Third Marine Regiment, Third Marine Division
Home of Record: Philadelphia, Pennsylvania
DOB: 03 November 1948
KIA: 16 June 1969
Body Recovered
Location: Quang Tri, South Vietnam
Panel 22W Line 059

James "Daddy Wags" Wagner
United States Marine Corps
Ninth Regiment Third Marine Division
Home of Residence: Philadelphia, Pa
DOB: 21 February 1945
Died 2 November 2002 massive brain tumor

Douglas R. White
Private First Class, United States Army
Alpha Company. Second Battalion, Twenty-Seventh Regiment, Twenty-Fifth Division
Home of Record: Doylestown, PA
Home of Residence: Lansdale, PA
DOB: 17 August 1946
Parsons College and Spring Garden College
Current Condition(s): tinnitus, hearing loss from artillery rounds

John Joseph Donnelly111
Seaman, United States Navy
E Platoon SEAL Team 1, Task Force 116
Home of Record: Philadelphia, PA
DOB: 20 October 1949
KIA: 23 June 1970
Body Recovered
Phong Dinh, South Vietnam
Panel 09W Line 083

Paul E. Galanti
Lieutenant, United States Navy
VA-216, USS *Hancock*
Home of Record: Lodi, NJ
DOB: 11 July 1939
Prisoner of War: 17 June 1966-12 February 1973
Country of Loss: North Vietnam

Six degrees of separation refers to the idea that everyone is at most six steps away from, or connected to, any other person on Earth.

While the Vietnam War was raging, silver bracelets were created to raise awareness of, and show support for, American servicemen who were prisoners of war (POW) or missing in action (MIA). After the war, black bracelets were produced to pay homage to any of our armed forces killed in action (KIA). The orange bracelet is more recent and symbolizes all those, living and deceased, who have suffered from diseases, combat wounds, and post traumatic stress resulting from their Vietnam service. These bracelets honor the memory and sacrifice of our troops—one of the central goals of this book.

In December 2009, John Siegfried discovered the silver POW/MIA bracelet that his mother-in-law had worn for over 20 years. Curiosity urged him to contact the person named on the bracelet, a contact that inspired him profoundly and set him on a path that resulted in this book. Colonel Myron Donald willingly shared the story of both his service and imprisonment as a POW in Vietnam. In a personal meeting with Colonel Donald, Siegfried learned the harrowing details of how Donald overcame over five years imprisonment in the horrid conditions of North Vietnamese prisons.

This story opened his eyes to the harsh reality and bitter tragedy of a savage war and inspired him to begin researching the stories of others affected by the Vietnam War. This book contains many of those stories, as well as compelling insights into Siegfried's own journey of discovery. All interviews within this book are true accounts and were conducted in person throughout the United States.

You will be riveted by the indescribable stories told by veterans, about veterans, and for veterans, and by the families of the lost or still missing

MIAs. More than 3,400,000 men and women served in Southeast Asia. Although close to 60 percent of all Vietnam veterans who served in-country are no longer alive, the families of all these veterans will continue to be affected by the Vietnam War for *generations*. This book illustrates the misery and despair experienced by both soldiers and victims of this visceral war, but also the exhilaration of combat, and the camaraderie felt, during their respective tours, to present day.

The understanding of warfare, combined with the appreciation of all the elements derived from combat, is necessary to better comprehend the effects of battle on those who have sworn to protect our country. Even if our soldiers did not incur flesh wounds, they may have suffered irreparable damage to their emotions, their psyche, and their soul. We civilians may never know or be able to comprehend the degradation caused to their human spirit and the violence and brutality they encountered. We need also to continue to support these men and women in the aftermath of their courageous service.

JOHN SIEGFRIED is a military historian who has worked as a marketing research consultant since 1993. He has spoken at Veterans Organizations, universities and high schools throughout the country. John resides in Pennsylvania, with his wife Donna and their daughters, Heather and Allie. Murphy, John's 7-year-old Golden Retriever, has been at his side ever since Murphy's rescue in 2004.

Made in the USA
Lexington, KY
06 January 2014